THE NEW CLARENDON BIBLE

OLD TESTAMENT

VOLUME IV

ISRAEL UNDER BABYLON AND PERSIA

ISRAEL UNDER BABYLON AND PERSIA

BY

PETER R. ACKROYD

Samuel Davidson Professor of Old Testament Studies in the University of London, King's College

OXFORD UNIVERSITY PRESS

1970

Oxford University Press, Ely House, London W.1

GLASGOW NEW YORK TORONTO MELBOURNE WELLINGTON
CAPE TOWN SALISBURY IBADAN NAIROBI DAR ES SALAAM LUSAKA ADDIS ABABA
BOMBAY CALCUTTA MADRAS KARACHI LAHORE DACCA
KUALA LUMPUR SINGAPORE HONG KONG TOKYO

PRINTED IN GREAT BRITAIN

PUBLISHER'S PREFACE

WHEN it became necessary, a few years ago, to contemplate revision of the Old Testament volumes of the Clarendon Bible series, the publishers were faced with two important decisions: first, on what text the revision should be based, and second, whether any significant change should be made in the form and plan of the series.

It seemed to them, after taking the best available advice, that the Revised Version could not expect to hold the field for much longer in face of the developments in scholarship which have taken place since its publication in the eighteen eighties, and which have been reflected in more recently published versions. On the other hand, the New English Bible Old Testament is only very recently published, and it will be some time before its usefulness for schools and universities can be evaluated. In these circumstances, the Revised Standard Version has seemed the obvious choice, the more particularly since the decision by the Roman Catholic hierarchy to authorize the use of their own slightly modified version in British schools. The publishers would like to express their gratitude to the National Council of Churches of Christ in the United States of America for the permission, so readily given, to make use of the RSV in this way.

With regard to the form of the series, the success of the old Clarendon Bible over the years has encouraged them to think that no radical change is necessary. As before, therefore, subjects requiring comprehensive treatment are dealt with in essays, whether forming part of the introduction or interspersed among the notes. The notes themselves are mainly concerned with the subject-matter of the books and the points of interest (historical, doctrinal, etc.) therein presented; they deal with the elucidation of words, allusions, and the like only so far as seems necessary to a proper comprehension of the author's meaning. There will, however, be some variations in the content and limits of each individual volume, and in particular it is intended that a fuller treatment should be given to Genesis, and to the Psalms.

The plan is to replace all the volumes of the old series gradually as stocks become exhausted.

AUTHOR'S PREFACE

THE study of any period within the range covered by the writings of the Old Testament inevitably leaves a multitude of questions unanswered, and in some cases, one suspects, unanswerable. This sobering reflection is particularly relevant to the period covered by this volume, and some of the reasons for it appear in the course of its pages. It is the more to be regretted since the understanding of this period is of such tremendous importance for the right appreciation of the period that follows, often rather inexactly termed the 'intertestamental period', largely covered by Vol. 5 in this series. The variegated patterns of thought during the times of Greek and Roman rule can only be fully appreciated if their sources are traced, so far as may be, in what precedes. The thought of the Babylonian and Persian periods—in which so much of the biblical text was brought near to its final form—is clearly further of importance for the subsequent developments both in Judaism and in Christianity. If the reader is at the end left with a recognition of many points on which there is uncertainty, it may be hoped that he will also be left with an appreciation of the very great richness and variety of thought which can be traced here. No simple systematization of this thought is possible or desirable. It witnesses to the life of a community which in size was so negligible but which in the measure of its influence on the subsequent history of human thought has been incalculably significant.

This volume replaces the one by W. F. Lofthouse entitled *Israel after the Exile* in the earlier series. The usefulness of the earlier volume is attested by its continued use. It will be observed that, although the present volume covers exactly the same period, in its emphasis and at many points in its choice of material to be discussed, it differs considerably from its predecessor. It would be surprising if this were not so; Dr. Lofthouse, who contributed richly to the interpretation of the

Old Testament, would have been the first to welcome a reassessment.

In accordance with editorial policy, quotations from the biblical text follow the Revised Standard Version (RSV). A short selection of books for further reading has been included, and in this a note will be found of other abbreviations used in the text.

I wish to express my indebtedness to the staff of the Clarendon Press for their general encouragement and help with the preparation of the illustrations. My thanks are also due to the Reverend R. J. Coggins of King's College, London, and to my father, the Reverend J. R. Ackroyd, for their valuable comments and help; to Miss Jean Kemble of King's College for the preparation of the final typescript; to Miss Ann Golden and Mrs. Judy Kidd for comments on the proofs; and to the Reverend John Goldingay for preparing the indexes.

PETER R. ACKROYD

November 1969

CONTENTS

CONTENTS

LIST OF ILLUSTRATIONS

LIST OF ILLUSTRATIONS

LIST OF SELECTED PASSAGES

I. THE EXILIC SITUATION

THE HISTORICAL BACKGROUND

A. *Introductory*

It is convenient, though not perhaps entirely accurate, to describe the period from the second fall of Jerusalem in 587 B.C. to the edict of Cyrus in about 538/7 B.C. as the 'exilic age'. Its beginning is marked by a major disaster in the life of the Judaean kingdom, the capture of Jerusalem and the destruction of city and temple described vividly in 2 Kgs. 25^{8-17}. Part of the population was taken away from Jerusalem and the Judaean area to be 'captives' in Babylonia. We shall have to look more closely at this description of the events and examine its significance. The end of the period is marked by the issuing of an edict by Cyrus, authorizing the rebuilding of the temple, and commissioning this work under the control of one Sheshbazzar (Ezra 1^{1-11}). This too will have to be considered in due course. But it is at once evident that there is a certain artificiality in the description of this period as the 'exilic age'. In the first place it lays very great stress upon those in exile, and we have to consider how far it is right to put the main emphasis there; only a section of the population was in fact exiled, and the part played by those in Palestine must be carefully estimated. In the second place, it presupposes that there is here a clearly marked period, with a defined beginning and end. But this is not really so, for the taking into exile of some people in 587 was only one stage in the action against Judah by the Babylonians; others had been taken into exile in 597, and there was to be a further small deportation in 581 (Jer. 52^{30}). The evidence for the return from exile in 538/7 is problematic, and in any case there is evidence both of subsequent 'returns'—for example with Zerubbabel, *c.* 520 B.C., and with Nehemiah and Ezra—and also of a continuing and important Jewish community in Babylonia for centuries after this.

But though these points need to be observed, it is nevertheless important to recognize that this period of about fifty years, inseparably linked as it is with what precedes and with what follows, marks a turning point in thought and experience for the Old Testament community. It is convenient, even if historically not quite accurate, to describe this community as Israel, as is done in the title of this book. It is indeed very difficult to know just what is the right term to use. It is clear that the term Israel often means the northern kingdom and its people, but it may also refer to the whole people regarded as descended from the one tribal ancestor Jacob/Israel. At a later stage, particularly clearly in the writings of the Chronicler, the term Israel is used for the true people, the obedient community; and often this is interpreted to mean the tribes of Judah and Benjamin seen as the loyal adherents of the ancient covenant, whereas the northern tribes are considered to have broken away from it. That this is not a historically accurate description is clear from the study of the histories of the pre-exilic period in Samuel and Kings, for while it is true that they pass a similar judgement on the north, they also make it clear that the division was not by any means so simple. And from prophetic collections in the books of Amos and Hosea we can see that the religious life of the north was very far from being merely a breakaway from a 'true' faith. Indeed the significance of northern tradition may with great probability be detected in the movement of theological thought which we describe as 'Deuteronomic', which reaches its climax in about the sixth century B.C. and of which we must therefore give some account alongside other indications of the thought of the time. If we use the term Israel, we use it in a somewhat idealized sense, noting that such a use is becoming common in the writings of the time. At the same time, we must also refer to the Judaean community which in many respects marks the centre of life and thought so far as the evidence which is available to us depicts it. It is probably better to speak of Judah, and Judaeans, than to use the term Jew and such a wide term as Judaism, which may be better kept for a somewhat later stage. But neat use of terms is not always possible.

In the first chapter of this book we shall be considering what happened in 587 B.C. and after, during the fifty years described as 'the exile'; in the second chapter we shall consider the closely related theme of what changes and developments in thought and understanding can be traced roughly to this period. The overlap will be evident, and no entirely firm lines will be drawn at the end of the period, since human thought does not start and stop at convenient dates; we must all the time be conscious of its richness, and of its links back into the past, into the period before 587 B.C. which is the subject of Volume 3 in this series. Many people, and some of them very influential indeed—we may mention Jeremiah and Ezekiel—lived through the disaster of 587 B.C. They may help us to understand both what led up to these events, what it was like to live through them and how those who experienced them were able to learn from them. The overlap will be evident too into the third and fourth chapters which look at what happened and how Israel developed its thinking under Persian rule.

B. *The disaster of* 587 B.C.

The previous volume in this series has traced the events leading up to the fall of the city in 587 B.C., and reference is made there to the light which has been shed on the circumstances of the last years of the kingdom of Judah from various Babylonian records—covering the period up to about 595 and actually mentioning the capture of Jerusalem in 597 (Vol. 3, p. 128)—from tablets referring to the allocations of provisions to the captive king Jehoiachin and to his family (Vol. 3, p. 132), as well as to craftsmen who may be some of the skilled foreign workmen active in Jerusalem during the period of Jehoiakim's substantial building activities (cf. Jer. 22^{13-15}). For the period of the final disaster no such direct records are available, but we have some indications of the difficulties of the inhabitants of Judah during the years of warfare and siege—a period of two years (2 Kgs. 25^{1-2})—from the letters discovered in the ruins of the city of Lachish, a very important centre in Judah, vital to the defence of the capital. The insecurities of the period are suggested by the references in these letters to military preparations, to fire signals, to a prophet involved in the events. (For the texts of these letters, see *DOTT*, pp. 212–17 and *ANET*, pp. 321 f.; and see Vol. 3, pp. 129 f.)

For the final stages of the fall of Judah we are therefore entirely dependent on the biblical narratives in 2 Kgs. 25^{1-21} and in Jer. 37^{1}–39^{18} and another later account in 2 Chron. 36^{11-21}. From Jer. $37^{7-9, 11}$ (34^{21}) we hear of the advance of an Egyptian army which caused the Babylonians to withdraw during the two-year siege. Lachish Letter III records that

> The commander of the army, Konyahu, son of Elnathan, has gone down on his way to Egypt, and Hodawyahu, son of Ahiyahu, and his men he has sent to obtain . . . (*DOTT*, p. 214.)

The text breaks off, so that we do not know the reason for this mission. It could have been to negotiate for Egyptian support, but there are other possible explanations. The Egyptian advance evidently only delayed the final disaster a little, though it must have brought a welcome relief for the besieged inhabitants. The possibility of making contact with the outside world—taken advantage of by Jeremiah (Jer. $37^{12\,\mathrm{ff.}}$) and misunderstood in his case as an intention to desert—would presumably have given some easement to the food shortage, though this was in the end to become desperate (Jer. 37^{21} 'all the bread of the city was gone', cf. also 2 Kgs. 25^{3}). But even the area outside cannot have been in a position to help much, for the presence of the Babylonian army living on the land it occupied is likely to have made conditions very difficult for the local population. At whatever point this short relief came, the long occupation and siege must have meant that little of the Judaean area, except in so far as it was less accessible to

LACHISH LETTER III. For a brief description of these letters, cf. p. 4. A quotation from this letter appears in the text. It has 16 lines of text on one side (left-hand picture) and lines 17–21 on the other (right-hand picture). The words quoted from this letter on p. 4 appear at the bottom left (up to '. . . Egypt, and') and continue at the top right. In the final lines occurs the one reference to a prophet, but he is indicated only as a messenger, carrying a letter from Tobyahu ('Yahweh is good') 'servant of the king', to Shallum (from the word meaning 'peace, prosperity'); the letter evidently gave a warning: 'Take care!' but we do not know to what this warning refers. The name Shallum appears several times in this period in 2 Kings and Jeremiah; a number of the other names in the letters are also attested from this period in the biblical material.

the invading army, can have been spared privation, destruction, and death. The evidence of excavations in the area indicates that few places escaped destruction and many were very slow indeed in making any kind of recovery. From Jerusalem itself, the excavations carried out by Dr. Kathleen Kenyon from 1961–7 on the south-eastern hill, the main area of the ancient Jebusite and then of the Davidic city and still in occupation in the early sixth century, reveal the clearest evidence of the destruction of the city walls and show that in all probability the walls that Nehemiah repaired a century and more later followed a different line because of the extent of the collapse. We need hardly be afraid of exaggerating the extent of the disaster to both Jerusalem and the whole area of Judah. This is important when we come to assess the position in Palestine during the exilic age.

The actual account of the taking of Jerusalem is given in 2 Kgs. 25^{3-8}, Jer. 39^{1-7}. The two accounts are clearly closely related and some parts overlap precisely; in other respects they provide slightly different information. According to 2 Kings, the situation had become desperate, with the famine so severe that no food was left for the ordinary people. (The phrase 'people of the land' in 2 Kgs. 25^{3} would seem here to mean this, though there are cases in which this phrase appears to denote influential people of some status in the community.) In such a situation, the king and his bodyguard attempted to escape. It is not quite clear what had happened. The text states that 'the city was broken open' and this could mean that the enemy breached the walls. The Jeremiah text (Jer. $39^{3\,f.}$) indicates that the Babylonian rulers were already in the city before the king's attempted escape. (RSV 39^{3} adds at the beginning the words 'When Jerusalem was taken' from the end of ch. 38. But such a transposition is not really necessary: does the text perhaps imply that part of the city was occupied, but not the royal palace where the king was?) If we link the phrase in 2 Kgs. 25^{4} 'a breach was made in the city' with what precedes in v. 3, we might think that it means that the people themselves, seeing no hope with the desperate shortage of food, decided to open up the city to the enemy, fearing death or captivity less than the horrors of a still longer siege. At all events, the royal house could not expect mercy, for Zedekiah was king only by Babylonian permission, having been put on

COLLAPSED BUILDINGS OF JERUSALEM 587 B.C. The city of Jerusalem in the time before and after David occupied the south-east hill, outside the present walled 'old city'. The eastern slope here is very steep, and buildings had to be built in terrace form up the side, inside the city wall which was low down the slope. When the city was sacked by the Babylonians in 587 B.C., the buildings on the slope were completely ruined, and when the city was re-established, this area was abandoned. Nehemiah's wall ran much higher up the hill (see pp. 254 f., 257 f.). The city had gradually extended northwards, where royal palace and temple were built; how much further it developed at this later time is not known with any certainty.

the throne after the previous capture of the city in 597. His attempt at escape was frustrated; he was captured and taken to the Babylonian headquarters at Riblah in the north. Nebuchadrezzar was not at this time involved solely in a campaign against Judah; we know that Ammon was also involved (Ezek. 21[18ff.]) and that Tyre was unsuccessfully besieged by the Babylonians for thirteen years from this date.

Presumably the control of the various campaigns was undertaken from Riblah. Zedekiah was sentenced for rebellion, his sons were executed and thereby that rebel line was cut off from the Davidic dynasty; Zedekiah himself was blinded and taken captive to Babylon. He is not mentioned again, and we may reasonably assume that he was never released.

The treatment of Jerusalem was severe, not surprisingly in view of its record of rebellion. An important Babylonian army officer, Nebuzaradan, was evidently sent to carry out large-scale destruction. The temple was burnt, so too was the royal palace; these were part of the same complex of buildings, and quite apart from their political and religious significance, would offer a strong point of resistance in any siege. (We may compare the importance of the control of the temple in Maccabaean and Roman times, especially in the disastrous Jewish War of A.D. 66–73.) The destruction in the city was also widespread; 'all the houses', qualified as 'every great house' (2 Kgs. 25⁹), were burnt, and the walls were broken down. The narrative in 2 Kings goes on to tell in detail of the destruction of the objects in the temple, and of the removal of the valuable vessels of bronze, silver, and gold. The compiler of the history clearly had a great interest in and love for the temple, and having included a detailed description of its building (1 Kgs. 6–7), he now dwells sadly on the fate of such wonderful treasures as it possessed (2 Kgs. 25[13-17]). We may glimpse his sense of the magnitude of the disaster as he makes the comment 'the bronze of all these vessels was beyond weight' (v. 16).

The people were also treated with severity. We are told that all the people left in Jerusalem were deported, together with the deserters and 'the rest of the multitude' (25[11])—this last word may mean 'the army', but we may note that the parallel texts in Jer. 39[9] and 52[15] have 'people' and 'artisans' respectively. This latter word is almost identical in form with the one for 'multitude' (*'āmōn* is a word of some difficulty, here translated 'artisans'; *hāmōn* means 'multitude', i.e. the crowd of ordinary people. The word for 'people', *'am*, is also very similar in sound). Thus we have different versions of who was involved, and it is perhaps the case that the more limited term 'artisans' has been extended into the idea that everyone was deported, the similarity of the words making this extension easy. The statement is in any case qualified by the comment that some of the 'poorest of the land' were left to attend to agricultural pursuits. How many were taken into exile is uncertain. 2 Kgs. 24^{14} states 10,000 for the exile of 597, but no figures are given for the later years. Jer. 52^{28-30} gives a more modest estimate: the total of 4,600 for the three exiles, 597, 587, and 581. Since we do not know the total population of Judah at this time and we cannot estimate the casualties of war and siege, it is impossible to do more than guess. But if the smaller figures of Jer. 52 are accepted—and they are more probable than the larger round number 10,000—it is reasonable to suppose that there was still a quite substantial population in Judah after 587.

Some of the leading officials—the chief priest Seraiah and his second Zephaniah; temple officials, the military commander of the city, members of the royal council, the army commander's scribe who was responsible for mobilization—together with some sixty 'men of the people of the land' who were in the city were taken to Riblah and executed. This latter group may here again simply be 'ordinary people' in contrast to the leaders, or they may be notable persons from the surrounding area. Among those executed may have been some of those who had most strenuously urged resistance to Babylon, and thus the conquerors sought to break down any possibility of further rebellion. But we can also see in Babylonian policy a method of selective reprisals which is very abhorrent (2 Kgs. 25^{18-21}).

The fortunes of Jeremiah at this juncture are described in Jer. 39 ff., and this narrative, with its opening recognizing the influential position of the prophet, allows us to detect that Babylonian policy was not so ruthless and without discrimination as we might suppose. Not only was a wise choice made of a governor, Gedaliah, of whom more must be said subsequently, but here we have a tradition that Jeremiah was treated with special consideration and given free choice of future—

whether he would go to Babylon and enjoy protection there or stay in Judah with the new governor. He elected to do the latter. Even if this story owes something to the tendency, so clear in many biblical narratives, to present vividly and picturesquely the fortunes of the outstanding characters, it shows that a Babylonian official could be depicted in a favourable light. The further account of the life of Jeremiah will be discussed in relation to the text of Jer. 40–44 (see pp. 34 ff.), and the conditions in Judah after the disaster are also considered subsequently (see pp. 13 ff.).

Any assessment of the situation during the years that followed the capture and destruction of Jerusalem must take seriously the extent of the damage inflicted both on the actual city and its buildings and also on the economy of the area. The withdrawal of the main Babylonian forces—a company was left with Gedaliah at Mizpah (2 Kgs. 25^{25})—would bring some easement. The Judaeans who remained could begin to re-establish agriculture and attempt to re-build their economic life. But recovery was evidently very slow and many of the towns of Judah remained underoccupied and impoverished, as may be seen from the archaeological discoveries.

With the fall of Jerusalem, Judah came even more fully under Babylonian control, with the governor and the Babylonian armed force stationed at Mizpah. Subsequently, with the assassination of the governor Gedaliah we enter a period for which we have no direct internal information. We can only sketch in the general background and see, as we shall do in the succeeding pages, what is likely to have been the situation in Judah and elsewhere. The reign of Nebuchadrezzar continued until 562 B.C. During this period there are indications of the involvement of the Western lands of Asia in Babylonian affairs—the inconclusive siege of Tyre lasting from 585–672 (reflected in Ezek. 26–28, though it is possible that some parts of these chapters reflect the later successful siege of Tyre by Alexander the Great; and note especially Ezek. 29^{17-20} which promises Nebuchadrezzar Egypt as a reward to compensate for his lack of success at Tyre), an intervention in Egypt in

569/568, following on an army rebellion there (cf. Ezek. 29–32 and Jer. 43^{8-13}). With Nebuchadrezzar's death, Babylonian power began to weaken. His successor Amel-marduk (known from the Old Testament record of 2 Kgs. 25^{27-30} as Evil-merodach) reigned only two years. His release of Jehoiachin from prison must have evoked speculation and probably hope. It is related as the last event in the books Joshua to 2 Kings which cover the whole period from the conquest to the exile, and it is clearly therefore important since it provides a climax and may point to the historian's understanding of the experience of the time. It must be considered when we look at that great work of historical and theological interpretation (see p. 145).

The successor of Amel-marduk, Nergal-shar-usur (Neriglissar), may have been a usurper, and when he died after only four years leaving a young son, Labashi-marduk, the opportunity was ripe for further rebellion. The successful rebels placed one of their number on the throne in 556; this was Nabunaid (Nabonidus) who was to remain ruler of the empire during its final period, until its overthrow by Cyrus the Persian, ruler of the empire of the Medes. Cyrus indeed, as ruler of the small subject kingdom of Anshan, part of the Median empire, began to reveal his abilities soon after the accession of Nabonidus, rebelling against his overlord and taking control of the Median empire. In the years that followed, he extended his control north-west into Asia Minor, overcoming the power of king Croesus of Lydia. This constituted a direct threat to Babylon, first because Cyrus now controlled the whole of the eastern and northern frontiers of the Babylonian empire, and second because Lydia and Egypt had become allies of Babylon, the three having joined forces in the face of the increasingly evident threat from the Median power. It was only a matter of time before Babylon fell and the empire changed hands, and in due course the whole of the vast area controlled by Babylon became part of what was the empire of the Medes and Persians but which may be more conveniently and briefly described as the Persian empire.

Nabonidus, on whom the power of Cyrus ultimately fell, was in one sense a victim of circumstance; but it is evident that he was a man of great energy and ability, for though already middle-aged at his accession, he appears to have carried through substantial reforms and maintained the life of the Babylonian empire in a difficult economic situation. The exact nature of his policy and the reasons for his actions are not to be stated with complete certainty, but inferences can be drawn from what is known. It is clear that he earned considerable unpopularity with the Babylonian priests of Marduk for his neglect of the rituals associated with Marduk and with the kingship, particularly during the period in which he was absent from Babylon and operating from Teima in northern Arabia. It appears that he was attempting some kind of religious reorganization, giving prominence to the moon-god Sin; this can be traced in his building activities at Harran, a great centre of the cult of this deity, and it is possible that Nabonidus, through his mother Adda-guppi, evidently a rather remarkable woman, was connected with the Aramaeans of that area. His activities at Teima have been variously interpreted; it used to be thought that he was somewhat of a recluse, interested in archaeological matters, and that he withdrew from the responsibilities of government. It now appears much more probable that his removal to Teima for considerable periods was connected with economic problems, and that he was endeavouring to build up trade with the west and south through this important centre of trade-routes and thereby secure the economic life of the empire. The pressures of the Medes in the east may well have been one of the factors which made a move westwards desirable.

When Cyrus took control of the Babylonian empire and it became part of the Persian domain, there were many to welcome the change, and Cyrus himself issued a propaganda document, the 'Cyrus cylinder', designed to affirm that he had been chosen by Marduk to restore the god to his rightful place in Babylon (see pp. 197 ff.). Nabonidus' unpopularity with some sections of the community has led to misunderstanding of his motives, and due allowance must be made for the very biased pictures of him which are provided in the Babylonian records. Some account will be taken subsequently of these

TEIMA. The Teima oasis became an important centre in the sixth century B.C. when it was conquered and developed by Nabonidus (cf. the text quoted on p. 200). The massive walls still stand prominently; they surround a very large area and provide protection to a whole settlement from raiders from outside. The size and strength of these walls are a measure of the importance of the place for the control of trade in the northern area of Arabia.

records. It is possible that the policy of Nabonidus is reflected in the Old Testament itself (see pp. 23 f.).

C. *The situation in Judah*

The captivity of king Jehoiachin in Babylon since 597 and now the deposing of Zedekiah who had been set on the throne in his place, brought to an end the Davidic dynasty. Zedekiah is clearly described as king, though from the fact that the book of Ezekiel offers datings reckoned from the captivity of Jehoiachin (e.g. 1^{2} explicitly; 40^{1} with a reference to the period of exile; other dates evidently calculated from the same point), it appears that the exiled king was still, in some circles, accorded royal status and regarded as the legitimate though captive ruler. Eventually he was to be released from prison in 562 (2 Kgs. 25^{27}). But with the removal of Zedekiah, it was not Babylonian policy to choose another member of the Davidic family, but Gedaliah the son of Ahikam the son of Shaphan who was now appointed as governor over the land of Judah (2 Kgs. 25^{22}). His precise position is not clear. The text, when it describes his office, simply says that 'he was appointed', he was 'set over' the Judaean community; no term for 'governor' is used such as might have been expected. (The RSV rendering, e.g. in Jer. 40^{5}, obscures this by introducing the word 'governor'.) The absence of a precise term may suggest that his office was simply that of intermediary between the Babylonian forces and the members of the Judaean community who were endeavouring to re-establish their life. He is described as the one who will 'stand before the Chaldeans [Babylonians] who will come to us' (Jer. 40^{10}). The organization of the Babylonian empire was almost certainly that which was inherited from the Assyrian which had preceded it, and much of this political organization was subsequently taken over by the Persians. Later indications, as we shall see, strongly suggest that Judah was at times at least subordinated to the provincial governor in Samaria. Possibly this was already the case in the exilic age.

Gedaliah's family is likely to be the one which figures not infrequently in the narratives of this period. At the time of Josiah's reform there was a Shaphan who was secretary—a high government official (2 Kgs. 22^{8-10}); he had a son named Ahikam (2 Kgs. 22^{12}), and it is therefore most probable that this Gedaliah was his grandson. Other members of the same family appear as Jeremiah's supporters in Jer. 36. A completely positive identification cannot be made because we have to beware of assuming that the same name or even group of names must refer to the same people (cf. also Shaphan in Ezek. 8^{11}). But there is every probability that this is the same family, and Jeremiah's support of Gedaliah (cf. Jer. 40^{1-6}) suggests that he saw in this man a real centre of hope for a new and better ordered life. And initially success did look possible. Gedaliah was joined at Mizpah by a group of important leaders who had escaped the disasters—evidently men whose posts were out in the countryside away from Jerusalem. Jews from neighbouring lands came too and a harvest was gathered which would seem to have augured well for a re-establishment of security. Evidently not every area was totally devastated, and it is possible that the placing of the centre of government at Mizpah, just north of the area where the severest conflicts had taken place, was deliberately done in order to make possible such a revival. Here the vines and olives and other fruit trees had escaped destruction (Jer. 40^{10-12}).

But we have only to think of modern analogies to realize how delicate Gedaliah's position was. Jeremiah had come under suspicion of desertion when he went out of Jerusalem during a lull in the siege (Jer. 37^{11-15}). Deserters there evidently were, and they were much in the mind of Zedekiah when Jeremiah was advising him to submit to Babylon: would he not be handed over to deserters who would have gained favour with the Babylonians (Jer. 38^{17-20})? The deserters, we are told, were taken off into exile (2 Kgs. 25^{11}). Gedaliah was a collaborator, and to some of the community he would clearly be regarded as a traitor, a 'quisling'. The fall of the Davidic house had not removed all Davidic claimants to the throne, and one of these, Ishmael, and a small band with him, assassinated Gedaliah in spite of the fact that he had been warned by some of the military leaders that this was Ishmael's aim. Indeed, they claimed that Ishmael was supported by Baalis, king of the Ammonites. We can only guess at the intrigues which lie behind these events. Was it a genuine attempt at re-establishing the Davidic kingdom? Were the Ammonites seeking some advantage of their own and using

Ishmael as a pawn? In Jer. 49^{1-5} we have an oracle against the Ammonites which suggests that they had taken advantage of the weakness of Judah to settle in areas formerly regarded as belonging to the tribe of Gad. If this oracle belongs to this situation, it may suggest that the neighbouring lands were only too ready to prey upon a weakened Judah, and this can be seen too by the outcry against Edom found in two forms, one in the book of Obadiah and the other in this same chapter 49 of Jeremiah (49^{7-22}). (On Obadiah see pp. 55 ff. and for other elements of the Gedaliah material see pp. 35 ff.). The hope of a new Judah faded. The supporters of Gedaliah in a panic resolved to escape, and against the advice of Jeremiah they went as refugees to Egypt (see pp. 24, 38 f.).

This is all the information we have directly concerning Judah during the exilic age. It leaves unanswered a whole series of questions which would help us not only to understand the period but also to understand the emergence of a newly organized community under Persian rule. What may we legitimately suppose to have happened?

On one point we may be reasonably sure: the Babylonians can hardly have let the incident of Gedaliah's assassination pass unnoticed, especially since their garrison at Mizpah had been wiped out too. Intervention would take the form of reprisals and probably further deportations. Jer. 52^{30} refers to such a deportation of 745 persons in 581. This may be the sequel, or it may be an independent action. If it is the sequel, then the period of Gedaliah's control may be longer than we might immediately infer from the very abbreviated account given in Jer. 40–41, an account which is clearly very selective in its treatment of the period.

We may also not unreasonably assume that come what may the ordinary folk who survived the disaster, especially those who lived in more out-of-the-way areas, would soon begin to recover their relatively meagre way of life. Some of them, like their later compatriots in the time of the Jewish War of A.D. 66–73, would have taken refuge in the caves in the dangerous valleys in the area to the south and south-east of Jerusalem—

the same caves in which relics of later refugees have been found in recent years, caves overlooking the bare rocky country bordering the Dead Sea near En Gedi, not far from the great rock fortress which was later to be called Massada. Such refugees would return to their home areas as opportunity offered, re-establish their simple agriculture, tend their flocks and live as they had done before, at a low subsistence level, relatively unmoved by the great political events, but no doubt perplexed, in so far as they thought about such things, at the overthrow of their country and the apparent inability or unwillingness of their God to protect his own.

Of the towns we know little other than that their ruined state would make full reoccupation slow. But we have a glimpse of Jerusalem as a place of worship in Jer. $41^{4\,\mathrm{ff.}}$, for though the sanctuary is not named it is difficult to believe that any place other than Jerusalem was intended. Here we read of loyal worshippers from Shechem, Shiloh, and Samaria coming to mourn and make offerings. There had been terrible destruction in the temple; but it is difficult not to suppose that some attempt would be made at clearing the ruins, removing the burnt woodwork and in all probability engaging in some act of rededication, of cleansing, which would permit some form of worship there. But what? Does the mention of only cereal offerings and incense in Jer. 41^{5} mean that the full sacrificial system could not be resumed, or was this limitation simply appropriate to the particular celebration of lamentation in which these worshippers were preparing to engage? It has been sometimes thought that psalms, such as 40 or 51, which appear in part to repudiate sacrifice, belong to such an age as this, but it is very difficult to be sure. The emphasis, as in the prophetic writings of the earlier period (cf. e.g. Hos. $6^{1\,\mathrm{ff.}}$), is really on what God requires. And Ps. 51^{18-19}, possibly an addition to reapply the psalm to such a situation as that of exile, does not necessarily mean that no sacrifices are offered but rather that the full joy of such a worship will only be possible when the tokens of divine favour are seen in a restored sanctuary and city.

Can we detect anything clearly in the book of Lamentations, so closely associated with this period, though, as poetry, not a very satisfactory source from which to reconstruct an exact picture of conditions? The wording of Lam. 2 (cf. also pp. 46 ff.) indicates the measure of the disaster and the distress (so esp. vv. 5–10), but the phrases cannot be taken merely literally. The question, however, which we may ask is: for what kind of occasion were poems such as these composed? Using the motifs and language of much more ancient psalms of lamentation, they appear now to allude clearly to this greatest moment of distress. But in their poetic descriptions they are not just recalling disaster. They are expressing penitence, acknowledging the causes of the calamity, looking to the hope of release which rests only in God.

> Thou, O Lord, abidest for ever;
> Thy throne is from generation to generation.
> Wherefore dost thou forget us for ever,
> And forsake us so long time?
> Turn thou us unto thee, O Lord, and we shall be turned;
> Renew our days as of old.
> But thou hast utterly rejected us,
> Thou art very wroth against us. (Lam. 5^{19-22})

Here, in this climax to the collection, is the appeal. Hope in this situation lies only in God and to him appeal must be made. It is most natural to suppose that such psalms as these belong to occasions of mourning, festivals celebrating disaster, fasts in which the people can acknowledge their condition and call upon God in his mercy. If we compare some of the psalms in the psalter (cf. pp. 41 ff.), we may see how the invocation of God is made in terms of what he has done in the past, what he is, merciful and faithful to his covenant, what he is in himself, one whose glory must not be dimmed among the nations. These are themes which will recur. They belong appropriately to a worship, restricted perhaps, but real, during the period of frustration and desolation. When later in Zech. 7–8 we find reference to different occasions of fasting, we may see a possible setting for such laments.

But whatever was done in the temple during the exilic age, it did not remove the sense of desolation. To those who spoke outside Palestine—the prophets and others in Babylonia—the conditions of Jerusalem remained pitiful, and the need for restoration was felt acutely. We should not minimize the magnitude of the disaster.

D. *The situation in Babylonia*

Apart from the tablets which mention Jehoiachin and which belong to the period between 597 and 587 B.C. (see p. 3), we have no non-biblical evidence for the exiled members of the community in Babylonia and for their treatment and fortunes there. From the second half of the fifth century B.C.—more than a hundred years later—there are records available from a Babylonian business company at Nippur, south-east of Babylon—the company of the Murashu family—and among those mentioned in these records are some with Jewish names. The continuing existence of a Jewish community in Babylonia from the sixth century B.C. onwards is attested by various indications in the biblical material—new impetus to development and reform came from the eastern part of the Persian empire on more than one occasion—and later still, influential Jewish rabbinic activity is attested for the period of the development of the final form of the Hebrew text of the Old Testament and of the Talmud and other Jewish writings. But this is in the first millennium A.D. The Murashu tablets are important because they are nearer to the time with which we are concerned, but it would be hazardous to deduce from them firm conclusions about the life of the exiles under Babylonian rule.

One of the tablets, a tax receipt, runs as follows:

> From 1½ minas of silver, the taxes on a field for the 33rd year of Artaxerxes the king belonging to Enlil-aha-iddina, the son of Gahla, which is at the disposition of Enlil-nadin-shumi, the son of Murashu—therefrom Enlil-aha-iddina received (and) obtained payment of 1 mina from the hand of Enlil-nadin-shumi.
>
> (witness, date, and thumbnail impression of the recipient)
>
> (*ANET*, pp. 221 f.)

These are simple business documents. The Murashu firm was not Jewish, and only a small proportion of its customers bore Jewish names. All that we can deduce is that in the period of these tablets some Jews were engaged in trade with men of other nationalities. Little can be deduced about the degree of their prosperity and influence, and all that this tells us about the preceding century is that some of the families who were settled in Babylonia remained there and were engaged in business transactions. Perhaps one day more information than this will come to light in new documentary evidence.

From the biblical material, various pieces of information can be deduced, but we have to realize that at no point is there any attempt at giving a description of life in Babylonia. When Jeremiah exhorts the exiles of 597 to

> build houses and live in them,
> plant gardens and eat their produce (Jer. 29[5])

he is presumably referring to real possibilities, though a poetic saying of this kind should not be overpressed. His primary emphasis here is on accepting the exile, accepting Babylonian rule:

> seek the welfare of the city where I have sent you into exile . . . (Jer. 29[7]).

No indication is given of the degree of freedom enjoyed, though the carrying on of correspondence revealed by this chapter of Jeremiah points to a measure of independent life.

Were conditions identical after 587 or should we suppose that the further provocation of the Babylonian authorities might be expected to lead to a severer treatment of the exiles at the next stage? The book of Ezekiel provides some slight clues, but the drawing of inferences from them is not easy. If Ezekiel was, as the book implies, already in exile in 597, then passages which refer to his sitting 'in my house, with elders of Judah sitting before me' (Ezek. 8[1]) may equally reflect the earlier situation and not necessarily the later (cf. also 14[1]; 20[1]). If Ezekiel was in Judah until 587—a view which has been argued (see pp. 64 f., 81 f.)—then such statements may reflect the later period when the teaching of the prophet was being reapplied in exilic assemblies. But these passages do not

THE ZIGGURAT OF BABYLON. The picture is of a model made to depict this great religious monument of Babylon, called E-temen-an-ki, 'The house of the foundation of heaven and earth', evidently intended to convey the relationship between the realm of the gods and that of men. It was destroyed and rebuilt many times, most splendidly by Nabopolassar and his son Nebuchadrezzar in this period. A little over a century later, it was described by the Greek historian Herodotus; 'The temple is a square building, two furlongs each way, with bronze gates, and was still in existence in my time; it has a solid central tower, one furlong square, with a second erected on top of it and then a third, and so on up to eight. All eight towers can be climbed by a spiral way running round the outside . . .' (*The Histories*, Book I, Penguin ed., p. 86). The ziggurat was part of the great temple complex dedicated to Marduk. It may serve here to symbolize the splendour of Babylonian buildings and Babylonian religion and to suggest how overpowering their effect must have been on exiled Jews. The 'tower of Babel' tradition in Gen. 11 is likely to be linked in some way with the existence of such great tower temples in many places in Mesopotamia.

really tell much; they provide a rather conventional setting for teaching. The elders appear at the beginning of a section, but do not reappear once the teaching has begun, nor does it necessarily follow that the teaching is given in direct reference to the elders (so Ezek. 20$^{3\text{ff.}}$ which appears to move over into a much more general condemnation, applicable to the whole people). In this, the settings are not unlike those found in the Fourth Gospel (e.g. John 12^20–22), and they may simply follow a traditional pattern (cf. 2 Kgs. 6^32). We cannot deduce from them anything clear about the ordering of the community or its freedom.

Certain parts of the Old Testament were in all probability shaped in Babylonia, and from this we may make some general deductions about conditions. The so-called Holiness Code (Lev. 17–26, see pp. 152 ff.) and the Priestly Work (mainly in Genesis–Numbers, see pp. 148 ff.) were almost certainly shaped there and subsequently brought to Palestine. The book of Ezekiel is likely to have received its final shape there, and probably the unknown prophet, usually referred to as the Second Isaiah (or Deutero-Isaiah—i.e. Isa. 40–55), worked there, though this has been seriously questioned. The great historical survey known as the Deuteronomic History (Deuteronomy, Joshua—2 Kings, cf. pp. 141 ff.) may have been shaped there too, though a Palestinian setting is also possible. The only evidence in all these cases is internal; no direct statement appears anywhere, but it is evident that wherever this work on the literature continued there must have been an influential and capable group of men, with sufficient resources and freedom to undertake the work. Ps. 137 (see p. 59) sheds a different light on the distressed state of mind of the exiles.

How can we picture this activity, whether in Palestine or in Babylonia (or even among some other Jewish groups)? Writing is a serious matter; it implies the skill of the trained scribe. It suggests the availability of documentary material on which the newer works are based. All this suggests a centre of religious life and of administration, and may therefore imply a greater degree of freedom and organization in Babylonia, as well as a certain revival of life in Palestine during the period in question. Conclusions can be drawn only with hesitation.

For the last years of Babylonian rule, when Nabonidus was on the throne, there are some other though still somewhat elusive clues. As we have seen (pp. 12 f.) the policy of Nabonidus is not altogether clear. His religious policy led to his conqueror Cyrus being welcomed by some of his subjects. Is it possible to detect in the welcome given to Cyrus by Second Isaiah and in the presentation of the history of the return in Ezra 1, a recognition not only that Babylon was viewed as the conquering and destroying power of the disaster of 587, but also that there may have been pressures on the Jewish exiles in Babylonia of a harsher kind than earlier? Clearly the earlier years of the exile must not be idealized; to live in a foreign land after deportation involves the kind of social and family upheavals which are all too familiar in the twentieth century, and personal sufferings must often have been acute. But after the show of favour to Jehoiachin, which may indicate some degree of relaxation, hostility to Babylon does appear more sharply in Isa. 40–55 (cf. the ridiculing of the Babylonian gods in 46^{1-2} and the harsh judgements of 47), and it may be that the anti-Babylonian oracles of Isa. 13–14 and Jer. 50–51 belong to this moment, in urgent anticipation of a conquest about to take place.

Did Nabonidus' religious policy, with its promotion of the worship of the moon-god Sin, involve an attempt at producing some kind of religious conformity? The multiplicity of deities in Babylonia may well have suggested a need for reform! Did such a reform involve Jews who were unwilling to pay even lip-service to other gods? No precise evidence is available, but we may note that later traditions concerning this period of exile lay considerable stress on hardship and persecution for the sake of religion. The stories included in the book of Daniel belong in their present form to the early second century B.C. and are set in the context of religious persecution at that time. But they purport to relate what happened in Babylonia in the sixth century B.C. How far do they contain genuine reflections of the earlier period? The story of the mad king in Dan. 4 may now be paralleled in a fragment found at Qumran which attributes a similar experience to Nabonidus. What is said of Nabonidus in Babylonian documents could very well have led to the growth of the tradition that he was mad at one time. It could also conceivably be the case that the story of the great image in Dan. 3 originally referred not to Nebuchadrezzar but to Nabonidus and represents an allusion to his policy of religious uniformity. (Some of these points are discussed in Vol. 5, pp. 200 ff.) In addition, other legends of Daniel were in circulation, and two of them—Bel and the Dragon, found in the Apocrypha—similarly lay stress on idolatrous practices in Babylonia. But such clues to the conditions of the sixth century B.C. are inconclusive. Like the story in the book of Esther, which originated in the Babylonian area, they may equally reflect experience of religious antagonism and anti-Jewish prejudice in the years of Persian and Greek rule. Such anti-Jewish prejudice is certainly attested in the Persian period in Elephantine (see pp. 279 ff.) and in Alexandria in the Greek period.

E. *Other exiles from Judah*

It is evident from Jer. 40[11f.] that at the time of the siege and fall of Jerusalem in 587, many of the inhabitants of Judah were scattered, either driven out by the invading armies or going voluntarily into remoter areas—'in Moab and among the Ammonites and in Edom and in other lands'. Some of them returned when Gedaliah established himself at Mizpah, but not necessarily all. (The text of Jer. 40 says that they all returned, but allowance needs to be made here for the purpose of a narrative which is linked with the description of Gedaliah as the chosen leader of what appeared to be a new people.) In any case, with his assassination a new dispersal took place, and in particular a description is provided in Jer. 42–44 of the events by which a party of unknown size went to Egypt. (Again the implication of the text at Jer. 42[2] is that it was the whole population, though this is most improbable.) The fortunes of this party of refugees can be traced in Jer. 44 (see pp. 38 f.), but no information is available about their subsequent fate. The text implies their total disappearance, but some must have returned, bringing the message of Jeremiah with them to be linked with the other traditions about the prophet. Some may have survived to form part of that eventually much larger Jewish community which existed in Egypt in the Greek and Roman periods.

The existence of a Jewish military colony at Elephantine at the southern border of Egypt in the sixth and fifth centuries B.C. is attested by documents which reveal some aspects of its life (see pp. 279 ff.). There is no doubt that this colony had been in Egypt from before the time of Cambyses (529–522 B.C.) for more than once the documents refer to the existence of the temple at Elephantine which was protected in Cambyses' time:

> Already in the days of the kings of Egypt (i.e. before the Persian conquest of Egypt by Cambyses) our fathers built that temple in the fortress of Yeb, and when Cambyses came into Egypt he found that temple built and the temples of the gods of Egypt all of them they overthrew, but no one did any harm to that temple (Cowley No. 30, lines 13–14).

But we do not know the actual origin of the colony. Probably it was a small mercenary force and its function at Elephantine was to assist in protecting the southern border of Egypt. Its significance is greater for us when we consider the problems of the history of the fifth century, but here we may simply observe that the adherents of the ancient faith were already scattered far and wide. The people was no longer to be thought of as one geographically conditioned entity; it was a complex and scattered community.

F. *Religious practice in the exilic age*

We have already seen (pp. 17 f.) the uncertainties which surround the question of the use of the temple or its site in Jerusalem during the exilic age. In some degree the questions about what its condition was and what was practised there need to be answered before we can go on to consider other aspects of worship and religious practice. It is difficult to imagine a community in the ancient world living without any kind of religious observance—the example of Jer. 44 shows us how with the fall of Jerusalem older religious practices such as that of the worship of the 'queen of heaven' could come ot the fore. What we do not know is how far worship apart from the temple site continued or was developed in this period, and in part the question depends upon other points on which there is no clear information available to us.

We know that in the time of Josiah, dating especially from the reform in 621 B.C., an attempt was made at centralizing all worship in Jerusalem and abolishing all other sanctuaries (2 Kgs. 22–23). It seems likely that an earlier attempt of this kind had been made in the time of Hezekiah (cf. 2 Kgs. 18[1–4, 22] and Jer. 26[19]), equally as part of a strongly nationalistic movement. But how completely successful the reforms were is less certain. The law of one sanctuary, clearly stated in Deut. 12[1–14], which may be in some way associated with the reform movement, was eventually to be applied stringently. But laws have a way of being disobeyed or simply disregarded, and there are at least some indications of worship at other places—Elephantine in Egypt, Leontopolis in Egypt (built probably by Onias IV, son of a notable high priest Onias III, for whom continued practice in Jerusalem had become impossible; cf. Vol. 5, pp. 36 n., 105 f.). We do not know how far the full sacrificial worship was observed at these places. It has also been suggested, though the evidence for this is very slight, that a new sanctuary was set up at Mizpah in the time of Gedaliah, and again, that during the exilic age, the ancient sanctuary of Bethel, which had been a royal shrine of the northern kingdom, came into its own again. The question of the Samaritans and their shrine on Mount Gerizim presents problems of a different kind which must be examined later (see pp. 000).

On none of these points is there clear evidence; nor is it possible to be sure what happened in Babylonia. The book of Ezekiel refers to God himself being to his people in exile 'a sanctuary . . . for a while'—or 'a sanctuary . . . in small measure' (Ezek. 11[16]; cf. p. 85). This may mean 'they need no shrine, because I myself am with them'. It is the presence of a deity which counts; without it a temple is nothing. It can also mean 'I will be with them, as in the Jerusalem temple, but only for a short time' or 'only on a small scale'. This implies either a temporary temple in Babylonia or a temple recognized to be only a shadow of the Jerusalem temple. From a somewhat later period—in Ezra 8^{17}—there is a reference to 'the place Casiphia' to which Ezra sent because he found that he had in his company, setting out for Jerusalem, no priests and temple attendants of the Levitical family. Does 'place' here mean simply 'locality', or does it, as so often in the Old Testament, mean 'holy place, shrine'? And if the latter, was this possibly yet another temple used during the exilic period, though perhaps not for full sacrificial worship?

The greatest danger in interpreting this material is that of imposing on it later ideas. That there should be one temple was an idea which grew only gradually to become dominant; the reasons for its growth were various—nationalist pressure, the prestige of the royal shrine at Jerusalem, the practices at other sanctuaries which were regarded, and perhaps rightly, as corrupted by idolatry, the recognition that it was appropriate that Israel's one and only God could have only one earthly dwelling as counterpart to his heavenly abode. But what was a natural development and intelligible in Palestine may not have been everywhere regarded as obligatory—the later Samaritan community could reject Jerusalem and so it appears could the Qumran group—and what could be urged as applicable while the people were still in their own land did not necessarily meet their needs in the years of exile. While still longing to be in the sanctuary at Jerusalem and to see it gloriously restored (cf. Pss. 42, 137), they must praise God aright wherever they were, and how could this be done without what was laid down in the law concerning sacrifices and other kinds of offering and worship?

If the full sacrificial worship was not possible, what did the people do instead? This is a question relevant for the period of Josiah's reform too, for though the country was small, worship at Jerusalem could be only occasional—three times a year at the great festivals for the men according to Deut. 16^{16}. But could this be all? Again the answer is not known to us. We must not import our ideas of regular religious practice back into the Old Testament situation without warrant. It is often suggested—and perhaps rightly—that it was in such a situation, before or during the exile, that the institution which was later to be known as the synagogue came into being. But this is purely a supposition. We have information concerning a practice of reading the law once every seven years at the Feast of Tabernacles (Deut. 31^{10}) at the central shrine; is it possible that such a practice was more widespread, observed on other occasions too? Later the synagogue was to be the great place for the reading and expounding of the law. Neh. 8 perhaps provides us with a picture of a stage in the evolution of the institution, with reading and exposition specially stressed. The synagogue was very much a place of instruction; this perhaps originally rather than a place for worship in the narrower sense. The synagogue is not therefore really an alternative to the temple and its sacrificial worship, and only became a substitute at a much later date when the temple no longer existed (i.e. after A.D. 70). For the institution itself no direct evidence is available until a much later date, and then only outside Palestine until we come to the Christian era.

What perhaps points towards such exposition of older traditions and prophecies is the recognition that in the prophetic and historical books particularly of this period there is a good deal of what we may call 'sermon' material. Thus Jer. 7^{1}–8^{3} can be seen as a long sermon, built up of various elements, linked with a particular utterance of Jeremiah which appears in a somewhat different way in Jer. 26. The 'sermon' elaborates various aspects of the prophet's teaching. Similar 'sermons' may be found in the book of Ezekiel and in the historical writings extending from Joshua to 2 Kings (e.g. 1 Sam. 12; 2 Kgs. 17). Later 'sermons' appear in the writings of the Chronicler (e.g. 2 Chron. 13^{4-12}). In what contexts were these 'sermons' originally composed and used? Perhaps in assemblies, small or large, in which the traditions of the past, the story of Israel's covenant and blessing by God, the stories of her heroes and prophets, and the words of the prophets were read, recited, and shown to be still meaningful to a new generation. Exposition of the laws may be found especially in the book of Deuteronomy and in the Holiness Code in Lev. 17–26. The poems of Second Isaiah (Isa. 40–55) often have a strongly rhetorical tone. Were they perhaps delivered by the prophet on occasions when it was appropriate to exhort and warn and encourage? Later still in the book of Malachi we find the question and answer style, very appropriate to teaching and warning.

But all precise description of the places and occasions for such exhortations is lacking. For the people to have survived the disaster of 587 and to have learnt from it how to reorganize their life, there must have been those who led and encouraged them, who had insight into the events of the time and into the meaning of the past so as to speak with discernment of what the future might hold. We have considerable collections of material very much of this kind. But just how and when and where it was used is no longer known to us; we can only attempt a reconstruction working back from the material we have.

The people in exile found themselves living alongside other nations who worshipped other gods, and who engaged in different religious practices. One of the problems must have been that of preserving the identity of the people which believed itself to be the 'people of God'. One way to do this would be such a study of ancient traditions. Another way would be by the development of special customs and practices by which they would know themselves marked off from other people.

Three practices in particular could be held at a later date to be the special marks of the Jewish community—the observance of the sabbath, the strict food laws, and the practice of circumcision. None of these practices was new in the sixth century B.C. The sabbath was evidently an ancient institution (cf. 2 Kgs. 4^{23}; Isa. 1^{13}). We find it interpreted in the decalogue in Exod. 20^{11} with a reference to Gen. 1—the later form of the creation story which took its final form possibly in about the sixth century B.C.—and differently interpreted in the Deuteronomic form of the decalogue in Deut. 5[15]. We find it alluded to in Ezekiel (ch. 20) and in Isa. 58 (perhaps just after the exile) and in Jer. 17[19–27] (probably later than Jeremiah and akin to Neh. 13[15–22]). The greater emphasis on the institution may indicate that it was being given a new and deeper meaning than it had at an earlier time (cf. pp. 155 f.).

That the food laws separate Jews from other peoples is still evident today, and if these laws seem strange, we should remember that they are ancient practices, whose origin is in any case very obscure, but which have become an expression of allegiance to Judaism. For their preservation, many Jews through the centuries have been willing to die with a faithfulness which commands respect and honour. The book of Daniel opens with just such a story of faithfulness. (Cf. Vol. 5, pp. 224 ff.) Much of the legislation about foods, about clean and unclean, is undoubtedly very old, but it is in the collections of laws which were given their final form in and about the exilic age—in Deuteronomy, in the books of Leviticus and Numbers—that we find the fullest setting out of the regulations. These are not just ancient laws being preserved as interesting relics of the past. It would appear rather that ancient practice is taking on a new meaning.

Reference to the Philistines as 'uncircumcized' (2 Sam. 1[20]) shows that at an early date Israel could be distinguished from some of her neighbours by reason of this religious rite (cf. also Gen. 34), probably in origin an initiation rite into sexual maturity. But apart from one or two stories which seek to explain its origin or to give it significance as marking a new beginning (Gen. 17; Exod. 4[24–26]; Josh. 5[2–9]), little is said about the custom. Later it came to be understood as marking entry into membership of the Jewish community, and even to be considered the most distinctive mark of the Jew (cf. Paul's discussion of it in his letter to the Galatians). Possibly this too was a custom which was given new meaning and emphasis in about the same period, though we have no precise indications of the process.

In each of these three cases, we can do no more than say that such developments could well belong to the exilic age. In reality, just as there is no sharp division between that age and what precedes and follows, so these customs will already have been in the process of change, or reinterpretation. What the crisis of the years of exile may have done was to sharpen men's perception of their meaning and importance as they tried to understand what it really meant to be part of that community which God had, as they saw it, made to be his own special people.

G. *The experience and its effects*

How does a community feel when its whole life is broken by military invasion and by political and social collapse? What reactions take place within a people's life and thought? Subsequently we shall be looking at some of the major works which appear to have come into being at this time; here we may simply make some general comments.

At the outset it is important to be imaginative in considering what people would think and feel. Some tentative parallels from more recent history might be drawn to suggest that for many of the ordinary people, the poorer members of the community—and that means the majority, living off the produce of small pieces of land, maintaining a livelihood by some such trade as that of a potter—the change of political life and the change of ruler would make very little material difference. Poverty is always there. Some are dead and some are refugees from the terrors of war and invasion. But with peace, life has to go on and the land has to be cultivated; flocks and herds have to be tended and built up again; houses are restored as opportunity offers, crops must be sown and harvested, and the routine of the year continues. What time and opportunity is there for thinking? No doubt many, without consciously thinking out what these great events could mean, simply continued with the religious observances of the past, being conservative in outlook as such people often are. They are aware of the ancient traditions of their people, and without any clear attempt at explaining, they go on worshipping the God of their fathers, adhering to ancient custom. No very striking reaction is to be seen here, yet here is the backbone to the community's life, even where the larger issues are not in discussion.

To some, misfortune seemed to argue that their God had deserted them, defeated by the superior power of the Babylonian gods. The worship of other deities—those of the conqueror or those of older cults which still persisted—can readily be understood. We find it condemned by the prophets (e.g. Ezek. 8 which describes a variety of idolatrous practices even in the temple at Jerusalem in the period between 597 and 587; it is very difficult to know precisely what cults these are, apart from the mention of 'weeping for Tammuz', a deity well known from the Mesopotamian area as a god connected with fertility. Jer. 44 provides another typical example; cf. pp. 38 f.). What is remarkable is not that this happened, but that it did not outweigh the pressures of religious conservatism, faithfulness to the old ways. When we read the criticisms which prophets such as Jeremiah and Ezekiel levelled at their contemporaries—as, for example, in Jer. 5 and Ezek. 16—we might be excused for thinking that all was black. But the prophets characteristically describe in the vivid terms of poetic hyperbole a situation which is much more complex. The castigations of idolatry and of social evils were no doubt deserved; but the words which the prophets spoke were remembered and cherished and they found a response in those who were anxious to preserve what was good. There were those who did 'sigh and groan over all the abominations' (Ezek. 9^4), and Jeremiah, in moments of crisis, found support even among the high officials (cf. Jer. 26 and 36 for examples of this).

The preservation of prophetic words may be seen not only in the writings associated with the contemporaries of the events, but also in the collections which are linked with the great names of the previous centuries. A careful study of the prophecies collected under the names of Amos, Hosea, Micah, and Isaiah reveals that the words of the prophets have often been reapplied to new situations and in particular to the disasters which finally overtook Judah. The same is true also of the collections in the books of Zephaniah, Nahum, and Habakkuk where original words of judgement, or, in the case of Nahum, of triumph, are shown to have more than one application. The judgement pronounced upon the northern kingdom by Amos and Hosea was seen to be meaningful to Judah when the north collapsed. Subsequently collections of the words of these prophets, and those of Micah and Isaiah, were handed down and reinterpreted, seen to be applicable to new situations. The last verses of the book of Amos (9^{11-15}) are most naturally understood as referring to the period after 587 when the Davidic monarchy had fallen; there may well be other late passages in the book. But this means that when we read the book as a whole, we are being invited to appreciate that what Amos said to Israel in the middle of the eighth century has been proved true and so is still meaningful in the situation of disaster in the sixth century. Those who heard the words afresh then were being invited to take them to heart as applicable to themselves. The judgement had been proved right; but the God whose purposes Amos declared had more yet to say to his people beyond judgement in mercy and promise.

We cannot always distinguish what is early from what is later. Isa. 3^{1-3} may contain both earlier words of judgement and a later reinterpretation of these words applied to the siege of 589–587. The words of the prophet have come down in the larger context of a book which contains much—not only in chapters 40–66 but also elsewhere—which is of sixth century or even later origin. The earlier words were not preserved out of antiquarian interest, but were given new meaning in this larger context. We have to learn to read the prophetic books as collections not merely put together for one moment of time, but seen as meaningful for many new situations.

Earlier prophets had proclaimed a great day of disaster, a coming 'Day of Yahweh' (Amos 5^{18-20}; Isa. 2^{9-22}; Zeph. 1^{7-18}). To some of their successors, it must have appeared clear that now in the moment of exile that great day of judgement had come. Later still, in the writings described as 'apocalyptic' (cf. Vol. 5, pp. 219 ff.) this idea of a great day of judgement is yet further developed. Some who experienced the disaster of 587 found it possible to see in the events the hand of God; this was what had been proclaimed as right, this was what God had spoken through his prophets. Judgement had fallen and was to be accepted as a true expression of the divine will.

Such an acceptance can be narrow and fatalistic. The contemporaries of Jeremiah and Ezekiel had a proverb:

> The fathers have eaten sour grapes
> and the children's teeth are set on edge.

It is quoted in the prophecies of Jeremiah (31^{29}) and of Ezekiel (18^{2}) and both prophets build upon it teaching about the true meaning of events. But that men could say such a thing points to a certain feeling of hopelessness. Ezekiel describes the people as saying: 'Our bones are dried up and our hope is lost, we are clean cut off' (37^{11}). But it was possible also for a poet to express his conviction of the rightness of judgement and also the distress which it occasioned him (see Lam. 1), and it was possible for men in this time to look at the past and to attempt to understand the will and purpose of God and so to set out a new picture of what the past had been and what, by inference, the future might be. This may be seen most clearly in the history from Joshua to 2 Kings; but we may see it also in prophecies and other writings which are in some measure to be associated with this period.

NOTES ON SELECTED PASSAGES

A. JEREMIAH 40–44*

In the second half of the book of Jeremiah, chapters 26 to 45, we have a number of stories concerning the last years of

* On Jer. 37–45, cf. also Vol. 3, pp. 387–9.

the kingdom of Judah, in some parts very like the narrative in the last chapters of 2 Kings. Here, in an account which corresponds to the short version in 2 Kgs. 25^{22-26}, we are shown the part played by Jeremiah, who till then had been in custody (38^{28}); he was put in the charge of Nebuzaradan, the captain of the guard, who in turn committed Jeremiah to Gedaliah (39^{11-14}). The story implies the measure of Jeremiah's influence in the political events of the time; and it may well be that Gedaliah, chosen to be governor of Judah, was able to ensure this protection for the prophet, just as his father had rescued Jeremiah on an earlier occasion (26^{24}). The various narratives in chapters 40–44 indicate some of the sequels to this.

40^{1-12} *Jeremiah and Gedaliah*

The passage begins formally with a phrase which is perhaps intended to cover the whole of what follows: this is Jeremiah's message in this time of trial. We may have here an alternative form of the story related in the previous chapter. We find the author putting into the mouth of the Babylonian Nebuzaradan the prophetic judgement upon Judah (vv. 2–3). Then Jeremiah is offered the choice of going to Babylon with the other exiles, with a promise of special protection there, or of staying where he pleases in Judah, though he is encouraged to join Gedaliah (vv. 4–5). We may note that in chapter 24 Jeremiah likens the exiles to good figs and the leaders in Jerusalem to bad figs, but this was clearly a judgement on a particular situation, and not to be taken as a general statement, since we know that Jeremiah could also be strongly critical of some at least of the exiles (cf. $29^{20\text{ff.}}$). Jeremiah's decision to stay with Gedaliah suggests that he saw here, in submission to Babylon, a real hope of revival, the possibility of the fulfilment of his own hopes as expressed in his redemption of a piece of family property (32^{1-25}). (On Gedaliah, cf. also pp. 14 ff.)

Jeremiah joined Gedaliah at Mizpah, about six miles north of Jerusalem, quite near Ramah where he had been released (v. 1). Probably Gedaliah chose this place as convenient for liaison with the Babylonians (v. 10) and it had presumably escaped the devastation of the war. Certainly it was possible for those who now gathered about him to collect an abundant harvest (v. 12) which would stand them in good stead at a difficult time. The establishment of Gedaliah attracted commanders of various military groups as well as fugitives from the war in neighbouring areas. All appeared to be set for a modest revival of life.

40[13]–43[7] *The assassination of Gedaliah and its consequences*

But all was not well. It is not surprising to find that even now there were still those who hoped for a revival of the Davidic monarchy in Judah, and Ishmael, described in 41[1] as belonging to the royal house, contrived with Ammonite support to assassinate Gedaliah and his associates as well as the Babylonian garrison at Mizpah. Gedaliah had refused to be warned of the danger, and would not permit a secret attack on Ishmael. Was he too good-natured to believe evil of a fellow Jew? Or did he suspect Johanan, who warned him, of some ulterior motive? We have no precise information, nor do we know the reason for Ammonite involvement in this coup. We do not know precisely how long Gedaliah was in control, for no year is given in 41[1] where the assassination is dated in the seventh month. This could be the autumn of the same year in which Gedaliah had been appointed, just after his encouraging words to the Jewish remnant (40[9–10]). The mention of pilgrims coming to the ruined shrine in 41[5] would suggest that all these events took place almost at once, but such pilgrims might have travelled to the shrine at a later time too. In Jer. 52[30]—as part of a passage almost identical with 2 Kgs. 25—there is mention of a further group of 745 Jews being carried away captive. This is dated in Nebuchadrezzar's twenty-third year, i.e. *c.* 581 B.C. Although there may be no connection between this event and the murder of the Babylonian garrison at Mizpah, it is reasonable to suppose that the Babylonians would take retaliatory action, and this might suggest that the narrative in Jer. 40–41 has telescoped the events into a shorter period than they actually covered. (A similar apparent telescoping of events may be seen in the opening chapters of the book of Ezra; cf. pp. 205 ff.)

Ishmael's next action is difficult to understand. A group of eighty pilgrims from the central part of the land on its way to the ruined shrine in Jerusalem is intercepted and enticed into Mizpah. All but ten were murdered, the ten managing to bribe Ishmael to spare them. Why did he commit this crime? Did he mistake these men for loyal supporters of Gedaliah who would be a danger to him? Or did he, perhaps more probably, fear that they would carry a report of Gedaliah's death back to the Babylonian authorities in Samaria? Samaria was undoubtedly an important administrative centre, as it had been under the Assyrians; after the exile, we find Judah for long periods under the control of the governor there (cf. pp. 169, 253). It has been suggested that these pilgrims were on their way to Mizpah, on the assumption that Gedaliah had moved the religious as well as the political centre there. But their coming in mourning (41[5]) shows that they were in fact on their way to the ruined Jerusalem temple, and evidently offerings could still be made there. The reference to cereals and incense alone could suggest that the worship was limited, but although in the sacrificial laws the word *minḥā*, translated here as *cereal offerings*, is used in this narrower sense, elsewhere, particularly in older passages, it is used quite generally of sacrifices of all kinds. What is particularly important is to see that the temple at Jerusalem was regarded as a centre of worship for people outside Judah; even from the ancient centres of Shiloh (cf. 1 Sam. 1–3) and Shechem (cf. Josh. 24), and from the administrative centre of Samaria, former capital of the northern kingdom, there were many who looked to Jerusalem as their holy place. After the exile, the temple in Jerusalem was to be even more clearly the focal point for the scattered Jews of Palestine and of further afield.

The story goes on to tell how Johanan and his associates rescued at Gibeon those who had been taken prisoner by

Ishmael, though Ishmael himself escaped. Then, in fear of Babylonian reprisals, the whole group who had joined Gedaliah at Mizpah fled to the south, intending to go to Egypt as refugees. (Chapters 42–43 tell how Jeremiah was consulted about this flight to Egypt and advised against it, foretelling disaster upon those who went. His words went unheeded and he was taken with his disciple Baruch and the rest. We are also told of a message of Jeremiah against Egypt, indicating judgement of that land at the hands of Babylon. A campaign did take place in about 569 B.C.)

44^{1-23} *Refugees in Egypt*

It is natural to connect this passage directly with what precedes since here Jeremiah passes judgement on Jews in Egypt as also in 42^{9-22}. But two factors suggest that the original judgement has been extended in scope. On the one hand, we have here a passage which is very much like Deuteronomy in its sermon-style. The repetitions, the formal phrases, are very much like other sermons to be found in the book of Jeremiah (e.g. in 7 and 8) and in Deuteronomy (e.g. 28, cf. p. 146). On the other hand, the places mentioned in 44^{1} cover a fairly wide area (see map, p. 164). *Tahpanhes* is in the northern delta of the Nile; *Memphis* is on the Nile just south of the delta area. *Migdol* is mentioned in Ezekiel (29^{10}, 30^{6}) as marking the northern extremity of Egypt (Syene, Elephantine, cf. p. 279, marks the southern). *The land of Pathros* means upper, i.e. southern, Egypt. Jeremiah is pictured as addressing all the Jews now scattered in Egypt, whether they belong to the party which brought him or had come on other occasions. The condemnation exactly parallels that of Judah in Jer. 7; it is apostasy which calls down doom. These people are worshipping other gods, and in particular the *queen of heaven* (v. 17), perhaps to be regarded as identified with the goddess Anath (cf. p. 283); but this reflects a long-standing tendency to worship a female deity alongside Yahweh, God of Israel (cf. Judg. 6^{25}; 2 Kgs. 21^{7}). The Jews at Elephantine also appear to have been guilty of such unfaithfulness. The female deity, who was thought to be particularly concerned with fertility and child-bearing, would naturally be an object of worship for the women. They, claiming their husband's support (v. 19), allege that all the disasters which have come upon Jerusalem and Judah have been due to neglect of the goddess. Here is an interpretation of the calamity radically different from that of Jeremiah and Ezekiel and the other prophets. Small wonder then that the prophet's judgement is so absolute, though there is a reference to *some fugitives* from the total destruction in Egypt in v. 14 (as also in v. 28), perhaps added by a subsequent commentator who knew of the later Jewish community in Egypt and recognized that the preservation of this judgement story—as indeed of other material concerning Jeremiah—suggested that some of these refugees remained faithful and ultimately were to return.

B. PSALMS 44, 74, 79*

Dating the psalms is always uncertain, for they belong to Israel's worship and as such may well have been used over many centuries and have been interpreted to meet the needs of many different situations. Yet we should suppose that those who experienced the disaster of 587—whether they were in their home country or in exile—expressed their distress by using ancient psalms, as they also probably composed new laments such as the book of Lamentations contains. Here and there in such psalms we may perhaps detect a direct reference to the situation of the time, though this must always be uncertain; and indeed it would seem likely that other and later occasions of disaster could also have had their effect in the final shaping and wording of such a psalm. So we may equally properly read such psalms as these in the context of the persecution of Antiochus IV Epiphanes in the second century B.C. (cf. also Vol. 5, pp. 289–91) and of the destruction of Jerusalem and its Temple by the Roman Titus in A.D. 70.

* On Hebrew poetry, cf. the Additional Note on pp. 43 ff.

If we now consider three psalms which provide fitting comment on the disaster, this does not then mean that these psalms are to be dated in 587 or shortly after. It means that older psalms, perhaps originally connected with some other historical disaster, or more probably deriving from a cultic situation, are now being used afresh and even more meaningfully to meet the needs of worshippers in such a terrible moment of collapse. Such reapplication of psalmody may be observed within the Old Testament, as when we find a 'royal psalm' put by the compiler into the mouth of Hannah as a prayer of thanksgiving for the birth of her son Samuel (1 Sam. 2^{1-10}), or when we find that Ps. 30 is headed 'at the dedication of the Temple', in spite of the fact that it is clearly in origin a much more limited expression of distress and thanksgiving. (It is just possible that this note applies really to the preceding psalm, 29, part of which, in a somewhat different form (cf. Ps. 96) is included by the Chronicler in the description of the worship at the bringing in of the Ark to Jerusalem, 1 Chron. 16. Ps. 29^{1-2} cf. Ps. 96^{7-9}; 1 Chron. 16^{21-30}. We may note also that the Greek translation has an added note to the title of Ps. 96, 'When the temple was built after the captivity', showing an application of this to another such occasion.)

Pss. 44, 74, and 79 are all laments, and similar therefore to the poems of Lamentations. They follow similar patterns of thought, and may be compared with other ancient, non-Israelite psalmody, which reveals the same structure. We may quote extracts from an Accadian text:

> Into Eulmas thy sanctuary the foe entered
> Thy holy chamber he defiled
> In thy holy place he set his foot
> Thy far-famed dwelling he destroyed.
> Thy precious rituals he . . .
>
> How long O my lady, has the mighty foe plundered
> thy sanctuary?
> In thy city Erech lamentation is raised.
> In Eulmas, the house of thy counsel, blood like
> water was sacrificed.

In all thy lands fire he cast and heaped them like
roasted grain.

(Langdon's trans., *Oxford Cuneiform Texts*, vi, p. 37)

This is very similar to Ps. 79, and this suggests that behind the Old Testament psalms there is a long tradition of psalmody, using similar phrases and similar motifs. The wording is often very conventional, so that precise allusions to the kind of disaster envisaged are absent. This is why it is probably better to describe the situation of such a psalm as a 'cultic situation' rather than a historical one. For while it is true that a defeat in war might well provide a suitable occasion for using such a psalm, other situations too could be appropriately expressed by such language—any kind of national distress or any kind of situation which hindered the normal ordering of worship in the shrine. In Old Testament psalms we find such moments expressed in statements about God's anger against his people, his people's consciousness of sin or their professions of allegiance and obedience, their confidence above all in his saving power. Such psalms belong not to one moment but to many.

44 *Rouse thyself! Why sleepest thou, O Lord?*

The psalm opens with two expressions of confidence in God's power to save. In vv. 1–3, there is recalled the great tradition of the mighty acts of God in the past, the entry into Canaan which is attributed to the direct action of God. It is of note that the psalm interprets Israel's victories as being in reality those of God. This is in line with the belief in 'holy war', fought in the name of God and regarded as being under his control (cf. 1 Kgs. 8[44–45]). The Chronicler (cf. p. 303) goes a stage further in the same direction by describing victories in which the action of God replaces human efforts (e.g. 2 Chron. 13[15]). In vv. 4–8 the theme is elaborated in more general terms. The people's only trust is in God. (For ideas similar to these cf. Judg. 7.)

A sharply contrasting section (vv. 9–16) depicts the distressed state of the people—defeat, despoilment by the enemy, exile among the nations (a point at which we might detect the influence of the exilic situation), and more general indications of the exposure of the people to mockery and scorn (cf. Deut. 28^{37}; Jer. 18^{16}).

The psalm then expresses the people's conviction of their faithfulness to God (vv. 17–22), and their recognition that if they were turning away from him, then they would expect disaster. The phrase *place of jackals* (v. 19) may simply indicate the desolate places, though it could mean the realm of the chaos-monster, that is the realm of darkness and death (cf. notes on Isa. 51^{9-11}).

The psalm ends with an appeal to God, in the bold metaphor of awaking from sleep, that he should no longer turn away from his people (vv. 23–26). It is because of his *steadfast love* (v. 26) that he will act: the word so rendered, and also translated as 'mercy' and in older translations as 'loving kindness', expresses the loyalty of man to man, and of God towards man.

74 *How long, O God, is the foe to scoff?*

The same themes are differently handled in this psalm which begins with the cry of distress (vv. 1–11). Here various themes are developed. The appeal is made to God's ancient works, his choice of Zion as his dwelling (cf. Ps. 78^{67-69}). The sanctuary itself is depicted as destroyed by the enemy (vv. 4–8), but the exact meaning of these verses is not clear; probably we should think rather of metaphors of destruction, enemies likened to woodcutters, though a more precise application of the phrases may have been made to the actual situation. The destruction of *all the meeting-places of God* (v. 8) perhaps originally indicated local shrines, or better 'all religious celebrations'; it may later have been thought to denote 'synagogues' (on synagogues cf. p. 28). The next verses express still more strongly the apparent absence of God; he does not reveal his will (cf. 1 Sam. 28^{6}), and is reproached for his inactivity.

Confidence rests in God who is now (vv. 12–17) described as the great victor in the struggle against the forces of chaos, *the sea* and *the dragons*, and *Leviathan* (vv. 13 f.) the 'fleeing serpent, the twisting serpent' (Isa. 27[1]). He is the creator and orderer of the world (cf. notes on Isa. 51[9–11]; and Gen. 1 for a more stylized presentation).

The psalm appeals to God to act (vv. 18–23). Will he let his enemies mock? Will he forsake the people for which he cares? Will he not remember his *covenant* with them?

79 *How long, O Lord?*

The opening description here (vv. 1–4) certainly fits the situation of Jerusalem's fall in 587, but the similar Accadian lament quoted above may remind us that these are general statements. The same thoughts are often expressed by Jeremiah (cf. 7[33]–8[2]). An appeal is made to God to turn his anger towards the enemies which have attacked his people (vv. 5–7). Forgiveness and release from the past are sought (vv. 8–9), and an appeal is made to God to show his true nature to the nations (cf. Ezek. 36[17–21]), and to show pity on his suffering people (vv. 10–12). The confident note on which the psalm ends reveals the trust which the people have in God (v. 13).

These brief notes can only touch on the richness of the themes in these psalms. We can perhaps imagine those who remained faithful in the period of the exile finding in such words an expression of their own needs, and experiencing afresh the reality of the faith of their forefathers in the action and purpose of God.

Additional Note on Hebrew Poetry

Many parts of the Old Testament are written in poetry and the RSV translation shows this by setting out the lines in verse form. In Hebrew manuscripts only the books of Psalms, Job, and Proverbs (and some few isolated passages elsewhere) are set out in verse form, but in modern editions of the text and in translation it is right that much more—particularly in the prophetic books—is recognized as poetry. There are some cases where it is not easy to be sure whether the form is poetic or not, and, as in other languages, there are passages which are clearly prose but where poetic language and structure may be detected in some measure. Thus, while most of the Second Isaiah is clearly in poetry, 44^{9-20} is set out in the RSV as prose; yet it has features which have suggested to some scholars that it is in reality a poetic passage.

To understand the difficulty here, it is necessary to know a little about Hebrew poetic form. There are some points which are quite clear and others on which there has been and still is much discussion. It has for long been recognized that the basic feature of Hebrew poetry is a parallelism of thought; the first unit is found to correspond to the second, and sometimes also to a third. Ps. 1^{1} offers an example: here the first clause 'Blessed is the man' is introductory, but the next three are closely linked in thought:

who *walks* not in the *counsel* of the *wicked*,
nor *stands* in the *way* of *sinners*,
nor *sits* in the *seat* of *scoffers*.

In each unit there are three ideas which we might denote a, b, and c; thus in the first 'walks' is represented by a, 'counsel' by b, 'wicked' by c. So the whole pattern could be described as $a+b+c$, $a'+b'+c'$, $a''+b''+c''$. Often the relationship is a contrasting parallel. Thus Ps. 1^{6}:

for the *LORD knows* the *way* of the *righteous*,
but the *way* of the *wicked* will *perish*.

Here we have a similar threefold structure in each of the two lines.

Such simple groups of two and three units occur very commonly. Further observation will show groups in which instead of a simple parallel or contrast we find a development of the thought of the first unit in the second (cf. Ps. 29^{1-2}); and others in which in a fourfold unit there is a chiastic effect (i.e. the first and last units have some correspondence and the second and third are linked together). An example may be seen in Ps. 28^1 though here the relation between the first and fourth is not close, and we may in fact see how the idea of the first is further elaborated in the next verse. There are immense possibilities in this kind of poetry, and sometimes there can be difference of opinion as to how the lines may be best set out.

Larger units or strophes are sometimes observable. These are clear in the poems of the book of Lamentations or in Ps. 119 where the alphabetic structure indicates them. They may also be seen where there is a refrain, as in Pss. 42 and 43, probably really one psalm, and in Ps. 46, where the refrain is perhaps missing after v. 3. It is not clear whether we should look for regularity in such strophic arrangement, or whether, as seems likely from the texts as they now stand, we should recognize a considerable freedom.

The units of the poetry are of varying length, and there are differences of opinion about the way in which the metre should be reckoned. Most scholars are content to recognize that the chief units of thought provide lines of two, three, or four (rarely more) stresses; some have believed it possible to trace a greater complexity of structure as between accented and unaccented syllables. But this does not affect the basic recognition of parallelism.

In prose—such as Isa. 44^{9-20} appears to be—we may often detect, particularly in sermon-like passages, or exalted prose, a certain rhythm and a degree of parallelism which suggest poetry. Thus we may note that, for example, Isa. 44^{18} has a considerable degree of repetition and parallel. Such poetic or rhythmic prose may also be found in Gen. 1. It is probably more satisfactory to treat such passages as prose, rather than try to force the passage artificially into a rigid rhythmic structure.

The structure of Hebrew poetry may be closely paralleled in the poems from Ras Shamra–Ugarit (Canaanite poetry) and more generally in the literatures of Mesopotamia and Egypt. A full description of Hebrew poetic structure cannot be given here; reference may be made to books noted on p. 353.

C. THE BOOK OF LAMENTATIONS (LAMENTATIONS 2)

In our English Bibles the five 'lamentations' are placed immediately after the book of Jeremiah, and described as 'The Lamentations of Jeremiah'. But in the Hebrew Bible, this little collection is grouped with four other books—Ruth, Song of Songs, Ecclesiastes, Esther—and the whole group is known as the 'Five Scrolls' (*Megilloth*). Each of these books came at some stage—we do not know how early—to be associated with an annual celebration; not surprisingly Lamentations was connected with the anniversary of Jerusalem's destruction. The traditional indication of authorship by Jeremiah is derived partly from the content of the poems and partly from the reference in 2 Chron. 35^{25}, where we are told that 'Jeremiah also uttered a lament for Josiah; and all the singing men and singing women have spoken of Josiah in their laments to this day. They made these an ordinance in Israel; behold, they are written in the Laments'. Evidently a collection of laments was known to the Chronicler, either directly or by repute. It is not, however, stated that the other laments were associated with Jeremiah; indeed, the implication seems rather to be that Josiah was the subject of various such poems. Nor have we any means of knowing whether this particular collection was in any way related to the book which we now have, and even the association of one lament with Jeremiah can only be regarded as a tradition which existed by the time of the Chronicler. So many examples occur in the Old Testament of works which are ascribed to famous figures (psalms to David, proverbs to Solomon) that we can only take note of the tradition and consider it in the light of other evidence.

Discussion about the authorship of the Lamentations is not very profitable and certainly does not affect their value. Some scholars have emphasized the differences of thought from that of Jeremiah, contrasting his certainty of divine judgement on Jerusalem with the distress expressed in the poems. But the differences are not really so very marked, and in any case the poems are in characteristic psalm style. As we have already seen (pp. 39 ff.), psalmody contains many conventions and stereotyped phrases; there is a strong measure of formalism about its presentation of theological thought and religious experience. The book of Jeremiah itself contains a number of 'psalm' passages, some of which are often termed the prophet's 'confessions' (cf. Jer. 11^{18-20}, 12^{1-6}, 15^{15-21}, 17^{14-18}, 18^{19-23}, 20^{7-18}; but note also other passages such as $14^{2-10,\ 17-22}$, 15^{5-9} which are not to be so described). It is not impossible that the prophet could readily make use of the forms and style of psalmody; such a use of psalm forms is particularly characteristic also of the Second Isaiah (cf. pp. 106 f.). But the conventional and formal aspects which invite comparison are an inadequate basis on which to argue for identity of authorship.

The form of the lament at the downfall of a city is in addition attested from a much earlier period outside Israel. The following short quotations from the very long Sumerian lament at the destruction of Ur (quoted from *ANET*, pp. 455–63) may serve to illustrate the style. The poem dates from the first half of the second millennium B.C. The first part of the text, very repetitive in style, speaks of the abandonment of their sanctuaries by the gods; the form is similar in each case:

> The lord of all lands has abandoned his stable,
>   his sheepfold has been abandoned to the wind;
> Enlil has abandoned . . . Nippur, his sheepfold has been
>   delivered to the wind.

This is followed by a lament over the city:

> O city, a bitter lament set up as thy lament;
> Thy lament which is bitter—O city, set up thy lament.
> His righteous city which has been destroyed—bitter
>   is its lament . . .

The poem goes on to speak of the god's concern for the city:

> My city on its foundation verily was destroyed;
> Ur where it lay verily perishes . . .

But it is Enlil himself who summons the storm:

> Enlil called the storm; the people groan . . .
> The storm that annihilates the land he called; the
> people groan.
> The evil winds he called; the people groan . . .

Subsequently, aspects of the disaster are described:

> On that day . . .
> Its walls were breached, the people groan,
> In its lofty gates, where they were wont to promenade,
> dead bodies were lying about;
> In its boulevards, where the feasts were celebrated,
> scattered they lay . . .

The gods express their distress; the appeal is made to them to bring relief, and the poem closes with a word of rejoicing at restoration.

The existence of such comparable material suggests that Israel too was accustomed, in its worship, in regular or special celebrations, to rehearse the experience of disaster by appropriate words of lament. Apart from the poems of this book, we may find examples of such lamentation in prophetic passages which refer to the downfall of great cities and nations (see Isa. 23 and Ezek. 27 on Tyre; Nahum 2 and 3 on Nineveh; Jer. $50^{2-3, 23-27}$, 51^{8} on Babylon. The theme is often, as in Jer. 50–51, combined with other elements, and a later use of the style, again with a new interpretation, is to be found in Rev. $18^{2f., 10ff.}$).

But the importance of these poems in Lamentations lies in their revealing of aspects of the thought of those who experienced the disaster of 587. Taking up older themes and phrases, the poets depict what men felt when confronted by this experience and they offer their own prayers for deliverance and forgiveness.

It is difficult in fact to draw a clear line between the use of older material and original composition in the period of the disaster. Nor can we give any precise date to the composition of the poems, for their vividness is not so much due to their being eye-witness accounts of the events and of the situation in Judah after 587, but to their being sensitive expressions of faith, the result of reflection on the meaning of what had happened in the light of the religious tradition in which those who composed and used them stood. To attempt to discover in these poems precise allusions to the events of the period is hazardous. The references are stylized, as is the poetry itself; for we note that it is arranged on an acrostic pattern, following the letters of the Hebrew alphabet. Such a structure introduces a measure of artificiality, and provides a limitation of the expression, though no more so than does any strict poetic form such as the sonnet. It may, because of the need to introduce a particular word, influence the order in which the ideas are presented. The poems do not have identical structure. Poems 1, 2, and 4 have 22 verses each, one for each letter of the Hebrew alphabet, with the first word of each verse beginning with the appropriate letter, v. 1 with *'āleph*, v. 2 with *bēth* and so on; this structure is also found in Ps. 145 (one line here, 13*b*, is missing in the standard Hebrew text, but is supplied in RSV from ancient evidence). Poem 3 has 66 verses, three to each letter; this is similar to Ps. 119 where each letter has 8 verses. Poem 5 has 22 verses, but no alphabetical arrangement; with this we may compare Ps. 103. Curiously enough, the order of the letters of the alphabet is not identical in each case. Poems 2, 3, and 4 have the same order but one which diverges at one point from the normal alphabetic arrangement, whereas poem 1 has the normal order. Possibly this difference points to different authorship. The use of this alphabetic acrostic, which seems very strange and artificial to a modern reader, has been variously explained; perhaps there is felt to be a certain completeness in such a structure. But it is probable that the origin of the form lies far back and that it later became simply a poetic convention.

The five poems do not present an entirely unified statement of the meaning of the disaster, but underlying them all is the conviction of the rightness and absoluteness of divine judgement, of the closeness of the bond which exists between God and the chosen city and temple of Jerusalem, of the distress experienced by the faithful worshipper. With these goes also a deep conviction of God's mercy and power to restore, as, for example, in 3^{31-33}:

> For the Lord will not
> cast off for ever,
> but, though he cause grief, he will have compassion
> according to the abundance of his steadfast love;
> for he does not willingly afflict
> or grieve the sons of men.

or as in 5^{19-22} (quoted on p. 18).

Lamentations 2. *The experience of disaster*

1. Like Lam. 1 and 4, the poem begins with the word *How*—better perhaps 'Ah, alas' for it is a word which is characteristic of the lament over the dead (2 Sam. 1^{19}; Jer. 48^{17}, and other passages where actual funeral dirges are quoted). Jerusalem is seen here in her special relation to God: *daughter (of) Zion*—the description of city and temple as a person; *splendour of Israel*—the symbol of the people's pride of place as God's chosen; *his footstool*—as God sits enthroned he rests his feet upon Zion (we may compare Isa. 66^{1} where the earth is his footstool, and 1 Chron. 28^{2} where it is the ark of the covenant). But God's anger is not restrained by this intimacy of association; judgement knows no partiality. The phrase *casting down from heaven* suggests an allusion to a mythological theme known from Isa. $14^{12\text{ff.}}$ (cf. p. 58)—the fall of the Day star—which was subsequently much elaborated in ideas of fallen angelic beings (cf. Luke 10^{18}).

2–3. These verses continue the picture of divine wrath, detailing more precisely the overthrow of Judah. The artificiality of the alphabetic structure becomes clear here, since the opening of v. 3 links closely to the end of v. 2, the word rendered *might* being really 'horn', a word often used of royal power (e.g. Ps. 132^{17}; Dan. $7^{7\text{ff.}}$). To some extent, therefore, verse division must be ignored in examining content. The *right hand* of God is a frequent expression for his protective and conquering power; now it is *withdrawn* and Judah is left exposed to the enemy.

4–5. Indeed, God has himself become as *an enemy*. The prophets (see, e.g., Ezek. 21[18ff.]) and the theologian-historians (see, e.g., 2 Kgs. 25[1ff.]) see the Babylonian power as the destroyer and may depict Nebuchadrezzar as the instrument of the divine will, the servant of God (Jer. 25[9]). The poet here speaks more directly of God himself as active. This is the obverse of the description of God fighting on his people's behalf when the conquest is described; we may compare the directly theological statement of Ps. 44[2–3] (God as conqueror of the land) with the interpretations of the events offered in the books of Joshua and Judges in which a different and often less directly theological statement is given (cf. p. 41). It is important to recognize here the stress on the interpretation of historic experiences as revealing divine purpose, whether in judgement or in deliverance. In v. 4, it seems better to make a division after *pride* (lit. delights) *of our eyes* and to link the last two clauses.

6–7 describe the overthrow of the sanctuary and its worship (cf. Pss. 74 and 79), already perhaps suggested by the *tent* of v. 4. The religious celebrations are brought to an end, and a noise is heard like that of a religious festival—this implies either the cry of distress of those who lament disaster or the triumphant shouts of the conquerors as they despoil the shrine.

8–10 depict the city and the overthrow of law and order and of leadership. Again there is stress on this being the direct result of divine purpose (*The LORD determined*). The walls are symbolic of God's protection (cf. Ps. 38); the gates are both protective and also places of public assembly, indicative of a social order which is now lost. Poetically the walls themselves are said to cry out in lament (contrast Luke 19[40]). The removal of leaders brings a consequent loss of public order and religious guidance. It is probable that we have here a reminder of the king's responsibility for law (cf. Deut. $17^{18\text{ff.}}$), though we may also recognize law (*tōrāh*) as the vehicle of priestly revealing of the divine will. The loss of the word of God is due to the withdrawal of God from his people, because by their failure they have made access to him impossible (cf. Amos 8^{11} and for the inaccessibility of God see the story in 1 Sam. 14^{24-46}, especially v. 37, and Isa. $59^{1\text{ f.}}$). A mourning ritual is undertaken by elders and young maidens; the latter appear often in the context of worship (cf. Judg. 11^{34}; 1 Sam. 18^{7}).

11–12. As often in the psalms, a vivid change of person introduces a new section; the distress of the poet is expressed in terms which have a more personal ring, and in v. 13 he addresses the city directly. RSV *in grief* is a paraphrase of the Hebrew 'to the ground' which might better be rendered 'utterly' (v. 11). The words rendered *soul* and *heart* are actually terms for the internal organs of the body (intestines and liver) conceived of as the seat of emotions. The phraseology, often to be found in psalmody and prophecy (cf., e.g., Ps. $22^{14\text{f.}}$; Jer. 4^{19}), vividly expresses the intimate relationship between emotional stress and physical experience. The starving of children in siege conditions (vv. 11*c*–12) again brings home the intensity of the disaster.

13–17. These verses, with their direct address to the city, show the utter impossibility of finding consolatory words. We may compare the command to Jeremiah not to intercede for his people (see Jer. 14^{11}) in the context of a statement of the people's distress in time of drought. The state of Jerusalem is such that no consolation is available. It is clear that, like Jeremiah, the poet is aware that it is normal to give words of consolation in a time of disaster, and that the assurance of divine help is a central feature in Israel's faith; but such assurance is not automatic, its sureness lies in the nature of God. The people's condition is such that consolation is not forthcoming. The final question: *who can restore you?* is an emphatic way of saying 'There is none to restore'.

As in Jeremiah, there is here (v. 14) the recognition that Jerusalem has been too often assured that all is well. Her prophets have said, ' "Peace, peace" where there is no peace' (e.g. Jer. 6^{14}, 8^{11}). They have failed to reveal the nature of Jerusalem's failure. Verse 15 depicts the distressed city as if she were a condemned criminal exposed in the pillory, to be mocked by every passer-by. The gestures are evidently typical of such mockery, and the wording, like that of the funeral dirge (cf. Amos $5^{1 f.}$), contrasts the former glories with the present miserable state. The verse thus echoes the opening of the poem. The theme is elaborated with the brutal boasting of the enemies (v. 16) who engage in an exultant shout of triumph at the defeated city. But v. 17 again reminds us that this is no accidental occurrence. We are back in the theme of the opening verses; it was God who decreed this, and it belongs in his long-established purpose. The enemy can only rejoice because he has permitted it.

18–21. It is God who decreed the disaster; there is no word of hope. What then can Jerusalem do? There is nothing possible but acceptance of his will and appeal to his mercy. The opening of v. 18 is obscure and the text is in disorder; RSV offers a possible opening: *Cry aloud*, and this may best be followed by another conjecture: 'Groan, O daughter Zion'. The imperatives of the following clauses strongly suggest that the text should be corrected in some such manner. The weeping of the city is not simply an expression of distress; it is a powerful religious act, part of a ritual aimed at moving God to pity. Weeping in ritual may be seen in the celebration envisaged in Joel $2^{12, 17}$ and in the intensity of appeal expressed in the allusion to the Jacob story of Gen. $31^{22 ff.}$ in Hos. 12^{4}: 'he wept and sought his [the angel's] favour'. Verse 19 continues the appeal, and leads on into v. 20 with its motifs of pity, a common theme in psalms of lament (e.g. Ps. $74^{18 ff.}$). This in its turn leads on to echo the loss of leadership (cf. v. 9) in the latter part of v. 20 and v. 21. The leaders and the best members of the community are dead, destroyed by the merciless action of divine anger.

22. The last verse offers yet another movement of thought. Now it is the city itself which speaks; those for whom Zion as a mother has cared (for the metaphor cf. Isa. 3^{25-26}, 49^{19-21}) have been destroyed by her enemy. The experience of disaster has been that of *the day of the anger of the* L*ORD*, that 'day of Yahweh' of which the prophets speak (cf. Amos $5^{18\text{ff.}}$; Isa. $2^{12\text{ff.}}$; Zeph. $1^{7\text{ff.}}$), the day of gloom and darkness and divine judgement (cf. pp. 33 f.).

The poem at first sight appears to be totally black in tone and outlook. Yet a number of points of profound theological interest shine through. The events, so disastrous, are no accident; they are part of God's purpose, decreed long ago, and decreed because of Jerusalem's sin. There can be no suggestion of God's failure; he has not been powerless to protect but has himself decreed judgement. The judgement is not an isolated event; it is an expression within the confines of history of the eternal judgement of God on human failure. If Judah was to survive and again to express its faith as people of God, in a deeper and fuller manner, it would be through the acceptance of this understanding of God's will. One of the miracles of Old Testament faith is the discovery of the divine will in disaster. It was in such faith that a psalmist could speak of his confidence that 'Yahweh of hosts is with us', even though the earth shakes and the power of evil is engaged in full-scale assault (Ps. 46). It is such a faith which has preserved the Jewish community through its many vicissitudes, and it is an essential element in Christian faith. No accident then that the description of the crucifixion of Jesus at so many points alludes to the words of these poems in the book of Lamentations and that they were traditionally among the chosen Old Testament readings for Holy Week.

D. THE BOOK OF OBADIAH

It appears clear from vv. 10–14 of this little prophetic book that the events of Jerusalem's fall in 587 B.C. do not lie far from the moment of the judgement here spoken against Edom. The brotherly relationship between the people of Judah and of Edom is a theme expressed in various ways in the Old Testament. It is enshrined in the ancient traditions of Jacob and Esau which preserve the recollection of ancient rivalry. Jacob, the younger, nevertheless claimed first place (Gen. 25^{27-34}, 27), and the Old Testament sees in this the working of God's purpose for his people (see also Mal. 1^{2-5}). These verses in Obadiah give us some insight into the events after the fall of the city, and suggest the probability that the more outlying areas of Judah were taken over by neighbouring peoples. The fate of fugitives at the time is vividly suggested. The historical account in 2 Kgs. 24^{2} mentions Moabites and Ammonites among the troops used by Babylon against Jerusalem, but does not include Edomites; it is possible that they too were engaged in this attack, but certainly they took advantage of the weakness of Judah to gain something for themselves. The old rivalry between the two peoples, claiming a common ancestry, no doubt became more bitter, and Edom seems in some Old Testament passages to become a symbol of the hostile world (see, e.g., Isa. 34, 63^{1-6}). This may be seen subsequently in the hatred of the Idumaeans in the last two centuries B.C., expressed particularly in hostility to the family of the Herods.

The prophet expects dire judgement for Edom, and it is possible that he saw this coming in the pressures of Arab tribes from the south. During the centuries after the exile, such pressures became strong, and the kingdom of the Nabataean Arabs, with its capital at Petra but with other important centres too, for example at Avdat in the Negeb, was firmly established by about the end of the third century B.C. Excavations in recent years have brought to light the early history of these Arab peoples, though this lies later than the period with which we are concerned. No precise description of the coming disaster for Edom is, however, given in the prophecy.

But the book contains more than just this judgement on Edom. The words of doom are set in a broader context by being related to a prospect of judgement on all nations, pictured in terms of a great feast on Mount Zion, like that described in Isa. 25^{6}; Jer. $25^{15\text{f.}}$. Such a portrayal of an attack on Zion by the nations may be found in the psalms (see Pss. 2 and 46); it is found elsewhere in prophetic oracles (see Zech. 14 and Ezek. 38–39). Here, as in other passages, it provides the occasion for a picture of a restored Israel, with its land again in its possession and its scattered members gathered. So the judgement of Edom has become—probably by a later reinterpretation of the prophet's message—a symbol of God's judgement on all the powers set against him, and the occasion for a word of hope for a new kingdom with its centre in Zion.

1–14, 15*b* (this last appears to be slightly misplaced) *Judgement on Edom*

The security and pride of Edom, thinking herself safe in her rocky fortresses (*rock* in v. 3 is Sela, the name of a chief city of Edom, often identified with Petra—which also means 'rock'—but possibly another of the fortresses in the wild mountainous area), is to be brought low. Edom's doom is complete. The reason for this judgement is set out in vv. 10–14: a series of pictures shows the complacency of Edom in the time of Judah's distress. So, v. 15*b*, she will be paid back in her own coin. The fact that much of vv. 1–10 is to be found in Jer. 49^{7-22}, combined with other prophetic material, may suggest that use is being made in both passages of older oracles on Edom, now reapplied to the exilic situation.

15*a*, 16–21 *The coming Day of the Lord*

The Day of the Lord concept (cf. pp. 33 f., 54) is here extended to cover all nations. The hostile powers are pictured as men who have drunk the cup of God's wrath, and are powerless as drunken men to bring disaster upon Jerusalem and God's people. The theme of judgement on Edom returns in v. 18, and this leads on into the promise of an extension of the realm of God's people, to include the surrounding lands. The whole area of the ancient kingdom is to be recovered, and the dispersed members of the community will return. These last verses express a concern naturally felt in the post-exilic period that all who are faithful Jews should be preserved and gathered into a new people of God.

E. PASSAGES EXPRESSING HOSTILITY TO BABYLON

It is no surprise to find the theme of the coming fall of Babylon, the conqueror and oppressor of the exilic age, in prophecy and psalmody. It is set out at considerable length in Jer. 50–51 and in the doom oracle of the Second Isaiah in Isa. 47; it is probably right to see in Isa. 13–14 and 21 reflections of the same situation. Among the psalms, Ps. 137 makes specific reference to this situation; it offers the only precise reference to the exile in the psalms, though there are other passages (e.g. Ps. 106^{47}) which refer to the gathering in of the scattered members of the people from among the nations. The prophetic passages in each case have a complex structure; not improbably some parts of Isa. 13–14 referred originally to the situation of Isaiah's own time, when Babylon was in rebellion against Assyria and encouraged Judah to join in rebellion (cf. Isa. 39 = 2 Kgs. 20^{12-19}). Subsequently, it would appear that there has been a reapplication of these oracles to the exilic situation. Isa. 13^{17} foretells a conquest of Babylon by the Medes (cf. also 21^{2}), a natural expectation in view of the power of this empire to the east, though one which was to be fulfilled only when Cyrus the Persian had taken over control of that power. (It is possible that the book of Daniel is in some measure dependent upon this passage in speaking of a Median empire under Darius taking over from Babylon, cf. Dan. 5^{31}.)

Isa. 14^{12-21} *The fall of the king of Babylon*

Babylon appears in this context as oppressor (14^{4}), and this fits best the exilic situation. In this part of the poem, use is made of a mythological theme, that of the fall of the *Day Star* (v. 12) from heaven. Apparently there is an allusion to a myth in which an angelic being boastfully claims to be enthroned in heaven, to set himself up as equal to God *Most High* (v. 14). But such boasting leads to disaster. So the king of Babylon who has claimed to be ruler over all (and on this theme cf. also Dan. 4) is brought down to Sheol, the realm of the dead. Vividly, we are shown the shades in this realm of darkness noting the contrast between *the man who made the earth tremble* (v. 16) and his present low state. Phrase after phrase in vv. 19–20 pictures the fearful fate of the proud king. Isa. 21^{1-10} provides a similar picture of the terrible downfall of the hated power.

Jer. 51^{59-64} *A symbol of judgement on Babylon*

The short narrative provides a summarizing conclusion to the long series of poems on the fall of Babylon in chapters 50–51. In these two chapters, poem after poem comments on the coming disaster—the overthrow of the gods of Babylon (50^{2}), and the pride which must fall ($50^{11\,ff.}$), the terror evoked by her ($50^{21\,ff.}$), the destroyer who will come ($50^{41\,ff.}$, $51^{1\,ff.}$). Here all the bitterness of the experience of exile is drawn out, and all the confidence that God cannot in the end allow such evil power to go unpunished. So to a note about an occasion when officials of Zedekiah were summoned to Babylon (in 595 B.C.; probably we should in v. 59 read not *when he went with Zedekiah*, but 'from' Zedekiah)—presumably the officials were summoned in connection with some irregularity, perhaps some report of disaffection at a time when there was stir in Babylonia (cf. also Jer. 29)—there has been attached a story of the writing by Jeremiah of a scroll of judgement upon Babylon, to be sunk in the Euphrates as a symbol: *Thus shall Babylon sink, to rise no more* (v. 64). In view of the injunction in the letter of Jeremiah that his readers should 'seek the welfare of the city where I have sent you into exile' (Jer. 29^7), it is not easy to believe that this is correctly attributed to Jeremiah, at least not at this period. But it is understandable that such a tradition should have grown up with the associating with Jeremiah of this great series of judgement poems. It is worth noting how, in chapters 50–51, themes of restoration and promise for Israel and Judah are interwoven with the words of judgement; the judgement on the nations is the prelude to the restoration of God's people (cf. below, pp. 90 ff., on Ezek. 25–32).

Ps. 137 *The bitterness of exile*

The distress of those who are exiled from their land, far from Zion, is poignantly expressed in this psalm. The captors mock, asking for *one of the songs of Zion*. But how can this be, remote from the temple? The psalmist proclaims his allegiance to Jerusalem, and pronounces dire judgement upon Edom (cf. Obadiah, pp. 55 ff.) and upon Babylon. Such bitterness as this is part of the reaction of the exiles. As we read it now, we should recall that Edom (cf. notes on Obadiah) and Babylon (cf. the use of the name in Rev. 18) came to be symbols of the hostile powers ranged against God and ultimately to be overthrown in the final battle.

II. THE THOUGHT OF THE EXILIC AGE

THE preceding section has attempted to provide an outline of the situation in which the people of the former kingdom of Judah found themselves after the fall of Jerusalem in 587 B.C. In Palestine itself, and also in Babylonia and Egypt, those who had experienced the events, and their children after them, had to come to terms with a situation of great difficulty. Some of the more popular reactions which may be detected in the literature of the period have already been indicated.

With this period may be associated also several of the most significant and influential writings of the Old Testament, and it is to these that we now turn. In some respects the thought that they represent overlaps with ideas presented elsewhere; it would be odd if it did not, for the men responsible were themselves members of the same community, with its strong religious traditions. It is proper to recognize the links back to the past, for in these we may see the way in which new interpretations are built upon old. At the same time, it is important to see the ways in which new emphases lay the foundation for the further development of the community and lead to newer ways of life and thought. The great thinkers of the exilic age were the transmitters of an older tradition, but their handling of that tradition enabled them to serve their contemporaries and their successors, both by offering an intelligible comment upon the situation in which they found themselves and by providing a basis upon which, in due course, a new community life could be built. The relation between the ideals propounded in the exilic age and the subsequent formation and development of the community in Palestine and elsewhere after the fall of Babylon, is, as we should expect, a very complex one. Ideals, no matter how well expounded, do not necessarily immediately lend themselves to practical application. But the relationship is there, and we should neither look for exact correspondence nor dismiss as pedestrian the attempts at reforming and reviving the community because they do not precisely measure up to some ideal standard.

Three of the great prophets of the Old Testament belong to this period—Jeremiah, Ezekiel, and the Second Isaiah. Some mention has already been made of the first of these in the description of the exilic age itself, because of the importance of evidence found in the book which bears his name. But since Jeremiah has been treated at some length in Volume 3 in this series (pp. 348–89), it is not appropriate to offer a further discussion here. It is, however, important to emphasize the significance of Jeremiah, especially in view of the many points of contact with Ezekiel and the Second Isaiah and with the Deuteronomic History. The reader should not allow the division dictated by the conveniences of the series to stand in the way of a full appreciation of the crucial position occupied by Jeremiah, bridging as he does the disasters to Judah and reflecting within the very rich body of tradition associated with him a variety of ways of thinking about the problems of the time.

Ezekiel too bridges the disaster. He is treated in this volume in the series since so much more of the book associated with his name belongs to the exilic age, and so much is concentrated on understanding what has happened in the disaster and why, and on examining the nature of future hope and its embodiment in actual forms. The Second Isaiah belongs to a somewhat later date, and is to be associated with the last years of Babylonian rule; it is possible that some parts of the material belong to the early years of the Persian empire, and if the last chapters of the book, 56–66, are closely linked with 40–55, it is possible to detect some of the acute problems of a community re-establishing itself in Palestine.

Two works of a different kind are also to be associated in greater or less measure with this same period—the Deuteronomic History covering the books from (Deuteronomy) Joshua to 2 Kings, and the Priestly Work, essentially the first four books of the Old Testament, sometimes known as the Tetrateuch. The chronological problems are here much greater but of a similar kind. The Deuteronomic History has already been very largely drawn upon in the preceding volumes of the series because its separate component parts comprise the primary sources for the history of Israel from the time of the conquest to the period of the exile. We are here concerned not with its value as such a source book, but with its significance in relation to the moment at which it reached its virtually final form. The Priestly Work also incorporates a very large amount of earlier material. It contains virtually all that is available to us for an assessment of the pre-conquest period (cf. Volume 2 in this series); it is of vital importance also for the understanding of the nature and development of Hebrew Law. Its final form is very difficult to date, and it may be that it should be associated with a period somewhat later than the sixth century B.C. But some parts of its content, and the purposes which may be detected within it, suggest that it is not inappropriate to place it alongside the Deuteronomic History and to see it as offering a comment on the past and on the meaning of older tradition, and also a project for the future in an attempt at understanding what the religious community really ought to be. In this respect it is convenient to treat it here, though some further reference will have to be made to it in relation to the developments of thought in the Persian period.

A. EZEKIEL

The book of Ezekiel is a large and complex work. Its study has produced widely divergent views of its origin and nature, and different estimates of the nature of the prophet with whose name it is associated. The more extravagant theses need not detain us. There are no good grounds for dating the prophet before the sixth century, though there are many points at which Ezekiel may be seen to take up ideas and forms which belong to earlier prophecy. Nor is Ezekiel to be taken out of the period with which he is associated in the book and regarded as a virtually fictional figure of a much later age, though it would not be surprising if some features in the book were to suggest that the words of the prophet have been re-applied in many new situations long after the time at which he lived and spoke. Again it is not appropriate to divide up the material of the book into prose and poetry and regard only the latter as original, the former representing subsequent re-interpretation of the oracles of the prophet; or on some other basis to dismiss large sections of the book as non-genuine. Yet it is clear that the structure is not a simple one, and it is not easy to see the precise relationship between the prophet who appears in the opening chapters, speaking with foreboding of the coming disaster on Jerusalem, and the prophet who appears in the later chapters, particularly in 40–48, with its meticulous attention to architectural and legal detail.

The book as it stands places Ezekiel in the first half of the sixth century B.C., dating the earliest moment of his experience in 'the fifth year of the exile of King Jehoiachin' (1^{2}) and indicating as his place of activity the community of the exiles 'in the land of the Chaldeans by the river Chebar' (1^{3}). It dates the opening of his visions of the restored community in the twenty-fifth year of the exile (40^{1}), thus providing a space of twenty years, from *c.* 593 to 573 B.C. (There is one later date than this, in 29^{17}, where a particular pronouncement concerning Egypt is dated in the twenty-seventh year. This is in the section of the book, 25–32, in which are gathered the oracles on foreign nations. Cf. pp. 90 ff.) The book states that while Ezekiel was active in Babylonia, he was transported by 'the Spirit' to Jerusalem, and able to see there both the condition of the temple and the onset of divine judgement (8^{3}, and see the whole of the section 8–11). The nature of this experience is not easy to elucidate, and both this section and other passages have raised questions about the place of the prophet's activity.

The book is structured in a familiar form—oracles of judgement (1–24), oracles on the foreign nations (25–32), oracles of restoration (33–48). A similar structure may be seen in the book of Isaiah, in Jeremiah (in its Greek form where the foreign nation oracles stand in chapter 25) and in Zephaniah, though in each case there are some differences. In the case of Ezekiel, there is some measure of promise in the opening section, and the note of judgement is by no means absent from the third section. As with other prophets, judgement and promise are not two diametrically opposed notions, but are related in that they represent the impact of the divine purpose: where it meets with sin and rebellion, there is judgement; where it meets with the will to obedience, there is promise. As in earlier prophetic collections, there is grouping of material in accordance with similarity of theme: thus 4–5 contain several prophetic symbols related to the disaster to Jerusalem and to Judah, and to the experience of exile; chapter 7 opens with more than one pronouncement concerned with the coming end, and the Day of Yahweh. As particularly also in Jeremiah, such oracular and symbolic material is expounded in shorter or longer sermonic passages. 5^{5-17} begins as an exposition of the symbolic action of 5^{1-4} in which the prophet divides up and destroys his hair, a complex symbol which may well contain elements of reinterpretation within it; the passage continues in more general terms, and thus provides a sort of commentary on the whole preceding collection of symbols in 4^{1}–5^{4}. Similarly, the words concerning the end and the Day in 7^{1-13} are elaborated in more general comment in 7^{14-27}.

Such arrangements and groupings of material may be due to the prophet himself. Did he, after the fall of the city, see that oracles pronounced and symbols performed before the disaster were not outdated by the events, but took on a new meaning? By placing these together, he or his followers could underline the divine ordering of events, and by sermonic exposition could exhort their contemporaries to avoid the sins of their predecessors and to learn obedience to the divine law. If, as some scholars believe, Ezekiel was first active as a prophet in Jerusalem, and only subsequently in Babylonia, such re-presentation and reinterpretation would be both necessary and appropriate. But in any case, the preservation of a prophet's words cannot be regarded as due to their being recorded at or near the moment of their first utterance. They gain their place in the preserved tradition by reason of the effect they have, and by reason of their continued relevance and applicability in new situations.

Such an understanding of the growth of the prophetic tradition does not remove the problem of deciding whether this or that passage really derives from the prophet, and of attempting to discover in what kind of situation the oracle was originally pronounced or the symbolic action performed. But it does lay a firm emphasis on the value of the actual handing on of the material, and its reapplication. We have received the prophetic sayings in contexts which may not be original; but this shows how these words were understood and treasured. In the case of the book of Ezekiel, it may be right to decide that the whole section 40–48, with its rather different language and its often curiously different impression of the prophet, really belongs either partly or entirely to a later development, and is only partly or indirectly attributable to Ezekiel. At some points, in details of legislation about the priesthood and sacrifice, it may be very much later, representing the attempts of later scribes to harmonize the Ezekiel tradition with what was found in the Pentateuch—the first five books of the Old Testament. But even if this is so, and it is extremely difficult to find sure criteria of judgement, it nevertheless gives us an insight into the effect of Ezekiel's teaching upon his contemporaries and his successors. It is in fact difficult to suppose that so detailed a statement of the rebuilding of the temple—closely dependent at many points on knowledge of what the former temple was like—would have been formulated after the rededication of the restored temple after the exile; and the details of the plans for the priesthood and for the more political organization do not sufficiently correspond with what happened then to make it seem likely that these too are later. This would suggest that during the fifty years between the fall of Jerusalem and the fall of Babylon, Ezekiel himself, his associates, and his disciples were working out their understanding of the disaster, and their view of how, under the will of God, there could be a proper re-establishment of life. Whether Ezekiel himself was personally responsible for more or less of the material affects only very little the recognition that to those who gathered the material into its present form he was a teacher whose influence they had felt deeply, and to whom therefore they gladly attributed such developments of his teaching as had come about in their own handling of it. In what follows of comment on individual passages, therefore, no sharp distinction is attempted between what may be original and what may be later. Our aim is to understand the mind of the prophet and his influence, and this is to be done by discerning within the tradition the kind of man he was, the kind of emphasis which he laid, and where he stood in the religious community to which he belonged.

If we take up the latter points first, we may usefully recognize that Ezekiel stands close in thought to his contemporary Jeremiah and also to his younger associate the Second Isaiah. The emphasis on the total corruption of the people and on the need for total renewal places him close to Jeremiah; his appreciation of the absoluteness of the divine will, expressed in his use of the idea of the name of God (see especially 36[22]), brings him near to the differently expressed emphasis in the Second Isaiah on the sole right and power of God to act, over against the futility of all others who claim to be gods (cf. p. 107). For Ezekiel, the name of God, that is, his actual person, is the one source of action; God does not act for Israel's sake, but because he is God. If this sounds harsh, and often Ezekiel's language is harsh and violent, it is important to realize that he is expressing a profound truth. There can be no external pressure which makes God act as he does; what he is and what he does are one. His nature is what it is, and because it is what it is, he acts; and his action involves the restoration of Israel, not because Israel deserves to be restored, not because she has any claim upon God, but because God is God. What he does for Israel is part of a total and consistent purpose.

Very close also to Ezekiel is that part of the book of Leviticus, chapters 17–26, which has often been called the 'Holiness Code' (cf. pp. 149, 152). The stress on holiness—the holiness of God and hence the holiness, separateness, and purity of his people—is characteristic of both works. Ezekiel was of a priestly family, and the laws of the Holiness Code are priestly laws; it is understandable that the prophet couches much of his material in terms which are closely reminiscent of such laws. It may serve to remind us that Israel's religious reformers belonged just as much to the ranks of the priesthood as they did to those of the prophets.

Ezekiel stands in a prophetic line. There are links with Jeremiah and through him with Hosea. The sexual symbolism of chapters 16 and 23 is like a violent caricature of the use by Hosea of such language to portray the intimacy of relationship between God and his people. In a situation of such extreme danger as that of the exilic age, Ezekiel was not one to mince words in describing the utter corruption of a people which had received such love and care from God. The foundling child of chapter 16 grows up to be the covenanted bride of God; but she becomes unfaithful, engaging in political and religious harlotry, and so meets the judgement of exposure to mockery and of destruction at the hands of those with whom she has defiled herself. In chapter 23, the same point is made in terms of the two sisters, Oholah and Oholibah (both names play on the word *'ōhel* which means 'tent' and suggests the tabernacle expressive of God's presence with his people). Both are unfaithful, and so judgement comes upon both. Like Jeremiah and like the historian-theologians (see 2 Kgs. 17), Ezekiel sees the failure of Judah to learn from the downfall of her elder sister Israel. Ezekiel also resembles closely the prophetic figures Elisha and Elijah; the strange stories which are told about Elisha in 2 Kings contain many elements which are reminiscent of the strange actions performed by Ezekiel, the emphasis on his being under the hand of God, possessed and controlled by God's spirit. Such stories are not easy to interpret. In the case of Elijah and particularly of Elisha, there are likely to be many elements of popular tradition concerning the activities of these famous men, and the miraculous nature of these activities no doubt owes something to popular imagination. When we consider the actions attributed to Ezekiel, we are confronted with similarly difficult problems of interpretation. Did Ezekiel really lie on one side for 390 days to represent the years of the punishment of Israel, and for 40 days to represent that of Judah, tied with cords so that he could not turn (4^{4-8})? Was he really taken by the hand of God and carried to Jerusalem, or was this in reality, as is suggested by the reference to 'visions of God', a trance-like experience (8^{1-3})? The preciseness of his descriptions in this latter case of what was taking place in the temple at Jerusalem raises further difficulties of understanding. It is inappropriate to accept all such statements at their face value, without trying to understand the situation and climate of opinion to which they belong; we are dealing with an ancient world which frequently describes experiences in ways which would be inappropriate in a modern scientifically interpreted world. It is equally unsatisfactory merely to dismiss the statements as unreliable without trying to discover the nature of the experience which is being described. We need an adequate psychology of the prophets; but this is not available to us for the simple reason that the information is not there. The best we can do is attempt to understand the milieu in which they operated, taking due account of comparable evidence from other parts of the ancient world; to see the value of analogies in other periods and areas, perhaps particularly in the area of oriental religion in which many strange experiences are attested; above all, to try to get inside the experience of the prophet by discerning what kind of man he was.

This is a point of very great importance, since a first reading of the book of Ezekiel is apt to leave the reader with a very odd impression. The harshness of the language is at times abhorrent, though we may, with such a modern analogy in mind as George Orwell, be aware that harsh language can conceal a very sensitive personality. The meticulous detail, particularly of the closing chapters, is not very exciting reading, and the oddity of the geographical descriptions at the end is most striking. There are long stretches of rather repetitive sermonizing, much longer than the more immediately interesting short poetic oracles and descriptions of symbolic actions. It is perhaps not surprising that, apart from some few well-known passages—such as chapter 37—the book has often been classed with the long sections of legal material in books such as Leviticus and Numbers; and this has in some measure been assisted by a commonly held view that Ezekiel belongs rather with the priests than with the prophets. To some who have written about the Old Testament, this has seemed to place him low in the prophetic line, for it has often been believed that priests and prophets were in opposing parties, the former representing the conservative element and also representing an artificial understanding of the nature of God, bound up with legalistic notions, where the latter are the progressives, open to the word of God, untrammelled by official position. The study of the Old Testament in recent years has shown the total inadequacy of such a position, but the impression persists. One way in which a better understanding can be reached is by a sympathetic approach to Ezekiel.

He was of priestly family, and probably, though not certainly, a priest himself. The statement at the beginning of the book 'the word of the LORD came to Ezekiel the priest, the son of Buzi' (1^{3}) represents the traditional understanding of the Hebrew at this point; but it could be rendered 'Ezekiel, the son of Buzi the priest'. Nevertheless, the association of Ezekiel with priestly circles is clear, and in this he resembles also Jeremiah who was of priestly family (Jer. 1^{1}). His concern with matters of ritual and holiness, and his frequent use of legal language (so, e.g., in chapter 18), show this connection with the priesthood. He was married, and we are told that his wife died not long before the fall of the city and the destruction of the temple (24^{15-27}). This information is given because the death of his wife, like the personal experiences of other prophets (cf. especially Hosea), is seen to be bound up with the message he has to give. So he is commanded not to mourn her death.

Oddly enough, this has sometimes been taken to suggest that he was a harsh and unsympathetic person. But a closer reading of the text shows that this is not so; he could refer to his wife as 'the delight of your eyes' (24^{16}) and the command not to mourn was evidently as alien to him as was the command to Jeremiah not to marry (Jer. 16^{2}). The loss of his wife was to him symbolic of the loss to his people of the sanctuary, the 'pride of your power, the delight of your eyes, and the desire of your soul' (24^{21}). In a powerful symbol, occurring twice in the book (3^{16-21}, 33^{1-9}), Ezekiel depicts himself as a watchman, upon whom is laid the responsibility of warning the people of coming disaster. If he fails to warn, the whole responsibility falls upon himself; if he warns and men do not heed, then it rests upon them. Again this has been thought to suggest a harshness of outlook, as if the prophet could not care less about the outcome, provided he has saved his own life by carrying out his appointed task. But again a closer reading indicates that what the prophet feels is the burden of responsibility which rests upon him. The prophet as watchman is really the prophet as pastor, and through the harshness of his words and the ruthlessness of his judgement there shines a deep care and love and distress which are at times so overpowering that he cannot speak.

It is always dangerous to simplify the nature of a prophet's message, but with Ezekiel this might be done by indicating that the one pole of his teaching is his conception of the centrality and absoluteness of God. 'To know that I am Yahweh' is a phrase which occurs not infrequently in the book, in various types of context; what God does, what the prophet does and says, lead in the end to this conclusion. God will be known for what he is; the whole range of his purpose will become clear, his nature be revealed. The other pole of his teaching could be said to be 'responsibility', and here the prophet begins with himself and his own calling, and sees the response which his people ought to make in the same terms. He does not ask of them anything which he does not know to be asked of himself. That God has laid upon him the obligation to be a watchman corresponds to his recognition that each man is responsible before God to be obedient to his will. That will Ezekiel shows to be set out in the laws and traditions of the faith in which the people have been called to live. The possibility of obedience is given in the willingness of God to give life even to a dead community (see chapter 37) and to give to his people a new heart (see 36[22 ff.]). The context of obedience is a newly ordered land and people with the holy temple of God at its centre (see chapters 40–48, developing 36[38 ff.]).

1[1–3] *Ezekiel and his ministry*

The opening verses provide more than one date. That which appears in v. 2 is clear; *the fifth year of the exile of King Jehoiachin* is 593 B.C. and it is interesting to note that Ezekiel's message is dated in relation to Jehoiachin, and not to Zedekiah who was placed on the throne as his successor. It appears that Jehoiachin was still recognized as the official king, even though he was in captivity, and this is suggested also by the Babylonian tablets which refer to the allocation of rations to him and his entourage (cf. p. 3). The date in v. 1 is problematic; to what does *the thirtieth year* refer? Is it the prophet's age? Is it an error for some other figure? Is it a date from some otherwise unknown chronological scheme? The simplest explanation would seem to be that it is due to a scribe who observed that whereas Jeremiah spoke of 70 years of exile (Jer. 25[12], 29[10]), Ezekiel spoke of 40 (4[6]); by this note, the scribe reconciled the two figures. Of course, in reality both 70 and 40 are to be taken as conventional figures, suggestive in the one case of a whole lifetime and in the other of a full generation. On v. 3, cf. also p. 69. The experience took place in Babylonia, by the great canal (*the river Chebar*); presumably the exiles at Telabib (3[15]) are one of the groups of Jews settled in various centres in Babylonia. No more precise information is available about either the place or the actual conditions of exile, though Ezekiel's activity (cf. 14[1], 20[1]) suggests not inconsiderable freedom in the ordering of their own lives. With this we may compare the hints in Jer. 29.

1^{4-28a} *The heavenly throne*

The vision here described may be compared with the much simpler visions of Isaiah (Isa. 6) and Micaiah (1 Kgs. 22$^{19\text{ff.}}$); the essential point of similarity is the centrality of God, enthroned in judgement. The description here, however, enters into great and complex detail, and a comparison with the overlapping text of chapter 10 suggests that in all probability the very repetitive style owes something to accidental double copying of some phrases and perhaps something also to the desire of later scribes to add to the mystery evoked by the wording.

4. What is eventually to be identified as the throne of God (v. 26) is only gradually introduced, but to those familiar with the ancient traditions of God's appearance to his people, the storm and cloud of the opening already suggest a theophany. It comes *out of the north*, and it is natural to see this, in the light of chapters 10–11, as linked with the departure of God's glory from Jerusalem, and his journeying to make himself known to his prophet in Babylonia. (The normal route from Jerusalem to Babylon would be northwards and then eastwards and southwards, along the main routes.) But it would be oversimple to limit the idea in this way. The north is particularly associated with the dwelling of God and with the place from which he comes in judgement. So we find Zion described as 'in the far north' in Ps. 48^{2}; this term, Zaphon, traceable also in the Canaanite religious literature, is used for the dwelling of God. (On this psalm, cf. Vol. 3, pp. 157 f.)

5–14. The picture of the throne of God is built up in stages, and the complexity of the detail is such that any representation of it in picture form is quite impossible. The first stage is marked by *four living creatures* (v. 5). The image would appear to derive from the kind of representations which are found in

Mesopotamian art where various combinations of animal and human forms can be seen (cf. p. 74). These are winged creatures; they have the *form of men*, that is, they stand upright, but they have four faces each, of man, of lion, of ox, and of eagle. What particular symbolism these features have is not made explicit. We may note one development in Rev. 4[7]; much later tradition associated them with the four evangelists. In the centre there is fire, and lightning flashing. This fire is in 10[2] used for the destruction of the city, but here it simply suggests both brightness and mobility, for the *living creatures* move *like a flash of lightning* (v. 14).

15–21. A new element now appears, and its relationship with what precedes is not altogether clear. A complex structure of wheels is described as being *upon the earth beside the living creatures* (v. 15). Is there perhaps an indication here of various elements being built together, perhaps by the prophet, perhaps by his successors, to suggest more elaborately the mobility of the throne of God, and indeed to describe it not simply in terms of a throne but in terms of a chariot? In addition, the wheel-rims are *full of eyes* (v. 18), and this may represent yet another concept, that of the all-seeing nature of God (cf. Zech. 4[10]). The fact that the living creatures and the wheels move simultaneously, *for the spirit of the living creatures was in the wheels* (v. 21), may suggest that there is an attempt at suggesting a relationship between the heavenly throne of God, remote and inaccessible and the earthly dwelling in which he manifests himself, here thought of in terms of a mysterious chariot.

22–25. The next stage is the description of a *firmament* (v. 22), the same word as is used in Gen. 1[6]; the word suggests something which is beaten out, firm and flat, as one might beat out gold to make an overlay. The implication would seem to be that God is enthroned on the firmament of heaven, and the impression of mystery and awe is heightened by the mention of the sound which issues from it, *like the sound of many waters, like the thunder of the Almighty, a sound of tumult like the sound of a host* (v. 24). Not one

WINGED BULL FROM NIMRUD. No precise representation can be given of the figures described in the vision in Ezek. 1. But we may usefully compare figures found in Assyrian and Babylonian buildings, of which the one illustrated is a good example. It shows the combining of features of different creatures in one figure; a bull's body and legs, eagle's wings, human head, lion's mane. The figures of Ezekiel's vision also combine man, lion, ox, and eagle, having four faces, wings, and feet like those of a calf.

symbol but three to suggest the appearance of God, for whom the thunder may be described as his voice, and who with his heavenly host rides out to battle (cf. Judg. 5).

26–28*a*. Very obliquely, the final stage of the vision is described; it is not a throne, but *the likeness of a throne*; upon it is seated a figure, *a likeness as it were of a human form* (v. 26). Isaiah's description of the enthroned deity does not hesitate: 'I saw the LORD sitting upon a throne' (Isa. 6[1]). Ezekiel's description is less direct and even more mysterious. What terms can one use to describe God? We have to use the best we have, and these must be human terms. But even to suggest that God looks like a man is dangerous and misleading; and to picture him as a king sitting on a throne is a symbol which we treat literally at our peril. So the prophet avoids direct statement, and overshadows the terms of the description with a brightness linked to the brightness of the rainbow against the stormcloud.

For the full appreciation of the vision, the details need to be examined; but its main impact must be in this sense of overwhelming majesty, of splendour and brightness, and a mystery which cannot be described. It makes a fitting start to the teaching of a prophet for whom the holiness and splendour of God are the central theme.

1[28b]–2[7] *The prophet's commission*

The opening of this passage, which runs straight on from what precedes, emphasizes again the nature of God in his holiness and shows its impact upon the sensitive person of the prophet. To see God directly is often indicated in the Old Testament as dangerous, bringing the risk of death (cf. Exod. 33[17–23]; Judg. 13[22]). The words here again suggest indirectness of statement; it is not God whom the prophet has seen but *the appearance of the likeness of the glory of the LORD* (v. 28). But this is sufficient to evoke awe and bring the prophet into the appropriate worshipping position of utter prostration. As he lies upon his face on the ground he hears 'a voice speaking' or 'the sound of one speaking'. He is addressed as *son of man* (v. 1); the phrase does not carry the kind of technical sense which appears in some New Testament contexts, but emphasizes the quality of humanity over against that of deity. So in Ps. 8[4] it is used, in parallel with 'man', to indicate the condescension of the God who gives honour and authority to man. The prophet knows himself for what he is, but knows himself also lifted by *the Spirit* (v. 2) on to his feet. In 1[3] and elsewhere, Ezekiel's experience is described in terms of the 'hand' of God, which takes hold of him, rests upon him, exerts compulsion upon him. Here and elsewhere, it is the *Spirit* of God, which might equally be rendered as 'wind' or 'breath'. There are various ways in which this sense of possession and compulsion may be expressed. It is said of Gideon that 'the Spirit of the LORD clothed itself with Gideon' (Judg. 6[34], RSV, has 'took possession of' which is a paraphrase). Such expressions are to be found in relation to various early prophets, rarely in the great prophets of the eighth and seventh centuries, but again in the exilic period and after. Equally it may be said that the hand of God was upon a man, to empower him for action; for the hand of God is particularly the symbol of his action to deliver in battle.

The words of the commission in vv. 3–7 provide a fairly general and comprehensive statement; we may compare the general message given in Isa. 6. It is an absolute commission, to be fulfilled whether the people listen or not. The overtones are suggestive of the inevitability of disobedience, as also in Isa. 6. But in any case, *they will know that there has been a prophet among them* (v. 5). The call narratives of the prophets are their warrant for speaking; this is their claim to authority. We might compare Mark 1[9–15]. The recognition of the prophet of God is the recognition of God himself, for it is he who has commissioned the prophet. So this phrase forms the counterpart to that other phrase 'They will know that I am Yahweh' to which reference has already been made (cf. p. 70).

2[8]–3[3] *The scroll of woe*

As the text stands, this passage is simply a continuation of the more general commission of the previous verses, and if we look at the whole of the section chapters 1–3 it is clear that there is a unity of structure in it. As is the case with other prophetic books the opening gives the setting (Jer. 1 provides a good example); it provides the basis for understanding the prophet's message, and outlines its essential elements, by the process of combining into one unit various smaller sections which may originally have come from different periods. The vision of the scroll which is here described in no way conflicts with what precedes, but it introduces a new element, and some scholars have felt, and with considerable justification, that this is really another commissioning tradition. Does it represent an earlier moment in Ezekiel's experience, perhaps even preceding what is described in chapter 1, and now woven appropriately into the whole structure? The symbol is of a *written scroll* (v. 9), and it is of interest that such a symbol should appear, for whereas in earlier prophecy there is little reference to the written word, and when reference is made it appears to be the exception rather than the general rule (cf. Isa. 8[1, 16], 30[8]; and also Jer. 36), here the idea of the prophecies being in written form is accepted as normal. Have we perhaps begun to move into that period when older prophecies were being collected together and read in the light of newer events? This would help in our understanding of the present form of earlier prophetic collections such as those of Amos, Hosea, Micah, and Isaiah of Jerusalem. The symbol makes clear that judgement is the central element in the message; the eating of the scroll indicates its total acceptance by the prophet; its being *sweet as honey* (v. 3)—that woe should be sweet is again a harsh concept—indicates that the word of God, no matter how uncongenial in itself, must be accepted and recognized for what it is.

3[16–21] *The prophet as watchman*

The idea of the prophet as *watchman* (v. 17) is not found only in Ezekiel. Isa. 21 has two uses of the expression, employing different words. In Isa. 21[5–8] (with which we may compare Hab. 2[1]), there is pictured the appointment of a watchman, apparently distinct from the prophet, who is to give a report on what he sees. In Isa. 21$^{11-12}$, an obscure passage, the inquiry is addressed to the prophet as watchman, asked—as the ordinary watchman might be—concerning the passage of the night. Ezekiel's use of the term shows a fuller development of the concept, and brings out its meaning both in relation to the prophet himself and to his people. In the other occurrence of this material, in 33$^{1-9}$, the exposition of the prophet's function is preceded by a more general statement, describing the appointment and functioning of the secular watchman and the nature of the responsibility which rests upon him (33$^{2-6}$). Here only the application is given, and its wording is rather repetitive, suggesting that it has probably been elaborated, perhaps in relation to the similar statements about sin and repentance and responsibility in chapter 18. But the essence of the message is clear. God issues his warning of judgement on the wicked; it is for the prophet to see that the warning is given. If he does, then responsibility rests upon the wicked man—whether he repents or pays no heed. If the prophet fails to give warning, the wicked man still falls under judgement—he can plead no extenuating circumstances. But the prophet is himself held responsible: *his blood I will require at your hand* (v. 20). For the prophet there is no choice; he has been commissioned by God. If he gives warning, it is well: *you will have saved your life* (v. 21)—a phrase which should be understood simply as the obverse of the previous one quoted. The prophet will be free of blood-guilt. But what a dire responsibility rests upon the prophet, to see that the whole community is warned of the coming disaster, so that there is opportunity of repentance. It is no light matter to be under the hand of God and to sense the compulsive nature of his word (cf. Jer. 20$^{7-18}$).

4$^{1-3}$ *A symbol of siege*

The prophet is commanded to perform a complex symbolic action, an expression of the word of God who is bringing relentless siege against Jerusalem. The *brick* (v. 1) is the same word as is used in the Exodus narratives; it is used of the sun-dried mud or clay bricks, largely used throughout the near east for cheap building. Most probably here the term is intended to imply a clay-brick or tile of the kind used so very commonly in Mesopotamia (and elsewhere) for writing purposes. Maps and plans are also found recorded on such tiles, and the portrayal of the city of Jerusalem here follows a pattern well known to us from Babylonia (cf. p. 80). The brick with its plan is to be treated as if it were the actual city. Representation of the siege is to be carried out by *siegeworks*, a *wall*, a *mound*, *camps*, and *battering rams* (v. 2); we are not told precisely how such detail could be undertaken. Verse 3 introduces a new element, the placing of an *iron plate* between the prophet and the city. No explanation is given of this, other than that it is to be *as an iron wall between you and the city*; it is most natural to suppose that as the prophet expresses the word of God, so the iron barrier indicates the relentlessness of the divine purpose and the exclusion of any possibility of deliverance. As so often, in this passage the description of the symbol and its interpretation are interwoven; the phrases *let it be in a state of siege* and *press the siege against it* appear as commands to the prophet, but in reality they are expressions of the meaning of the symbol for the people of Jerusalem.

This symbol and its interpretation raise two more general points. In the first place, it illustrates the use by the prophets of symbolic action alongside the speaking of the prophetic word. Numerous examples of such actions are found in the prophetic books (e.g. Jer. $13^{1\text{ff.}}$) and in narratives (e.g. 1 Kgs. 11^{29-32}, 22^{11}); in Ezek. 4–5 we have four such symbols grouped together, and others occur elsewhere in the book. 21^{18-23} has a symbol representing the divine will that Nebuchadrezzar should choose to attack Jerusalem rather than Rabbah of the Ammonites; 37^{15-23} one concerned with the reunion of Judah and Israel. What is their nature? They are not simply vivid illustrations of the prophetic message; they are to be taken as part of the message itself. There is nothing to suggest that the symbolic action was thought to be more effective than the

PLAN OF THE CITY OF NIPPUR ON A CLAY TABLET (*c.* 1500 B.C.). This example of a city plan on a tablet illustrates the prophetic symbol in Ezek. 4. The plan shows various features of the city. The lower left-hand corner is the south, and the narrow double line which runs south-east and south-west marks the city wall. In the south-west wall are three gates indicated by the lettering giving their names. Just by the third, the wall turns to mark the north-west side and the only gate here is marked just at the break in the tablet. The double line which runs across the centre from north-west to south-east is the 'central canal'. Outside the wall to the south-west lies the Euphrates, shown by a wider double line; on the north-west edge runs another canal. Important buildings are outlined and named—two temples together on the north-east, a large building against the south-east wall, an enclosure described as a park in the corner formed by the junction of the south-east, south-west walls. The name of the city appears as the short vertical line of writing in the very centre, damaged by the crack which runs across. The purpose of such a city plan is not quite clear. Perhaps it is best understood as prepared to be placed before the god of the city, a perpetual reminder to him of its need of his protection and blessing. So in Isa. 49[16] God says of Zion: 'Behold, I have graven you on the palms of my hands; your walls are continually before me', as if it were not just a plan on a tile which reminds God of his city, but an even more permanent engraving.

prophetic word; the word which the prophet speaks, being the word given by God, is itself effective, it produces its result as surely as the word of blessing spoken by Isaac to Jacob (Gen. 27). It is effective because it is God's word. So too the action is an expression of the divine will. We have no means of knowing why sometimes the prophets used such actions rather than simply using words; the action normally, as here, would need some verbal comment for it to be intelligible.

In the second place, this passage raises a question which has already been briefly mentioned (cf. pp. 64 f.). Was Ezekiel only active as a prophet in Babylonia? When, as here, he concentrates his attention on the siege of Jerusalem, does this perhaps suggest that he is speaking to its people directly? The issue is not a clear one, since the exiles too were closely concerned in the fate of the city. When in chapter 8 we find a detailed description of the idolatry being practised in the temple, does this not imply that the prophet is there? But how far is this precise description and how far is it visionary experience? Ezekiel is elsewhere described, also when transported by 'the Spirit' to the temple, as prophesying and one of those actually there is said to have fallen dead (11^{1-13}). How are we to understand first the effect of the prophetic word and second the prophet's knowledge of it? Did he subsequently discover a coincidence, or is he perhaps describing an event at which he was actually present, in Jerusalem, not in vision but in person. When he performs a symbolic action portraying escape from the besieged city to go into exile (12^{1-7}), does this belong in Jerusalem or in Babylonia? There is much in the book of Ezekiel which points to a Babylonian setting—details of vocabulary, allusions such as that to the plan on the tile; but there is much also which points to his close knowledge of Jerusalem. The extent of the former could be explained in the recognition that the earlier parts of the prophet's message were subsequently reapplied in Babylonia. The extent of the latter could be simply due to his knowledge and experience before he was taken into exile in 597, and it is not impossible that some of the passages, like chapters 8 and 11, which show more precise knowledge, derive from an earlier stage of his activity, before even the first capture of Jerusalem. The possibility cannot, however, be absolutely ruled out that the present form of the book obscures the earlier stages of the prophet's activity.

8 *Idolatry in the temple*

The opening of this chapter gives a setting of a kind which appears again in 14[1] and 20[1]; a similar setting is given for an Elisha story in 2 Kgs. 6[32]. It introduces a long section covering chapters 8–11, for in 8[3] we find Ezekiel transported by *the Spirit* and brought *in visions of God to Jerusalem*, while at the end he is brought back: 'Then the vision that I had seen went up from me. And I told the exiles all the things that the LORD had showed me' (11[24f.]).

The material of chapter 8 is arranged in a highly stylized manner; a series of descriptions of idolatrous practice is given, and each leads on into the next with the expression: *You will see still greater abominations* (vv. 6, 13, 15). This suggests the probability that here various accounts of such practices and the prophet's judgement upon them have been drawn together to provide a climax. The downfall of city and temple which follows is directly linked here with the apostasy of Jerusalem. Four particular evils are indicated.

5–6. The first (already prepared for in v. 3) is of an *image of jealousy, north of the altar gate, in the entrance* (v. 5). It is not indicated what this is; the description simply means that the very presence of such an image provokes the wrath of God, the jealous God of ancient tradition. Jealousy as attributed to God means that he claims absolute allegiance, he will allow no rival claimant to his position of supremacy; for Israel he is the one and only (cf., e.g., Exod. 20[3–6]). The position of this image —whether it is the representation of a human figure or a pillar decorated perhaps with mythological motifs—may suggest that it was originally seen as a protective creature at the temple gate, and that in course of time worship had been transferred to it *to drive me far from my sanctuary* (v. 6), i.e. to provoke the anger of God so that he will deliberately withdraw himself from the temple, as indeed he is subsequently shown to do.

7–13. The second raises some curious practical questions. How could the prophet dig through the wall and find a concealed door if in fact it led into a room occupied by seventy elders engaged in idolatrous worship? Is there perhaps a conflation of differing elements here? What is clear is that here we have prominent and responsible members of the community engaging in secret rites for *each had his censer in his hand* (v. 11) and portrayed on the wall of the room were *all kinds of creeping things, and loathsome beasts, and all the idols of the house of Israel* (v. 10). The representation of animal figures marks a direct contravention of Israelite law (cf. Exod. $20^{4\,\text{ff.}}$), but what exactly the elders were worshipping remains undisclosed.

14–15. The third is clearer, for here we find *women weeping for Tammuz* (v. 14). This deity, known under this name and others, is of very ancient origin, known in Sumerian as Dumuzi. There survive many dirges connected with him, and it is often claimed that he was a deity connected with the fertility of the earth whose death—in the period of heat—was lamented. The obscurity of the texts has led to much discussion about whether he was thought of as a dying and rising god—it is difficult to understand the intention of the lamentation unless it was thought to be possible that he would revive. The occurrence of motifs of this kind connected with Baal in the Canaanite texts of Ras Shamra suggests that there was a widespread popular belief that such a cyclic pattern occurred. Here in Ezekiel, the mention of the name Tammuz would indicate the direct influence of the Babylonian religion in Jerusalem, though it may be that the fact that the text actually has 'the Tammuz' indicates that the name has become a title, applicable to a ritual rather than denoting a particular deity.

16–18. The fourth shows a contempt for God by men who worship the sun with their backs to the temple. Is this perhaps also evidence of Babylonian influence? Or is it simply a revival of practices recorded as having been removed from the temple during Josiah's reform (cf. 2 Kgs. 23^{11})? The expression *Lo, they put the branch to their nose* is quite obscure; it must refer to a particular ritual which was felt to be in some way specially insulting to God.

The obscurity of the allusions throughout the chapter is perhaps due to later scribes who may well have removed more precise references which might cause offence. The Old Testament shows many signs of having been to some extent 'censored' to avoid creating difficulties for the pious worshipper and reader.

9–10 *The doom of the city and temple and the departure of God*

The sequel to the idolatry is the doom of the city, and the opening of chapter 9 depicts the agents of divine destruction, *six men . . . every man with his weapon for slaughter in his hand* (v. 2). This offers a description of the disaster in mythological terms, for these are evidently heavenly beings. As in Lam. 2 (cf. p. 51), the disaster is attributable directly to God, though in 2 Kings and elsewhere to Babylon and its armies. Significant here, however, is the appearance of a seventh man *clothed in linen, with a writing case at his side*. Analogies for this have been sought in the Babylonian pantheon where Nebo is particularly denoted as the scribe (cf. p. 120). But there is no reason why, since Israel thought of God as enthroned like a king in a royal court, she should not also have supposed there to be the appropriate officials associated with him (cf. 1 Kgs. $22^{19\text{ff.}}$; Job $1^{6\text{ff.}}$). The function of this man is clearly to keep the records of the heavenly court (perhaps we might compare Ps. 87^{6} and Mal. 3^{16}), and so here to *put a mark upon the foreheads of the men who sigh and groan over all the abominations* of Jerusalem (v. 4). *Put a mark* is literally 'mark with a *tau*', the last letter of the Hebrew alphabet: in the older script this would appear as a cross (+). The idea of a protective mark is found in the story of Cain (Gen. 4[15]), but a closer analogy is to be found in the Exodus narrative (Exod. 12[21–30]) where the houses of Israel are protected from the destroyer by the mark upon the door. Here it is not Israel which is protected, but only a remnant which is faithful. Ezekiel is affirming a principle (as also in chapter 18); he does not deal with the practical question of how the innocent will be spared in the destruction of the city. In the description of the destruction itself, we are led into the picture of the enthroned holy God, in the same terms as in chapter 1, the recurrence of this material emphasizing its importance in Ezekiel's understanding of God's nature.

11[14–21] *A word of judgement and hope*

These verses hardly belong to their present context, but their presence illuminates the way in which different elements of the prophet's teaching may be used to elaborate a particular point. In the preceding verses, the self-confidence of the people in Jerusalem has been indicated; are they not better than those who have been taken away into exile (v. 15)? To this, the reply is given that, though the exiles have been scattered abroad, yet God himself has been *a sanctuary to them for a while in the countries where they have gone* (v. 16). The precise meaning of this phrase is uncertain (cf. the comments on pp. 26 f.), though it is clear that it emphasizes the reality of the presence of God with the exiles. The promise is then given that the exiles will be gathered and restored to the land; they will purify it, and will themselves be purified; and a new covenant people will be established, *for they shall be my people, and I will be their God* (v. 20). The passage thus alludes to parts of chapter 36 and anticipates the broader conclusions of 40–48.

11[22–25] *The departure of the divine glory*

The relationship between God and his temple is variously indicated in the Old Testament. In the prayer of Solomon in 1 Kgs. 8[27] we read: 'But will God indeed dwell on the earth?

Behold, heaven and the highest heaven cannot contain thee; how much less this house which I have built.' Here is the recognition that God can never be confined to a temple. Yet the intimacy of his relation to it is shown by the vision of Isaiah, who saw God enthroned in judgement in his temple; and many of the psalms indicate such a closeness of relationship. There were some in the time of Jeremiah who believed that the very existence of the temple in some way guaranteed the presence and hence the protection of God (Jer. 7[4]) and who needed to be warned that God would destroy the Jerusalem shrine as he had destroyed that of Shiloh (Jer. 7[14]). Ezekiel preserves a recognition of both the intimacy of relation and of the independence of God; while he is there, his glory present in the temple, who can possibly prevail against him? But if he decides, in judgement upon his people, to withdraw his presence, then there is none to protect. So here the description is a vivid comment on the deliberation with which God hands over his own dwelling-place to be destroyed because it has been so defiled by the practices of those who frequent it.

18 *Responsibility*

1–4. The people (the *you* of v. 1 is plural) are repeating a proverb which appears also in Jer. 31[29], expressive of the experience that those who sin do not reap the result of their sin, it falls on their successors. More emphatically than in the Jeremiah passage, the proverb, no doubt a popularly repeated one at this time, is rejected by God himself. The comment is different in the two passages, but the sense is the same. It is the same thought as is found in Deut. 24[16]: 'The fathers shall not be put to death for the children nor shall the children be put to death for the fathers; every man shall be put to death for his own sin.' The Ezekiel passage expresses the certainty that all men belong to God, and he therefore controls their destinies.

5–29. The main section of the chapter, very repetitive in style, which suggests that the individual points have been underlined in the transmission of the material, is concerned with setting out in detail the implications of this initial affirmation. Its main point is that of responsibility. It is usual to stress that this is a matter of individual responsibility, and to compare and contrast this with earlier ideas about the corporate nature of responsibility within Israel, ideas of which the condemnation of Achan and his family (Josh. 7) provides the clearest example. But this is to oversimplify the matter. On the one hand, it is a mistake to isolate this part of the book—and some other similar passages—and give them undue prominence. While as we have seen, in chapter 9, Ezekiel recognizes the need for sparing the innocent in the disaster, for the most part his condemnation of Jerusalem and Judah is absolute. It comes almost as a surprise, after the harshness of the judgements in the opening chapters, to discover that he even entertains the idea of there being any who deserve to be spared. This shows the danger of generalization. By and large the book of Ezekiel is concerned with the overall fate of the community, its right judgement at the hands of God, and its re-establishment in purity by his will. Just how the individual fits into this is not really made clear. On the other hand, it is equally a mistake to suppose that the idea of the responsibility of the individual was a new idea, found at this period in Jeremiah, in Ezekiel, and in Deuteronomy. For Old Testament law certainly works on the basic assumption that it is the guilty who are to be punished, and the corporate understanding of responsibility comes out more clearly only in certain instances, as in the Achan case where the infringement of a basic law of the holy war demands the excision from the community of the whole offending group.

It is more appropriate to read this chapter in the light of what has already been said about responsibility in relation to Ezekiel himself (cf. p. 70), and also in the context of the historical situation to which Ezekiel belongs. It would be only natural to find that the prophet who is so conscious of his own responsibility as watchman should express his concern for obedience in terms of what rests upon each man—and here he belongs very much to the priestly line with its stress on law. It is also important to recognize that the proverb which ushers in the discussion is double-edged. It can of course be a complaint—why should we suffer for the sins of others?—with the implication that those who suffered the disasters of exile and the loss of their kingdom were not to blame. Ezekiel is very concerned to bring home responsibility to his own generation; they are being punished for their own failure. The proverb can also be understood as an expression of distress—how can we escape from the weight of the past?—and this is a theme which is to be elaborated in chapter 37.

So Ezekiel's exposition here is to be read in the light of an urgent pastoral situation. Those who make light of sin are to be warned of the stringency of divine justice. Those who are in distress because they see no hope are to be encouraged in the obedience which represents the right response to God's purpose.

5–9 deal with the first positive case, the man who does right. The basic statement, in vv. 5 and 9*b*, is clear; the righteous man shall live. The intervening lines provide a brief summary of the basic requirements, in terms which are very closely linked to those of the decalogue. Here is an appeal to a known standard, absolute in its demand for whole-hearted allegiance to God and loyalty to one's neighbour.

10–13 state the opposite case, in terms of a wicked son of a righteous father. Two points are made here. On the one hand, the wicked man is fully responsible and cannot escape judgement. On the other hand, he cannot rely upon his father's righteousness. The same detailing of particular evils stresses the point.

14–18 go a stage further by developing the second point, but in reverse. The grandson in this line, which is being taken as an illustration, turns away from his father's sins; again the details are set out. He is judged for what he is; and what he does in no way affects the judgement on his wicked father.

19–20 again set the matter out in general terms, repeating the point. 'The person who *sins shall die*' (v. 20; 'person' is often a better rendering than *soul* as the RSV has it, since 'soul' now has overtones not proper to the Hebrew word).

21–24 provide yet another elaboration of the point. Such detailing is characteristic of legal material, where each case must be covered, using the casuistic form 'if a man . . .' for each instance. It is also appropriate to the sermon, in which warnings and encouragements suitable for each hearer can be included. Here the possibility of release from past sin is made clear, and it is important to read vv. 21–22 in context; to isolate them and conclude that behaviour does not matter provided you are found in a righteous condition at the crucial moment is to misunderstand the kind of argument here being used. It is further interpreted by v. 23, which stresses the desire of God that men should find life in obedience. The same danger of isolating the words is present in v. 24 which states the obverse, concerning the man who turns from good to evil.

25–29 represent a further homiletic passage drawing out the consequences and repeating the phrases of the preceding section. Its fundamental concern is responsibility.

30–32 round off the whole 'sermon' with a warning: *I will judge you* (v. 30), a note of encouragement to repentance, again speaking of a new heart and a new spirit which elsewhere is seen to be in fact the gift of God, and a concluding affirmation about the nature of God, the one who desires that men should live. Ezekiel gives here his most urgent warning to his people. They must recognize responsibility, but they must also repent; it is God's will that there should be life.

25–32 *The foreign nation oracles*

It is part of the established prophetic tradition that pronouncements are made concerning the fate of the nations with which Israel came into contact. We have already in fact taken note of some of these from other prophetic books (cf. pp. 55 ff., 63 f.). Such oracles have both a political and a religious basis. On the one hand, it was recognized as proper in the ancient world, that a nation engaged in maintaining its own life over against opposition from other nations, would be not infrequently involved in war. On the other hand, such warfare, in the contemporary climate of thought, could not be undertaken without the assurance of divine favour, and this included the pronouncing of words of curse and doom upon the nation's enemies. A good example of the employment of a prophet to utter such curses is to be found in the Balaam narratives of Num. 22–24; the king of Moab employs Balaam to curse Israel. (The fact that in the event Balaam is prevented by God from doing this and instead is under an obligation to pronounce blessings does not affect the point.) There is evidence from Egypt in what are known as the 'Execration Texts' (for examples cf. *ANET*, pp. 328 f.) of a more ordered and regular ceremonial of cursing enemies, both external and internal, by way of ensuring the protection of the community from all ills; and it has been suggested that similar practices were known in Israel. The prophetic judgements on other nations and on Israel itself may be explained in part on such an assumption. We might be inclined to view the cursing of national enemies as a sort of psychological warfare. But what we can understand of the conception of the word of God given through the prophets indicates that we should see rather the efficacy of the divine pronouncement. If Egypt is condemned, the events by which disaster is brought are decreed by the divine will. In part this represents a development of ideas which are found associated with the concept of the 'Holy War', that in which God decrees that *his* nation shall fight *his* battles against *his* enemies (cf. the end of the Song of Deborah in Judg. 5).

CLAY FIGURINE WITH EXECRATION TEXT. This is one of a number of figurines, representing the upper part of the human body in the form of a prisoner, probably from Saqqarah, just east of Memphis in Egypt, and probably belonging to about 1700 B.C. The texts on the figurines, as also on potsherds, listed the enemies of Egypt, and most frequently her foreign enemies. The pots were broken, the figurines probably buried, in an act designed to call down effective curses upon the enemies. We may compare Jeremiah's action in breaking a jar as he pronounced doom upon Jerusalem and Judah (Jer. $19^{1 \text{ff.}}$). We may also see an analogy in the pronouncing of judgement upon the foreign nations in many Old Testament passages, though we know nothing of any rite performed to accompany such pronouncements (cf. pp. 79 f., 90 ff.).

The collecting together of pronouncements on foreign nations as we find them in the prophetic books, as here, is partly a political matter. In some measure, such groups of oracles reflect particular historical situations, and in Ezek. 25–32 we may find numerous references to the events of the exilic period. But it becomes clear as we look more closely at such groups of oracles that they have a much more significant theological point. They reflect the conviction that God is engaged in a conflict with all the hostile powers, typified in certain foreign nations; his conflict with them is part of a cosmic struggle, to be wound up in a last great battle which will usher in a new age of peace and righteousness. Thus in Isa. 13–23 a collection of such oracles, some clearly reflecting the period of Isaiah, others probably of much later origin (cf. pp. 57 f. on Isa. 13–14, 21), is given a climax in chapters 24–27 which go far beyond simple historical considerations. The same is true of Ezekiel, though here in a rather different manner. The oracles in chapters 25–32 contain comments on many aspects of the contemporary situation, though quite probably also some material which is later in origin. They serve as a bridge from the primarily judgement material of 1–24 to the restoration themes of 33 ff. But the more general and theological point is picked up subsequently in chapters 38–39 which depict a mysterious battle against Gog king of Magog (cf. pp. 99 f.). There may be a historical basis for this battle picture, but it is now more clearly a picture of final events. Full restoration comes after such an overthrow of the powers of evil by God himself.

Such themes as these are closely linked to ideas to be found in the Psalms. Thus Pss. 2 and 46 both depict a concerted attack on Jerusalem by the armies of the nations, and the assurance of the divine presence which brings about the ultimate victory. These ideas are themselves bound up with Israel's understanding of kingship, ideas of world sovereignty such as are to be found in Ps. 72 (on this, cf. Vol. 3, pp. 158 ff.). The important thing is to recognize the theological significance of this material in both psalmody and prophecy. Of course it had its political aspects; Israel, like the nations of the modern world, was concerned about security, and this could express itself in war and in atrocities committed in the name of God. But the Old Testament presents not simply the history of a little nation in its changing fortunes; it shows how that history was seen to have theological meaning. The conflicts with other nations did not cease, but the theme became a central one in men's endeavour to understand how, in the end, God and the reign of peace and righteousness would prevail. The exile was an important period for the kind of rethinking that this represents, and so too was the period of political subjection which followed in which some of Israel's best thinkers—for example, the Chronicler—were more concerned to think out how the will of God is to be understood than to see how political independence could be achieved again. Not surprisingly, there was much tension between the more political and the more theological types of thought.

It is in the light of such considerations that these oracles in Ezek. 25–32 are to be read—not as a dull catalogue of nations condemned, but as part of an interpretation of experience. The chapters include (chapter 27) one of the most magnificent of Old Testament poems, a picture of judgement upon Tyre which is portrayed as a rich merchant ship. In chapter 28, further themes concerning Tyre are developed, and the overthrow of the king of Tyre is interpreted in the light of ancient myths related to those found in Gen. 3. The detail of such passages requires full-scale commentary such as is not possible here; but they should be read so that the impact of the poetry may be felt.

33–37 *Themes of restoration*

Not inappropriately, this new section of the book opens with the watchman theme (33^{1-9}) and with a reiteration of the teaching on responsibility, closely similar to that found in chapter 18. What is said in these chapters about the will of God to restore his people is thus prefaced by the reminder that the appropriation of the new hope rests in the response that God's people will make.

33^{23–33} *False confidence*

Immediately, we are again reminded of the dangers which still remain, the over-confidence in themselves which can make those still in Judah, in *these waste places*, sure that as *Abraham was only one man, yet he got possession of the land; but we are many; the land is surely given us to possess* (v. 24). But the prophet makes it clear that their future does not depend upon any such simple reading of God's workings in the past; it depends upon the willingness to give full allegiance to God, in total obedience. And judgement falls upon those who pay no need, who are insincere in their professions, to whom the prophet is *like one who sings love songs with a beautiful voice and plays well on an instrument, for they hear what you say, but they will not do it* (v. 32). These verses clearly contain two elements: a judgement upon those in Palestine, a statement which includes a series of condemnations of particular evils and which is to be understood in the light of that view which saw the hope for the future solely in the exilic situation; and a comment, presumably on those who gather to hear Ezekiel's words in Babylonia, on their insincerity and unwillingness to obey. But the placing together of these, with the final comment: *Then they will know that a prophet has been among them* (v. 33), provides a general warning. Judgement is not simply a thing of the past, and the chapter which follows (34) deals with another aspect of the general problem, the condemnation of false shepherds, that is rulers, and their replacement by a new David, a genuine prince in a land purified and made secure.

36^{16–38} *The basis of restoration*

Judgement on the past, judgement upon the nations (typified by Edom in chapter 35), usher in words of promise. But it is important to see the basis of that promise. Ezekiel, as may be seen from the earlier part of the book, is fully conscious of the history of God's dealings with his people, and is the more impressed by the utter corruption which has marked the people from the beginning. Now in the exile they have been *scattered among the nations, dispersed through the countries* (v. 9). But the result of this has been that *they profaned my holy name, in that men said of them, 'These are the people of the LORD, and yet they had to go out of his land'* (v. 20). There is a reminiscence here of a theme found in other parts of the Old Testament, particularly in the descriptions of the wilderness period. When the people are disobedient, they are threatened by God with rejection; but the appeal is made to him that if he does reject them, the nations will think that God's intentions were evil or that he has failed (cf., e.g., Exod. 32[7–14]). His name would thus be profaned, that is, his nature would be so misunderstood and misrepresented that it would be equivalent to treating him in a totally wrong manner. The name of God is another way of speaking of his being, his nature, for it is by knowledge of his name—which he has been willing to reveal (see Exod. 3[13f.])—that men may worship him as he really is. So Ezekiel expresses his conviction that God will act in terms of God's *concern for my holy name* (v. 21). The nations must not be allowed to think that he could fail; they will be shown what he really is (cf. notes on 39[21–29], and on Isa. 52[3–6]).

Restoration therefore takes place because God is God, and not because Israel has any claim (v. 22). The people will be gathered, they will be cleansed (this is referred particularly to the removal of every idolatrous practice, because central to Israel's place as people of God is the absoluteness of allegiance). They will be given *a new heart, a new spirit; and I will take out of your flesh the heart of stone and give you a heart of flesh* (v. 26). Restoration of the land, the rebuilding of the destroyed cities, the tilling of the land—all these are directly undertaken by God. So those who pass by, those who mocked at Israel's downfall (cf. Lam. 2[15f.]), will now say: *'This land that was desolate has become like the garden of Eden; and the waste and desolate and ruined cities are now inhabited and fortified'* (v. 35). The nations will know that it is God who has done this.

The whole passage is full of hints of the kind of restoration which is subsequently described in such detail in chapters

40–48. The covenant will be re-established (see v. 28) and *then they will know that I am the LORD* (v. 38).

37 *Three restoration prophecies*

37[1–14] *The vision of life*

This, the most familiar passage in the whole book, occupies a central point in the promise and hope of restoration. As elsewhere (cf. on chapter 8), the prophet describes the experience in terms of being transported by *the Hand* and *Spirit* of God, here to a great battlefield in a plain, strewn with bones so dry that the hope of restoration to life is utterly remote (vv. 1–2). The message is presented in double form. First, in vv. 3–6, we find a series of questions and answers—a style to be found further developed in Zechariah and Malachi—by which the effect is heightened and the miraculous nature of the restoration is underlined. The command to prophesy to the dry bones in v. 4 is followed by the affirmation of God's purpose to give flesh and life to the bones. Second, in vv. 7–10, the same theme is developed in the actual prophecy, with its vivid description of the bones coming together and their being clothed with sinews, flesh, and skin; and, again with emphasis, a new command to prophesy to the wind (this seems more appropriate than RSV *breath*; we may note how the same Hebrew word *rūaḥ* is understood here in three senses—Spirit of God, breath in man, the winds of heaven). *The slain*—for it is the bodies of a dead army—become a living *host*. Finally, the message of the dialogue and action is made explicit (one can sense in the whole structure the sermon technique by which repetition brings home the meaning). *These bones are the whole house of Israel*; their complaint is that their *hope is lost* (v. 11). The disaster of exile is as the gloom of death. So the picture shifts, and it is no longer the dead of a battlefield, their bones exposed to the elements (cf. the judgement in Jer. 7[33]; exposure of the dead was a terrible fate), but that of the buried dead in their graves. The graves are to be opened and the people restored.

The Old Testament only at a late date affirms the belief that there is to be a resurrection of the dead—so Dan. 12^2. But the picture of restoration from death is used here and in Isa. 26^{19} for national restoration. It is not surprising that the picture has caught the imagination of artists, and provided a theme to be loved by both Jewish and Christian writers (cf. p. 98).

37^{15-23} *A new people*

The theme of a united Israel is one which appears in many Old Testament contexts. Under David the nation was one. It claimed its descent from one ancestor. Must not this unity be one day re-established? In the time of Josiah, there appears to have been a substantial move in this direction, and probably also already earlier under Hezekiah when, with the fall of the northern kingdom, the political barriers to unity might seem to have been broken; the Chronicler (2 Chron. 29–32) makes much of this theme. The ultimate disaster to Judah, which brought her to the same state as her sister Israel (cf. Ezek. 23), offered a further opportunity for a rethinking of the nature of the people. So we find here the performance by the prophet of a symbolic action in which two sticks, one representing Judah and the other representing Israel, are joined together. We are not told precisely how this was to be done, and the passage is somewhat overloaded in its present form as a result of explanatory notes written into it, but the main point is clear enough. The people is shown asking for an interpretation, and the declaration is made that there will be a restoration of the whole community of Israel—'Israel' (that is, the whole people), made up of 'Israel in Judah' (so, v. 16*a*) and 'Israel in Ephraim' (so, v. 16*b*). The different senses in which 'Israel' is used, perhaps in part due to the annotations of later scribes, result in some confusion in the passage. It is to be a people united in their own land, united under one king, and restored to covenant relationship (note v. 23).

37^{24-28} *A new David*

The third section picks up an element from the second—should we perhaps see the grouping of these three sections as a

THE RESURRECTION OF THE NATION (Ezek. 37^{1-14}). At Dura-Europos on the Euphrates, already an important centre in the Greek period, the discovery of a third-century A.D. synagogue brought to light a wonderful series of paintings of biblical scenes. They indicate the way in which particular biblical incidents were understood in the life of the Jewish community. Hope for the future of the people is vividly portrayed here in the bringing to life of the dead bodies; this shows how Ezekiel's vision was found meaningful in a later situation.

deliberate exposition of the prophet's message?—and develops the theme of David *my servant* (v. 24). The term *servant* is often used to denote the relation between king and God. The restoration of covenant is expressed in the presence of God in the sanctuary, and the nations will recognize what God has done. In a few verses, the whole range of restoration themes is brought together. It is not altogether easy to reconcile this conception of a renewed Davidic monarchy with the portrayal of the 'prince' (cf. 44^3, 45^7, etc.) in the last chapters of the book. These chapters do not use the word 'king' for the ruler of the new age, and this is perhaps a deliberate avoidance of a term which to some of Israel's thinkers had come to have too many evil overtones. The Davidic ideal, which remained active in one form or another through the following centuries (cf. pp. 294 ff. on the Chronicler), has here given place to a different conception of the secular leader. The close links between chapters 40–48 and the priestly laws (especially in Lev. 17–26) may suggest that those responsible for these chapters have linked ideas from Ezekiel with ideas found in the ancient traditions (where the term 'prince' often appears for the leaders) and were attempting to evolve a better conception of secular rule, freed from the dangers of a kingship which had been so much involved in the failure of the nation in the past.

38–39 *The final battle*

It has already been suggested (p. 92) that the apparently twice described great battle against Gog, king of Magog (the names later came to be regarded as the names of two figures, Gog and Magog), presents a conception of a final onslaught of the nations, the evil powers, overthrown by God himself. As in much later apocalyptic writing there is much vivid and gruesome detail here, heightening the effect of victory. The purport of the section is to present the conviction of the ultimate victory of God, and it seems to hold out little sympathy for the nations other than Israel. But this impression is corrected by its final verses.

39^{21-29} *The nations as witnesses of God's purpose*

The nations are to see divine judgement, and Israel is to recognize God for what he is. The nations will understand what has happened to Israel, committed to *captivity for their iniquity* (v. 23); so they will discern the depth of the divine purpose. With restoration there will come a new situation in which Israel itself acknowledges God afresh in the fulfilment of his purpose of gathering and restoring them. But the keynote lies in the opening words: *I will set my glory among the nations* (v. 21); they will be witnesses of what God has done. The witness in the Old Testament is not one who stands apart from the event; he is himself involved and, like the hearer of a parable, is committed to what he acknowledges to be true. If the vision of the future is concentrated upon Israel, God's purpose for Israel nevertheless has meaning for the whole world. This is a theme which is to be further developed in the teaching of the Second Isaiah and of Zechariah.

40–48 *The new temple and land*

The detail of these chapters is immense, and may easily obscure the central stress. At the outset (40^{1-4}) the prophet describes a visionary experience; there is to be a new city, a new temple, a new land; and this is the work of God. To the new temple, pure and kept free of any possible defiling contact, 'the glory of the God of Israel' returns (43^{1-4}) and so the answer is given to the departure of that glory when the city and temple were handed over to destruction (see notes on 11^{22-25}). The laws are set out for the government of the priesthood, and the ordering of worship. The land is so ordered as to express more adequately the will and purpose of God, and this theme is developed in full detail in 47^{13}–48^{35}, culminating in the renaming of the city of Jerusalem as 'The LORD is there' (48^{35}. This renaming is based on a play on the sound of the name—*Yᵉrūshālaim* will become *Yahweh-shammāh*). The theme of renaming is found in other passages, notably in Isa. 1^{26}, 60^{14}, 61^{4}; Zech. 8^{3}.

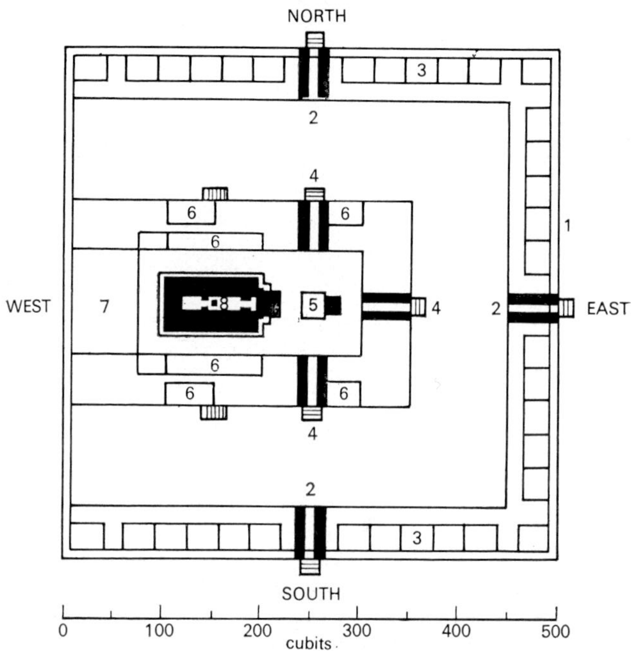

PLAN OF EZEKIEL'S TEMPLE. (All measurements for the temple are in the 'long cubit' (40^5) of about 21 inches.)

1. Outer wall, 500 cubits each side (40^5, 42^{16-20}), 'to make a separation between the holy and the common'.
2. Gates into outer court, with guardrooms to control entry ($40^{6, 20, 24}$).
3. Rooms in outer court (40^{17}).
4. Gates into inner court (40^{28}).
5. Altar of burnt offering, shaped like a ziggurat tower, with horns (43^{13-17}. Cf. p. 102).
6. Priests' buildings (40^{44}, 42^1).
7. West building (41^{12}); no purpose is indicated for this.
8. The temple proper (40^{48}–41), divided into porch, nave, and most holy place (41^4), with a table before the holy place ($41^{21\text{ f.}}$).

Many of the details in the description of the temple are obscure; in any case, this temple was never built, but the many points at which it corresponds with Solomon's temple show that the tradition of the older building continued, and was presumably followed in the rebuilding after the exile.

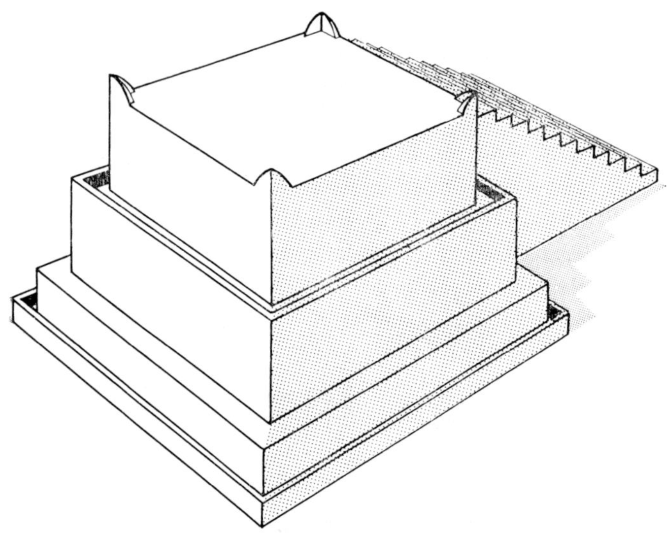

THE ALTAR FOR EZEKIEL'S TEMPLE (Ezek. 43^{10-17}). The construction of the altar as it is here described suggests that the model for it is ultimately to be found in the temple tower form known from the ziggurat of Babylon (cf. the illustration on p. 21). The first word translated 'altar hearth' in v. 15 actually means 'mountain of God'; the other occurrences are written differently and may be a proper name 'Ariel' (cf. Isa. 29^{1} where it is used of Jerusalem). Possibly there is a play upon words here. We might see the idea of the dwelling-place of God, and of the place in which God meets with men, combined with the place where sacrifice is offered. That the altar has horns brings it into line with earlier altars (cf. I Kgs. 2^{28}). It is measured in the long cubit of about 21 inches; thus each of the upper sections was about 7 feet high. It is not at all clear how this immense structure could have been used; like other of the projects for the future in these chapters, its significance lies rather in what it expresses than in practical considerations.

47^{1-12} *Life for the land*

The temple in the Old Testament is often pictured as the dwelling place of God, not in the narrow sense that he is restricted to it, but in the broader sense that he chooses to reveal himself there, and from it to control the life of the world. It is not indeed always clear whether it is the temple or the

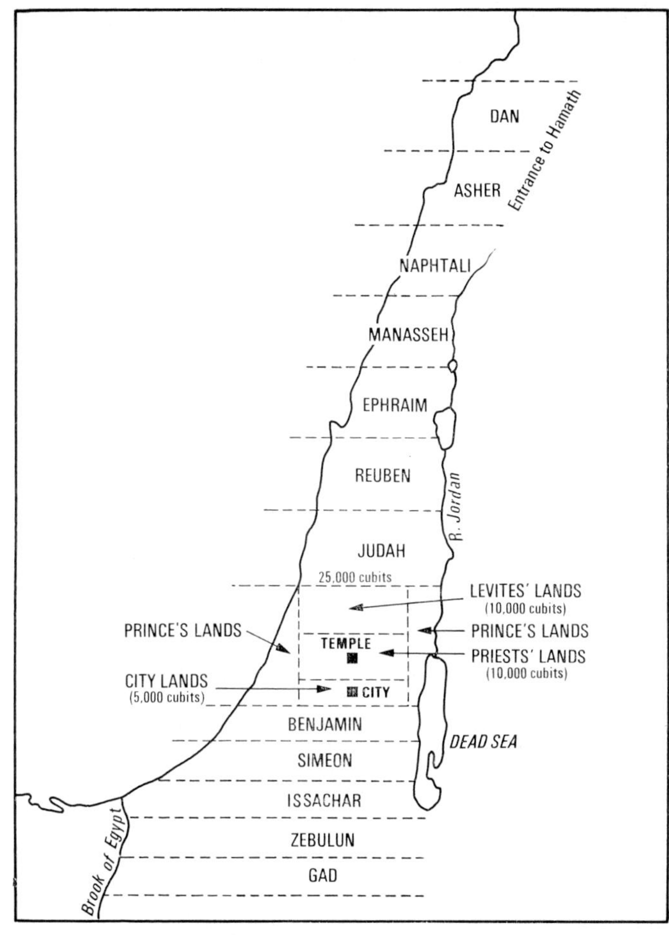

EZEKIEL'S NEW LAND. The new land is geographically reordered, all the tribes being brought to the west of Jordan (47^{15-20}), aliens who reside among the tribes being allotted inheritances in the tribes in which they live (40^{21-23}). The position of Jerusalem dictated that more tribes should be north of the central area than south of it ($48^{1-7, 23-29}$); the waters from the temple flow east into the Dead Sea (47^{1-12}). The dimensions of the central area are given in 48^{8-22}. The temple is kept free of direct contact with the city, being included in the priests' lands. Nearest to this central area are the tribes of Judah and Benjamin, the tribes of the kingdom of Judah (cf. 1 Kgs. 11^{32}, but made explicit in 2 Chron. 11^{1}), as the true and loyal Israel.

heavenly dwelling of God which is being described. Since God is the giver of life, it is appropriate that from his dwelling there should go forth waters which bring life. A mythological portrayal of this is to be found in Gen. 2^{8-14}, for the garden which God planted was clearly for his own use, to be tended by man; and from it the waters of the great rivers flow to bring life to the world. El, the supreme deity of the Canaanite pantheon, is also depicted as dwelling 'at the source of the rivers, amid the channels of the two oceans' (so in the Baal texts, and elsewhere in the Ras Shamra literature. Cited from G. R. Driver, *Canaanite Myths and Legends* (Edinburgh, 1956), p. 77). The idea of a river of God in the temple is also to be found in Ps. 46 and perhaps in Isa. 8^{6}. Here in Ezek. 47, the theme is developed. The river flows out from the temple to the east, miraculously becoming deeper as it flows (vv. 3–6). On either bank, the trees flourish, and the waters flow into the Dead Sea to bring freshness and life to it. Fish will thrive in it, and the fishermen will be active there. A practical detail intervenes in v. 11; the marshes will be left untouched so that there will be an adequate supply of salt, essential for food and worship. The trees which grow by the river will never *wither*, and *will bear fresh fruit every month. Their fruit will be for food*, *and their leaves for healing* (v. 12). With these themes, the links to paradise legends again become clear; for this is a miraculous new world, with life-giving trees and perpetual harvest. The prophet sees beyond the vicissitudes of time to an ideal age to come.

B. THE SECOND ISAIAH

It has long been recognized that there is a totally different atmosphere and historical background in the second part of the book of Isaiah, beginning at chapter 40. The situation of the prophet and people is that of the exilic age, during the period of Babylonian rule, with the anticipation of Cyrus' conquest of Babylon (44^{28}, 45^{1}). The problems of the book of Isaiah cannot, however, be solved simply by making this division, for it is not to be supposed that the two sections of the book came together accidentally; there is a deeper relationship between them. So we must recognize that the message of Isaiah of Jerusalem, incorporated in the first part of the book, has itself been reinterpreted and in some measure elaborated during the years that followed his activity. We have already noted that this may be seen in some of the opening chapters and again in chapters 13–14 and 21 (cf. pp. 33, 57 f.). A clear and precise example of such reinterpretation occurs in 23[13], which appears to mean that the judgement upon Tyre set out in the oracle of 23[1-12] is now to be seen as effected not by Assyria, the world-power of Isaiah's time, but by Babylon. We have also noted that the foreign nation oracles of 13–23 have been given a wider setting and hence a reinterpretation by what follows in 24–27 (p. 92). The words of the eighth-century prophet were not preserved as a dead record, but as a living message, meaningful for many generations.

It is with this in mind that we may best understand the inclusion, in the same prophetic collection, of material from a later age. In the present structure of the book, the main later section is ushered in by a series of stories about Isaiah in the time of Hezekiah (Isa. 36–39; an almost but not quite identical form appears in 2 Kgs. 18[13]–20[19]). This passage ends with a word of judgement in terms of captivity in Babylon, and this would seem to be a case where the message of the earlier prophet has been updated to meet the needs of the later situation. The judgement fittingly introduces the message of comfort of Isa. 40[1]. It is generally agreed that 40–55 belong together, though there may be some later material as well here; it is also clear that these chapters are more or less closely connected with 56–66 and also probably with 34 and 35, but the precise relationship is still very much under discussion. Are these chapters all from the same prophet, or are 34–35, 56–66 from a disciple or disciples of the Second Isaiah? Do they reflect one particular period and situation, or do they cover a wider range of time and place? In general, the relationship must clearly be recognized. Moreover, although there is no absolute certainty, it seems most probable that 40–55 at any rate derive from a Babylonian setting, almost certainly before the fall of Babylon to Cyrus the Persian, whereas 56–66 quite possibly reflect a somewhat later situation, perhaps the early years of Persian rule. But whatever the truth of the matter, we have in this whole collection a rich treasury of prophetic material, from which we can gain a considerable understanding of the thought and the problems of the later period of the exile and probably of the early years of Persian rule. Again, as in the case of Ezekiel, we may devote more attention to the picture which emerges than to the minute discussion of detail on which opinions still differ sharply. It will be convenient, since we are for the moment looking at the thought of the exilic age, if we take first what is generally agreed to be the section attributable to the Second Isaiah, namely chapters 40–55. Subsequently we shall be looking at some other passages in the context of the problems of restoration (cf. pp. 233 ff.).

An attentive reading of the whole of these chapters immediately impresses us with the poetic quality of a great deal of the material. And if we make a comparison with other Old Testament poetry, we may find particular resemblances to the style and language of psalms of the kind often described as 'hymns'—psalms such as 96–98. But this is not the only point of contact with other literary forms in the Second Isaiah. We find oracles of salvation in which there is pronouncement of words of blessing appropriate to occasions of lamentation for the past disasters of the community. If we picture some such occasion, when words of psalms of lamentation such as are found in the book of Lamentations have been spoken—and we know from Zech. 7–8 that various fasts were observed in this period, probably commemorations of the stages of disaster—then what more appropriate than that the prophet should speak a word of rebuke and comfort like that in 40[27–31]. The opening words indicate that a statement of distress has just been spoken:

> Why do you say, O Jacob,
>   and speak, O Israel,
> 'My way is hid from the LORD,
>   and my right is disregarded by my God?'

To this expression of doubt of the power of God, common to psalms of lament in which the worshipper vividly states his present uncertainties, the prophet's reply comes in affirmation:

> Have you not known? Have you not heard?
> The LORD is the everlasting God,
> The creator of the ends of the earth.

He continues in words of assurance both of the power of God and of the strength which he gives to those who look to him in hope and faith. Something of the same effect is produced when we find the prophet using legal terminology to rebut the doubts of those who see the exile as defeat, and to challenge the claims of other deities to control the destinies of the world. The answer, often here too in hymnic phrases, affirms the reality and the power of God.

The thought of the Second Isaiah centres around his conviction of the reality and power of God, his assured faith that the God who has revealed himself in creation and in his action in regard to Israel in the past remains the same, the one who will deliver Israel from exile, who answers her lack of faith by the reality of his action. This central conviction enables him to interpret the contemporary experience of his people, to comment on the future, to relate her experience to the nations, to proclaim the utter impotence and indeed unreality of other gods. The various themes are closely interwoven so that there is continual movement from one to another. In what follows, a selection of passages is examined with the intention of drawing out more clearly the elements of the teaching. The choice of these passages is designed to illustrate the various ideas, and if the remaining chapters are read with this in mind, the same emphasis will be discerned over and over again, with the use of other words and other pictures. This interwoven character of the material makes analysis difficult; it is not easy to be sure whether we should examine short units, and see in them examples of the prophet's spoken messages to his people, or whether we should also look at the broader structures. By some scholars it is believed that the Second Isaiah was a great literary artist, using older forms but presenting them in larger compositions. By others the emphasis on the immediacy of the spoken message suggests that the units are small and that the ordering is haphazard or due to some purely external principle such as that of the linkage of catchwords and phrases. Perhaps we may admit an element of truth in both approaches, keeping clearly in mind the likelihood that the message was delivered, like that of other prophets, in spoken form to specific occasions, but also recognizing that the prophet and his successors were conscious that the word once spoken, if truly the divine word, could not lose its validity. So the units of the message were built together, and larger, perhaps in some cases liturgical, structures were formed from them.

40^{1-11} *Comfort for Jerusalem*

The prophecy begins with a direct address, but we are not told to whom the command is given. It is plural in form, so that perhaps we should think of a command by the prophet to those who are lamenting, to change their statements of woe into triumphant words of comfort. The complaint of Lam. 2^{13} (see notes) that there is none to comfort here receives its answer, for it is God himself who changes the fortunes of Jerusalem. *Her warfare is ended* (v. 2), perhaps better as RSV margin 'time of service', the period of military service or of compulsory labour. The *iniquity* which led to disaster is forgiven, the 'equivalent' having been paid in compensation. (This is the sense rather than *double*.)

3–5. The initial words of vv. 1–2 are followed by a series of loosely connected sayings. The first of these introduces the words of an unidentified speaker who gives a further command; the processional, triumphal road across the desert back to Jerusalem is to be built (cf. $35^{8\text{ ff.}}$), a raised highway from which all obstructions are removed, so that God himself can march in glory to his city. His glory will be revealed (a thought similar to that of Ezekiel) so that all men may see it, for, as we shall see, what God now plans to do for Israel is part of a larger purpose which involves the nations. The march across the desert will be a new and more glorious Exodus (cf. chapters 51, 52).

6–8 introduce a new and contrasting theme, perhaps suggested by the reference to *all flesh* in v. 5; the appearance of a first person form in v. 6 may indicate that the prophet himself is here expressing the doubts and hesitations which his people feel. The transitory nature of human life, a feeling apt to the situation of gloom of the exiles, now perhaps forty years after the disaster, with no hope in sight, is expressed in words reminiscent of Ps. 90[5f.] which reflects upon the limitations of life. But the words are the occasion for a sharp contrasting of the permanence of the word of God. *The mouth of the LORD has spoken* (v. 5) is echoed in the *word of our God will stand for ever* (v. 8).

9–11. The interlude makes the positive command here even more striking. Again with a movement of thought and a change of person, Jerusalem is now summoned directly. Such changes are characteristic of Hebrew poetry, and here aptly the city to which the words of consolation are first addressed herself becomes the messenger, speaking now to the *cities of Judah* to welcome the appearance in glory of their God. (The RSV margin indicates an alternative interpretation which avoids the direct address to the city, but has the disadvantage of introducing a new singular subject. It is more natural to see Zion itself as the herald.) Verse 10 depicts God as himself the victorious ruler, and v. 11 as the shepherd of his people, a term commonly used for the ruler (cf. Ezek. 34). It has been suggested that the *reward* and *recompense* (v. 10) are to be understood on the analogy of the Jacob tradition, for Jacob received his wages in the form of flocks which he then led back to his own land; so we may picture God coming in triumph, bringing those whom he has delivered.

Other sections of the prophecies of the Second Isaiah reveal more precise historical allusions, particularly where there is reference, direct or indirect, to Cyrus, or to the coming downfall of Babylon. This passage does not look to a precise moment; it proclaims a fact of the prophet's faith. God is already victor, whether or not the outward signs can be seen. Jerusalem can already herself be consoled, and as a bringer of good news can proclaim the coming of God. The tone for the whole prophecy is set in this conviction.

41^{1-4} *God in control of history*

With greater precision, the nature of God's saving purpose is now declared, and it is done in terms of controversy, inviting the nations to acknowledge that he has decreed the rise to power of Cyrus, *one from the east whom victory meets at every step* (v.2). Summoned to testify are the *coastlands*—the word could mean 'islands'; it is a favourite with the Second Isaiah, and (cf. 41^{5}) most aptly suggests the remotest places—and *the peoples*. For *renew their strength* (v. 1) which is out of place, being a repetition from 40^{31}, read 'draw near and come', words which occur, probably redundantly, in 41^{5}. It is to the judgement scene that they are called, and they are invited to acknowledge what is evident, namely that God himself is supreme, having planned from long ago the events which now take place. This is a theme which recurs. The gods of the nations cannot foretell anything (cf. $41^{21\text{ ff.}}$); they are worthless. Only Yahweh is God. The final phrase of v. 4 *I am He* is a striking affirmation; it suggests 'I am God, I alone' but also seems to depend upon an attempt at interpreting the divine name. This name, usually nowadays written as Yahweh, though its actual pronunciation is not certainly known, is explained in Exod. 3^{14} as meaning 'I am' (this is appropriate in the mouth of God who speaks of himself in the first person, *'ehyeh*, where man may properly be thought to speak of God in the third person, *yahweh*). But in many Hebrew names, the name of God appears either at the beginning as *Yᵉhō* or *Yō* (so Jonathan, Jehoiakim) and at the end as *yāhū* (so *yᵉshaʿyāhū*—Isaiah). The prophet seems to be working from this form and interpreting the name as 'He' (Hebrew *hū*'). The comment is a common one in the Second Isaiah, so that evidently it held some importance in the prophet's thinking (cf. also Ps. 99 [3,5].

41[21–29] *Who but God can control events?*

The theme of God's control and of the inability of any other to say what is to come to pass or to exercise any control is here worked out in fuller detail (cf. 41[4]). The legal procedure appears again, and it appears that the gods of the nations are summoned to show their ability to comment on *former things* (v. 22), which here presumably refers to events which in the past they can demonstrate to have had under their control, or to foretell *what is to come hereafter* (v. 23). Their inability to do so proves their total worthlessness, and from this the moral is drawn that the man who gives them his allegiance (*chooses them*, v. 24) is totally abhorrent to God. The term *abomination* is common in Ezekiel and in the laws of the Priestly Work; it is a technical term for something which is utterly forbidden to the worshipper.

Here is a theme which is subsequently more fully elaborated, in derisive terms (44[9ff.]). The Second Isaiah makes bold claims for the God of his people; he claims that he is absolute sovereign, indeed that he alone is God. It is often said that this is the first time that there is in the Old Testament an outspoken monotheistic claim, and in one sense this is true; in earlier writings, we find over and over again the stress that for Israel there is only one God to whom allegiance can be given. Other nations have their gods, but that is nothing to Israel. Whether the term monotheism should be used for the earlier period is largely a matter of definition; it is probably better to recognize that no total repudiation of the existence of other gods appears, while at the same time, so far as Israel is concerned, the situation ought to be that no other god counts for anything. But before this, Israel's thought had gone far towards claiming not only the absoluteness of her allegiance to God but also the supremacy of his claims; he is often in the psalms described as 'supreme God above all gods' (so we might paraphrase Ps. 95^{3}, where Yahweh, God of Israel, is depicted as king in the heavenly court). We even find, in a remarkable psalm, 82, the claim that Israel's God exercises judgement over the other gods in such a way that they are condemned, for their failure to

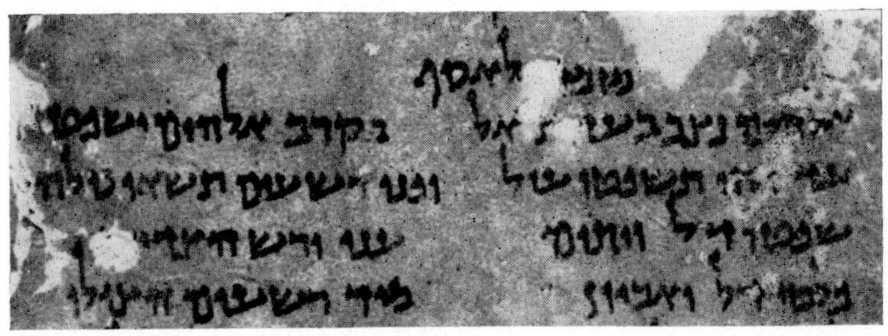

THE TEXT OF PSALM 82 (Title and vv. 1–4). This fragment of Hebrew text was found in the excavations of Masada by the Dead Sea, the rock fortress where the last refugees in the Jewish War of A.D. 66–73 were besieged and killed themselves rather than fall into Roman hands. It is thus part of a very early biblical manuscript, though older material has come from the Qumran area. It shows how the text was set out in clear poetic-lines (cf. the note on Hebrew poetry, pp. 43ff.).

maintain justice (presumably among the people allocated to them, cf. Deut. 32^{8}), to die like ordinary men. The Second Isaiah continues and develops this type of thinking about the position of God, supreme in the pantheon, supreme in the heavenly court, with the other gods becoming subordinate angelic beings, 'sons of god' (cf. Job 1–2), or even expelled for failure. The same theme is developed in the verses that follow (vv. 25–29), now combining the summoning of the new ruler who is to conquer the world, with the conviction that this is the expression of the anciently established will of God; and picking up once more the message of good news for Jerusalem and the ridiculing of the gods who can do nothing. Here it is *one from the north* and also one who *has come from the rising of the sun* (v. 25). This is not a contradiction, but a use of the traditional language (cf. the comments on Ezek. 1[4 ff.]) in which the north is especially the realm from which God, and hence his messenger, appears, alongside the more direct pointing to the east, to Persia. *He shall call on my name* is one way in which the dependence of Cyrus upon the will of God can be expressed. Elsewhere the different emphasis is laid that 'you do not know me' (45[5]). Sometimes it has been thought strange that a prophet should speak thus of a foreigner, one who did not acknowledge Israel's God, but worshipped his own national deity. (Cyrus was presumably an adherent of the then prevalent form of Persian religion; it is not possible to be sure whether or not the reforms of Zoroaster had yet had full effect, but this does not affect the issue). Politically, as we may judge from the Cyrus cylinder and from the similarly constructed declarations in Ezra 1 and 6 (cf. pp. 197 ff., 202 f., 208), the Persian ruler could describe his conquests as due to the will of the deity of the people with which he was at that moment concerned. But here the prophet is making a declaration of the real meaning of events; the one whom God calls to his purposes is controlled by him, whether or not he acknowledges it.

42[1–9] *God's purpose declared in his servant*

This passage, or the first part of it, is the first of those sections of the Second Isaiah which have often been singled out for separate treatment and entitled the 'Servant Songs'. A note on this approach and its problems is appended to this section (pp. 137 ff.). But since it has now come to be very generally recognized that these passages are part and parcel of the teaching of the Second Isaiah, it is best in the first instance to treat them as they occur and attempt to interpret them in relation to other aspects of the prophet's message. To detach them or to handle them as a group may well do violence to their significance. The interpretation offered in these pages is therefore concentrated on understanding their place in the message of the Second Isaiah. The additional note indicates some of the consequences which follow from other types of interpretation.

It is important at the outset to note that the term 'servant' which appears in the opening phrase here occurs in 41⁸; although no rigidity in the use of words is necessarily to be expected in the prophet's work, it is most natural to examine the ways in which such an obviously important expression is employed. In 41⁸, the term is applied directly as a description of Israel, the people gathered by God, chosen by him, strengthened and upheld. In reply to those who might suppose that God has cast off his people the affirmation is clear, and again here we may suggest the use of language which represents a reply to words of lamentation. Such language is used in Ps. 89[38]: 'thou hast cast off and rejected, thou art full of wrath against thy anointed'; and this provides a link to an important feature of the use of the word 'servant' in the Old Testament; it is used of many individuals, but it is particularly appropriate for the king (e.g. 2 Sam. 3[18] of David) and for notable religious leaders such as Moses (e.g. Num. 12[7 f.]). The description of *my servant* in 42[1–4] stresses the support which God gives to him, that he is *my chosen*, that God *delights* in him, that is, he is acceptable to God. The *spirit* of God is *upon him* (for this, cf. Isa. 11[2]), and *he will bring forth justice to the nations*. The precise meaning of vv. 2–3 is not clear, other than that it culminates in the reiterated stress upon the establishing of justice; there appears to be some contrast with a wrong method of proclaiming justice and also a stress upon the protection of the weak. Possibly there are allusions to customs unknown to us. The servant will fulfil his task so that eventually the whole earth knows justice. The nearest analogies to this are to be found in Isa. 11 in the prophecy of an ideal ruler and in such a psalm as Ps. 72; the servant appears in many ways to fulfil the royal role, exercising a beneficent rule and upholding right. Judah had no king at this time, for it is not likely that Jehoiachin, released from prison in 561, had long survived (cf. pp. 11, 145). But what kingship stood for is here expressed as a hope.

5–9 may not really be part of the same section, but there are many links. The creator God (v. 5) has called the one addressed, and again the language suggests a royal figure, taken *by the hand* (v. 6), performing acts of right and of protection. It would be possible to regard these verses as a continuation of the Cyrus theme of chapter 41, ending as they do in v. 9 with the reiteration of the idea that what God formerly ordained—the *former things*—is now fulfilled, and that his new purpose of deliverance is now set forth. Perhaps we might suppose that the prophet uses the same language because to him the political act of release from bondage to be brought about by the conquests of Cyrus, decreed by God, has a counterpart in the establishment of new life not only for Israel but for the nations, as expressed in his presentation of the servant. If these verses are read side by side with 41^{8-10} it is difficult not to see in them an interpretation of the purpose for which Israel is being called afresh. The passage is immediately followed in 42^{10-13} by a psalm of praise to the victorious God.

42^{19-25} *Israel, the servant of God*

(The RSV paragraphing includes v. 18 with these verses, but it seems better to regard the reference in them to the blind as referring to those who put their trust in gods that are no gods. The words *blind* and *deaf* then provide a link with the new section which is really concerned with a quite different matter.) Again here we have *my servant*, also described as *my messenger* (v. 19). Many commentators, observing that the description of the servant in the opening verses of the chapter indicates one who is apparently responsive to God's will, treat this passage as quite separate; v. 22 with its description of the *people robbed and plundered, a prey with none to rescue* and v. 24 with its questions about Jacob/Israel, seem to make it clear that we are dealing with the people here. But before we overstress the contrast, we may conveniently set together all three of the passages with which we have so far been concerned. In 41^{8-10}, the servant is Israel, a chosen people needing reassurance and faith—a fitting comment on the condition of the exiled and depressed community; in 42^{1-9} the servant is described in glowing terms, fulfilling God's will, establishing justice and giving relief; in 42^{19-25} the servant is blind and deaf, unresponsive to the will of God, though under his control, sinning against him and therefore brought to disaster. May not these things equally be said of the exiled community, which fails to understand but which is divinely chosen for greater purposes? We might not improperly compare the contrasting things which can be said, with equal propriety, of the Church—the disobedient and often faithless community which may at the same moment be described as the true body of believers, even as the body of Christ. If we are looking for an ordered development of ideas, each passage leading on neatly from the preceding one and the whole built into a completely coherent and logical system, then we shall look as vainly for it here in the Second Isaiah as we might look for a systematic theology in the letters of Paul. But if we are looking for sensitive interpretation of the position in which he and his people found themselves, with a recognition of the lack of faith, of the sense of distress, of the awareness of the past, of the consciousness of God's power, then all these are present.

43^{1-7} *The redeemed people*

Central to this passage are the words of v. 3: *I am the LORD your God, the Holy One of Israel, your Saviour*. The second phrase recalls the stress upon holiness which is characteristic of Isaiah of Jerusalem; the Second Isaiah stands in that tradition. The emphasis on his saving power is also a marked element in the theological tradition both of the Exodus (cf. notes on 51^{9-11}) and of the Jerusalem cultus (cf. Pss. 96–98). Other elements appear here. In v. 1 the stress rests upon the creative and redemptive activity of God, both directly linked with Israel. In v. 2 the protection promised by God to his people recalls the experience of the Exodus and wilderness periods, while adding even more vivid pictures to this, pictures suggestive of the disasters of destruction and exile (cf. 42^{25} with which this is appropriately linked verbally).

3–4 emphasize the prophet's sense of the value set upon his people by God; the special relationship, the special calling of the people of God, involves the paying of a high price to ensure their deliverance from slavery, the bondage of the exile. Probably we should not look for any precise allusion in the references to Egypt, Ethiopia, and Seba (to the south of Egypt); the names, perhaps intended to suggest wealthy lands, are to be set beside the more general terms of v. 4, where for *men* we may more appropriately read 'lands'. Verse 5 with its *Fear not* (so also v. 1) is also an Exodus echo (Exod. 14[13]; cf. Hag. 2[5]), and the promise follows of a complete gathering in of *every one who is called by my name* (v. 7), that is, all those who belong to God.

In this brief passage, rich in allusions, much of the wide range of the Second Isaiah's thought is drawn together. It demonstrates how in reading these oracles we need to be sensitive to the ideas which are suggested by the words and phrases, and to observe how themes which are touched on in one place are developed more fully elsewhere.

44[1–5] *The chosen people*

As an example of the elaboration of one theme, we may see here the further indications of what is meant by the 'people of God'. Again we have the emphasis on the creation and choice of Israel, as servant of God; even before birth, the people was chosen in the foreknowledge of God. For this idea, we may compare the sense of being foreordained which is expressed in Jeremiah's call (Jer. 1[5]). The name *Jeshurun* (v. 2) occurs only here and in Deut. 32[15], 33[5, 26], in two probably fairly early poems, the Song and Blessing of Moses. The name appears to be a title of honour, perhaps to be connected with the word *yāshār*, 'upright'; it suggests here in that case the idea of the obedient servant of God. Such a sense is appropriate in Deut. 32[15] which refers then to the chosen and blessed people becoming rebellious. But the meaning of the form is not completely clear. God will give to them the blessing of rain, essential to Palestine and often used as a symbol of divine favour (cf. Ps. $65^{9\text{ff.}}$); its withholding is a sign of judgement (cf. Hag. $1^{10\text{f.}}$). The gift of the *Spirit* (v. 3) is a sign of a new age (cf. Joel 2^{28} and Acts 2); children as a blessing is a common Old Testament theme. Verse 5 uses a whole series of expressions to suggest the intimacy of relationship between the restored people and God; each member of the community attests his belonging by invoking upon himself the name of God or of his people's ancestor.

44^{9-20} *The folly of idolatry*

The Second Isaiah over and over again proclaims the absoluteness of God, the sole creator and redeemer. He pictures God challenging the other gods in the law-court, inviting them to produce evidence of their ability to control or foresee events, and ending with the affirmation that they are nothing. A number of poetic sayings refer to the futility of finding any kind of comparison adequate for God: 'To whom then will you liken God, or what likeness compare with him?' (40^{18}), which is followed by a short saying on the making of idols, verses which might be taken as the text of the sermon which we have here. This passage appears to be a prose description, though attempts have been made to find poetic structure. We should probably recognize that the 'preacher' with his rhetorical style often uses rhythmic patterns of speech. The line between prose and poetry is not always completely clear, and the parallelism of lines characteristic of poetry comes readily into prose forms too. (Cf. the Additional Note on pp. 43 ff.) Read the passage noting its repetitiveness.

The passage makes a number of general statements about the folly of those who make idols, and of those who accept them, including the shaping of metal or of wood (40^{19} adds the practice of overlaying such a core with gold or silver). In particular, there is portrayed the ridiculous situation of a man who chooses a well-grown tree, of which he uses part for fuel, to warm himself and to cook his food, and then *the rest of it he makes into a god*. Worshipping this, he prays to it for help:

'*Deliver me, for thou art my god!*' (v. 17) The concluding verses (vv. 18–20) draw out the meaning again. The other gods—or the idols (the two are not sharply distinguished)—cannot see or hear (cf. Ps. 115^{4-7}); men who accept them are so foolish that they cannot see what they are doing, making a god out of the remains of the wood used for heating and cooking. They are totally deluded.

Two lines of thought run together here. On the one hand, there is the principle (cf. on $41^{21\text{ff.}}$) that Israel's relationship is to one God alone, with its concomitant statements in the decalogue (Exod. 20^{3-4}) that no representation is to be made of God. On the other hand, there is the affirmation of the complete non-existence and therefore impotence of all other gods. We may compare the statement in Jer. 2^{11-13} which notes the unheard-of evil that a nation should change its allegiance to its gods—even the other nations do not do this, though their gods are not real; but Israel has changed God 'the fountain of living waters' for water in a cistern and the cistern is in fact broken so that there is no water in it! The same mocking tone is present here as in the Jeremiah passage. Israel did in fact at various times have objects which represented the presence of God—the ark, the ephod, the bronze serpent; in the northern kingdom bull images were set up, probably intended as thrones of an invisible deity, and not as representations, though the bull was a clear symbol for fertility and strength. Such symbols were not substitutes for God, but tokens of his presence. Yet very easily the symbol came to be regarded as the reality. The representations of deities found among other ancient peoples were similarly symbols; but here too the danger of misunderstanding was very evidently present. And while the ancient world was perfectly familiar with the idea of deities whose dwelling was in heaven and who were by no means tied either to localities or to objects, the confusion between symbol and reality was easy. The prophet ridicules such a confusion; but his deeper concern is with the worship of alien deities which is involved.

We must assume that this sermon is addressed to members of

THE GOD NEBO. 'Bel bows down, Nebo stoops' (Isa. 46¹). This is the only passage in which this deity is actually named in the Old Testament; it has been suggested that the conception of the scribal figure in Ezek. 9² (cf. p. 84) might owe something to the idea of a deity who was patron of literature and science and regarded as the inventor of writing. His name appears as the first element in the name Nebuchadrezzar (*Nabu-kudur-uṣur*—'Nebo protect the son') and in other Babylonian names.

the Jewish community who are tempted by the rich religious life of their environment. Elsewhere, the gods of Babylon themselves are spoken of (46^{1-2}) as mere idols carried on beasts of burden, unable to save their worshippers. No direct allusion is made here to these gods, but we may detect both the danger that some will turn from their ancestral faith to give allegiance to the gods of the conquering power and the danger that the splendours of statuary and decoration in Babylonian shrines may tempt some to wish for such representations, and, in accepting the symbols, to be led away from the strictness of their allegiance.

To the prophet all idolatry is folly because God alone is real and powerful; those who turn aside will find the emptiness of the hopes which alien religion and idolatrous practice hold out.

44^{24}–45^{8} *Cyrus, the anointed of God*

This passage is probably made up of more than one unit; the sections have been put together because they deal with one theme. It is that of the divine choice of Cyrus the Persian to be the instrument of God's saving purpose, the restoration of his exiles to their own land, the rebuilding of Jerusalem. Again we may observe how the theme of salvation is set in the context of the proclaiming of God's ultimate creative power (v. 24), the one who shows up the utter uselessness and folly of all who endeavour to set themselves up as interpreters of events (v. 25), the one who by his work confirms *the word of his servant* (v. 26, probably better 'servants' in view of the plural *messengers* which follows, for the reference here is to the prophets who have proclaimed the coming salvation). Not only does God, through his prophets, pronounce the coming deliverance, the restoration of *Jerusalem* as an *inhabited* city, and the rebuilding of the ruined *cities of Judah*; he lays his choice upon the conqueror Cyrus. (The similarity of such a pronouncement to the Cyrus Cylinder is of interest as showing that Israel shared with other ancient communities such an interpretation of events as the outcome of divine action, and spoke as they did of God's choice and appointment of individuals. Cf. pp. 197 ff. The Old Testament writers are found to use the style of their time, as revealed in contemporary documents. In v. 28 Cyrus is described as *my shepherd*, the term for a ruler but one which emphasizes protection and care; in 45[1], which probably marks the beginning of a new pronouncement, he is described as *his anointed*, taken by the *right hand* as a royal nominee. With superb poetry, the prophet speaks of the conquests and achievements of Cyrus, affirming that though he does not know the God who is responsible for these, he will come to *know that it is I, the* LORD, *the God of Israel, who call you by your name* (v. 3). The passage moves again into affirmations of the sole power of God, the creator of *light* and *darkness*, of *weal* and *woe*, blessing and judgement (v. 7), and a final word of blessing upon the whole earth (v. 8).

Fundamental here is the conviction that it is God who creates and saves; Cyrus is only the instrument of his purpose, and in this he resembles the Assyrians chosen to be the agent of divine judgement (Isa. 10[5]), and 'Nebuchadrezzar, the king of Babylon, my servant' (Jer. 25[9]) sent to destroy Jerusalem. The Second Isaiah goes even further in his description, calling Cyrus the *anointed*, and the *shepherd*, terms appropriate to the kings of his own people. The former term, the Hebrew *māshīaḥ*, gives us the technical use of the word when transliterated as Messiah and translated into Greek as Christ. It is small wonder that both Jewish and Christian tradition, and some modern interpreters, have found this rather much to accept. Some have boldly reinterpreted, saying that it cannot refer to Cyrus, but must refer to Abraham, or to Jesus; some have excised the Cyrus references as due to later hands, though it is difficult to see how this solves any of the problems. It is best simply to recognize that the prophet is making a bold use of terms, expressing his conviction that God can choose the alien Cyrus for his purposes, deputing him as his agent in delivering his people. Did the Second Isaiah subsequently feel disappointment that Cyrus did not in fact acknowledge that it was God who had called him? The moves towards restoration, as we shall see, were less decisive than his words would seem to have led him to expect. But to look at the situation in this way is to put too literal a meaning on the words, and to overlook the significance of the overriding conviction of the prophet. Political and material restoration is certainly part of what he envisages, but if he continued active in the early years of Persian rule, and if some reflection of his thinking is to be found in the last chapters of the book and in influence on the other prophets of the time, then we may recognize his ability to see the working out of God's purpose even in less favourable political circumstances. Part of the legacy of the Second Isaiah was the subsequent rethinking of the nature of the people of God and its function.

47^{1-13} *The judgement on Babylon*

The dirge on Babylon, the virgin princess reduced to menial tasks, exposed to mockery and vengeance, condemned to disaster in her pride, serves as a reminder that the Second Isaiah is fully aware of the pressures of the conquering power. Babylon is pictured, like Assyria (cf. Isa. 37^{22-29}), as priding herself in her achievements. But her overthrow of Judah was possible only because God permitted it, passing judgement upon his people. Nothing, not even her prevalent magical and astrological practices (vv. 12–13), will be able to deliver Babylon from his will. In this, the Second Isaiah stands in line with Isaiah of Jerusalem, for he too passed judgement upon the instrument of God's purpose (Isa. $10^{5ff., 12ff.}$).

49^{1-7} *The servant's call and commission*

The resemblance between the opening of this passage and chapter 44 is clear, and the analogy suggested in the notes on that section with Jer. 1^{5} makes it all the more appropriate that we should see here a handling of the idea of the servant's call and commission similar to the way in which the call and commission of a prophet may be treated. In v. 3, the servant is plainly identified with Israel, and although the evidence of the poetic structure or of one manuscript which omits the name has led some scholars to argue that it should be omitted here, the similarity with chapter 44 and the use of the term servant for Israel elsewhere makes such an omission very dubious. The problem, however, becomes clear only in the subsequent verses, for in v. 5 we find the servant called and commissioned *to bring Jacob back to him, and that Israel might be gathered to him.* Subsequently, the mission is enlarged, and the servant's commission is to all nations. How can the servant be Israel if his mission is to Israel? The answer to this dilemma is not really to be found by talking in terms of an 'ideal Israel', a 'remnant within Israel'; and certainly not by avoiding the issue by taking out the word Israel in v. 3. The problem must be approached with a recognition of the character of Hebrew poetry. We might recall the curious apparent change of standpoint in chapter 40; a message of comfort is proclaimed for Jerusalem, Jerusalem is the messenger giving comfort. If we are to understand the present passage, it must be with a due regard for the movement of thought.

This raises a further point. It is noteworthy that nowhere in these chapters do we get a description of the prophet or of his call such as we find in other prophetic books (though not in all). If chapters 56–66 are linked, then we may note the opening of chapter 61 which has something very near to a call statement; but this also very markedly resembles other passages in which the 'servant' is mentioned, so much so that some scholars have classed 61^{1-4} as a 'servant song' (cf. pp. 238 f.). Is it possible to see in 49^{1-7} some expression of the prophet's own experience (the question must be asked of chapter 53, and also of 50^{4-9}). This is not to say, as some have felt bound to say, that the servant is to be identified with the prophet, though quite a good case can be made out for such a view. It is to suggest that just as we may see Ezekiel's sense of responsibility expressed in the watchman sayings (cf. pp. 70, 77 f., 93), so we may discern the Second Isaiah's understanding of his own position in terms of this idea of the servant which appears—with or without mention of the actual word—so many times in these chapters. It is as if, like other prophets (e.g. Hosea), he projects his own personal experience of God into his understanding of the position and destiny of his people; the intensity of this experience is perhaps to be sensed in the wording of vv. 1–2 and 4 here. So, in the poetic statement, he moves from his own experience to that of Israel; he moves from the rehabilitation of Israel to the *light to the nations* (v. 6) which Israel is called to be. It is, so v. 7 explains—and the theme is brought out more fully in chapter 53—as the nations see what has happened to Israel, see her low position, *deeply despised, abhorred by the nations, the servant of rulers*, and see also the faithfulness of God *who has chosen you*, that they will acknowledge God, *prostrate themselves* to him.

The full nature of this acknowledgement of God is not made plain; but it is clear that there is in the fortunes of Israel in exile not just a statement about her failure in the past. It was an act of judgement, dictated by the anger of God (cf. 47^{6}), at the sins of this people; but it was more than this. It was a revealing of the purposes and nature of God, so attested in the experience of Israel that the world might come to know and acknowledge him.

49^{14-21} *Zion restored*

Much of the concentration of the Second Isaiah is on the exilic situation, on what the experience of exile means, on the need for faith and the answering of doubt, and on the proclamation of the coming deliverance. But the future of the people is never far from his mind; Cyrus is appointed for the rebuilding and restoring of Jerusalem and Judah (44^{26-28}). The people are to return to their land, with God marching victoriously along the processional road across the desert ($52^{11f.}$). So it is fitting that we should consider this passage with its viewing of the situation from the other end. It follows verses which echo the opening words of consolation in chapter 40, the bringing in of the exiles from all lands—not just from Babylon but also from Egypt. Now we are shown Zion's distress. The words of a lament are put in her mouth: *The LORD has forsaken me, my Lord has forgotten me* (v. 14). The prophet's answer isin the form of a pronouncement by God, of his continuing care, deeper even than a mother's love (v. 15). The precise sense of v. 16 is not clear; does it perhaps mean that the plan of the city is thought of as carved on the hands of God so that it can never be forgotten? (cf. p. 80). In that sense the *walls* of the city *are continually before me*. Verse 18 elaborates what is to happen to the city, as it is restored; it must refer to the gathering in of the exiles (some scholars think that v. 12 belongs here; certainly its sense is applicable at this point), so that Zion is adorned as a bride, given honour in the sight of the nations. Here is the total reversal of her destiny which will evoke the wonder of the nations. The picture is continued in the following verses, where the city and land, at present still desolate, are shown that in time to come there will be too large a population (cf. Zech. 2[4]). So the complaint of the desolate one (v. 21) is answered in the miracle of restoration. Verses 22–26 continue the theme, both with the gathering in of exiles, and with the subordination of the nations. Fortunes are reversed, and 'all flesh shall know that I am the LORD your Saviour . . .' (v. 26).

50[1–3] *Has God repudiated his people?*

The lack of faith of the exiles is here rebuked. Are they saying that God has cast off his people utterly, as a man might divorce his wife? (For the metaphor, cf. Jer. 3[1].) Or is it to be supposed that he has used his people to pay off a bad debt (cf. Ps. 44[12])? There was a reality in their sense of being sold, in the thought of divorce, but this is not to suggest that God cannot save. The implication of v. 2 is that when God asks this question, no one dare make an accusation against him. His power is not in doubt. The drying up of the sea could be an Exodus reference, or it may, alongside the other pictures of v. 3, be an indication of the absoluteness of God's control over the natural order as a sign of his power (cf. Ps. 107[33 f.]).

50^4–11 *Suffering and strength in the experience of the servant*

We may note the contrasting ideas in the sections of this passage. It opens with a confession of experience on the part of the speaker—is this the prophet?—(vv. 4–6) in which he reveals his task, with a particular emphasis on the sustaining of the weak, and suggesting that day by day he learns from the tradition in which he stands so that he may transmit to others the faith he has received. Like Jeremiah, he stresses that he has been obedient, accepting the anguish which was inevitably his in the delivering of the word of God (cf. esp. Jer. 20^7–18). It is natural that v. 6 has been thought to refer to actual physical sufferings, suggesting the idea of persecution whether by his own compatriots or by aliens. But in view of the rich poetic language elsewhere in the Second Isaiah and in psalms of lamentation and of trust, it is more natural to see the words as descriptive of the inner distress which comes from the delivery of the divine word. Here, as in chapter 53, to labour points of resemblance to the New Testament passion narrative is to oversimplify the relationship between Old and New Testaments (cf. the general comments on pp. 139 ff.).

7–9 recall the confidence expressed by Jeremiah and Ezekiel in the power of God to sustain his prophets. In a vivid series of law-court pictures, the opponents of the prophet are summoned and assured that their guilt will be declared. It is only with v. 10 that there is mention of the servant. Both verses, 10 and 11, are very obscure. Verse 10 may suggest again the contrast between the anguish and the confidence which the obedient servant of God experiences, but the verse may also be rendered: 'Whoever . . . fears the LORD . . . obeys the voice . . . walks in darkness . . . has no light . . . let him trust . . . let him reply'—i.e. expressing the assurance that those who have experience like that of God's servant, who are obedient and yet experience anguish, may, like the servant, find reassurance and strength in God. Verse 11 presumably contrasts with the obedient the man who lights a fire which gets out of control—i.e. engages in evil which will eventually overtake him and bring judgement. The precise relationship of these verses with what precedes is not clear. Perhaps they provide a comment, offering further interpretation of the experience described in vv. 4–9, in which the prophet's own position appears to be revealed. Perhaps in reality they belong with what follows; for in the following chapter (cf., e.g., vv. 7–8), similar contrasts are drawn between the obedient and the wicked.

51^{1-3} *The basis of assurance*

In these verses, we find a positive use of the Abraham tradition which contrasts with the criticism of false confidence in Ezek. 33^{24} (cf. p. 94). To those who put their firm trust in God (v. 1), there is assurance to be found in the witness of the past, for the blessing which God gave to Abraham and Sarah is a token of the reality of his present purpose. Another point of resemblance with the Ezekiel tradition is to be found in the use of the Eden theme in v. 3, a theme further developed in $55^{12\text{ f.}}$ (cf. pp. 93, 137).

51^{9-11} *The creator and redeemer*

This is a central passage for understanding how the Second Isaiah thinks of the coming deliverance as both a new act of creation and as a new Exodus. A common theme in psalms of lamentation is the appeal to God to awake from sleep (so Ps. 44^{23}; cf. the use of the picture in Ps. 78^{65}). When his people are in distress, as in the exilic age, it looks as though God has deserted them, pays no heed to their condition, as if he sleeps while they call in vain. One way of meeting this complaint is to affirm the barrier which men set up by their sin between themselves and God; it is not God who sleeps but men who will not hear. Another way is to use the picture to suggest vividly how God comes to the rescue of his people, waking from sleep 'like a warrior sobering up from wine' (so Ps. 78^{65}, rather than RSV 'shouting'); it is a daring metaphor, but the Old Testament prophets and psalmists were not afraid of using such language. Here in v. 9, the picture is linked to another, drawn from ancient mythology; the *arm of the* LORD, symbolic of his power for victory, overthrew *Rahab*, pierced *the dragon*. Creation myths expressing the idea of a great conflict at the beginning of time are well known in the ancient world; the Babylonian form described Marduk, king of the gods, in conflict with Tiamat:

> . . . she opened fully wide her mouth.
> He shot therethrough an arrow, it pierced her stomach,
> Clave through her bowels, tore into her womb;
> Thereat he strangled her, made her life-breath ebb away,
> Cast her body to the ground, standing over it (in triumph).
> (*DOTT*, p. 10)

The name Tiamat is almost certainly equivalent to the word used in Gen. 1[2] for 'the deep' (*t^ehōm*), that is, the primeval waters, the waters of chaos. Elsewhere, for example in Ps. 104[5 ff.], God is portrayed as controlling these waters, after permitting them to cover the earth in the judgement of the Flood (cf. Gen. 6–8). In Gen. 1, the mythological element has been so re-interpreted that it can only be traced with difficulty; in Isa. 51, its terms are more plainly used. But v. 9 goes a stage further; it uses the name *Rahab* for the conquered opponent of God (cf. Ps. 89[10]); elsewhere (Isa. 30[7]) we find Egypt being described as 'Rahab who sits still' (cf. also Ps. 87[4]). This paves the way for v. 10 which moves on from God's conflict with the powers of chaos at creation to his leading of his people out of Egypt; and a further link is provided by the use of the phrase *the great deep* to describe the crossing of the sea. God's deliverance of his people from Egypt is thus closely compared with his victory in creation. This is an important point for understanding the significance of the Exodus narratives in which Egypt and her Pharaoh are identified with the enemies of God with whom he is engaged in a great conflict. Such a conviction about the past is the basis for hope in the present. The God who defeated the hostile powers, who rescued his people from Egypt, leading them through the sea, is the one who now will bring his people back to Zion, to a new age of rejoicing (v. 11).

This short passage contains a wealth of theological statement and allusion. A whole range of biblical thought is opened up, without which the interpretation of the Exodus and of the exilic experience cannot be adequately undertaken. Allusions to creation are frequent in the Second Isaiah; so too are phrases which suggest the experience of the Exodus. It is in the light of such a passage as this that we are to see how the prophet views past and present and future as essentially parts of one great experience of the saving power of God.

52[1–12] *The themes of deliverance*

This passage contains a number of elements, but since they cover a variety of themes all connected with the coming deliverance, it is appropriate that they stand together.

1–2 should perhaps be linked back with the preceding chapter, where v. 17 'Rouse yourself, O Jerusalem' is a variant on *Awake, awake* in v. 1 here. We have the theme of the deliverance of Jerusalem, pictured from two angles. It is the city which is henceforth to be pure (cf. Ezek. 40–48), preserved from the entry of those who are not fit to be in the holy place. It is worth observing that the Second Isaiah here shares with Ezekiel and with the Priestly Work (cf. pp. 100, 151 f.) the insistence on ritual purity. The captive city is also now to be released. Of course this can be said of Jerusalem the actual city, under Babylonian rule; but more appropriately it is here the exiles themselves who are described as being *captive Jerusalem*. (We may compare Zech. 2[7] which should be rendered 'Ho there, O Zion, escape, you who are dwelling in the realm of Babylon'.)

3–6 are set out as prose in RSV, but we may observe a poetic quality in the language. The experience of the past is here too evoked—with an allusion to both the Egyptian captivity and to Assyrian conquest. The distress of the people is noted (there is some confusion in the text of vv. 5 f.), and the fact that as a result of the exile *my name is despised* (cf. Ezek. 36[22]). *In that day*, so often used to denote the coming 'Day of Yahweh' in its judgement aspect, but now expressing the new age of salvation, the experience of deliverance, will enable the people to recognize that it is God himself who both speaks and acts.

7–10 provide an obvious link back to the opening of chapter 40, with the picture of the watchmen of Jerusalem proclaiming with rejoicing the return of God to Zion, the king ruling over his people (cf. Pss. 96–98). The ruins are restored, and the bringing of victory—he *has bared his holy arm* (v. 10)—enables the whole earth to see what he has done.

11–12 again echo the Exodus theme. A purified people, not to be defiled by any unclean contact, is exhorted to set out from exile. Those who *bear the vessels of the* LORD (v. 11) are to purify themselves for their contact with these holy objects. It is a sacred procession to Zion. Whereas in the first Exodus, the people had to go *in haste* and as fugitives from their oppressors (cf. Exod. 12), now the situation is reversed (v. 12); but the same God who went before them in the pillar of cloud and fire (cf. Exod. 13^{21}) will be with them to lead them and to protect the rear of the marching assembly (cf. Exod. 14^{21}).

52^{13}–53^{12} *Rejection and acceptance*

This passage, considered as the fourth of the 'servant songs' (cf. pp. 137 ff.), presents major difficulties of interpretation, quite apart from the question of how the figure of the servant is to be identified. There are many textual problems, and problems of language, and these vitally affect the overall understanding of the passage.

52^{13-15}. These verses open the passage with a proclamation of exaltation, and of the effect that this will have upon the nations. It might be more appropriate to put in brackets the words in v. 14: *His appearance was so marred, beyond human semblance, and his form beyond that of the sons of men* which interrupt the main statement of triumph. (Some scholars think, and not inappropriately, that these words belong in chapter 53, perhaps after v. 2; this would be more logical, but it is not impossible that the opening of the poem should contain a contrasting hint of the degradation from which the servant has been lifted). The main point is a reversal of fortune; from being in a downcast state—the theme which is subsequently fully elaborated—he is given a glory and honour which evoke stunned silence from the rulers of the nations. They are confronted with an unexpected reversal, and v. 15 implies that they *see* and *understand* what otherwise has been a mystery to them. Already there are hints that the passage is related to the kind of psalm which laments the distress of the psalmist, or speaks of the rejection of the king, and then points to vindication and honour. (In Ps. 89 the theme of rejection follows a long statement of divine favour; the implication of its concluding verses is that God will not allow the enemies of Israel to mock for ever.)

53[1–3]. The opening verse echoes the amazement expressed in what precedes. Now we pass over from the divine pronouncement of the change of fortune, picked up again at 53[10b–12], to the comments upon what has happened by those whom it most nearly concerns. Part of our difficulty in understanding the whole passage lies in uncertainty about the identification of the speakers; here the context suggests that it is the rulers of the nations who make the statement. The latter part of v. 1 could be interpreted: 'The arm of the LORD—that is, his victorious might—who could have realized that it was visible here?' The situation is so strange that it is hardly surprising that the reality of divine action has been overlooked. This is further made plain by the descriptions of vv. 2–3, in which several different metaphors are used to suggest how strange it should be that divine victory should be seen in so untoward a figure. Verse 2 suggests a thin, weedy plant, which *grew up* 'straight' (rather than *before him*), like one which grows *out of dry ground*. This could be compared with the corn which grows on rocky ground where there is not much soil (Mark 4[5]); it has little body and no strength. The picture shifts to suggest that there is no comparison to be made with those normally divinely chosen, who possess *beauty* such as that of Joseph (Gen. 39[6]) or David (1 Sam. 16[16]: RSV 'of good presence'); physical appearance, height (cf. Saul), grace, are divine gifts and signs of favour. Verse 3 develops this to point yet more clearly to the lack of divine blessing; one who is not shown the divine favour is to be regarded with despite by the righteous (cf. Ps. 15[4]); he withdraws himself from men (so, rather than *rejected by men*), for he is afflicted with distresses, 'humbled by' (perhaps rather than *acquainted with*) sickness. The words used may as appropriately suggest mental as physical distress; we might compare the expressions of anguish in psalms of lamentation (e.g. Ps. 22, 88) or in the book of Job (cf. pp. 319 ff.). 'We despised him' (rather than *he was despised*). The whole purport of these successive pictures is to suggest that here was no sign of divine favour; what then more appropriate than that those who saw this figure of distress should withdraw from him and treat him as surely he must deserve. If God withdraws his favour, it is natural that men should have nothing to do with such a person. This is a harsh view of life, but it is one which is, in general, taken by the Old Testament.

53[4–6]. These verses develop the contrasting reflection, which arises out of the recognition that the estimate of the servant was in error. *We esteemed him stricken*—this last is a word particularly used for the infliction of divine judgement—but actually this was not a correct view. While it appeared that he was under divine disfavour, in fact it was the speakers themselves who were in error (so, v. 6) and this leads to the conclusion that they had sinned but he suffered. The words of v. 4 echo those of v. 3 and bind the passages together. Such a response as is here made implies the revaluation which arises out of the divine act of victory. God has vindicated the servant—the affirmation appears at the beginning and end of the whole section—hence a reassessment of the meaning of his distresses must be undertaken. It is expressed in terms of a psalm of lamentation.

53^{7-10a}. Again there is a clear verbal link between the sections, for the *sheep* that *have gone astray* of v. 6 provides a link to the *lamb that is led to the slaughter*, the *sheep that before its shearers is dumb* of v. 7. The verses continue with the theme of vv. 2–3, elaborating more fully the experience of distress which is observed by the commentators of vv. 4–6. There is no mitigation to the distress. The wording of vv. 8–9 is very strong, so much so that it has often been supposed that we must have here the description of the actual death of an individual, even a violent death. But before we jump to such a conclusion, we must recall that this is poetry, not necessarily to be given a literal interpretation. It is as hazardous to derive 'historical' information from these verses as it is from many another passage in the prophets. The language is conventional, using a series of phrases and pictures for the depiction of the distress. Furthermore, we must recognize that 'death' in the Old Testament is a somewhat broader concept than mere physical dying. Death is the opposite of life; to give life means to restore health, to bring blessing, well-being, all that makes life full and evidently divinely favoured; to experience death is therefore the opposite, and what is said here can as well be regarded as the expression of distress as of death. A comparison may be made usefully with Ps. 88 in which the psalmist speaks of his sense of isolation and distress as making him 'like one forsaken among the dead, like the slain that live in the grave' (v. 5). The exact meaning of a number of the phrases in these verses is not clear. Instead of *for the transgression of my people* (v. 8) we should probably read 'for our transgression'. He has been treated as if he were wicked and so brought low; the parallel phrase in v. 9 should read as 'with doers of wickedness' rather than *with a rich man* which does not fit the context. Verses 9*b*–10*a* should be taken together; it was God's will that this innocent figure should bear displeasure. (Another interpretation would link 10*a* with what follows: 'But God took delight in his bruised one, strengthened (healed) the one who gave his life as a guilt-offering'.)

The interpretation of these verses very much depends upon

the way in which the figure of the servant is understood; but whether a decision is made for a more individual or a more corporate interpretation, it nevertheless remains more likely that they should be understood as indicating distress, separation from God, a sense of isolation, than regarded as literal descriptions of judgement and death.

53^{10b-12} (beginning *he shall see his offspring*, but note what is said above about v. 10*a*). We return to the divine declaration. The fact that this righteous servant accepted distress, that he gave himself and went through anguish, is answered by the will of God that in him the divine pleasure will be fulfilled. Verse 11 may be rendered 'because of the distress of his own person he shall drink his fill and be satisfied; by his humiliation (or submission) my servant shall declare many to be accounted right'. The precise definition of the words and division of the lines remains uncertain; many commentators have despaired of finding a satisfactory sense.

If we now look back over the whole passage, some general comments may be made. It is perhaps important first to raise a question about its unity. Having noted that there are a number of close linkages, verbal echoes, which join the sections together, we might well ask whether the arrangement is due to this rather than to any original unity. The changes of person, though possible within a single poem, might also point to the bringing together of separate units. If this is so, then we may need to be even more cautious about trying to find an exactly consistent line of interpretation. Even if the sections do belong together, we may again recall the way in which the prophet can move from one angle of vision to another, picturing the different objects of his concern in different ways. This is not a flat painting; it is a three-dimensional sculpture. With this in mind, we may recall the other passages in which the term 'servant' has been employed, and while not demanding complete unity of treatment in a poetic work, we may most naturally ask first whether the picture of an Israel suffering the distress of exile may not fit into our understanding of the passage. In asking this, we must be aware that this is then the Israel which is the obedient people of God, the servant viewed in terms of faithfulness; of this Israel it could be said that though the exile from one viewpoint was a just judgement upon past failure, it was nevertheless something more. We may recall that Ezekiel could think of a restoration of disobedient Israel because of the name of God which is to be glorified by the nations. The Second Isaiah thinks in terms of an Israel which undergoes suffering in exile not simply for her own sake but that God may be acknowledged by those who see and understand. The terminology of this section is not infrequently linked to sacrificial ideas (so in particular vv. 4 ff., 10); the idea of a substitute victim, through which in some unexplained way God removes sin and guilt, has contributed to the explanation of this understanding of exile. To this, having in mind the royal elements in earlier passages and the idea of the rejection and humiliation of the king found in Ps. 89, we may add the question whether in some way the prophet has seen in the long-drawn-out captivity of Jehoiachin, from 597 to 561, followed by his release and honour at the royal court, another element in his picture. And, recalling chapter 49, we must surely ask whether there may not be here too an interpretation of the prophet's own experience and of his people's experience in the light of it, which accounts for the very deeply personal atmosphere in which this section moves.

That this is only one possible line of interpretation will be made clear in the note on the 'servant songs' (pp. 137 ff.); but if we are to attempt an understanding of the mind of the prophet, then it is most reasonable to make an approach which brings out the interwoven character of his thought, rather than one which divides up his prophecies into sections which can only with difficulty be presented coherently.

55 *A climax of hope*

The last two chapters of the Second Isaiah are filled with hope, and the stress upon hope and reversal of fortune in 54 with reference to the whole community may not improperly be held to provide a further basis for the interpretation of 52^{13}–53^{12} just offered. With 55, yet further elements of hopeful teaching emerge. The new age, so we learn from vv. 1–2, is one of full life in which none is in want; blessing comes from God. A new covenant relationship is to be established, which the prophet here, and only here, links directly to God's sure bond with David. Does this too suggest that the Second Isaiah was not without perception of the meaning of Jehoiachin's release? The new action of God in saving will bring nations to the acknowledgement of who he is (vv. 4–5). But there is no easy entry into the new age, and a note of hesitation creeps in (vv. 6–9) similar to that which we find in the post-exilic prophets Haggai and Zechariah (cf. pp. 211 ff., 220 f.). The final assurances come in the promise that what God decrees he will do (vv. 10–11), and in the picture (vv. 12–13), again with Exodus echoes, of the rejoicing of a new entry into a promised land in which the harmony of nature will be restored as in the garden of Eden (cf. 51^{3} and for a similar picture cf. Hos. 2^{18}). The climax, like the opening, rests in the absolute assurance of the will of God, of his re-creative power, of his intention to save.

Additional Note on the Interpretation of the 'Servant Songs'

It would have substantially overburdened the discussion of the prophecies of the Second Isaiah if at every point each of the many different types of interpretation had been set out. This is particularly true in the case of the so-called 'servant songs'. The use of the term 'so-called' is, of course, question-begging, but it emphasizes the conviction which is increasingly being expressed in modern scholarship, that the division of the Second Isaiah by separating out certain passages and denoting them 'servant songs' does violence to the prophet's thought. Particularly is this the case since the four passages commonly extracted in this way—$42^{1-4\ (5-9)}$, $49^{1-6\ (7)}$; $50^{4-9\ (10-11)}$, 52^{13}–53^{12} (the parentheses indicate differences of opinion)—are not the only 'servant' passages in these chapters, and one of these, in 50, does not name the servant at all. To extract these and handle them separately, supposing them to be in some sort of order, is arbitrary. The language of these passages differs in no way materially from that of the remainder, with the possible exception of chapter 53; but here the recognition that the Second Isaiah uses the language of the psalms repeatedly and elsewhere uses the language of lamentation, makes us realize that there is no special reason to attribute this material to a different author.

If the passages are taken out of context, then their interpretation becomes quite open and may be very arbitrary. If they are kept within the Second Isaiah, there is still room for immense diversity of view. Echoing the question of the Ethiopian to Philip (Acts 8[27-39]), we may ask: 'About whom, pray, does the prophet say this, about himself or about someone else?' Is it about himself? If chapter 53 were taken literally, we should have to suppose, as some commentators have rather scornfully remarked, that the prophet composed his own obituary notice; but this is to degrade the poetry of that chapter to prose. It would be surprising if we were not able to discern some elements of direct and intense personal experience in these prophecies, and, as we have seen, some of these passages echo the conception of call and commission found in other prophetic books. Is it about some other? But if so, what particular individual could be meant? Many names have been suggested, and it has already been indicated that the experience of the captive king Jehoiachin could well have contributed something to the prophet's understanding. With his emphasis on a new Exodus, we might expect there to be features of the figure of Moses, of whom it is said that he expressed a willingness to be blotted out of the book of God (Exod. 32[32]); did such an idea of vicarious suffering contribute to the prophet's interpretation of contemporary experience? Of the variety of other individuals suggested at one time or another, one can only say that some are so remote as to be totally improbable, others, granted the sensitiveness of the prophet to the experience of his people, could have contributed something to his presentation.

Traditionally, Jewish interpretation has seen in the servant a representation of Israel, and it is to this kind of view that many scholars today have returned. The view has, however, been represented in a variety of ways. A simple equation—'the servant is Israel'—is not adequate to the richness of the prophet's thought. As we have seen, there are differing understandings of what Israel is within the prophecy, and differing viewpoints from which she is considered. Such an interpretation has been helped by the recognition that it is possible to see in the Old Testament many indications of a way of thinking somewhat strange to the modern world. The relationship between an individual and the group to which he belongs is subtle, and often the Old Testament uses language which makes it clear that the life of the individual is bound up in that of the group to which he belongs, and that the life of the group can be thought of in highly personal terms. Clear examples of this may be found in the patriarchal stories in the book of Genesis. The term 'corporate personality' is often used for this. The servant Israel is then pictured as an individual, personal terms are used in the description, and at times so highly personal is the language that it is small wonder that an individual has been sought. Some scholars have maintained that the personification becomes more intense as we work through the 'servant songs', but this is very doubtful; it is more appropriate at each point to recognize how the language of psalmody has been used to express convictions about the community in exile. There are overtones which must be heard if we are fully to apprehend the prophet's meaning.

What is the relationship between the idea of the servant and the idea of the Messiah? This further question is provoked partly because of New Testament use of 'servant' language; the Christian interpretation of these passages, and others like Ps. 22, has given them new overtones of meaning. This is part of the development of the tradition and must be taken seriously. But the question of 'servant' and 'Messiah' may also be raised apart from Christian interpretation. In so far as kingship ideas appear, it may be recognized that these passages

—and other material in the Second Isaiah—show an aspect of the development of Old Testament thought which is understandable in the exilic age. Kingship had come to an end; hopes raised by Jehoiachin's release may not have lasted long. Was kingship wholly negative, an institution to be condemned? Some Old Testament narratives strongly suggest this. But psalmody and prophetic oracles in particular show something of the understanding of the king which existed; the king was divinely appointed, he was to be the vehicle of God's blessing. Such an institution could not just fade out. So we get, in various forms, the development of 'royal' into 'messianic' thought; some aspects of this appear in Ezekiel and in the Second Isaiah, and we shall see further aspects during our study of the Persian period. Without saying that the servant is in any sense the Messiah, we may recognize that the understanding of the function of Israel in these terms owed something to the interpretation of kingship and so marks a move on in the presentation of the relationship between people and Messiah.

The relation between the thought of the Second Isaiah and Christian interpretation is more complex. Some would say that the prophet, directing his message to his own age, nevertheless spoke more than he knew, pointed to something which could not be fulfilled in his own time and which is fulfilled in the New Testament. Crudely put, this is not very satisfactory; it suggests that we ought to be looking for hidden meanings in Old Testament passages in a way which is unrealistic. Whenever an artificial correspondence is sought between the Old Testament and the New there is an impoverishment of understanding of the Old. But if we put the matter in a different way, its meaning can be seen. The prophet is proclaiming the word of God as he sees it relevant to his own situation; his revealing of that word is conditioned by himself and the limitations of his own time, but it does nevertheless disclose something of the eternal reality and purpose of God. To subsequent generations, what he said remained meaningful and was reinterpreted. Such reinterpretations might easily be misinterpretations, failing to see the real value of what was said; but they might well be right insights into the nature and purpose of God, taking further what the prophet discloses. The interpretation of New Testament material is not the purpose of this volume and it raises many problems of its own; but in the disclosure of God which Christians claim is made absolutely in Jesus, there must be correspondence with every right perception of his nature and purpose in the tradition in which he stood. He himself acknowledged that tradition, and could not but express himself in its terms. But it was a tradition which had not stood still. So it was not, in the New Testament, a matter of taking up this or that out of the past; it was rather that the whole Old Testament tradition, with its right insights and its deficiencies, went to make up that out of which a new statement could be composed. The mind of a great prophet could not fail to contribute deeply to that new statement.

(The inevitably abbreviated survey offered here needs to be carefully supplemented by some of the additional reading suggested. Since this study presents a particular viewpoint, in an attempt to give coherence to the understanding of the prophet, it is important that other ways of interpreting the material should be examined more fully than they can be discussed here. Cf. also the short discussion in Vol. 1 in this series, pp. 150 ff.)

C. THE DEUTERONOMIC HISTORY

The analysis of the books of the Old Testament is a complex and much debated matter and in recent years one of the main areas of discussion has been the nature and construction of the books which form the first two sections of the Hebrew Bible—the Law (Torah, Pentateuch, the Five Books of Moses) and the Former Prophets, the books from Joshua to 2 Kings. (This title differentiates them from the Latter Prophets, Isaiah, Jeremiah, Ezekiel, and the Twelve Minor Prophets, and does something to characterize their theological rather than historical aim.) Older criticism tended to divide these two sections fairly clearly, while seeing within the books of the Former Prophets a continuation of the main sources found in the Pentateuch. More recent criticism does not necessarily deny that there is a close relationship between the underlying sources, even maintaining in some cases the continuity of strands into the subsequent books—thus the J and E sources of the Pentateuch are seen to underlie parts of Deuteronomy and to continue into Joshua and Judges at least. But greater emphasis has come to be given to the larger structures, and here it is observed that there is a marked difference between Deuteronomy and what precedes, and a marked resemblance between Deuteronomy and what follows. So an alternative view has commended itself to many scholars. On the one hand, we have the first four books—sometimes called the Tetrateuch, but also the Priestly Work from its final shaping; it is recognized that related materials may be found in the books that follow. On the other hand, we have what is generally known as the Deuteronomic History, a survey of the whole period from the Exodus to the exile, beginning with a work of law, Deuteronomy, and then covering the period in a series of now separate books, themselves based upon a great wealth of earlier traditions and sources. (For the discussion of the literary questions, cf. also Vol. 1, pp. 3 ff., and Vol. 3, pp. 60 ff., for the Deuteronomic History.)

These two major works, as well as the third, that of the Chronicler, fall to be discussed in this volume because their final form was reached only after 587 B.C. Since the Deuteronomic History has been very fully discussed in the preceding volume, and extracts from both Deuteronomy and 1 and 2 Kings have been annotated there, only a little needs to be said here because of the importance of the light that this work sheds upon the kind of thinking which went on during the exilic period. The very fact that during the years which followed the disaster, the already existing writings and traditions concerning the earlier period could be worked over afresh and read in the light of the most recent events, argues for the existence of a very lively group of thinkers (cf. p. 22). The latest event mentioned is the release of Jehoiachin in 561 B.C. (2 Kgs. 25^{27-30}); the final stages must be later than this. Much of the rethinking could, however, already have taken place; the absence of any account of what took place between the assassination of Gedaliah (2 Kgs. 25^{22-26}) and the release of Jehoiachin makes the latter passage look rather like a late appendix, though we must remember that the authors of this great work were clearly not concerned with complete coverage of the history but rather with an interpretation of its meaning. The absence of any hint that Babylon has fallen to the Persians strongly suggests that the work must have been completed before 540 B.C.

Were the authors in Palestine or in Babylonia? There is no means of knowing for certain. The account of the fall of Jerusalem shows little real interest in the fate of the exiles, and perhaps a little more interest in what went on in Palestine; but since it describes those left in the land as 'the poorest of the land', this does not suggest a very high opinion of their standing. 1 Kgs. 8 contains a long prayer attributed to Solomon at the dedication of the temple; parts of it reflect a much later situation, probably that of the exile (especially vv. 46–53). Prayer is several times described as being 'toward this place' (so, v. 35) or 'toward their land' (so, v. 48); this suggests the viewpoint of the exile. On the other hand, the great concentration upon the temple as a place for prayer here has suggested that the author of the prayer is trying to show what significance the temple still had during the exile, and might rather suggest someone on the spot. The arguments are inconclusive. What is important is the testimony which the work provides for the existence of a group of thinkers, standing in the tradition of thought represented by the book of Deuteronomy, closely allied in their thinking with Jeremiah and his successors (much in the book of Jeremiah is very similar) and also having much in common with Ezekiel, the Holiness Code, and the Second Isaiah. Israel during the exile may have been in a state of depression, but it was not without much liveliness of mind.

The basis for the judgement of the past and for the interpretation of the contemporary situation is twofold. On the one hand, there is the law, given by Moses, set out and expounded in Deuteronomy, which provides the norm for the people's life, the standard of obedience by which it is judged. Failure to obey this law has resulted in the downfall of the state in a judgement from which there could be no escape even though Josiah carried through major reforms; but the real intention of the law was to provide the opportunity for a long and blessed life in the land which was God's gift to his people. (So repeatedly in Deuteronomy, but note especially Deut. 30^{15-20}, cf. pp. 146 f.) On the other hand, God in his wisdom had given his people the Davidic kingship, and with that royal line a covenant had been established (cf. esp. 2 Sam. 7). The king had responsibility for upholding the law (cf. Deut. 17^{14-20}) and the judgement upon the kingdoms was expressed as a judgement upon the failure of the kings to conform to that right standard which the law laid down.

The Deuteronomic theology expressed in this great work did not come into being all at once, and it is clear that behind Deuteronomy there lies a great legal tradition, linked with earlier theological movements both in Jerusalem and in the old northern kingdom. Behind the narratives of the books from Joshua to 2 Kings, there are not simply isolated elements now put together for the first time, but larger presentations. If the J and E traditions traced the working of God's purpose with his people down to the beginnings of the monarchy or even beyond, there was already precedent for engaging in such a survey and continuing it. The story of the kingdom of David and the succession to it (mainly 2 Sam. 9–20; 1 Kgs. 1–2) provides a unified reflection on the meaning of that particularly significant moment of Israel's experience. The stories of Elijah and Elisha are already woven into a larger unity, presenting various aspects of the life and thought of the northern kingdom of Israel in a crucial period. The Deuteronomic theologians built upon all this, but saw its meaning in a new light because now the judgements of the prophets had reached a climax; their gloomiest forebodings had been justified. Israel had to learn afresh in the exile what her place in the purpose of God was to be.

What did this mean for the future? Here the authors are very cautious. Much of the material of the book of Deuteronomy, whatever its origin, appears to be saying to the readers: This is what God's people is intended to be; this is how obedience is to work out in practice. The picture of Israel poised at the entry to the promised land must have taken on a new meaning when in a sense the land had been lost; whether the authors modified what they had before them, or were content to let it speak to the new situation—and around this whole question there is much contemporary discussion—the people in the exilic age could hardly help seeing themselves as back where their ancestors had been. What would be the outcome, if a new opportunity were to be given them? For the modern reader to appreciate this, it is necessary to read the whole work, but particularly Deuteronomy, putting oneself in the exilic situation and seeing what the words could mean then.

There is no statement of what will happen, only the implication which cannot be missed that the God who brought his people out of Egypt and into the promised land, who gave them the law and the dynasty of David, who time and again delivered them from disaster and when they were disobedient relaxed the severity of judgement right up to the final moment (cf. 2 Kgs. 14^{27}, $17^{19\,f.}$, $22^{16\,ff.}$), could not just repudiate everything that he was. He is the God who has caused his name to dwell in Jerusalem; and here 'name' carries the same weight that it does in Ezekiel and in the Second Isaiah. It is the very expression of the person and presence of God, of his nature; God is true to his name, and in this rests the only source of hope.

So there is no blueprint for the future, only an outlook which rests in Israel's acceptance of God and what he has done. The last words of the book are surely hopeful; Jehoiachin the captive king has been released from prison. It is immaterial whether he lived long after that release or not; the meaning of the event must be plain. Even after years of captivity, the Davidic king is a symbol of the enduring love and goodness of God.

(Volume 3 in this series provides detailed discussion of a number of passages from Deuteronomy (pp. 213–30); attention here is therefore limited to some brief comments on two passages only. So far as the remainder of the work is concerned, two passages of particular importance are also covered in the previous volume—2 Kgs. 17 (pp. 105 ff.) and 2 Kgs. 25^{27-30} (p. 132); it is sufficient therefore to draw attention to some other passages which deserve special note because of what they reveal about the interpretation of the history.)

Deut. 28 *A sermon on obedience and disobedience*

The opening verses of the chapter (vv. 1–14) set out the positive results of obedience; the remainder (vv. 15–68) concentrates on disobedience. This imbalance is an indication of the soberness of the appraisal of Israel's history here offered. In fact, within the latter section, it is possible to see a correspondence between the opening part (vv. 15–35) and the passage dealing with obedience. The blessings of the opening find their counterpart in words of curse and judgement. From v. 36 on, there is a concentration upon exile as judgement which, though not impossible before 587—for the northern kingdom had suffered such a fate already and the policy of Assyria and her successor Babylon was well-enough understood—most probably reflects precisely upon the experience of siege and exile as Judah came to know it. The gruesome descriptions of siege in vv. 52–57 suggest the horrors which Jerusalem itself did undergo. Similarly much of the detail of vv. 36–51 and of vv. 58–68 makes its best sense seen against the background of the exilic experience itself. We may perhaps best read this chapter as a sermon, an expansion of earlier sermons on the same topic but now given sharp definition by the situation of the exile.

Deut. 30^{15-20} *The way of life and the way of death*

The whole of this chapter again becomes most significant when seen against the exilic setting. Its last verses reiterate the theme of blessing and cursing, obedience and disobedience. But above all, setting the choice before the people of *life and good, death and evil* (v. 15), and indicating the consequences of both, the final appeal is a moving and heartfelt cry for obedience: *therefore choose life, that you and your descendants may live* (v. 19). This is what God wills for his people.

The passage is also of interest in setting out the idea of 'two ways' (cf. Jer. 21[8]), to be found also in Ps. 1, a theme which was developed in the Wisdom literature (often in the opening chapters of Proverbs), where it may have originated, and to be taken further in the writings of the Qumran community which speak of the 'ways of the sons of light' and the 'ways of the sons of darkness', in the New Testament (cf. Matt. 7[13 f.]) and early Christian writings (e.g. the Didache), and in Judaism.

1 Sam. 12[6–18] *A sermon interpreting history*

This is one of the punctuating statements which mark the history; into the mouth of a great figure of the past is put a sermon surveying the historic experience of the people, reminding them of the Exodus deliverance, and of the series of changes of fortune which are described in the Judges narratives, and drawing from this the moral for the contemporary situation. Though there is little or nothing here which demands an exilic date for the composition, the words of judgement take on a new meaning in that setting.

1 Kgs. 8[15–53] *Solomon's Prayer*

The detailed discussion of this long composition does not belong here but in the consideration of Solomon's reign (see Volume 2 in this series). Much of its content is clearly composed with direct reference to the position in which it stands, though it is likely to be largely of later origin. The brief poetic fragment in vv. 12–13 preserves an older prayer tradition. Some parts of the prayer must in any case reflect the situation before the fall of the kingdom, since v. 25 promises that *There shall never fail you a man before me to sit upon the throne of Israel. . . .*

But the promise is conditional upon obedience, and the words would have an added poignancy after the fall of the royal line, and would raise new thoughts when Jehoiachin was released from prison. Much of the prayer is concerned with particular occasions of worship, and it expresses many of the characteristic features of Deuteronomic theology. It has already been observed that it speaks more than once of prayer *toward this place*, suggesting remoteness from the temple (cf. p. 143). Verses 46 ff. develop in fuller detail the theme of exile, but include in this the important series of statements in vv. 47–48: if the people *lay it to heart in the land to which they have been carried captive*, if they make an act of penitence and their repentance is sincere, then (vv. 49 f.) the appeal may be made to God to *forgive* and *grant them compassion in the sight of those who carried them captive, that they may have compassion* (a similar thought is suggested in Jer. 29[7]). The motive of the appeal is also set out: *they are thy people, and thy heritage, which thou didst bring out of Egypt* (v. 51). God's action for his people in time past is the basis upon which hope of his delivering them again may be based.

D. THE PRIESTLY WORK

Again in considering this part of the Old Testament, covering the first four books (the Tetrateuch) and perhaps originally containing also some other material now found elsewhere, our concern is not with the earlier origins of the material, nor with the light which it sheds on the earliest periods of Israelite tradition, but with its final form. It includes a great mass of early tradition, much of it already incorporated in large-scale works (those known as J and E) which no longer have any independent existence. A great deal of legal material is included, some evidently very early, other representing the gradual development of Hebrew law. It is probable that traditions included here came from various centres of religious life—some from Jerusalem, some probably from the central and northern areas, some perhaps from other important sanctuaries of the south, such as Hebron. It includes a section of laws and expositions in Lev. 17–26 which has for many years now been regarded as a separate collection, and named the 'Holiness Code' because of its stress upon the holiness of God and the corresponding response of man. Since this culminates in an exposition of the meaning of the exile in Lev. 26, and is in its language and style very closely akin to Ezekiel, it is reasonable to recognize here that older laws have been given a new interpretation just at this vital moment of Israel's history. The fact that this section is incorporated in the Priestly Work means that whatever may be said of the date of individual sections, the final shaping of the whole cannot be earlier than the exile; it may be later, but in so far as it is to be understood as an attempt at setting out a programme for a new community, it is appropriate to associate it with that moment when, as we have already seen, there was much concern with what kind of people, what kind of obedience, what kind of political and religious order, were proper, if there was not to be further disaster.

The reason for calling this the Priestly Work is that its final presentation depends upon that strand of the traditions which has for long been known as P—the Priestly strand. This is characterized by its interest in priestly matters—laws governing the priesthood, the cult, questions of clean and unclean; but it is much more than this, for it offers a presentation and interpretation of the earliest history of Israel, from creation to the entry into the promised land. It is therefore intelligible that it should have come to incorporate earlier presentations of the same period of history, presentations which appear to have acquired an authoritative place in the people's life and thought, and could not therefore be discarded even if in some respects men's understanding had changed. It is very characteristic of the Old Testament method of handling earlier traditions that it sets them in a new context, and thus gives them a new meaning. In this Priestly Work, the earlier traditions are given the context of its own survey, its own chronological system, its own view of the working of the divine purpose.

What this is may be seen by taking up one or two points by

way of example. The work begins with a creation narrative in Gen. 1¹–2⁴ᵃ. Since the opening chapter of a work may well help us to understand its nature and purpose, this passage will be looked at in somewhat more detail later. It has, like much of the Priestly Work, an orderliness, a formality of language and style, which make it quite different from what follows. In Gen. 2⁴ᵇ–3, there is another description of creation, so contrasting in its style and its interpretation that it is quite clear that the two come from different hands. But once the second has been put in the context of what precedes it, it takes on a new meaning. The story of man placed as guardian in the garden of Eden and of his failure in his trust is subordinated to the divine ordering of the world in its precise stages and to the climax of his purpose in resting on the seventh day. To this point we shall return in commenting on Gen. 1 (see pp. 154 ff.).

The structure of the Priestly Work is determined by definite stages, points of development in God's covenanted relationship with men. The creation marks the first moment, the Flood and covenant with Noah the second, the covenant with Abraham the third. The Priestly Work does not offer a new presentation of the Exodus covenant, though it has new understanding to offer of the revealing of the name of God in Exod. 6. But it provides a special emphasis on the setting of the Sinai covenant by the accumulation here of the enormous mass of legislation which runs from Exod. 25 to Num. 10, including all the directions for the making of the tabernacle in Exodus, all the legislation in Leviticus, and the ordering of the community in the opening chapters of Numbers. Only then does narrative resume. The result is that very great emphasis is given to the law, and to its relationship to God's ratifying at Sinai of his covenant with Abraham.

The whole work is carefully ordered chronologically. In this respect the Priestly Work resembles the Deuteronomic History, which also incorporates chronological schemes, particularly in the books of Judges and Kings. The chronology is carried carefully through so that the climax of the Sinai events is seen to be part of a history which began at creation.

Though it is quite proper to find mythological elements in the first chapter of Genesis (as we have seen in commenting on Isa. 51$^{9-11}$), it is the more remarkable to observe that the Priestly writer dates the events there in relation to what happens subsequently. The creation is tied in with history. This may be regarded as another aspect of that thought which we have seen in the Second Isaiah; God's creative and his redemptive work are all of one piece (cf. pp. 128 ff.).

What does this great work set out to do? To some extent we may judge this by seeing what it covers. It begins at creation, linking this, as we have just said, with history; it ends, so far as we can tell, for there are uncertainties here, with the people, ordered, encamped around the tent of meeting in which God reveals his presence, ready for the entry to the land. If, as many scholars believe, there is material belonging to the Priestly Work in Josh. 13–19, then the allocation of the land is part of the plan, but since there is no clear trace of a conquest narrative, it is perhaps most natural to suppose that this allocation was presented in anticipation. The scheme resembles most closely that of Ezekiel—a new land, divided among the tribes, a new temple to which here the tent of meeting corresponds, an orderly and holy people, ready for a more obedient life.

A large part of the legal material—and this too corresponds with the emphasis in Ezek. 40–48—is concerned with the problem of purity, that is, of acceptability to God. The people had shown themselves unacceptable by their disobedience; they were not fit to worship God (cf. Isa. 1$^{12-17}$). Although the Priestly Work gives no account of the period of history leading up to the disaster of the exile, it makes the same point by projecting this disobedience into the ancient traditions, particularly of the wilderness period. The people is pictured as being, as in Deuteronomy, on the threshold of the promised land, so that those in exile can see themselves in the same position as their ancestors. Hope for the future lies clearly in the willingness of God to give them again the land which was promised. But will they be an obedient people? The Priestly

Work, and the Holiness Code which it incorporates, take up older laws concerned with purity, with the ordering of worship, with regulations for clean and unclean, and set out a fresh pattern of life. The hope for an obedient people is seen to depend not on a single moment of divine action and human response but on a continuous provision by God for the mechanism by which the relationship, broken by failure, can be restored. The meticulous detail of the laws has its dangers, as we may see when we consider the place of law in post-exilic life (cf. pp. 311 ff.) but its basic point here is to show that there is a way of reconciliation divinely commanded. Central to this is the great ceremonial of the annual day of atonement, described in Lev. 16. Not only is there daily and other regular provision for purification at every level; once a year the whole community is to be cleansed.

The Priestly Work, like the Deuteronomic History, expresses its hopes for the future obliquely. It does so by setting out in a new form older material concerning the early traditions of Israel. But to those to whom this was directed in the exilic age, these ancient traditions took on a new meaning and aroused a new hope.

The Holiness Code (Lev. 17–26)

The legal sections which make up the largest part of this collection of material concentrate on purity and acceptability in every aspect of the community's life. Purity in sacrifice (17), right ordering of relationships within the community (18 and 20), exposition of laws concerned with every aspect of social life and with the maintenance of religious institutions (19), the ordering of the priesthood (21–22), sabbaths, religious festivals (23), offerings (24^{1-9}), sabbatical and jubilee year observances, particularly directed to the protection of the poor and the dispossessed (25)—all these are set out and expounded, with frequent injunctions to avoid defilement, to recall that the basis of obedience is that 'I am the LORD' (so 18^{5}, etc.) and to enjoin that 'You shall be holy; for I the LORD your God am holy' (19^2). At only one point is there narrative, in 24^{10-23}, but this is an illustration of the problem of blasphemy and how it is to be handled, closely connected with the general theme. The climax is reached in the sermon of chapter 26.

Lev. 26^{3-45} *The meaning of exile*

3–13. The opening description of obedience and its consequences is closely allied in style and content to the opening of Deut. 28. We may note the emphasis on God's willingness to dwell with his people when they are in this acceptable condition.

14–22. These verses offer the contrasting statement, and again a comparison may be made with Deut. 28. The positive statements of the preceding verses are balanced by the negative judgements here.

23–33. Again as in Deut. 28, the negative aspect is developed more fully. The judgements of the preceding verses are interpreted as *discipline* (v. 23), designed to bring back the people to obedience. The judgements move on now to a climax—we may compare the stages in Amos 4^{6-12} and in the long poem in Isa. $9^{8-21}+5^{25-30}$—in pictures of siege (v. 29), of destruction of holy places and cities (vv. 30–32), and of exile (v. 33).

34–45. What has been said so far is for the most part of a very general kind; now we move into the interpretation of the exile itself. First there is a markedly negative statement (vv. 36–39) which leaves little room for hope. With v. 40, however, the possibility of the acknowledgement of sin and of repentance is entertained, and the promise of God declared that he will remember his covenant with the patriarchs (v. 42). An alternative but similar statement is made in vv. 44–45 which promises relief from the total disaster on the basis of the deliverance from Egypt. Woven into all this is a repeated statement about the exile itself (vv. 34 f., 43) in which the position of the land is described. It is relieved of the burden of its inhabitants, and enjoys a sabbath rest. There is a link here with the sabbatical year laws set out in $25^{1\,ff.}$. The origin of the custom of the sabbatical year is not known. It is possible that it was originally a simulation of famine so that the blessing of fertility could follow. It is also possible that it was designed to allow to the owners of the land—that is the deities believed to control it—their share of the produce. But when the custom appears in the Old Testament, it has already been given a theological interpretation, and here this is made clear in relation to the exile. The sabbatical years which have been missed will now be enjoyed; thereby the land will be restored and ready for the new covenant which is to be established by God with his people. This last point provides a link with the Priestly Work, as we may see in commenting on Gen. 1; it also provides a basis for the interpretation of the exile which is to be found in 2 Chron. 36^{21} and for the further development of the idea of a prolonged captivity in Dan. 9 (on this cf. Vol. 5, pp. 238 ff.).

The Priestly Work

Gen. 1^{1}–2^{4a} *The sabbath as the climax of creation*

For the understanding of the Priestly Work it is useful to look at the beginning, to see from what starting-point its interpretation of Israel is offered. Much that appears in this chapter is not here our concern, but needs to be taken up in connection with the Old Testament understanding of God as creator (cf. Vol. 1, pp. 179 ff.). One point has already been made, though it does not appear immediately in the words of this chapter; it is that the moment of creation, in which the creation of man belongs to the sixth day, is linked into history by the subsequent provision of the dates of the first man's life (Gen. 5^{1-5}). To suppose that the days of creation are longer periods, or ages, is not warranted. They are described as 'evening and morning' because the Hebrew day is thought of as beginning and ending at sunset. We are not here dealing with a description of the ages of geological time, and attempts at providing a simple alignment of Gen. 1 with scientific discovery do less than justice to the theological statements here being made. Nor should the description be taken literally, for this is a statement of the meaning of creation, deriving from very ancient ideas—including mythological ideas (cf. pp. 128 ff. on Isa. 51[9–11]). As the starting-point of the Priestly Work, it provides the ultimate setting for the author's understanding of the eternal purpose of God in creation, bound in with the purpose as it is worked out in the history of his people.

For the Priestly writer, the climax of the actual creation is reached with man; his subsequent narrative shows how the blessing of mankind comes to be narrowed down through successive covenants until it is Israel which is the central concern. The purpose of creation is declared in 2[1–4a], for this day on which God *rested . . . from all his work which he had done* is set apart, *blessed* and *hallowed* (that is, 'declared to be holy'). In the setting out of the laws of the decalogue in Exod. 20 (and this may be contrasted with the similar material in Deut. 5 where a different point is made), the basis of Israel's observance of the sabbath is because 'in six days the LORD made heaven and earth, the sea, and all that is in them, and rested the seventh day; therefore the LORD blessed the sabbath day and hallowed it' (v. 11). Israel therefore, the chosen people of God, is called to perpetual observance of the creative work of God; sabbath by sabbath that creation is recalled.

The origin of the sabbath is obscure; it is possible that it was originally a day which was considered to be inauspicious and that work was not to be done on it because of this. But when we meet the sabbath in the Old Testament, it has been given theological interpretation. In the Deuteronomic interpretation, it is a day of rest, and the needs of dependent members of the community are particularly in mind, with a recall of Israel's slavery in Egypt. In the Priestly interpretation, the emphasis rests on creation. The stress on the observance of the sabbath as a day of worship only gradually appears in the Old

Testament; the emphasis in Ezek. (cf. 20^{13}), in the Holiness Code (Lev. 23^{3}), and in the Priestly Work and in later passages such as Neh. $13^{15\,\mathrm{ff.}}$ (perhaps we should also compare Jer. 17^{19-27} which is probably a late addition), suggests that in the exilic and post-exilic periods it was coming to have a new and deeper meaning, and taking on that central place in worship which eventually made it such a focal point in the life of the Jewish community and directly influenced the growth of the similar but also markedly different institution of the first day of the week in Christian practice. (The Christian Sunday is not the sabbath, though features of the latter have influenced both thought and practice in relation to the former.)

The Priestly Work, with this beginning, points to an understanding of the meaning of human life, and in particular to the place occupied by Israel; it is to be a worshipping community, acknowledging the God who created it from the beginning. Compare this with the picture of Israel in Num. 2 (cf. pp. 159 ff.).

Lev. 16 *The Day of Atonement*

1. The instructions for religious celebration are introduced with a reference back to *the death of the two sons of Aaron*, described in Lev. 10^{1-2} as due to their having infringed an important regulation, thus incurring the divine displeasure. We are brought straight into a basic religious problem. How can men rightly approach God? The problem is expressed in harsh terms, but it is vital to any kind of understanding of a relationship between man as he is and God; for if any adequate terms are to be used to describe God's nature, they must somehow include a recognition of his 'otherness'. Approach to God involves the understanding of relationship. How are men to avoid cutting themselves off from the one whom they believe to be the source of life and well-being?

2–5. Approach to God by the appointed priesthood is not to be casual but ordered. These verses contain various regulations about purification, about proper holy garments, and about offerings.

6, 11–14. It is convenient to look at these verses together as they are concerned with an offering designed to permit the approach of the priests, *Aaron . . . and his house*. The bull is a *sin offering* (v. 11), that is, it is in some way designed to compensate for sin. Incense is used to make a sweet smell; perhaps its original purpose was thought to be that of encouraging benevolence in the deity. Now it has become a symbol to veil the presence of the holy God (v. 2) from the priest *lest he die* (v. 13). *The blood of the bull* is sprinkled (v. 14), and perhaps here the idea is that of bringing about a reconciliation, a union of life, between the deity and his worshippers. At each point, we can only surmise what was really thought to happen; the Old Testament describes the rituals, but it does very little towards explaining how they were thought to be effective. This makes it possible for the main emphasis to be on the point that God has ordained this as his appointed way of restoring and preserving a right relationship with his people, removing their guilt and facilitating their approach to him.

7–10. The strangest part of the ceremonial is here introduced. Two goats are in question, which are allocated by lot, the one to *the LORD* and the other to *Azazel* (v. 8). The first is to be a sin offering; the second is to be presented alive before God before being sent away. The details of the two rituals are then developed in a fuller description.

15–19. The goat which is to be a sin-offering for the whole people is killed and its blood sprinkled; these verses compare it with the bull for the priestly house. The priest is instructed to do this to *make atonement*—the word used seems to mean 'to cover' and hence 'to avert evil'—*for the holy place, because of the uncleannesses of the people of Israel* (v. 16). This may be compared with the emphasis in Ezek. 40–48 on the holiness of the shrine at the centre of the newly organized land. Subsequently this is developed with reference to *the tent of meeting*, and *all the assembly of Israel* (v. 17). Priesthood, people, and shrine are all to be made acceptable.

20–28. The goat for Azazel presents a major difficulty of interpretation. The phrases of v. 10 are here developed so as to indicate that by the laying of hands on the goat and by confession, the sins of Israel are in some way transferred to the goat which is then taken away by an appointed person and let loose in the wilderness. Who is Azazel? At a later time, he is known as the prince of the fallen angels and it seems clear in this passage that he is to be directly contrasted with God. He appears to be connected with the wilderness and is therefore perhaps in origin a spirit of the desert areas. It is possible that the origin of the rite was the offering of a sacrifice to appease the hostile desert spirits and protect the people, but this has been refined into the idea that Israel's sin is appropriately to be carried away into the desert and there it will be in the realm of the one to whom it belongs. (A comparison might be made with Zech. 5^{5-11} where a woman in an ephah representing wickedness, and perhaps idolatry, is carried away and set up as an object of worship in Babylon; Israel not infrequently described other religions as being the exact opposite of her own, which is good polemic even if not accurate as a study of religions.) The last verses of this section are concerned with further purification, and in vv. 27–28 there appears to be another aspect of the ritual, namely the burning of the bull and goat. Everything connected with sin is to be destroyed completely.

29–34. The injunction to annual celebration of this ritual is here made precise. The tenth day of the seventh month is the appointed day. It is probable that this represents a late stage in the ordering of the ritual, for in Neh. 8–9 no place is given to such a celebration though the period in which it would occur is covered; a fast is held on the twenty-fourth day of the seventh month (cf. p. 273). It is probable that, as with other annual celebrations, there was an eventual standardizing of an earlier more occasional practice. Some further points about purification conclude the instructions.

The whole chapter is very complex and its detailed interpretation meets with many difficulties. We may recognize two distinct elements. On the one hand, there appears to be the ancient ritual of the two goats, itself including two important religious ideas—the transfer of sin or uncleanness (we may compare the leprosy laws of Lev. 14), and the idea of protection from hostile powers. On the other hand, there are rituals connected with the purification of priests, people, and sanctuary, with a variety of elements. The whole purpose of the ritual as now understood is summarized at the end; it is to be an annual celebration, a total purification of the community each year to ensure that nothing which hinders relationship with God is carried forward into the next year. The fact that elsewhere, in Lev. 23^{27-32} and Num. 29^{7-11} in calendar lists (and cf. Exod. 30^{10} which gives no date), this day of atonement is mentioned without any reference to the two goats shows that there were various stages in the development of the ritual. Here as elsewhere the Priestly Work shows how older practice, no doubt in part very ancient indeed, comes to have a new meaning in the development of a new and obedient community.

Num. 2 *The holy encampment of Israel*

Where Ezekiel (47–48, see pp. 102 ff.) pictures a new Israel in its land, the tribes ordered to either side of the area within which the holy temple is to be built, the Priestly Work reveals a similar understanding of the ordering of the people and of the centrality of the tent in which God reveals his presence. For the detail of the arrangement as it is set out in vv. 1–31, cf. the plan on p. 160. The tribes are divided into four groups, one group being appointed to encamp on each of the four sides of the tent. Each group is considered as forming a unit, described by the name of the leading tribe of the group—Judah, Reuben, Ephraim, Dan. The central area around the tent is occupied by the tents of the Levites (v. 17); subsequently we are told that in the area on the east side of the tent are to be 'Moses and Aaron and his sons' (3^{38}). A marching order is indicated; Judah (i.e. the Judah group), Reuben, the tent, Ephraim, Dan.

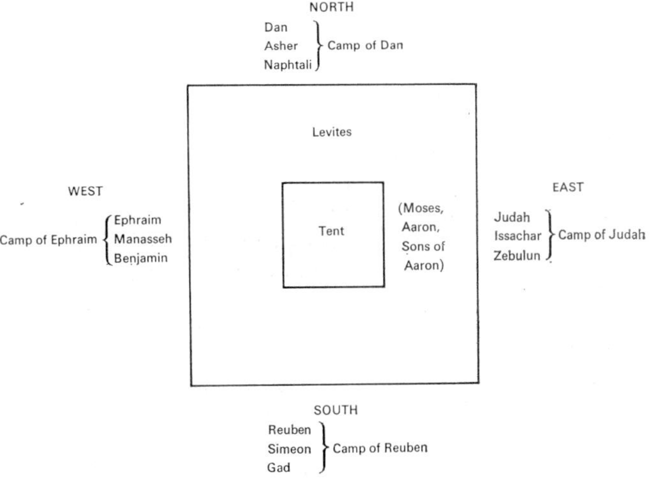

THE ORDERING OF THE ENCAMPMENT (Num. 2).

The terminology of this description is military, each group belonging to a particular *standard* (v. 2, etc.); the term indicates some kind of military division associated with it. The enumeration of the tribes is on a military basis, being the men 'who are able to go forth to war' (Num. 1^{3}. Num. 1 has a different account of the tribes, in the form of a military census. But the figures are the same as those used in Num. 2). But the military element is overshadowed by the religious, for the picture of the camp is not based on organization for war, but on meeting for worship. We may compare the Chronicler's interpretation of warfare (cf. p. 303). The closest analogy is to be seen in tent festivals of a kind still to be found in the Arab realm (cf. H.-J. Kraus, *Worship in Israel* (Blackwell, 1966), p. 131). Israel was evidently familiar with this kind of religious observance, so that what is here described was not an invention of the Priestly writer but a reflection of known practice. What they have done is to offer a picture of Israel in the wilderness in terms of this practice, and they have, by implication, depicted an ideal of religious life in these terms. To those who saw the people in the exilic age, the hope for the future lay in recovering a way of life in which God, revealing his presence in the *tent of meeting*, will be central to the people's life and worship.

Num. 34–36 *The allocated land*

The allocation here described should be compared with the more idealized conception of Ezek. 48 (pp. 102 ff.). The boundaries of the land are ideal as there, but closer to what Israel had once enjoyed in the time of David; tribes are to be settled on both sides of Jordan, as in fact they were. Cities are to be set aside as Levitical inheritances in addition to the cities of refuge for those who have committed manslaughter (this to enable them to be protected since they were not guilty of culpable homicide. The point is set out in detail in 35^{9-34}). It is worth noting that in the description of these cities of the Levites there is a precision of measurement again comparable with that of Ezekiel. So 35^{5} enjoins that *two thousand cubits* are to be measured in each direction to mark off the pasture-land for each city. A problem of inheritance, i.e. possession of the land, is dealt with in the last section of the book, 36^{1-12}, and although the passage is rounded off by v. 13, it would appear not improbable that the original ending of the Priestly Work has been curtailed, perhaps when this work and the Deuteronomic History were placed together and some attempt was made at reconciling the two. Yet with their different approaches to the problem of the people's life, they make essentially the same demands; it is to be an ordered people, a people entering the land which God gives, a people ready to accept and submit to the whole will of God.

III. THE PERSIAN PERIOD
RESTORATION IN JUDAH

THE period of the exile saw substantial rethinking and re-interpreting of the older traditions. The two centuries of the Persian period conceal important developments in both life and thought and in the shaping of the Old Testament books, though it is not possible to draw a neat line between this period and the Greek one which follows. Following on the kind of developments which we have been tracing in the exilic age, it is clear that there were continuing endeavours to stabilize life, to reorder the community, and that this involved a gradually changing attitude towards the writings which had come down from the past. These were re-used and re-presented, notably in the work of the Chronicler. But above all, they come, though only gradually, to be regarded as having a special and sacred position, as a standard of life to which recourse must be had for the resolving of problems of living. The subsequent association of the canon of the Old Testament with Ezra (cf. p. 266) is an appropriate expression of the regard which Judaism was to have for this formative period.

The history of this period is difficult to write. The sources at our disposal are limited, and they provide a very incomplete picture. The books of Ezra and Nehemiah, the last part of what now forms the Work of the Chronicler (cf. pp. 294 ff.), deal with only three great moments in the life of the people—restoration and rebuilding, and the activities of the two leaders Ezra and Nehemiah. Only one short passage, Ezra 4^{6-23}, appears to belong to the intervening years, and its precise relation to the remainder is uncertain. Even the dating of the activity of Ezra and Nehemiah is a matter of continuing debate (cf. pp. 191 ff.). Some other information may be deduced, though again with many uncertainties, from the writings of the Jewish historian Josephus. The prophetic and other books which belong to the period also provide indications of the situation; but even where these writings may be fitted precisely into the historical framework, there are here, as in older prophetic books, many problems of interpretation before we can use their evidence to give us more exact information. For so vital a period as the 200 years of Persian rule, we are in very considerable uncertainty, and this is the more unfortunate since it is so evident that these are years of great significance for the development of the Old Testament and of the life and thought of the Jewish community which comes into a somewhat clearer light in the succeeding centuries. Perhaps we may most conveniently remind ourselves that like other periods of that community's life, both earlier and later, this is not a time about which simple generalizations should be made. There were differing groups, some of which appear more sharply—so the Samaritan community; there were different lines of development of thought, expressed in a varied literature. There were personal tensions, such as can be seen in the story of Nehemiah. If it is too precise to speak of 'party divisions', there nevertheless existed side by side those who did not see eye to eye about the nature of the community's life and faith. To simplify this by implying that there was a clear normative line of belief and practice, an orthodox centre from which others deviated, is as untrue for the Persian period as it is for the subsequent period with its more defined parties, or as it is for the earlier period of the great prophetic and priestly reformers.

A. *The Period of Rebuilding*

The fall of Babylon to Cyrus the Persian in 539 B.C. ushers in a new stage in the life of the Jewish community. Persian policy was to prove very different in some respects from that of the empires which had earlier ruled the states of Palestine. But it would be a mistake to oversimplify the changes. The Persians had conquered; they were intent on ruling, and they could be as ruthless against their opponents as their predecessors. Rebellion met with sharp reprisals; the western

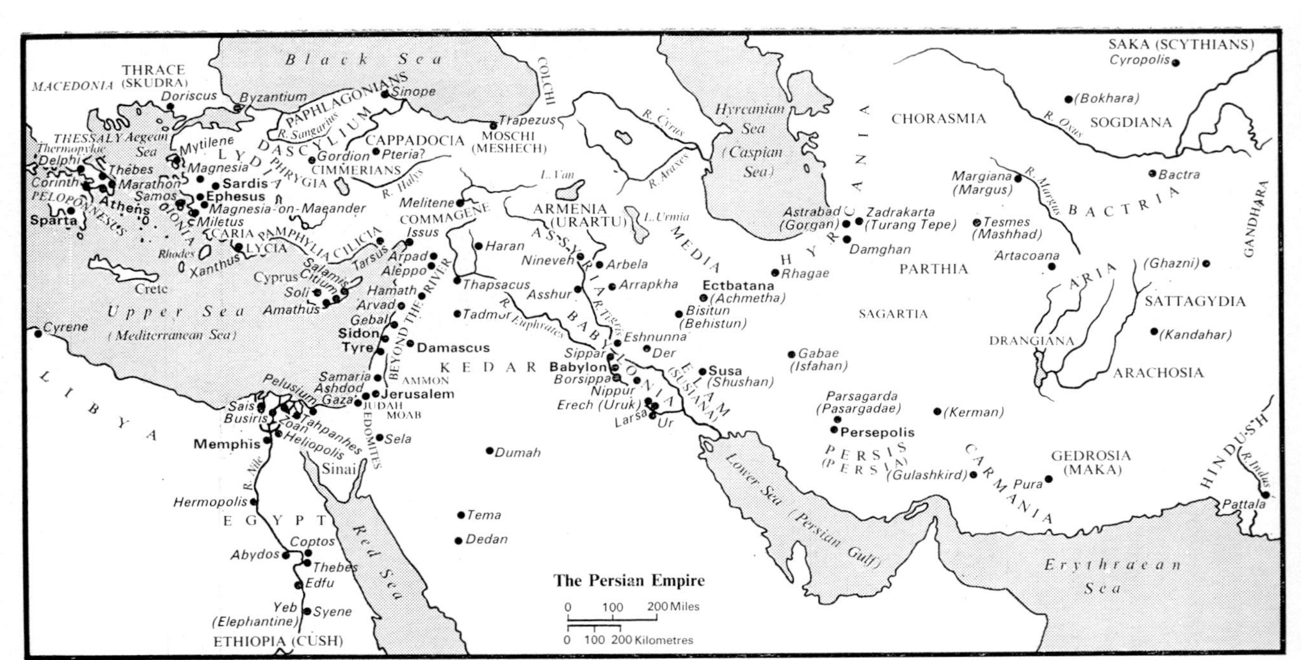
Black Sea
THRACE (SKUDRA)
MACEDONIA
Doriscus
Byzantium
PAPHLAGONIANS
Sinope
COLCHI
Trapezus
MOSCHI (MESHECH)
CAPPADOCIA
Pteria?
Gordion
DASCYLIUM
R. Sangarius
CIMMERIANS
R. Halys
PHRYGIA
LYDIA
THESSALY
Aegean Sea
Thermopylae
Delphi
Thebes
Marathon
Corinth
Athens
PELOPONNESUS
Sparta
Mytilene
Magnesia
Sardis
Samos
Ephesus
Magnesia-on-Maeander
IONIA
Miletus
CARIA
LYCIA
PAMPHYLIA
CILICIA
Tarsus
Issus
Rhodes
Xanthus
Crete
Cyprus
Salamis
Citium
Soli
Amathus
Upper Sea
(Mediterranean Sea)
Cyrene
LIBYA
Melitene
COMMAGENE
Arpad
Aleppo
Hamath
Arvad
Gebal
Sidon
Tyre
Damascus
BEYOND THE RIVER
Samaria
Ashdod
Gaza
Jerusalem
JUDAH
AMMON
MOAB
EDOMITES
Sela
Pelusium
Sais
Busiris
Zoan
Tahpanhes
Heliopolis
Memphis
Sinai
R. Nile
Hermopolis
EGYPT
Abydos
Coptos
Thebes
Edfu
Red Sea
Yeb
(Elephantine)
Syene
ETHIOPIA (CUSH)
L. Van
ARMENIA (URARTU)
Haran
Thapsacus
Tadmor
R. Euphrates
ASSYRIA
Nineveh
Arbela
Asshur
Arrapkha
R. Tigris
KEDAR
Dumah
Tema
Dedan
BABYLONIA
Eshnunna
Der
Sippar
Babylon
Borsippa
Nippur
Erech (Uruk)
Larsa
Ur
ELAM (SUSIANA)
Susa
(Shushan)
R. Cyrus
R. Araxes
L. Urmia
MEDIA
Ectbatana
(Achmetha)
Bisitun
(Behistun)
Hyrcanian Sea
(Caspian Sea)
HYRCANIA
Astrabad
(Gorgan)
Zadrakarta
(Turang Tepe)
Damghan
Rhagae
PARTHIA
SAGARTIA
Gabae
(Isfahan)
Parsagarda
(Pasargadae)
Persepolis
PERSIS
(PERSIA)
(Kerman)
(Gulashkird)
CARMANIA
Lower Sea (Persian Gulf)
The Persian Empire
0 100 200 Miles
0 100 200 Kilometres
CHORASMIA
Margiana
(Margus)
R. Margus
Tesmes
(Mashhad)
Artacoana
ARIA
DRANGIANA
SAKA (SCYTHIANS)
Cyropolis
(Bokhara)
R. Oxus
SOGDIANA
Bactra
BACTRIA
GANDHARA
(Ghazni)
SATTAGYDIA
(Kandahar)
ARACHOSIA
GEDROSIA
(MAKA)
Pura
HINDUSH
R. Indus
Pattala
Erythraean Sea

regions of the empire were still to be the route for armies marching to conquer Egypt which had more than once to be subdued. During the fifth and fourth centuries, there was also to be an intermittent but prolonged struggle with Greece, for the control of the Greek areas of Asia Minor and for the conquest of Greece itself. It was out of this struggle that there eventually emerged a Greece united under the Macedonian royal family of Philip and Alexander, and the armies which were to invade the Persian empire and bring about its total overthrow.

Persian policy was a mixture of firmness, skill in organization, and conciliation. The suppression of rebels and claimants to the throne can be seen clearly in the events which surround the accession of Darius I, described in propagandist terms in the Behistun inscription (cf. pp. 166 ff.); this was to be of some moment for the Jewish community working at the rebuilding of the temple. The organization can be seen in the division of the empire into satrapies, of which the one 'Beyond the River', i.e. west of the Euphrates, concerns us since it was within this satrapy that Samaria and Judah were situated (cf. Ezra 5[3]); a division of civil and military authority was made to discourage rebellion by the satraps, though this did not in fact prevent the satrap of 'Beyond the River' in the middle of the fifth century carrying out a very nearly successful coup. A well-ordered communications system, inherited from the past and developed, assisted control. Conciliatory policy can be seen in the declarations of the Cyrus cylinder and in other documents (cf. pp. 197 ff.); the Persian policy towards the Jewish community and towards other groups such as the Jewish colony at Elephantine (cf. pp. 279 ff.), shows sympathy for the religious susceptibilities of subject peoples. To call this 'toleration' is perhaps to give it too modern a title; there was not a little of political skill in the policy. When it suited, there could be a ruthlessness which did not match a true tolerance, as when the Egyptian campaign of Cambyses brought destruction to Egyptian temples. Rebels were rebels, and subject peoples remained under strict control.

THE BEHISTUN SCULPTURES AND INSCRIPTIONS. Darius I commemorated his victories over rival claimants to the throne and other enemies in a great relief carved in the cliffs at Behistun (Bisitun), about 200 miles north-east of Babylon, by the road to Ecbatana, capital of the former Median empire. The inscriptions are in three languages: Persian, Elamite, and Akkadian (Babylonian); fragments of other copies have been found, including papyri containing parts of two copies in Aramaic at Elephantine (cf. pp. 279 ff.). The trilingual text made possible the decipherment of the cuneiform writing of Mesopotamia. It seems evident that this propaganda document was widely circulated; this is perhaps not surprising, since its main intention is clearly to establish that Darius is the true successor to the throne, and that all his rivals have been successfully overcome. Darius announces himself: 'The great king, king of kings, king of Persia, king of the lands, son of

Hystaspes, grandson of Arsames, an Achaemenid (i.e. of that family and royal line)' (Section 1). Such a stress on ancestry and legitimacy is not uncommon in ancient documents and inscriptions; but it is clear from the

The policy of Cyrus towards the Jews is described in the opening chapters of the book of Ezra, and some parts of this material are subsequently examined in closer detail. That Cyrus should have been concerned to see that the God of the Jews was 'restored to his dwelling' fits with his known policy; that he should provide for the rebuilding of the temple at Jerusalem is also not improbable; we may compare the later benevolence of Artaxerxes I to Nehemiah (Neh. 1–2). The detail of what Cyrus ordered may be more open to question; the story has been told by those who were concerned about the meaning of the restoration and rebuilding. But the general impression accords with what is known from elsewhere.

When we endeavour to discover more detail about the political situation in Jerusalem and Judah, we encounter considerable difficulties. The narrative is by no means clear in Ezra 1–6 (cf. pp. 201 ff.). Sheshbazzar, the first commissioner, to whom is ascribed the laying of the foundation (Ezra 5^{16}), is

---

long list of those who were defeated that Darius' position was not automatically accepted. He claims to have put down all disorder: 'I rebuilt the temples which Gaumata the Magian had destroyed. I restored to the people their pastureland and their cattle herds and their dwellings in the houses which Gaumata had seized from them. I returned the people to their own places as they were before, Persia, Media and the remaining lands' (Section 14). In assessing Darius' claims and his assertions about his opponents, we must bear in mind the propagandist intention. Gaumata, who appears as a leading claimant to the throne, gave out that he was the brother of Cambyses, supposedly executed on Cambyses' orders; whether his claim was true or not, he gained a large following. Nidintu-Bel claimed to be a son of Nabonidus and called himself Nebuchadrezzer III; he established himself for a time in Babylon, but while it is stated at one point that 'the whole Babylonian population went over to Nidintu-Bel', it is clear that, with the defeat of the leader, the insurrection collapsed and there is no indication of reprisals against the general population. To exaggerate the strength of the opposition did after all increase the glory of the victor. A very colourful account of the events at the time of Darius' accession is given by Herodotus (*The Histories*, Book III). It was only to be expected that the Jewish community (cf. Haggai and Zech. 1–8; cf. pp. 210 ff., 218 ff.) and no doubt other subject peoples should have speculated about the possible outcome.

The sculpture itself shows Darius, pictured on a larger scale, standing with his foot on the defeated Gaumata to receive the submission of captive leaders; above them is the winged solar disc, symbol of Ahuramazda, supreme deity of Persian religion.

replaced, without comment, by Zerubbabel in the narrative of Ezra 3. The chronology is not clear, since no indication is given of the years in question. It appears most probable that a modest beginning was made in the years immediately after Cyrus' permission was given, though whether Sheshbazzar was responsible alone or whether Zerubbabel had already joined him is not clear. Since we do not know the condition of the temple area during the preceding years, we do not know just how much had to be done by way of repair. The altar was remounted—was this a reconstruction of it, or a replacement of it in position, or an act of rededication of it for new and purified use? But the temple was not fully restored. The first stages were followed by opposition and frustration (cf. 4^{1-5} and pp. 206 ff.); it is possible that in some measure this opposition came from political opponents who did not wish to see a rehabilitation of Jerusalem. Sheshbazzar's official position is not clear, nor is the degree of Persian control in the west; it could be that at this point Judah was under the control of an officer in Samaria (as appears to be the case a century later) and that he (was he the Babylonian governor still holding office as happened in many areas under the Persians?) did not want to lose an important area to a separate governor. Did Sheshbazzar find the situation impossible and return to Babylon, or was his term of office only quite limited?

The next stage of the work belongs to the time of Darius I (cf. Ezra $4^{5, 24}$ and 5–6), and here we find the figure of Zerubbabel clearly. This suggests that he was a newly appointed governor and that the author of the present form of the narrative has telescoped the history by putting Zerubbabel into the earlier stage as well. Other traditions (cf. 1 Esdras $4^{42\,\mathrm{ff.}}$) suggest that Zerubbabel came later, and the implication of the words of Haggai seems to be that it was only in the reign of Darius that he was in a position to take action towards the rebuilding of the temple (cf. Hag. 1^{1}–2^{9} and 2^{20-23}; cf. pp. 212 f., 217 f.). We have to recognize that the Chronicler, using older sources no doubt, was presenting a view of the period—a view in which the impetus to rebuild came entirely from exiles returning from

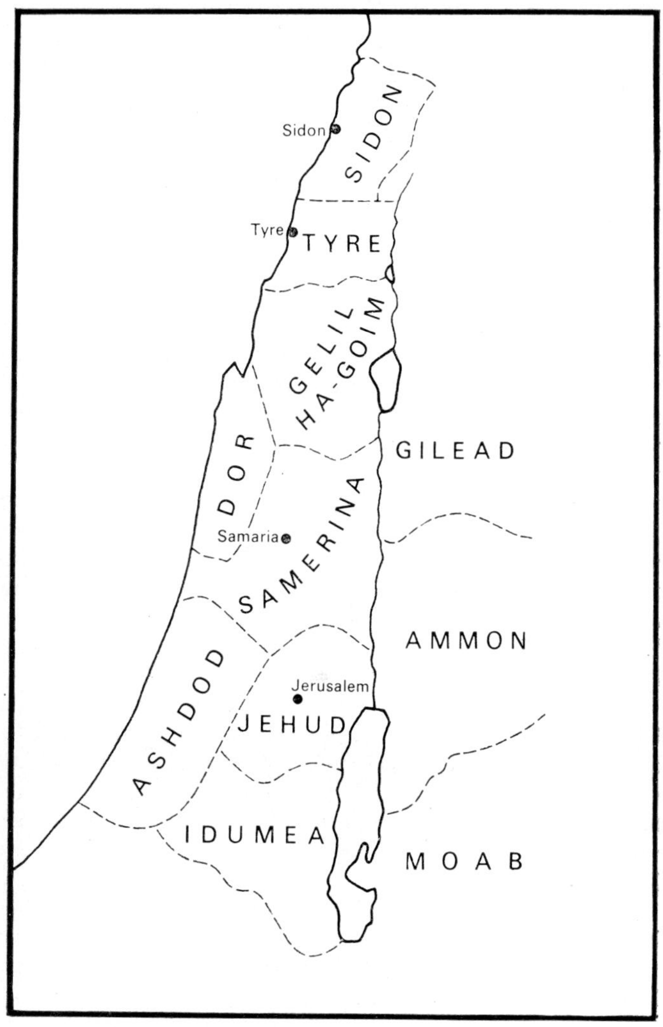

PERSIAN ADMINISTRATION—THE DIVISIONS OF PALESTINE

Babylon and in which the delays in rebuilding which the tradition recorded had to be explained away. The course of events remains far from clear (cf. p. 179 on Nehemiah for other examples of confusion of identity and chronology in this period).

Cyrus was occupied between 539 and 530 in many problems of control in the eastern part of the empire, and there is no evidence to show whether he really controlled the west or campaigned there. He was succeeded in 530 by his son Cambyses, who engaged in a campaign against Egypt and conquered it; but he died in somewhat mysterious circumstances in 522, and left behind a very complex situation in which various claimants to the throne contended and there was severe rebellion in Babylonia. Darius I appears as the main claimant to the throne, though he was not in the direct line of succession; but he was able only with considerable difficulty to bring the empire under his control and for a period there was much unrest (cf. pp. 166 ff.). At this juncture, we gain a new picture of the life of the community in Judah and Jerusalem, both from Ezra 5–6 and from the prophecies of Haggai and Zechariah (1–8). Again there are problems of interpretation in the evidence. Both our sources of information agree that the two prophets played an important part in the stimulating of leaders and people in the work of rebuilding, but the relationship between the Ezra narrative and the prophetic books is difficult to define precisely. According to the narrative, inquiry was instituted into the rebuilding programme by the governor

---

PERSIAN ADMINISTRATION—THE DIVISIONS OF PALESTINE. When Darius I had established himself as ruler, he undertook a reorganization of the empire. He inherited from his predecessors a system of provinces which went back at many points to Assyrian administration. According to Herodotus, *The Histories*, Book III (Penguin edition, pp. 214 f.), there were now twenty provincial areas called *satrapies*; Palestine was part of the fifth, which we know to have been called 'Beyond the River' (cf. e.g. Ezra 7^{21}). By dividing civil and military administration within each satrapy, the likelihood of a satrap being able to rebel was reduced. Within each satrapy, smaller subdivisions were made. Judah (Jehud or Yehud) was one such. At certain periods it appears to have been under a separate governor (so probably Nehemiah, and Bagoas, cf. the Elephantine papyri); at other times it is likely that it came under the governor in Samaria (cf. pp. 169, 253).

of the province 'Beyond the River'; investigation in the archives showed that Cyrus' decree had authorized rebuilding, and Darius confirmed and amplified the instructions so that whatever was needed could be supplied. As a result, the building was completed and rededicated in 515 B.C., in the sixth year of Darius' reign. The text could be so understood as to suggest that there was opposition to the rebuilding, but this is not directly stated; it could equally be taken that this was a routine investigation. As the narrative now stands, it provides a point for stressing the divine blessing of the work of rebuilding, mediated through the benevolence of the Persian ruler. At the end, both in 6^{16} which is in Aramaic (cf. pp. 202, 209) and in 6^{19} which is in Hebrew—and presumably this suggests separate source material—it is emphasized that it was returned exiles who were responsible, though others who purified themselves joined in the rededication. In Haggai and Zechariah, no clear division appears between those who returned from Babylonia and those who were in Judah, though there are some difficult passages here of which the interpretation is not clear (cf. pp. 216 f., 231 f.). Again we seem to have a particular type of presentation of the period.

The political uncertainties of this period, together with economic difficulties which appear clearly in Hag. 1, appear to have raised speculation about the meaning of events. The prophetic books contain a number of passages which suggest that to some at least this was a new age, the age of the fulfilment of promise; perhaps some believed that the great powers were soon to fall and Judah would come again into her own. Others may well have countered such ideas with a more sober appraisal of the situation. It was evidently a lively moment, beset by hopes and frustrations. If some parts of Isa. 56–66 belong to these years, we may detect indications of both aspects of thought (cf. pp. 233 ff.). The temple was rebuilt; the community life again had a focal point. For Jews both in the homeland and further afield, Jerusalem could again be the centre to which they looked, and as the years pass, evidence of such a looking toward Jerusalem appears.

But for the moment, we are left with this picture of the restored community, with little precise knowledge of what life was like, little real appreciation of economic conditions, with a recognition that politically the situation could hardly have been easy—and then, nothing at all; for information is virtually entirely lacking for the years after 515 B.C. There is only the rather limited light shed in the years of the next century by the book of Malachi (probably to be so dated) and by Ezra 4^{6-23}, until we again get a clearer picture with the work of Nehemiah.

B. *The Jewish Community in the Fifth Century*

If, as appears likely, the book of Malachi contains material which sheds light on the first part of the fifth century B.C. (cf. pp. 243 ff.), it suggests no very high level of religious life and thought. Its criticisms of the inadequacies of worship, of lack of faith, of social and religious ills, point to a rather depressed situation; its outlook towards a new age, heralded by a new Elijah, shows the continuing hope of changed fortunes for the people, but its emphasis is much more on judgement than on the promise of a new life characteristic of the Second Isaiah and Zechariah.

The next precisely defined moment is the appearance of Nehemiah in the twentieth year of Artaxerxes I, 445 B.C. (Neh. 2^{1}). The identification of the Persian king is virtually confirmed by the evidence of the Elephantine papyri which point to the position occupied by the sons of Sanballat towards the end of the century (cf. pp. 286 f.). This would fit the situation in which Nehemiah was active while Sanballat his opponent was at the height of his power as governor in Samaria. Although there is evidence to show that there was more than one governor of this name (cf. pp. 291 f.), and the Nehemiah narratives are not without their problems, there is general agreement about the chronology at this point. The relation between Ezra and Nehemiah is still the subject of much discussion. The assumption made here is that Ezra came later, and that, of the dates proposed, the most natural is 398 B.C., the seventh year of Artaxerxes II. This problem is discussed in Vol. 1, pp. 176–8, and a short résumé of the arguments is given in a note at the end of this section (pp. 191 ff.).

SAMARIA. The hill on which the city of Samaria was built by Omri in the ninth century B.C. occupies an important strategic position in the centre of the land, commanding main lines of communication to the west, north, and east. Its suitability as a seat of government is shown by its continued use under the Assyrians, Babylonians, and Persians as a provincial capital.

The description of Nehemiah's activity begins with the report of a message brought to him in exile, where he was cup-bearer at the royal court; this tells of the still ruined state of the walls and gates of Jerusalem. The implication is that nothing had been done to repair these since the destruction in 587. That destruction had been very radical, as the excavations have made clear. When Nehemiah came to rebuild the walls, it is clear that he met with major difficulties in certain areas (see Neh. 2[14]). But it has been speculated that perhaps there had been some attempt at rebuilding which had met with opposition and that the message which came to Nehemiah arose in part out of this situation. A number of separate points are here involved, and the reconstruction of the course of events is very hazardous. We know that in about 450 B.C., the satrap of 'Beyond the River', rebelled against Artaxerxes; this rebellion arose in part out of the rebellion of Egypt in 460, which had eventually been brought to an end in 454. Thus the Persians were faced with uncertainties in the western part of the empire not long before the appointment of Nehemiah. In Ezra 4^{6-23} we have the account of an attempt at building the walls of Jerusalem in the reign of Artaxerxes and of the report which was sent to the king suggesting that the Jews were engaging in rebellion. The account is a colourful one; it fits into what we otherwise know of the desire of some in Palestine to prevent the redevelopment of Jerusalem. But we have no precise knowledge of the situation, and the matter is complicated by the fact that in the book of Ezra the passage is quite out of place; it looks as though it was put where it is because it illustrated, alongside 4^{1-5}, the kind of opposition which the Jewish community met, though it derives from a quite different source. In 1 Esdras it is put in a different position (2^{16-30}), immediately after the commission of Sheshbazzar. It would be intelligible if at the time of the Egyptian rebellion or at the time of the rebellion of the satrap, some in Jerusalem saw a suitable moment for improving the city's defences and perhaps even for gaining some measure of independence. If so, the complaints made to Artaxerxes had some ground. Or it may be that the rebuilding was simply a matter of protection and that the opponents (those who are in Samaria are particularly mentioned, $4^{10, 17}$) saw this as an opportunity for preventing any fuller development at Jerusalem; Nehemiah's opponents made similar charges against him, impugning his loyalty to his Persian master (Neh. 2^{19}).

At all events, here we have a glimpse into the problems of the period. And this makes it all the more intelligible that the Persian ruler should have seen fit to send Nehemiah to

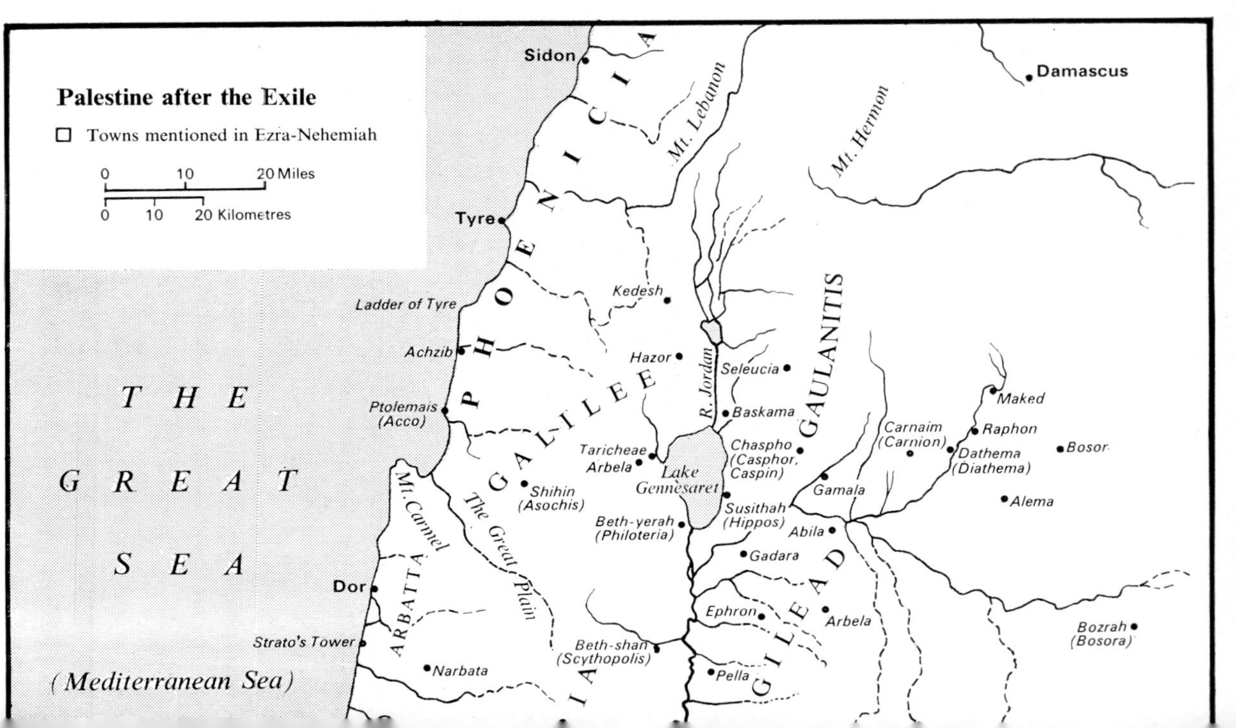
Palestine after the Exile
Towns mentioned in Ezra-Nehemiah
0 10 20 Miles
0 10 20 Kilometres
Damascus
Sidon
Tyre
PHOENICIA
Mt. Lebanon
Mt. Hermon
Ladder of Tyre
Achzib
Ptolemais (Acco)
Kedesh
Hazor
GALILEE
R. Jordan
Seleucia
Baskama
GAULANITIS
Maked
Raphon
Bosor
Carnaim (Carnion)
Dathema (Diathema)
Alema
Chaspho (Casphor, Caspin)
Gamala
Taricheae
Arbela
Lake Gennesaret
Shihin (Asochis)
Susithah (Hippos)
Beth-yerah (Philoteria)
Abila
Gadara
GILEAD
Ephron
Arbela
Bozrah (Bosora)
Pella
Beth-shan (Scythopolis)
The Great Plain
Mt. Carmel
ARBATTA
Dor
Strato's Tower
Narbata
THE GREAT SEA
(Mediterranean Sea)

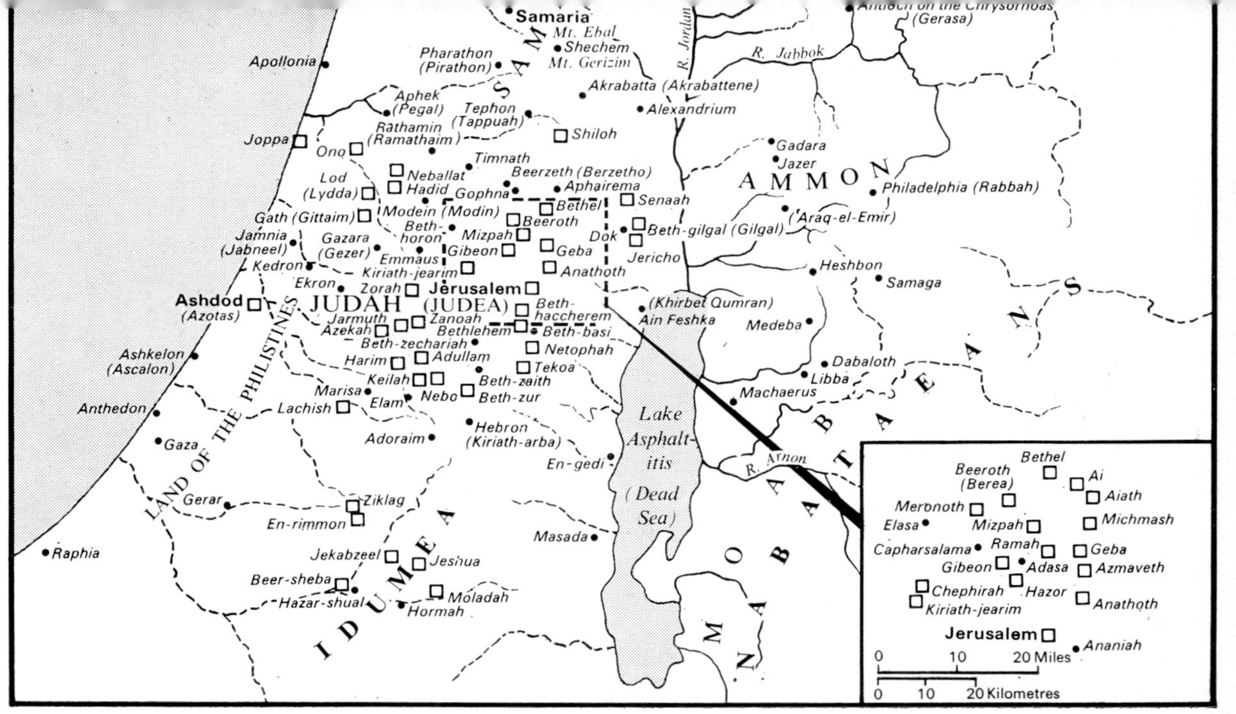

Samaria
Mt. Ebal
Shechem
Mt. Gerizim
R. Jordan
(Gerasa)
R. Jabbok
Pharathon
(Pirathon)
Apollonia
Akrabatta (Akrabattene)
Alexandrium
Aphek
(Pegal)
Tephon
(Tappuah)
Rathamin
(Ramathaim)
Shiloh
Joppa
Ono
Gadara
Jazer
AMMON
Philadelphia (Rabbah)
Timnath
Neballat
Beerzeth (Berzetho)
Lod
(Lydda)
Hadid
Gophna
Aphairema
Senaah
('Araq-el-Emir)
Gath (Gittaim)
Modein (Modin)
Bethel
Beth-
horon
Beeroth
Mizpah
Dok
Beth-gilgal (Gilgal)
Jamnia
(Jabneel)
Gazara
(Gezer)
Gibeon
Geba
Jericho
Emmaus
Kedron
Kiriath-jearim
Anathoth
Heshbon
Samaga
Ekron
Zorah
Jerusalem
Ashdod
(Azotas)
JUDAH
(JUDEA)
Beth-
haccherem
(Khirbet Qumran)
Ain Feshka
Medeba
Jarmuth
Zanoah
Azekah
Bethlehem
Beth-basi
Beth-zechariah
Netophah
Ashkelon
(Ascalon)
Harim
Adullam
Dabaloth
Tekoa
Libba
Keilah
Beth-zaith
Marisa
Machaerus
Elam
Nebo
Beth-zur
Anthedon
Lachish
LAND OF THE PHILISTINES
Lake
Asphalt-
itis
(Dead
Sea)
NABATAEANS
Gaza
Adoraim
Hebron
(Kiriath-arba)
En-gedi
R. Arnon
Gerar
Ziklag
En-rimmon
Masada
Raphia
Jekabzeel
Jeshua
IDUMEA
Beer-sheba
Moladah
Hazar-shual
Hormah
MOAB
Bethel
Beeroth
(Berea)
Ai
Aiath
Meronoth
Michmash
Elasa
Mizpah
Capharsalama
Ramah
Geba
Gibeon
Adasa
Azmaveth
Chephirah
Hazor
Kiriath-jearim
Anathoth
Jerusalem
Ananiah
0 10 20 Miles
0 10 20 Kilometres

Jerusalem at just this moment of time. A loyal governor there, who owed his position to the personal favour of the Persian king, could be a valuable support for Persian control of the west. Judah was important for the approach roads to Egypt, and Egypt was a continuing source of anxiety. Similar considerations may apply in the case of Ezra (cf. pp. 181 f.). Nehemiah was appointed for a fixed term (2^{6}) of twelve years (5^{14}, 13^{6}), and subsequently he returned to Jerusalem for a further period. There are, however, many gaps in the narrative and we know only a little of what went on during these years.

The detail of Nehemiah's work in Jerusalem is brought out in the discussion of some passages from the narrative concerning him (pp. 246 ff.). It is convenient here to attempt an assessment of what he attempted and achieved, and in this it is important to realize that the information we have comes to us in documents which have to be carefully considered so that the nature of their information may be clear. The Nehemiah narratives in the book of that name give information about him in the first person; certain moments of his activity are elaborated—his 'call', for so we might designate the stimulus of the report which reached him and the resolution which followed on his prayer (Neh. 1), his 'commission' and here too the analogy of prophetic appointment is perhaps not improper, for what Artaxerxes did is described as being due to the 'good hand of my God . . . upon me' (2^{8} and so frequently); his carrying out of the divine commands which are the royal commands—the building of the wall, the reordering of the social life of the community, the increasing of the population of Jerusalem, religious reforms within the temple and city. Like the prophets, Nehemiah is shown as meeting with opposition; like them he performs a symbolic action (5^{13}), like them he is tempted to obey a word of a prophet who has not been divinely sent ($6^{10\,\mathrm{ff.}}$, cf. 1 Kgs. 13 and Deut. 13). This is not to say that Nehemiah was a prophet, but to suggest that the presentation of his work is stylized, a description of what he did which is at the same time almost a legal defence. 'Remember me, O my God, for good' (13^{31}, etc.). So the narrative closes, and with this its purpose is declared; it is a presentation styled in some ways like the inscriptions set up by ancient kings, setting out before their gods the things which they had achieved as a lasting memorial. It is therefore selective and incomplete; it is apologetically and theologically motivated and not intended merely as narrative. To its compiler—for it is unlikely that Nehemiah actually wrote it (cf. pp. 247 ff.)—Nehemiah was a great figure; but more than that he was one who operated under divine control, sought the guidance of God in prayer, and worked as the instrument of God for the good of his people. His memory is to be revered.

Subsequent tradition takes the picture further. The survey of the heroes of the faith in the book of Ecclesiasticus (49[13]) in about 180 B.C. says:

> The memory of Nehemiah is also lasting;
> He raised for us the walls that had fallen
> and set up the gates and bars,
> and rebuilt our ruined houses.

The second book of Maccabees (1[10]–2[18]) has some very curious material about Nehemiah, which in effect puts Nehemiah and a priest Jonathan in the place of Zerubbabel and Joshua in the rebuilding of the temple after the exile. Such an identification, which is historically quite absurd, shows, however, that there was a great deal of confusion in the traditions about the restoration period, and makes it not so difficult to understand how the Chronicler in the opening chapters of the book of Ezra could apparently confuse Sheshbazzar and Zerubbabel. The 2 Maccabees narrative goes on to record another very interesting element of tradition:

> The same things are reported in the records and in the memoirs of Nehemiah, and also that he founded a library and collected the books about the kings and prophets, and the writings of David, and letters of kings about votive offerings (2 Macc. 2[13]).

With Nehemiah it compares Judas Maccabaeus who is said to have collected the writings which had been scattered by reason of the war (2^{14}). We may see here an overlap of the Nehemiah tradition with that of Ezra, for Ezra was later regarded as having been responsible for the rewriting of the ancient scriptures, destroyed in the exile (2 Esdras $14^{21, 42-47}$), and later still as being really responsible for the whole ordering of the canon of scripture (cf. p. 266). Other forms of the Nehemiah tradition are also to be found in the writings of Josephus and allusions in yet later writings show the way in which various elements in the story were elaborated.

It is evident that to some of those who followed, the period of his activity appeared as a high-water mark in the life of the Jewish community under Persian rule; his work was a sign of the continuing blessing and guidance of God, and it did much to show the tiny subject province of Judah that it was truly the successor of the past. In him we may hear echoes of the ideals of earlier thinkers. He is shown establishing a protected and enclosed community; as enriching its life and raising up its poorer members; as establishing more clearly the separateness of this community, so that it might be faithful to the ancestral laws; as making firm the religious ordinances and purifying the priesthood. There are links here with the reforming ideals of Ezekiel and the Second Isaiah, for whom the establishing of a new people in a new and holy Jerusalem was important; there are links with Haggai and Zechariah and with the Deuteronomic History and the Priestly Work in the desire for a new and obedient community. The thought of the past and particularly its representation in the exilic period come to have their expression in the more practical applications of a royally appointed leader.

An unexpected sidelight is cast upon the life of the Jewish community in this period by the fortunate discovery of documents relating to a military colony of Jews at Elephantine in Egypt. Some of these documents are discussed elsewhere (pp. 279 ff.). The existence of this group is traced by its members back into the preceding century; its origins are unknown, though it appears to derive from troops stationed for the control of the southern border of Egypt. By the fifth century, certainly, its military purpose is clear. From the documents, insights are gained into the economic and legal affairs of this community, in relation to one another and to their Egyptian neighbours. Towards the end of the century, we find them facing increasing pressure from the Egyptians; in 410 B.C. their temple was destroyed and they appealed for help to the governor and authorities at the temple in Jerusalem, perhaps after failing to get any help from the Persians in Egypt. Still getting no response, they wrote again in 407 both to Jerusalem and to Samaria. An authorization for rebuilding did follow from the two civil authorities jointly, to be communicated to the Persian governor in Egypt, who had been absent when the appeal was sent. The temple was probably rebuilt, but within the next few years Egypt was able to rebel against Persian rule and become independent and we can only assume that the Jewish military colony was wiped out.

This glimpse of Jewish life elsewhere, and the rather tantalizing indications of its contacts with Jerusalem and Samaria, emphasize the importance of realizing how, in this whole period, the life of the Jewish community was not concentrated in one place. At a later date, from the time of Alexander, there were very important Jewish settlements in Egypt; it is not impossible that there had been other groups there during the Persian period. In Babylonia there were many who still remained, as is indicated directly by the names in the Murashu documents (cf. pp. 19 f.) and also by the repeated stimulus to new life which came from leaders there; in the period of restoration, again with Nehemiah and Ezra, and probably again subsequently, we can see that the impetus to reform, to rethinking, owed much to the developments within Babylonian Jewry.

C. *The Jewish Community in the Fourth Century*

The coming of Ezra in 398 B.C. (cf. note, pp. 191 ff.) marks another vital moment in the development as we are able to trace it. And the reference just made to the Egyptian situation may well be relevant to our understanding of his commission from the Persian authorities. As in the case of Zerubbabel and Nehemiah, we need to see the evidence from different viewpoints; to the Jewish community, the appointments had a meaning which could only be expressed in terms of a divinely ordered purpose; to the Persian authorities, other motives are at work, perhaps personal like those suggested in the Nehemiah narratives, for he enjoyed the favour of the ruler, and, more significantly, political motives and above all that of protecting the far-reaching extensions of Persian rule towards and into Egypt. With the loss of Egypt in 401, and a great deal of uncertainty elsewhere, some part of which is reflected in Xenophon's narrative in his *Anabasis*, the appointment of Ezra to go to Jerusalem with special powers may well be seen as part of a wider policy of getting reorganization and reform, and of conciliating and giving rights to certain subject peoples. In such a context, the work of Ezra makes good political sense.

Some of the details of the Ezra tradition are discussed in relation to the texts themselves (pp. 263 ff.). As in the discussion of Nehemiah, we may here draw together what may be said about the nature of Ezra's activity and its significance. Again part of the problem consists in assessing the evidence available to us; the account given of Ezra is partly in the first person and partly in the third. Does this perhaps represent separate sources? Or is it a matter of presentation only? Much of the language has been seen as so close to that of the Chronicler that it is very probable that, using already existing material, he wrote the account and gave his particular interpretation of what Ezra was. But that interpretation is itself significant, for even if we cannot at every point be sure just what powers Ezra had and what he was commissioned to do, the writer of the story saw his work as vitally important. Hence his portrayal of Ezra as commissioned by God through the person of the Persian ruler: '. . . the king granted him all that he asked, for the hand of the LORD his God was upon him' (Ezra 7[6]). He is described as commissioned to teach the law and to impose it on all his people in the whole of the province 'Beyond the River' (7[25]).

In addition, authorization is given to those who wish to return with him, and financial support for the enterprise and gifts for the temple. This is a very remarkable conception. Whether Ezra really had such wide powers has often been questioned, but this is less important than the recognition that such an idea opens up a new understanding of what it means to be a member of the Jewish community. In fact Ezra's work is described as taking place entirely in Jerusalem, and the reading and enforcement of the law there is central; but the view that the law is operative throughout the whole province, and that, whatever their particular political situation might be, Jewish residents in that area were subject to Jewish law, indicates an important point. A member of the community is not just one who lives in Jerusalem or the immediate neighbourhood, not just one who for historical reasons happens to be in the exiled group in Babylon or in a settlement in Egypt; he is any one of the people, known no doubt by his ancestry, who accepts the obligation of the law. What is more, though there are indications of various legal codes in the Old Testament, what Ezra is described as imposing is one law, and that one which is expounded so that its precise application is understood. The people is defined as that community which accepts, learns, and is governed by, the law.

This conception was subsequently to be of very great significance. In the Ezra narrative, it is linked, as is also the case with Nehemiah, with a great concern for the defining and protecting of the community; hence a policy on marriage with aliens which appears harsh and narrow. But it was not necessarily so narrow, for acceptance of the law, acceptance of its obligations and therefore of membership of the community, could open up the way for the entry into the Jewish people of others from outside, the proselytes who undertook such full acceptance. The understanding of the community as a people of the law, however much it might in certain circles seem to restrict, in fact offered an openness which was to be in large measure taken over in all its ruthless logic by the Christian community, for whom origin mattered not at all, and acceptance not of the law but of the person of Christ, mattered supremely. If Ezra has been charged with being the exponent of the narrowest views, and some who claimed to follow in his footsteps did have that narrowness of outlook, it is only right to acknowledge that this understanding of the nature of the people of God was immensely broad. From the point of view of the immediate problems of the community under Persian rule, it also offered much; for this people of God, not enjoying independence nor having complete control of its affairs, was nevertheless shown to be the true community, obedient to the law as Deuteronomy and the Priestly Work and other of the great presentations had said it must be. Small wonder that we may detect in the writings of the Chronicler, for whom this appears to mark the climax of his survey, such a sense of achievement, of finality, of divine blessing.

Of the further life of the community during the years that remained before the fall of Persian power at the advance of Alexander the Great, virtually nothing is known. Troubles in the west in the middle of the century could have brought difficulties for the Jerusalem Jews, but attempts at discovering reflections of these in the Old Testament literature are too uncertain to be of any value. The writings of the Chronicler probably belong to this time, but apart from what has just been said about the appreciation of Ezra and his work, light is shed only on certain aspects of the life of the community, particularly in regard to its worship, a subject to which the Chronicler devotes much attention.

The Chronicler's concern for a united people is expressed in his emphasis on the unity of all Israel in the time of David and in his repeated portrayal of the faithful worshippers of God in the north recognizing their fault and returning to Jerusalem—as in the time of Hezekiah (2 Chron. 30). This fits in well with his picture of Ezra, bringing about a new conception of one people obedient to the law. Does it perhaps direct attention to the particular problems of the time, problems of division and discord which the Chronicler was seeking to resolve by an appeal for a return to what he saw as the true faith expressed in worship at Jerusalem? It is often claimed that this is the case, and that his attention was especially directed to the problem of the Samaritan schism which appears to have come to a head in about this period. With so many uncertainties about the history of the schism it is very difficult to be sure; all our sources of information are rather heavily biased in one direction or the other. There may have been other stresses within the community's life at this time of which we have no direct information. But the Samaritan schism does provide an example of the kind of problem with which the community was faced; and this was a division which was in course of time to become hardened into a rigid separation.

The very use of the term 'schism' begs the question somewhat. A schismatic is one who breaks away from the main, the orthodox, line. For such a division to take place, there must be an orthodox position firmly in existence, and it is doubtful if this is a true view of the situation in the Persian period. Later, in the Greek and Roman periods, it is clear that there were many divisions and groups within Judaism—of which the early Christian community was one—and that it was only after A.D. 70 that a really clearly defined Jewish centre could be regarded as the orthodox line from which there could be dissension. From the viewpoint of various groups, such as that of Qumran or that of the Christian community, theirs was the true centre, the true descendant of the ancient faith, and all others could be regarded as dissident. So we must beware of applying too rigid standards to the discussion of the division between the Jerusalem religious community and that which came in time to be centred in Samaria and in particular at Shechem and Mount Gerizim.

To understand the development, we need to go back somewhat in history. It is clear from the earlier stages of Old Testament history that the division between the two areas, northern and southern, expressed in the two kingdoms which were united under the personal monarchy of David, was very deep-rooted; various views have been taken of the relationship and of its origins. Both areas claimed, and rightly, to worship Yahweh, the God of Israel; both laid claim to the same religious traditions, though with somewhat different emphases. (On these points, cf. Vol. 3, pp. 42 ff.) The division

SHECHEM AND MOUNT GERIZIM. The ancient religious centre of Shechem (see Gen. $12^{6\,ff.}$ and Josh. 24) came to be important for the Samaritan religious community (see Ecclesiasticus 50^{26} and also pp. 291 f. on the Samaria Papyri). Mount Gerizim (see Deut. 27^{12} for this as the 'mountain of blessing') rises beside Shechem on the south; Mount Ebal (see Deut. 27^{13} for this as the 'mountain of cursing') on the north. The slopes of Gerizim may be seen rising beyond the excavations of the pre-Israelite Shechem in the foreground. Other parts of the Shechem site were found to have been considerably rebuilt in about the fourth century B.C., perhaps in association with the development of the Samaritan community. Recent examination of the mountain top has disclosed clear evidence of a temple of the Roman period—of which there is also evidence on later coinage; this appears to have been built upon an earlier structure.

was sharpened by history, but there was a recognition that the two groups belonged together, a recognition expressed in the traditions of a common ancestry and a common faith. Our Old Testament comes to us eventually through the southern tradition, that of Judah; it therefore presents the north as dissident and the south as faithful, but preserves many traditions which reveal that this is too simple a view. The fall of the northern kingdom in 722 brought a new emphasis to

A MEMBER OF THE SAMARITAN COMMUNITY TODAY. The very small Samaritan community today is centred mainly in the neighbouring town of Nablus, just west of Shechem. The ancient Passover sacrifice is still celebrated; the community claims to possess very ancient scrolls of the Law (*tōrāh*). The scroll here being displayed to visitors is probably medieval, though claimed by the community to be much more ancient. The very existence of this small community demonstrates the tenacity of ancient practice and belief.

southern life; it is not therefore surprising to find northern traditions being used and elaborated in the south, as for example the prophecies of Hosea, nor to find that at the fall of Jerusalem, worshippers could come from 'Shechem and Shiloh and Samaria' (Jer. 41[5]; cf. pp. 17, 36 f.) to mourn at the devastated shrine.

The situation after the exile is more complex still. To understand it, we must also take account of the political aspects of the situation. In 722, with the exiling of some part of the population of the northern kingdom, colonists from elsewhere were brought in. It is by no means clear whether this was just a ruling group, settled, so it is stated, in the cities of Samaria (2 Kgs. 17^{24}), or whether it involved a more full-scale movement of peoples. The story in 2 Kgs. 17 tells of the problems of the time, and of the interpretation of a plague of lions as due to ignorance on the part of the settlers of the national deity of Israel. The story continues by suggesting that the settlers accepted worship of the God of Israel, but also continued worshipping their own gods, and the passage concludes 'so they do to this day' (2 Kgs. 17^{41}). The narrative here must be read in the light of later developments, and this includes the ultimate division between Jewish and Samaritan communities. According to Ezra 4^{1-5}, there were those after the exile who claimed, as worshippers of the same God, to be allowed to share in the building of the temple, having been settled in the land in 'the days of Esarhaddon king of Assyria'. This would suggest a later movement of population, of which we have no other evidence, unless, as is quite possible, there has been a confusion over the names of the Assyrian rulers. How far the settlers intermarried with the local population, we have no means of determining, nor how widespread was the alien religious practice. But it is not to be doubted that there were many who continued loyally in their ancestral faith. Among the ruling party in Samaria, there was at least sufficient acknowledgement of Yahweh for Sanballat to name his sons Delaiah and Shelemaiah, names indicating his acknowledgement of Yahweh as his God (cf. p. 253). Did he also worship other gods? Nothing in the narratives in the book of Nehemiah suggests this at all, and one would have thought that if he could be accused of being an alien in this sense, the point would have been made.

The opposition between Sanballat and Nehemiah was, in fact, at the political level, perhaps also at the economic if the redevelopment of Jerusalem seemed to threaten the advantages which Samaria had in the control of the economy. The only point at which religious issues came to the fore was over the position of Tobiah, one of Sanballat's associates in opposition to Nehemiah, for whom, quite improperly, the priest Eliashib in Jerusalem had provided a room in the temple buildings, a room which was thus alienated from its proper, sacred purpose (Neh. 13^{4-9}); and over the position of a grandson of this same priest, here described as high-priest, who was son-in-law to Sanballat (13^{28}). Both of these men Nehemiah drove out, but one can see that religious questions and political ones are here interwoven, and that in a sense the person most involved was actually the high-priest in Jerusalem. Josephus has a rather curious story which appears to be linked to this, though he places it in the time of Alexander's campaigns. According to this, one Manasseh, brother of the high-priest Jaddua, great-grandson of Eliashib, was son-in-law of Sanballat. (We do in fact now know that there was more than one governor of this name (cf. pp. 291 f.), but the resemblances in the story make it unlikely that the same situation arose again; it is more probable that there is a chronological muddle.) The daughter of Sanballat was regarded as a foreigner and Manasseh was instructed to divorce her, in line with the policy against foreign marriages seen in the work of both Nehemiah and Ezra. Manasseh explained to Sanballat that he did not wish to give up either his wife or his priestly office (he is said to have been partner with his brother in the high-priesthood). Sanballat offered to give him full priestly rights and a new temple; so he seceded and the temple was built on Mount Gerizim. Hence, so Josephus is saying, the origin of the Samaritan community involved a piece of rather sordid intrigue; it is indeed just the kind of garbled story which might circulate to give a false impression of the nature of an opposing religious group. The history of the Christian church is not without its examples of attempts at discrediting opponents by the elaboration of specious stories about them.

Can we get at the truth from the other end, from the later life and thought of the Samaritan community? Today, the Samaritans form a small isolated pocket of religious life, carrying on very clearly ancient practice, and claiming authority and antiquity for their position. Although their writings show that their ideas have developed over the centuries, it is evident that they can best be thought of as extremely conservative in outlook. There is nothing to suggest that they were involved in alien religious practice or belief as some of the stories about them state. Such stories are part of a propagandist tradition in some Jewish circles. The New Testament too, while showing some influence of anti-Samaritan ideas (notably in John 4), shows much more clearly an acknowledgement of the Samaritan faith and life. Some affinities have been found with the Qumran community. All this suggests the possibility that the Samaritan community was in origin a conservative protest against Jerusalem practice. If the tradition is right which places the building of the temple on Gerizim in the time of Alexander—Josephus repeats this when he records its destruction by John Hyrcanus (134–104 B.C.)—then we might perhaps see this religious group as one which seceded from Jerusalem, as the Qumran community was later to do and as later still the Christian community did, in protest against its claims. There could have been personal quarrels involved; Josephus might be recording a piece of true tradition though in a muddled form. There may have been political aspects; the governor in Samaria might well offer his protection to a group which was in opposition to Jerusalem. But the Samaritan religious community itself seems quite clearly to have been concerned to re-establish a more ancient, and no doubt they believed, truer faith and practice by going back to the ancient religious settlement of Shechem (cf. Josh. 24) and to the sacred hill of Gerizim (cf. Deut. 27[12]). The name 'Samaritan' is itself a nickname; the group thought of itself as the *shōmerīm*—'keepers' (i.e. of the true law and tradition).

The whole problem remains at many points unresolved; it provides an illustration of the difficulties of interpreting the developments in the Persian period and later. But it also opens a window on the currents and cross-currents of religious life in this formative time.

Additional Note on the chronology of Nehemiah and Ezra

The arguments for the dating accepted in this volume are set out briefly in the first volume in this series, pp. 176–8, but it is desirable that they should also be presented here.

At a first glance, the traditional order appears clear. Ezra's activity begins in the 7th year of Artaxerxes (Ezra 7^{1}), his journey lasting from the first to the fifth months of that year. In the ninth and tenth months (no year mentioned), Ezra dealt with the problem of foreign marriages (Ezra 9–10). In the 20th year of Artaxerxes (Neh. 1^{1}), Nehemiah was granted permission to go to Jerusalem to rebuild the walls. According to Neh. 5^{14}, he was governor until the 32nd year. The rebuilding of the walls was completed during the 20th year in the month Elul, the sixth month (6^{15}). Neh. 7^{73} refers to a seventh month—no year is indicated—in which Ezra read the law to the people. The dedication of the walls is described in Neh. 12^{27-43} and though not dated must be assumed to have taken place later than the religious celebration on the 24th day of the seventh month mentioned in 9^{1}. Nehemiah's second period of activity is described in Neh. 13^{6} as later than the 32nd year. The Persian king is named throughout as Artaxerxes. If the same king is intended in all the references, then it could be either Artaxerxes I (465–424) or Artaxerxes II (404–358), but the evidence of the Elephantine papyri virtually excludes Artaxerxes II for Nehemiah (cf. pp. 286 f.).

This traditional account is still accepted by many scholars, who feel that the difficulties raised by the alternatives are too great. It must be clearly stated that the alternatives cannot be proved in any absolute manner, but the traditional view raises substantial problems, and these must be recognized. First, the gap of thirteen years between Ezra's arrival in Jerusalem and his carrying out of the major task for which he was sent, namely the implementation of the law, is quite unexplained. Theories that he met with this or that difficulty are without clear foundation, since in any case the foreign marriage reform is described as being put through at once. There is absolutely nothing anywhere in the text to provide a clue as to why such a delay should have occurred. Second, as the text is presented, Nehemiah and Ezra were operating at the same time in Jerusalem; but they appear together only at two points. In the story of the reading of the law in Neh. 8, 'Nehemiah, who was the governor' is mentioned in v. 9 but he plays no part in the events, and the corresponding passage in 1 Esdras 9[49] refers only to the governor, with no mention of a name. In 10[1] Nehemiah's name appears at the head of a list of those who adhered to a new covenant; but in this list Ezra is not mentioned, so that it would appear that the list has nothing to do with the passage which precedes. In Neh. 12[26] Nehemiah and Ezra are both mentioned, but this is simply in a summarizing statement commenting on the lists of names which precede. In Neh. 12[36], in the narrative of the dedication of the walls, 'Ezra the scribe' is named, but in view of his importance it is odd that this name is at the very end of the list; it looks suspiciously like an addition. The serious point here is that if these two men really were working in Jerusalem at the same time, there is no indication of any real contact between them. Their interests were not identical, but there is nevertheless considerable overlap; the supposition that they were at loggerheads is nowhere implied or stated. To these major points, we may add the recognition of the evidence for the dating of Nehemiah (cf. p. 173), and the implications of this for the date of Ezra.

If Ezra and Nehemiah were not contemporaries, then two problems have to be resolved. (1) To what dates are they to be assigned? (2) How can we explain the present disorder of the material?

The first question can be answered in three main ways: (1) Ezra entirely preceded Nehemiah; (2) Ezra followed Nehemiah but still within the reign of Artaxerxes I, some measure of overlap being then possible; (3) Ezra was active in the reign of Artaxerxes II, whereas Nehemiah worked under Artaxerxes I. Each of these answers has to be considered both in regard to evidence for and against, and in regard to the second question;

for in each case a comparable modification of the material is necessary.

(1) If Ezra came entirely first and was active in the 7th year of Artaxerxes I, then we must suppose that the reading of the law took place speedily after his arrival. This may most readily be done by assuming that Ezra 9–10 really belongs after the reading of the law. The month numbers follow neatly on this supposition—which is likely to be a very sound one—for then Ezra's arrival is followed by the reading of the law, and it is in the light of this that the foreign marriage problem becomes acute. The present order of the Ezra material can be explained as due to the Chronicler, who preferred a theologically significant order to a merely chronological one. The climax of Ezra's work is in the reading and acceptance of the law, and such a climax should not only come at the end, its celebration should have been preceded by the removal of alien elements. So a purified community hears and accepts the law. If this view is accepted, the arrangement of the Nehemiah material interrupts the Ezra narrative. There is no obvious reason why it was so placed since by its dates it would appear to belong later. Furthermore, the fact that Eliashib was high priest in the time of Nehemiah (cf. Neh. 13[28]) creates difficulty in view of the appearance of Johanan (Jehohanan) in Ezra 10[6] as son of Eliashib; Johanan appears in the list of priests in Neh. 12[22] as grandson of Eliashib, and appears in the Elephantine papyri as high priest in Jerusalem in the last years of the fifth century. It is this indication from the priestly line which most strongly suggests that Nehemiah in fact came before Ezra.

(2) It has been suggested that there is an error in the date in Ezra 7[7], and that reference should be to a later date in the reign of Artaxerxes I, probably the 37th year. This would place Ezra at about the time of Nehemiah's second period of activity; it has been suggested that they came together and that subsequently Ezra was active alone. This hypothesis allows for the appearance of the names together in Neh. 8[9], though probably not in Neh. 12[36]; it probably allows time for Johanan

to have become high priest, or at least for him to be an active participant. It has to be assumed that after the text had been accidentally (or deliberately) altered at Ezra 7[7], the material was rearranged because it was now supposed that Ezra had arrived much earlier. The literary aspects of this view are very involved, and its greatest weakness is that it is based upon an entirely hypothetical textual error.

(3) The view that Ezra came only later under Artaxerxes II, in 398 B.C., entails a complete separation of the activities of the two men. In this respect it resembles view (1) and the same ordering of the Ezra material is appropriate. But it has the advantage that it meets the problem of the high priestly names quite squarely. We still have the literary problem of why the different source material was arranged as it now is.

As can be seen from this brief outline of the various views, there is no neat and watertight answer to the problem. The literary aspects of it are very difficult to disentangle. Here a question arises in regard to the date at which the Chronicler compiled the work; for if he was responsible for the present order of the material, then we must ask how he could so misunderstand the events as to arrange them in such a confusing order. Again, however, it must be emphasized that this is a problem whatever view we take, for in addition to the indications already noted here of disorder in the material, there are other features of the arrangement—particularly in the Nehemiah narratives—which raise difficult questions.

The date of the Chronicler is not certain (cf. p. 295). If he worked very late—e.g. in the Greek period, perhaps in the third century B.C.—then the time lapse between Ezra and himself is long enough for misunderstanding, even if Ezra worked in about 398 B.C. But if, as seems more probable, the Chronicler was active in about the middle of the fourth century, not more than a generation after this late dating for Ezra, then the disorder would be very difficult to explain. Not impossible even then, for we can see enough of the Chronicler's practice of arranging material in a theologically significant order to realize that he subordinated mere history to meaning.

Nevertheless, the problem is a difficult one. This point militates against the later dating for Ezra, though not absolutely. For there is one further possibility which deserves serious consideration. The Nehemiah narratives clearly form a quite independent source. Is it possible that the Chronicler's work was originally composed without any reference to Nehemiah at all? We have already seen (p. 192) that 1 Esdras provides a sequence which does not include Nehemiah. The Chronicler's work shows many signs of having been subsequently enlarged. May not the Nehemiah material have been inserted, at what appeared to be the appropriate points, by way of setting this great leader alongside Ezra? Such a supposition cannot be proved, but there are several points, quite apart from this question of the chronology of Ezra and Nehemiah, which suggest that it may be the right one.

First, we may note that in many ways the two figures overlap; they perform similar actions, and subsequently traditions concerning them run in some measure parallel (cf. pp. 179 f., 266 for a comment on their relation to the formation of the Scriptures); in the present form of the text some conflation has taken place of a kind which we find also in many narratives in the Old Testament where divergent traditions lie alongside one another. A similar situation can also be seen in the interweaving and overlapping of the Elijah and Elisha traditions. Second, we may note that in Ecclesiasticus (49^{11-13}) and also in 2 Maccabees (cf. p. 179), Nehemiah appears without any mention of Ezra; this would suggest that there were circles in which the Nehemiah traditions were treasured, and someone from these circles might have introduced the Nehemiah material. Third, we may observe that whereas Ezra and his policy accord very closely with the general line of the Chronicler's thinking, particularly in the emphasis on the law, on purity, on the priestly functions, the rather more nationalistic element in the Nehemiah tradition is perhaps slightly less in that line. But the addition of such material would be very appropriate in a moment of national upsurge, and the most obvious moment would be the second century when the upholding of Jewish traditions was an urgent problem. A small detail here is suggestive; revival of Hebrew (alongside Aramaic) appears to have taken place in the Maccabaean wars (a similar tendency is evident in the Bar Kochba revolt of A.D. 132–5, and also in modern times), and the emphasis in Neh. 13^{23-27} on the preservation of 'the language of Judah' would make Nehemiah's work seem an important anticipation of the nationalism of the second century B.C. The references in Ecclesiasticus and 2 Maccabees would point in the same direction. If such an insertion of the Nehemiah material is assumed, some of the details of the present order may be due to the way in which the Chronicler ordered his Ezra narrative (cf. above) and to the way in which the compiler of the Nehemiah memoir set out his account—not in chronological order, but as he saw its meaning; other details may be due to the dovetailing and harmonizing process, a process akin to that which may be traced in many Old Testament narratives.

On the basis of such arguments, the present writer is persuaded that the 398 B.C. date for Ezra is the most likely. It enables us to make good sense of all the material; it provides a realistic historical setting for Ezra. On our present evidence, it can be only a hypothesis, but it is one which, since it was first suggested in the last two decades of the nineteenth century, has been often re-examined and challenged but nevertheless remains very widely accepted. Other less important points, which are sometimes introduced as arguments in favour of the later date for Ezra, but which really hardly prove anything by themselves, would fit neatly into this rearrangement. Thus it is sometimes claimed that the more radical policy of Ezra on foreign marriages is better seen as following the less drastic actions of Nehemiah, rather than preceding them. The impression of the Ezra narrative is of a people living in fairly large numbers in an already re-established (and walled, Ezra 9^{9}) city; this would fit well after Nehemiah's work of rebuilding and repopulating.

References to fuller discussions may be found on p. 353.

NOTES ON SELECTED PASSAGES

A. THE CYRUS CYLINDER

During the excavations in Babylon in the last century, a baked clay cylinder was discovered which shows how the successful Cyrus was presented to his Babylonian subjects. In the time of their distress:

(Marduk) had compassion. He scoured all the lands for a friend, seeking for the upright prince whom he would have to take his hand. He called Cyrus, king of Anshan. He nominated him to be ruler over all. . . . Marduk the great lord, compassionate to his people, looked with gladness on (his) good deeds and his upright intentions. He gave orders that he go against his city Babylon. He had him take the road to Babylon and he went at his side like a friend and comrade. His vast army, whose number like the waters of a river cannot be determined, with their armour held close, moved forward beside him. He got him into his city Babylon without fighting or battle. He averted hardship to Babylon. He put an end to the power of Nabonidus the king who did not show him reverence. The entire population of Babylon, the whole of Sumer and Akkad, princes and governors, bowed to him (Cyrus) and kissed his feet. They were glad that he was king. . . .

A text found at Ur describes the victory of Cyrus as granted by the power of Sin, the Moon-God. We have seen that the Second Isaiah attributes his calling to Yahweh, the God of Israel (p. 113).

The text continues, making Cyrus himself speak in the first person:

I am Cyrus, king of the world, the great king, mighty king, king of Babylon, king of the land of Sumer and Akkad, king of the four quarters, son of Cambyses, great king, king of Anshan, grandson of Cyrus, great king, king of Anshan. . . . When I, well-disposed, entered Babylon, I set up the seat of dominion in the royal palace amidst jubilation and rejoicing. Marduk the great god caused the big-hearted inhabitants of Babylon to . . . me. I sought daily to worship him. . . .

The blessing of Marduk on the royal house is affirmed, and the submission of all the kings, including: 'all the kings of the

THE 'CYRUS CYLINDER'. For an account of this document, cf. pp. 197 ff.

West Country who dwelt in tents, brought me their heavy tribute and kissed my feet in Babylon'. The text speaks of the ruined sanctuaries in many lands of the gods who had been brought to Babylon. These

> I returned to their places and housed them in lasting abodes. I gathered together all their inhabitants and restored (to them) their dwellings.

The text closes with a prayer for blessing:

> May all the gods whom I have placed within their sanctuaries address a daily prayer in my favour before Bel and Nabu, that my days be long, and may they say to Marduk my lord, 'May Cyrus the king who reveres thee, and Cambyses his son . . .' (Text quoted from *DOTT*, pp. 92–94.)

The opening chapters of Ezra (cf. pp. 201 ff.) offer their own interpretation of Cyrus' actions in relation to the Jewish community. The rebuilding of the temple at Jerusalem is there too linked with the requirement that 'they may . . . pray for the life of the king (of Persia) and his sons' (Ezra 6[10]).

The religious policy of the Persian rulers may be further illustrated by brief reference to inscriptions which deal with other occasions when they showed concern about the religious life of subject peoples. Cambyses, successor to Cyrus, campaigned in Egypt; although he appears to have destroyed much and shown great cruelty, he also showed concern for religious tradition. An inscription tells how he purified the worship at the shrine of the goddess Neith in the Delta city of Sais. '. . . the temple was purified . . . the property of the deity was given to the great mother goddess, Neith, and to the great gods in Sais, as of old.' (Quoted from M. Noth, *History of Israel* (London (1960), p. 305.)

For Darius I, evidence is provided by an inscription in Greek from Asia Minor. Its authenticity has been doubted, for it is available only in a late form, from the Roman period. Does its present form perhaps owe something to a desire upon the part of those who inscribed it to glorify their own deity? This may well be so, but this does not prevent its being based on an original text (cf. the discussion of Cyrus' decree in Ezra 1 and 6; pp. 202 ff., 208 ff.).

> The king of kings, Darius, son of Hystaspes, to his slave Gadatas, thus speaks: I have learned that you do not in all respects obey my injunctions . . . because you set at nought my policy towards the gods, I will give you, if you do not change, a proof of my injured feelings. For you have enforced tribute from the holy gardeners of Apollo and have ordered them to dig unhallowed ground, not knowing the mind of my forefathers towards the god, who told the Persians the whole truth. (Quoted from A. T. Olmstead, *History of Palestine and Syria* (Grand Rapids, 1931, 1965), p. 571. The last phrase, though not entirely unlike the claims of the Cyrus Cylinder, does look rather like religious propaganda.)

For a later Persian ruler, Darius II, we may compare the evidence of the Elephantine papyri (cf. pp. 288 f.).

B. THE 'VERSE ACCOUNT OF NABONIDUS'

This poem provides an account of Nabonidus' reign and of his overthrow and replacement by Cyrus as ruler. Parts of it are not clear because the text is fragmentary or difficult to interpret. It belongs to the reign of Cyrus and has something of a propagandist tendency, praising Cyrus for his restoring of order after Nabonidus.

[. . . whatever he (Nabonidus) had cre]ated, he (Cyrus) let fire burn up.
[. . . what he (Nabonidus) had cre]ated, he (Cyrus) fed to the flames.
[To the inhabitants of] Babylon, a joyful heart is given now.
[They are like prisoners when] the prisons are opened,
[Liberty is restored to] those who were surrounded by oppression.
[All rejoice] to look upon him as king.

The events of Nabonidus' reign are related, but in such a way as to imply the improper conduct of which he was guilty. Thus he is described as setting up the representation of a new deity, with a moon symbol, promising to build a temple, declaring:

When I have fully executed what I have planned,
I shall lead him by the hand and establish him in his seat.
(Yet) till I have achieved this, till I have obtained what is my desire,
I shall omit (all) festivals, I shall order (even) the New Year's Festival to cease.

It describes his expedition to Teima and his defeat of the prince of Teima:

And he, himself, took his residence in [Tei]ma, the forces of Akkad [were also stationed] there.
He made the town beautiful, built (there) [his palace] like the palace in Babylon. . . .

(Text quoted from *ANET*, pp. 312–15.)

The poem, placed alongside such a document as that of Cyrus' cylinder (cf. pp. 197 ff.), reveals much about the situation at the time of the political change-over from Babylonian to

Persian rule. At the same time, these documents show how many problems of interpretation exist in ancient writings. Neither of them can be regarded as providing a straight account of events. Concealed within them is valuable information, and the fact that here we find details about Nabonidus' building activities set in a context of criticism of him and approval of his overthrow, illustrates some important points which are relevant also for the study of Old Testament documents. These too often contain valuable historical information, but it is contained within writings offering a theological interpretation; what may well be sound and historical is given a slant due to the viewpoint of the author. The Old Testament documents are further complicated by the fact that they have been handed down and reinterpreted over the centuries within the life of an active religious community. They are not, like this poem or the 'Cyrus cylinder', writings turned up by an excavator's spade in recent years, untouched since the moment at which they were buried with the destruction of the cities of the past.

C. EZRA 1–6

These chapters form a part of the large work covering the books of Chronicles, Ezra, and Nehemiah, conveniently described as the Work of the Chronicler. A fuller discussion of the nature and purpose of this Work is given on pp. 294 ff. For our present purpose it is important to recognize that these chapters in Ezra offer the only biblical *narrative* evidence for the period of the restoration and rebuilding of the temple. (Indirect evidence, of considerable significance, is to be found in prophetic writings.) In handling this material, we must take due account of the author's method, of his interpretation of history in the light of his understanding of the divine purpose, and of the problems of deciding just what sources were available to him. We should expect, from our knowledge of the author's work elsewhere, to find considerable deliberate arrangement of the material according to a particular theological interpretation, and this means that the historical order and chronology may well need readjustment. So far as sources are concerned, we may observe that part of this section is in Hebrew and part in Aramaic; 4^{8}–6^{18} is in Aramaic (so also is 7^{12-26} which we shall consider later, cf. pp. 268 ff.). This bilingual character of the book is not easily explained; another example is to be found in the book of Daniel, and this too presents difficult problems (cf. Vol. 5, pp. 222 f.). It may be that the author of the book of Ezra had at his disposal two groups of material, one in Hebrew and the other in Aramaic, and that he preferred to offer these in the language in which he had them. But even so the exact relationship between the information they contain is not easy to sort out in detail.

1 *The first return*

The opening words (vv. 1–3*a*) overlap the concluding words of 2 Chron. 36^{22-23}, differing only in a single word. This overlap provides a necessary link because in the Hebrew Bible Ezra-Nehemiah stands before 1 and 2 Chronicles, the latter being the last part of the canon. These words thus provide both an encouraging ending to the Bible in its Hebrew form and a link to the sequel to be found in this book.

1. The emphasis on the fulfilment of prophecy in relation to the exile is a theme in the Chronicler's interpretation; disaster was because of the failure of Zedekiah to hear Jeremiah's words (2 Chron. 35^{12}), the exile fulfilled his word (2 Chron. 35^{21}), and so the restoration is linked, though quite loosely, to what Jeremiah had said. We cannot point to a precise saying of Jeremiah for this, though a comparison could be made with Jer. $27^{21\text{f.}}$, with the seventy-year prophecy (25^{12}, 29^{10}), and with other general statements in Jer. 30–33. There is a much closer link with the prophecies of the Second Isaiah (Isa. 44^{24}–45^{7}).

2–4. The words of Cyrus' proclamation are set out, and with this passage may be compared the alternative form in 6^{3-5}, which is in Aramaic. If we make a comparison with the Cyrus cylinder (pp. 197 ff.), we can see the general similarity of the proclamation as given here to other statements of the intentions of Cyrus. For the peoples of the west it would be most natural to find the Aramaic language used as the official means of communication. Already at an earlier period (cf. 2 Kgs. 18^{26}) Aramaic had such an international status, being then understood by officials in Jerusalem though not by the ordinary population. After the exile, Aramaic continued to be so used and its various dialects also came to be more generally used by the Jewish population in different areas where they lived. This might seem to suggest that the form of the proclamation in chapter 6 is more original, but it is better to assume that we have two accounts, based either on documents or on traditions of the decree, each representing a slightly different use of the tradition.

Cyrus claims that his conquests are due to *The LORD, the God of Heaven*, and that this God *has charged me to build him a house at Jerusalem* (v. 2). Thus, to use the language of the Cyrus cylinder, he could be said to 'restore (Yahweh) to his dwelling' (cf. p. 198); and no doubt the Persian government expected that prayer would be offered at Jerusalem for the King and the royal line. In chapter 1 the emphasis then rests on the permission for the exiles in Babylonia to return to Jerusalem, supported by the inhabitants of the place in which they lived. This is an Exodus motif, for as at the Exodus those who go to the promised land carry gifts of silver and gold (cf. Exod. 12$^{35\text{f.}}$). Thus the return is seen as a new Exodus.

5–11. The response to the proclamation is really a response to the working of the spirit of God (a comparison might be made with Hag. 1$^{12-14}$; cf. Ezra 5$^{1-2}$). We may observe that the words 'stirred up', common in the Second Isaiah, occur more than once in this passage. The sacred vessels are also brought out to be restored to Jerusalem (v. 7). This is a theme common in the writings of this period but one which raises a number of questions. In 2 Kgs. 25$^{14\text{ff.}}$ we are told that the vessels of the temple were taken by the conquerors; in 2 Chron. 36^{19} the 'precious vessels' are said to have been destroyed. Jer. 27–28, making reference to the fall of Jerusalem in 597, speaks of the restoration of the vessels taken then. Dan. 5 offers a later tradition about the sacrilegious use of the vessels by Belshazzar. Rather than try to sort this out and attempt a harmonizing of the various elements, we should recognize that they are used not to provide historical information but theological comment. The disaster of the exile meant the loss—by destruction and as booty—of the sacred vessels; restoration of the temple involves a recovery of the continuity of the past. So the words of judgement are answered by words of hope, and the new temple represents a restoration in the fullest sense; continuity with the past is re-established and the people of God, in the full sense, comes into being again.

The leader appointed to bring the treasures back to Jerusalem is *Sheshbazzar the prince of Judah* (v. 8). We do not know who he was; at an early date, he was thought to be identica with Shenazzar, son of Shealtiel, son of Jehoiachin, the captive king (cf. 1 Chron. 3^{17}) and thus uncle to Zerubbabel (described as 'son of Shealtiel' in 3^{2} and Hag. 1^{1}, the word 'son' perhaps being used more loosely for 'descendant'). It would not be surprising if the Persians chose a man of the Davidic family to control the restoration, but it is somewhat odd that Sheshbazzar is described by the expression *prince of Judah* which merely means 'one of the leading men' and that no indication is given of his family (contrast Zerubbabel in chapter 3). His function is not clearly defined; he is to supervise what happens, and in particular appears to be accountable to the royal treasurer Mithredath for the vessels. In 5^{14} he is said to have been appointed 'governor' by Cyrus; but the term is a very broad one, and perhaps may suggest simply the position of a commissioner whose appointment was limited in scope and perhaps in period.

How far was there a full-scale return at this period? The chapter which follows gives a list of returned exiles, but since 2^{2} refers to various leaders, not including Sheshbazzar, it may be that the list is a document from a different period, so that its numbers ($2^{64f.}$) do not necessarily refer to this one return. (The same document is used also in Neh. 7.) The impression given by the prophetic books of Haggai and Zech. 1–8 is that conditions were hardly such that more than a small body returned; the absence of any mention of permission to return in 6^{3-5} is not necessarily of any consequence, since that passage is concerned simply with the authorization to rebuild. Restoration implies resettlement, but this was probably on a relatively modest scale.

3^{1}–$4^{5, 24}$ *The beginning of restoration*

1. The mention of *the seventh month* appears to imply that these events took place shortly after those described in chapter 1, but we observe that Sheshbazzar is not mentioned, and instead we have Zerubbabel (in Haggai he is called 'governor') and Jeshua (Joshua) the priest (described in Haggai and Zech. 1–8 as 'high priest'). This opening verse is in fact very much a link verse, and it may conceal a quite considerable passage of time. In v. 8, there is a reference to the 'second year of the coming', and a comparison with the words of Haggai and Zechariah strongly suggests that this refers to the beginning of the reign of Darius I. The Chronicler has telescoped events, and, in order to show that rebuilding was fully undertaken immediately and also to explain why the temple was only completed over twenty years after Cyrus' edict, has transferred to the period of Cyrus events which appear to have taken place only under Darius. This is effected by the use of the little narrative of 4^{1-3}, with the comments in 4^{4-5} which record the frustrating of the building. In 3^{3-7} an account is given of the re-establishing of the altar, and of the celebration of the autumnal festival of 'booths' or tabernacles. The RSV wording: 'the foundation of the temple . . . was not yet laid' (v. 6), is a somewhat misleading rendering of the text. It is much more probable that the text means more simply: 'the temple was not yet restored' (a similar sense should be given to Hag. 2^{18}), for the word has a much wider sense, and no reference

is made to some supposed formal stone-laying ceremony. This first stage was marked only by such clearing and repair as was needed to enable the sacrificial ritual to be undertaken adequately. Verse 3 indicates fear of other peoples as a factor. The text is very obscure: it may refer to 'enmity', suggesting that this modest undertaking was all that was possible because of opposition. This would fit well with the general picture given by the Chronicler. It is possible that, having a tradition of this re-establishment of the altar in the early years of the restoration, he has associated it with Zerubbabel whom he transposes to that moment; it is also possible that even this only took place nearly twenty years later. It is not unreasonable to suppose that some move was made under Cyrus, but we have to remember that for the Chronicler there could not have been any real religious life in Judah during the exile (cf. 2 Chron. 36[21]). In his view, a completely new beginning had to be made at the moment of Cyrus' decree.

Verse 7 already points to a more definite beginning, and vv. 8–13 trace a new start, dated in the second year. This is represented as set under the control of the Levites; the concern which is expressed in Ezekiel for purity in the new temple is shown in this. Again in this passage, we should probably understand the reference to 'foundation' as meaning really 'restoration' so that the whole section refers to the rebuilding as a whole. Just as in Hag. 2[3], there is a comparison suggested with the former temple, and weeping at the deficiencies shown by the restored building; but it is also emphasized that a great celebration of rejoicing could be held. It really is most likely that this is one description of the actual rebuilding, and that it is in part paralleled by the narratives of chapters 5–6. The meaning of v. 11 is not certain; probably there is no reference to a particular method of singing psalms, but simply to the response of praise which is evoked by the appearance of the priests.

4[1–5] is a very difficult passage. It must be understood in the context of the Chronicler's view that only returned exiles could have been instrumental in rebuilding the temple, though he does allow that others who have suitably purified themselves may eventually join them in worship (cf. 6^{21}). It must also be recognized that the motif of opposition developed here and in vv. 4–5 provides a bridge between what the Chronicler saw as a first stage in rebuilding—set in the reign of Cyrus—and the second stage which is set in the reign of Darius. We do not know who *the adversaries* (v. 1) are. *Judah and Benjamin* describes the true people of God, those who remained faithful to Jerusalem and the Davidic line after the reign of Solomon. The *adversaries* describe themselves as being aliens, brought into the land in the time of Esarhaddon king of Assyria (681–669 B.C.). We have no other record of a settlement in that period, though Assyrian domination in Palestine could have brought it about. It is possible, however, that a confusion has been made between one ruler of Assyria and another, and that this passage really contains a somewhat garbled reference to the settlement of aliens at the time of Samaria's fall in 722 B.C. (cf. 2 Kgs. 17). The point being made is that these people are alien, in spite of their professions of faith in the same God. Perhaps the most likely explanation is that a tradition of religious divisions in the restoration period—and such divisions may have arisen from a variety of causes—has been linked by the Chronicler with divisions known to him, probably including what was later to be called the Samaritan schism (cf. pp. 185 ff.) though not necessarily this alone. Such alien groups, he believes, prevented the full restoration in the reign of Cyrus.

The historical problems of this passage are very great indeed. Both in these comments and in those on Haggai and Zech. 1–8, and also in the general account of the restoration period (cf. pp. 163 ff.), an attempt is made at showing possible sequences of events and possible explanations of the nature of the sources at our disposal. But we cannot be certain. The theological construction which has been placed upon the source material is, however, of very great interest. If we cannot be sure just what happened, we may nevertheless see the way in which the Chronicler could present a picture of the period which stresses the faith and persistence of those who returned, and which reveals the working of divine grace to remove the obstacles to full restoration.

5–6 *Another account of the rebuilding*

The Chronicler's presentation of the period of rebuilding is punctuated by interruptions and questionings. We have already seen this in 3^{1}–4^{5}, and a further opposition theme follows in $4^{6\,\text{ff.}}$ though this is totally out of its proper chronological position, for it belongs to the reign of a later ruler, Artaxerxes (cf. p. 175). This too is used to emphasize the difficulties of restoration; 4^{24} links it to the temple, though it is really concerned with the walls of the city. In chapters 5–6 a similar pattern of questioning and reassurance appears.

5^{1-2} brings a new summons to Zerubbabel and Jeshua (Joshua) to rebuild, attributed to the activity of the two prophets Haggai and Zechariah. The work of rebuilding is described as proceeding with prophetic support.

5^{3-5} introduces a question concerning the rebuilding; this differs in tone from the sharp opposition themes of the previous chapters, for it is expressly indicated that the work continued, since God protected his people and prevented any stoppage of the building. Thus the inquiry is depicted in a more positive manner, and serves to lead into a narrative which emphasizes the propriety of the rebuilding programme. The theme of Cyrus, the divinely appointed protector and instigator of rebuilding, is now elaborated.

5^{6-17} set out a letter of inquiry to Darius. It is couched in moderate and courteous terms, describing the diligence with which the rebuilding is being undertaken. It is clear that in this account the authorities making the inquiry are shown as sensible men, aware of the reputation of Jerusalem (v. 8). Verses 11–16 contain a very interesting statement of the Jewish view of what is going on, expressing their conviction of the vital importance of the temple, acknowledging the judgement which had come upon them, and describing the events by which the present situation had been reached. The beginning of work is attributed to Sheshbazzar, and it is said that rebuilding has been in progress ever since his time.

6^{1-12} record the search in the archives and the discovery of the original edict of Cyrus (cf. the account of this in chapter 1 and the comments on this). The result is the reaffirmation by Darius of the terms of the decree; the builders are not only given full permission to continue but are assured of substantial support from the provincial governor. Judgement is pronounced upon anyone who alters the edict or who in any way attempts to destroy the temple at Jerusalem.

6^{13-18} describe the completion of the temple and the dedication celebration in the sixth year of Darius, again with emphasis on the part played by the prophets.

6^{19-22} appear now as a simple continuation of the narrative, with an account of a Passover celebration undertaken by returned exiles and those who separated themselves from impure contacts. An interval of only a few weeks lies between the third day of Adar (the twelfth month, 6^{15}) and the Passover on the fourteenth of the first month (6^{19}). But the fact that the whole section from 5^{1} to 6^{18} is in Aramaic (as is also 4^{8-24} which may in part account for its present position in the book) whereas vv. 19–22 are in Hebrew, indicates that we have here a placing together of originally independent material. Is this perhaps the original conclusion to the narrative of rebuilding which we have seen in chapter 3? In 3^{8} we have the appointment of overseers for the rebuilding, dated to the second month; 6^{19} presents events which happened at the beginning of a new year, though we have no means of knowing whether this was the next year or several years later. The inclusion of the Aramaic section has resulted in a complete reshaping of the narrative.

Again in these chapters we observe the complexity of the historical problems. But again we may recognize that, with all the uncertainties that remain both in regard to details of interpretation and in regard to the order of events, we have a picture of restoration which is meaningful. Here in particular, the emphasis on the benevolence and favour of the Persian authorities shows an aspect of the Chronicler's thought which is important. To his people, living as they do under alien rule and no doubt sometimes chafing at it and wishing for independence, the reminder is given that it is possible for them to be the true people of God, to worship him and obey his law. Is there an implicit warning of the dangers of seeking to gain independence by political action? The heroism of faithful Jews in the second century B.C. and later attempts under Roman rule at winning freedom cannot conceal the fact that military and political action brought dire results, not least in the sharp divisions within the community, the intense rivalries and hostilities which led to so much disaster. The Chronicler's belief that the true life of his people could develop under alien rule was to be borne out again and again in subsequent history when the true witness of Judaism was to be seen in little Jewish communities which maintained their faith even in the most adverse circumstances.

D. HAGGAI

Nothing is known about the prophet Haggai apart from what may be deduced from the book which bears his name and the brief indications in Ezra 5[1] and 6[14] which speak of the impetus provided by him and his contemporary Zechariah in the restoration of the temple in the time of Darius I. It would seem not unlikely that the statements made in these latter passages are dependent on the prophetic tradition found in the two books of Haggai and Zechariah, and there are some indications to suggest that the collecting and presenting of the words of these prophets was finally undertaken in a period not far removed from that of the Chronicler. The sermon style of exposition found in both books and the exhortations based on the preaching of the prophets are not unlike what is to be found in the Chronicler's work. Such exhortations are particularly to be found in Zech. 1^{1-6} and $8^{9\text{ff.}}$ and perhaps also in Hag. 1^{12-14}.

Although the two prophets appear together in the book of Ezra and there are certain similarities—particularly in the datings—between the two collections, there is no real cross-reference from the one to the other, and it is a mistake therefore to treat them as if they were necessarily working together and still more as if they both said exactly the same thing. The concern of both with the rebuilding of the temple is clear; but this is by no means the only element in their teaching, and we gain a better understanding of the period if we recognize that in the same situation two prophets could offer somewhat different emphases and different interpretations of the needs of the time. It is also important to realize that the interpretation of the history of the period in Ezra 1–6, thought not unrelated to the evidence found in Haggai and Zech. 1–8, is not the same as the views presented by the prophetic teaching. We must beware of an oversimple acceptance of the evidence of the prophetic books, which needs careful interpretation and is at many points difficult to understand fully; this prophetic material is itself presented and interpreted, and it probably represents only a part of what the prophets actually said. We must therefore appreciate it as a view of the period, not so much concerned with giving precise historical description, as with interpretation.

The words of Haggai appear now in a carefully arranged presentation, with precise dates. It is not completely in order, for there is an odd, unattached date in 1^{15}. Separate elements have been combined into larger units, as seems likely in 1^{1-11} and in 2^{10-19}. But the main emphases of the prophet are clear. The rebuilding of the temple has absolute priority because it is the centre of the life of the community, the place in which God reveals himself in glory. No discouragement must be allowed to delay the rebuilding; God himself promises to set his glory in their midst. Hope centres on this, and various disasters are to be understood as due to the people's failure to respond. A yet more glorious future is at hand, for this is a new age in which God in his temple stands at the centre of the life of the world, blessing will rest upon his people, and his executive agent, Zerubbabel, governor of Judah, will be specially chosen for divine favour.

1$^{1-11}$ *The call to rebuild*

The prophet's address is described as given to the two leaders, *Zerubbabel . . . the governor* (v. 1) of the Davidic family (cf. p. 204) and *Joshua the high priest*. Elsewhere we find that he addresses also 'all the people of the land' (2^{4}), an expression which may indicate the remaining leaders, but here more naturally suggests 'the ordinary people'. They are also described, both in 2^{2} and in the narrative of 1$^{12-14}$ as being 'all the remnant of the people'. Here are two levels of understanding the community of this period of restoration. As 'ordinary people' they are summoned with their leaders to rebuild; there is no indication here of any division within the community between those who returned and those who had been in the country all the time. As 'remnant', they are described as those who have come through the disaster and judgement (cf. Zech. 3^{2}); this offers a theological interpretation of their status, for they are now the people of a new age, the inheritors of the promises of the past.

In this opening passage, emphasis lies, however, on their reluctance to act as befits the new age. They complain that the moment is not opportune for rebuilding the temple. But their complaint is countered by the twofold reminder; they are living in good houses of their own (*panelled* (v. 4) suggests a measure of luxury, but the word may mean only 'roofed', contrasting the roofed houses with the temple lying open to the sky) and this should suggest where priority lies; they are also suffering economic difficulties, and these should give them a clue to what is wrong. The reference in v. 6 to *a bag with holes* suggests the worthlessness of wages as costs spiral; since at this period minted coinage was coming into use (as distinct from broken silver which had to be weighed), the *bag* may be a purse for coins. Judaean coins are known from about 400 B.C., but coins from other areas would begin to be in circulation at an earlier date.

Verses 7–11 point out the meaning of the temple building. If it is restored, then God will appear there in glory, for it is his chosen dwelling, the place in which he wills to make his presence known to his people. It must not be supposed that God was thought to 'live' in the temple, or to be limited to it. The presence of God is the source of life (cf. Ezek. 47–48); so the unbuilt temple is related to the distresses of the natural order in which divine judgement is expressed. When the temple is rebuilt, the people will be able to acknowledge the presence of God in true worship, and God will no longer turn away in displeasure. The prophet uses very vivid expressions to show his sense of the centrality of a right relationship with God; to appreciate his meaning we need to translate into other terms, but the fundamantal point is clear. The people's life can only depend upon God, and upon the reality of his presence; their response must express their awareness of his nature.

The narrative which follows recounts the response and emphasizes the working of God's spirit, through the agency of the commissioned prophet. The same themes are drawn out in the encouragement to faith of 2^{3-5} and in the assurance of the divine presence in 2^{6-9}. This latter passage takes further the idea of the central place of God's temple at Jerusalem, not only for Judah but for the world. For this cf. also Ezekiel and the Second Isaiah.

2^{10-14} *The problem of failure*

The interpretation of this passage has been much [illegible]ssed, and no general agreement has been reached. But it [illegible]learly an important section for understanding both the [illegible]rophet

1
2
3
5
6
4
7

and the situation. The pronouncement of v. 14 marks the climax. It is prepared for by the questions and answers of vv. 12–13. The mechanism employed for disclosing the divine will is interesting because unusual. Where another prophet might find the occasion for a pronouncement in some natural object (cf. Amos 8[1–2]), or in a visionary experience (Amos 7[1 ff.]), Haggai makes use of a normal procedure of inquiry from the priests, asking for a ruling on a problem of clean and unclean. He asks for a 'directive'. (RSV *to decide the question* (v. 11) conceals that the word used here, *tōrāh*, the word used for law and eventually for the whole Pentateuch, has the technical sense of a ruling given by the priests. Cf. Jer. 18[18] and Ezek. 7[26] for an indication of the relation between such a directive and the prophetic word and the wise man's counsel; they are all means by which the divine will is revealed.) Did Haggai know what answer he would receive? Quite possibly, but this does not affect the issue. The point is that he sees a relationship between

---

COINS OF THE PERSIAN PERIOD

1. Silver stater of Byblos, inscribed 'Azbaal king of Gebal' (Byblos). **2.** Double shekel of Sidon. **3.** Stater of Tyre. These three coins, from Phoenician cities, have features which express the sea trade of the cities. In addition, **1** has a shell suggesting the purple dyeing industry; **2** shows the Persian king in a chariot. The Egyptian figure behind the king, and the emblems of Osiris (crook and flail) on **3** show Egyptian influence. In **3** the Baal of Tyre rides on a hippocamp.

4. Stater of Tarsus in Cilicia. On **4**, a lion attacks a bull above fortifications representing the city. The Aramaic inscription reads 'Mazdai who is over "Beyond the River"' (cf. pp. 174 ff.). The words by the seated figure announce him as 'The Baal of Tarsus', and the figure is very like a Greek Zeus. Aramaic was the language of the Persian administration in the west (cf. p. 203). **5** and **6**. Tetradrachms of Alexander the Great from the mints of Babylon and Alexandria, marking the taking over of the empire. (For further notes on these six coins, cf. P. R. Ackroyd, *The People of the Old Testament* (Chatto and Windus, London, 1959), p. 230.)

7. A coin of Judah. On the obverse, it has a bearded and helmeted head, as is common on Greek coins of the time. On the reverse, a figure in a winged chariot holds a bird; this is very like the coins of Alexander (**5** and **6**). Above the seated figure appear the three letters YHD—*Yehud*, the name of the province of Judah as it is found in Ezra 5[1, 8] in Aramaic form (cf. pp. 170 f.). This probably suggests that the right to mint their own coinage had been granted to the Jewish community; the coin probably belongs to the fourth century B.C.

the ruling on clean and unclean and the condition of the people. The emphasis of the ruling is that uncleanness is more contagious than cleanness: if a man is unclean, he will spread uncleanness to whatever he touches, but a holy object has a more limited effect. Concern with these questions is, as we have seen, very marked in the Priestly Work; the life of the people is seen in terms of the avoidance of unclean contact and of the right approach to the holy.

The interpretation of v. 14 must follow on from this. The most natural way is to take it as a reference to the present condition of the people. Their condition is such that their offerings at the shrine are unacceptable. We could understand this as a reiteration of the point made in 1^{7-9}, namely that true worship is only possible with a rebuilt temple and a purified and acceptable people. This perhaps suggests that this passage really belongs at an earlier point in Haggai's preaching, and that the date in 2^{10} did not originally refer to it. (Does the date perhaps refer to 2^{15-19}? The matter is uncertain, since nothing in the book—or in Zech. 1–8 where similar dates appear—indicates the significance of the datings.) We could also understand v. 14 to mean 'You rebuild the temple, the holy place, where God will reveal his glory. But you are not to suppose that this automatically guarantees that all will be well, for God requires an obedient people.' At an early date, a note was added to v. 14 (it appears in the Greek translation) suggesting that the people's failure was in oppression and the taking of bribes and the like. This points to such an interpretation.

Some commentators have felt that it is difficult to see how, after the encouraging words of 2^{1-9}, so negative a statement could be made here. They have therefore thought that the reference to *this people* and *this nation* is not to the community rebuilding the temple, but to an alien group who claim to be true worshippers but are not (cf. Ezra 4^{1-5}). It would be anachronistic to say that these are the Samaritans (cf. pp. 185 ff.); but it is not impossible that there were sharp divisions within Judah and that this pronouncement reflects some of the problems of the time. It is, however, difficult to reconcile this with the apparent lack of any sense of a division in the people in the words of the prophet in the preceding passages. And it is more natural to suppose that *this people* has the same meaning in 2¹⁴ as it has in 1².

2²⁰⁻²³ *Zerubbabel, the royal signet ring*

The words of this passage echo those of 2⁶⁻⁹. Just as the re-establishment of the temple as the world's centre is linked to upheavals in the life of the nations, so here the establishment of Zerubbabel stands out against the overthrow of the kingdoms. The first years of Darius I were years of turmoil. Does the prophet's word reflect the uncertainties and hopes of the time? Or is he making use of the temporary upheavals to point to a greater moment, a moment of onslaught by the nations, ushering in a new and final age? The theme of such an onslaught is familiar from the psalms (cf. Pss. 2 and 46); it is reflected also in prophetic passages, especially of an apocalyptic type (cf. Ezek. 38–39; Zech. 14). Zerubbabel is described as *my servant* (v. 23), an appropriate royal title for a descendant line of David. He is to be *like a signet ring*, which means that he will have executive power; for the ruler gives his ring to one of his officers so that his will may be carried out (cf. Esther 3¹⁰; 1 Kgs. 21⁸).

What did the prophet expect to happen? Did he believe that Zerubbabel was to be established as a supreme ruler like David, and that Judah would be independent as the Persian empire crumbled to ruin? Or is he speaking in such terms only to emphasize the will of God to bring in a new age, marked both by the rebuilding of the temple and by the leadership of a Davidic figure? Some commentators, noting that in Ezra 6 the name of Zerubbabel does not appear in relation to the final stages of the rebuilding, believe that a rebellion was attempted and suppressed. But the emphasis in Zechariah on Zerubbabel's completing of the temple goes against this (cf. Zech. 4⁹, 6¹²), and there is no evidence of Persian intervention in this period. If there had been, we might have expected the rebuilding of the temple to be halted. A less political interpretation seems more suitable, for while we should not deny to Haggai a strong fervour for the people to which he belonged, his understanding of the meaning of the presence of God among the people in the new age is very much like the emphasis of earlier prophets on faith in God, reliance upon his power, and not upon military alliances or rebellious endeavours. He was not a narrow zealot.

E. ZECHARIAH 1–8

The book of Zechariah, like the book of Isaiah, must be divided. In the first eight chapters, there is repeated reference to the prophet, and some clear indications appear of the period of the rebuilding of the temple when he was active. Chapters 9–14, sometimes called Deutero-(Second)Zechariah, contain no such references; the section consists of two groups of oracles, 9–11 and 12–14, both headed in the same way as 'An Oracle' (the word used is that which appears frequently as a heading in Isa. 13–23; it may also be translated 'burden', and Jer. 23[33 ff.] provides a word-play on this, suggesting that the 'oracle' of the false prophet is a 'burden'). The book of Malachi which immediately follows has a similar heading, and this suggests the possibility that three small collections of oracles have been placed at the end of the group of prophetic books, eventually known as the 'Book of the Twelve' (Hosea to Malachi). But just as there may be seen to be relationship of thought between Isaiah of Jerusalem and the Second Isaiah and other prophets whose words are to be found in the book, so too we may perhaps detect in the book of Zechariah a certain relationship between the thought of Zechariah himself and that of the author(s) of the material in chapters 9–14. The dating of this latter part is very uncertain; some parts of it are more fully discussed in Vol. 5, pp. 200 ff. (cf. also below p. 293).

We are here concerned only with the work of the prophet who appears with Haggai in Ezra 5[1] and 6[14] in connection with the rebuilding of the temple. He was the grandson (so 1[1]) or possibly the son (Ezra 5^1, 6^{14}) of Iddo. (The name Berechiah in 1^1 may be due to a confusion with another Zechariah mentioned in Isa. 8^2; or the term 'son of' may be loosely used to denote 'descendant'.) An Iddo is mentioned in Neh. 12^4 (cf. v. 16) as one of the heads of a priestly family who 'came up' with Zerubbabel. It is therefore possible that Zechariah was of this priestly family, though identification is not certain.

Zech. 1–8 consists of two main sections: a series of visions in 1^7–6^8, including descriptions and interpretations of visionary experiences of the prophet, as well as other prophetic material which now provides a kind of commentary on some of the visions; and a collection of teaching in 7–8, made up of loosely connected utterances and longer sermonic passages. The vision series is followed in 6^{9-15} by a passage of narrative. The whole collection is prefaced by a sermonic passage 1^{1-6}. The collection is provided with dates at 1^1, 1^7, and 7^1, but no indication is given of the significance of the dates; in this respect the structure closely resembles the book of Haggai, and it is not unreasonable to suppose that the final shaping of the two collections was undertaken in the same circle. It has already been noted that this final collecting and presenting may be from a period close to that of the Chronicler. Particularly in Zech. 1–8, there is a strong emphasis on the need for the community to learn obedience and to learn it by a consideration of the situations which led up to and accompanied the rebuilding of the temple.

The visions are difficult to interpret. They introduce strange images, their allusions are obscure. If, as seems likely, their present structure is due to a deliberate building together of visions, interpretations, and other prophetic sayings, then we must try to see their meaning at two levels. We must attempt to discover their original meaning, as they were experienced and recounted and commented on by the prophet; and we must try to see the overall impact of the collection on readers at a somewhat later date.

Such a collection of visions is found also in Amos 7–8, where a group of four visions (7^{1-9} together with 8^{1-3}) is combined with a narrative section, and is followed by a collection of teaching. In both cases, there are visions which may be seen to be linked to ordinary experiences: in Amos, locusts, a plumb-line, a basket of fruit; in Zechariah, a group of horsemen, a golden lampstand, a man with a measuring line. But in both, and much more markedly in Zechariah, there are other elements: in Amos, the fire which devours the great deep and the land; in Zechariah, horns and a flying scroll, a woman in an ephah and mysterious chariots. Indeed, the line between real objects as the basis of a vision and pictures which suggest a mythological background or a heightened sense of reality, is not easy to draw. In Zech. 3, we have a picture of a court scene involving the high priest Joshua; clearly this is the heavenly court, but at the same time it is closely linked with the ceremonial vesting of the high priest in the temple. We may compare the earthly and heavenly elements in the vision of Isaiah (Isa. 6). We may also compare the vision in Ezek. 1, and other of the visions and oracles of Ezekiel for similar strange imagery. Later, apocalyptic, writings show a further development of this style.

The individual visions relate closely to the needs and problems of the community at the time of the restoration. There is concern with the moment of restoration after long years of desolation (1^{7-17}), with release from external danger (1^{18-21}), with the new and glorious city (2^{1-5}); linked with these is the call to exiles to return, and a promise that Zion, in which God himself will dwell, is to be the central place in the life of the world (2^{6-13}; cf. Hag. 2^{6-9}). The purification of the high priest and its meaning in relation to the new age, and particularly to the 'Branch', are brought out in chapter 3. The theme of the temple is again developed in chapter 4. The community is to be purified of all evil practice and idolatry (so chapter 5, where the figure of the woman in the ephah appears to express the idea of idolatry, appropriate to Shinar (Babylon) but not to Judah). The renewal of the world under divine control is perhaps the theme of 6^{1-8}. With these expressions of confidence and hope in the visions go the elements of narrative which speak of the establishment of Zerubbabel in 6^{9–15}, and teaching concerning the nature of the new age, with warnings of the necessity of obedience in chapters 7–8. The climax is reached in a renewed emphasis on the central place of Jerusalem, to which the representatives of the nations will come; fittingly, it is a place of rejoicing and no longer one in which fasts are held to recall disaster (8^{18–23}).

Such a brief summary of Zechariah's teaching does not do justice to the impression of expectancy and hope which runs all though. Individual elements in these chapters point to aspects of the new age, or provide warnings of the things which can delay the coming of a full hope. The whole vision series, and still more that series placed in the context of other teaching, stresses the reality of the day which is dawning. If to some it seemed a 'day of small things' (4^{10}), to the prophet it is the moment of hope. He is conscious of the bitterness of past experiences and of his people's failure; he is aware that there is still reluctance to obey the will of God, to heed the warnings of the 'former prophets'. But he is still more conscious of the reality of God, of his all-seeing power, of his willingness to return to Jerusalem and to his people, of his protective love.

As the words of the prophet are now presented to us, we are encouraged—with the readers of earlier days—to look back to this moment of restoration. We may detect the economic and political and social problems of the time; we may be tempted to think of it as a day of disappointment after the high hopes expressed in the teachings of the great exilic prophets and theologians. But to see it aright, we must see the achievement of rebuilding the temple, of recreating the life of the people. The words of Haggai and of Zechariah, like the teaching enshrined in the Chronicler's narrative of this period in Ezra 1–6, invite a later generation to see in this the real meaning of restoration.

1^{7–17} *The promise of restoration*

Both in v. 7 and in 7^1, the Babylonian month names have been added alongside the month number; the use of these names reflects a practice which appears to have come in during the Persian period. The verse gives a formal introduction to the vision series which follows. The phrase *the word of the LORD came* is not grammatically linked with *and Zechariah said*, it serves simply to say: 'This is Zechariah's prophetic message.'

The vision is described in vv. 8 ff. It is a *night* vision, like a dream, but a conscious, waking experience; 4^1 makes this clearer by likening it to the moment of vivid awareness at waking. A similar statement is made about the transfiguration experience in Luke 9^{32}. The nature of divine revelation to a prophet is variously described; dream, vision, the sound of a voice, the experience of seeing ordinary objects with a heightened consciousness—all these are indicated as ways in which the revelation is felt to come. Often it is clear that the experience defies precise description.

This vision is of a horseman and of horses of various colours. No interpretation is given of the colours (cf. also 6^{1-8}); in later writings this aspect was developed (cf. Rev. 6). The *glen* (v. 8) with its myrtle trees may give a clue to the actual experience, which in the prophet's consciousness of the divine revelation is given a heightened description. But the word used for *glen* is a strange one, perhaps suggesting rather a 'depth', a place of mystery. Possibly the prophet moves from an actual experience to a vision of an action taking place beyond the human sphere, for the explanation shows that these horses (perhaps 'horsemen') are divine messengers. They are like the messengers of the Persian (and before it the Babylonian) system of dispatch riders; it is their task to report back to God the state of the earth. We may find an analogy in Job 1 and 2, where the heavenly court scenes suggest occasions when God's servants (the 'sons of God') report to him. The report here is of peace in the whole earth, and this is significant at the beginning of the reign of Darius I, for the upheavals then may have suggested to some (perhaps to Haggai, cf. 1^{6-9}, 2^{20-23}) that a great divine intervention was about to take place.

The vision thus leads on into question and answer. God's messenger himself asks: *How long* (v. 12)—a phrase common in psalms of lamentation (cf. e.g. Ps. 79[5])—is there *no mercy* yet for Jerusalem and Judah? *Seventy years*—a conventional figure—recalls the prophecy in Jer. 25[12], 29[10]. Is not the real end of the exile yet reached? At a later date, this was to be seen by the Chronicler (2 Chron. 36[21]) to mark the true length of the exile; and later still, the author of Daniel (9[1–2, 24–27]) was to interpret the seventy years as 490, seventy 'weeks' of years, an exile still not complete when he wrote in the second century B.C. It is God himself who speaks to proclaim his grace to his people, and the angelic messenger lays upon the prophet the message of hope, of God's returning to Jerusalem, and of his restoring of prosperity for his people. Zion is to be comforted, and Jerusalem chosen again, as it was chosen by God for the place of his temple (cf. the narrative in 2 Sam. 5, and, e.g., Ps. 78[67 ff.]).

Such an outline and comment conceals some of the uncertainties and difficulties of the passage. The precise part played by the various figures in the vision is not clear; possibly some of the confusion arises from accidental repetitions in the text (e.g. in v. 11). No precise explanation is given of who the persons are. There is the man on horseback; there is *the angel who talked with me* (v. 9), introduced without comment. In v. 10, the man on horseback gives an explanation of the messengers; but in v. 11 it is the angel who is among the myrtle trees, to whom the messengers report. The figure of the angelic messenger appears in the other visions; he is the interpreter of the experiences to the prophet (for a later and fuller development, cf. the angelic messenger in Daniel). But he is not only an interpreter, for we find him involved in the action, and himself making appeal to God.

Nor is it clear where vision ends and other prophetic utterances begin. We have a vision, we have interpretation; we also have further sayings, not exactly related, but loosely linked together with brief introductory phrases (cf. vv. 16, 17). Both here and elsewhere, other prophetic words are used to draw out more fully the meaning of the visions. The prophet, or his followers, may have seen that sayings belonging to various occasions could illuminate one another.

But with all the uncertainties, the central theme is clear. The real end of the exile has come; a new age dawns, and God in his mercy returns and restores. The theme of mercy is picked up again in chapter 3; the judgement on the nations in 1^{18-21}; the rebuilding of the temple in chapters 4 and 6; the restoring of Jerusalem in 2^{1-5}. The last vision in 6^{1-8}, which rounds off the series, echoes this opening picture; the divine messengers find their counterpart in the heavenly chariots sent out to bring about the will of God among the nations, and in particular to bring release to captives in Babylon and judgement upon the oppressor. (The sense of 6^{8} is open to discussion, and it is difficult to decide between the meaning 'set my spirit on', i.e. stir up the exiles to return (cf. $2^{6\text{ff.}}$; 6^{15}) and the meaning 'assuage my anger', i.e. bring due judgement upon Babylon (cf. 1^{18-21}).)

2^{1-5} *The new Jerusalem*

The promise of a new city is an important element in the future hope of Ezekiel (cf. pp. 100 ff.). Zechariah takes up a similar theme, expressed in the vision of a man surveying the new city. The message is given that Jerusalem will be so populous that it will be like *villages without walls* (v. 4)—settlements open and exposed, and not restricted like a walled city. God himself will be protection all round, and his glory will be within. There are two ways of interpreting this passage. We may suppose that, not unnaturally, at the time of the temple rebuilding, attempts were also being made to rehabilitate the city and to rebuild the walls; the message then may warn that trust in stone walls is inappropriate to a people whose protector is God. Or, not looking for such precise reference, we may see here the theme of a new and glorious city, far transcending anything known in its past history. This theme is picked up also in a number of sayings in chapter 8, where the return of God in glory, the renaming of the city as 'the faithful city', and the marvellous life and blessedness of Jerusalem, the centre of the world's life, are all touched on (cf. 8^{1-8}).

'AARON, THE HIGH PRIEST.' The symbolic clothing of the high priest Joshua in festive garments in Zech. 3 reminds us that these garments had an important place in religious celebrations. The full description in Exod. 28, which belongs to the Priestly Work, brings out some aspects of this, suggesting ways in which the relationship between God and his people was seen to be expressed in the figure of the high priest in his festal attire. So here, in one of the paintings from the synagogue at Dura-Europos (cf. p. 98), this figure is set alongside other pictures—the ark, the seven-branched candlestick (cf. pp. 228 f.), sacrificial animals, attendants. It reveals the importance of this range of ideas in the continuing life of the Jewish community. Cf. also for such thought the hymn of praise of Simon the high priest in Ecclus. 50.

3 *The declaration of forgiveness*

To give such a title to this chapter may seem to stress only one point; yet it is a central one. In this court scene—and we have already noted (p. 220) that it is both a heavenly and an earthly scene—the high priest Joshua stands accused. His accuser is 'the Satan'—not *Satan* as RSV (v. 1), since the word means 'adversary' and is here used with the definite article. Later the name became a title for the evil power (cf. also on Job 1–2 (pp. 321 f.), and note that 1 Chron. 21[1] uses the word without the article). This figure is a kind of prosecutor in the heavenly court, and he is here rebuked by God for the accusation. Verse 2 is crucial to our understanding of the passage. It makes two points. The God who rebuked the Satan is the one who has chosen Jerusalem. *This*—is it Joshua or Jerusalem?—is as one *plucked from the fire* (a proverbial phrase, suggesting the rescued remnant, appearing in a slightly different form but with the same meaning in Amos 4^{11}). Many suggestions have been made as to the nature of the accusation against Joshua: was he a priest who was suspected of being contaminated with idolatrous practices in Palestine during the exilic period, or was he one who came from Babylon and was considered by some of his compatriots to be unfit for that reason? But the stress on the choosing of Jerusalem and on the rescuing of a remnant strongly suggests that the accusation is not in any way personal to Joshua. It is the high priest as representative of his people who is accused, and the exchanging of his filthy garments—symbol of mourning, or of uncleanness—for 'clean white garments' (rather than RSV *rich apparel*, v. 4) are a sign of forgiveness and cleansing for the community.

Rather unexpectedly, v. 5 opens in the first person. The text may be in error, and a third person verbal form (referring to the angel) should then be substituted. If it is correct, then the prophet himself intervenes, and this would give a special emphasis to the placing of the clean turban described in detail in Exod. 28^{36-38}. The turban is particularly associated with atonement, with the acceptability of priests and people before God.

Verses 6–7 develop further the position of the high priest; his obedience to God's law will make it possible for him both to rule over the temple and hence to order men's worship, and also to have access in the heavenly court. So the high priest can present his people's petitions and know the decisions of the court. Such access is also a prerogative of the true prophet (cf. 1 Kgs. 22^{19-23} (Micaiah); Isa. 6; Jer. 23^{18-22}). Furthermore, vv. 8–10 affirm a relationship between the position of Joshua and his associates and the coming *Branch*, who is *my servant* (v. 9); 6^{12} (cf. 4^{6-10}) makes it clear that this is a title used for Zerubbabel, the chosen agent of God (cf. Hag. 2^{20-23}). The same title is used for an ideal ruler in Jer. 23^{5}, 33^{15}; Isa. 4^{2} (probably a late passage); a similar term is used in Isa. 11[1]. The function of the priests is to attest the coming of this ruler. Verse 9 links this with a stone, most probably associated with the high priest's turban though it may have some other reference. The whole act of cleansing, the promise of the restoration of the people and of the coming ruler, leads up to a day of salvation and peace (v. 10).

This chapter is again not easy to interpret precisely, but is rich in allusion to the ways in which forgiveness and reconciliation are effected between God and his people. There is a strong awareness here that the restoration is due to God's grace, and that he will fulfil what he promises for his people.

4 *The symbol of the lamp, and the assurance of rebuilding*

The interpretation of this chapter is complicated by the fact that it contains two separate elements. The symbol of the lamp and its exposition are found in vv. 1–6*a* (*Then he said to me*) and 10*b* ('*These seven* . . .'. The RSV marks this with a new paragraph)–14. The intervening passage, 6*b*–10*a*, is a separate group of sayings, beginning '*This is the word of the* LORD . . .' and although this now appears to be part of what the angelic messenger says, in reality it is a statement of the prophet's message to the civil leader. It is concerned with the rebuilding of the temple. The two separate themes are, however, connected. The assurance of the lamp symbol is that God himself is watching over the whole earth and over his people to bring blessing. As elsewhere in both Haggai and Zechariah, the rebuilding of the temple is central to faith in the reality of God's presence. Whoever put these two sections together saw that each could provide an illuminating comment on the other.

The vision of the lampstand is elaborately described, and not all its details are clear. In particular, the wording of v. 2 does not give a clear picture of what the lamp is like. Though often it has been thought to be a seven-branched lamp, it is more probable that it is like a lamp with a bowl, the bowl having

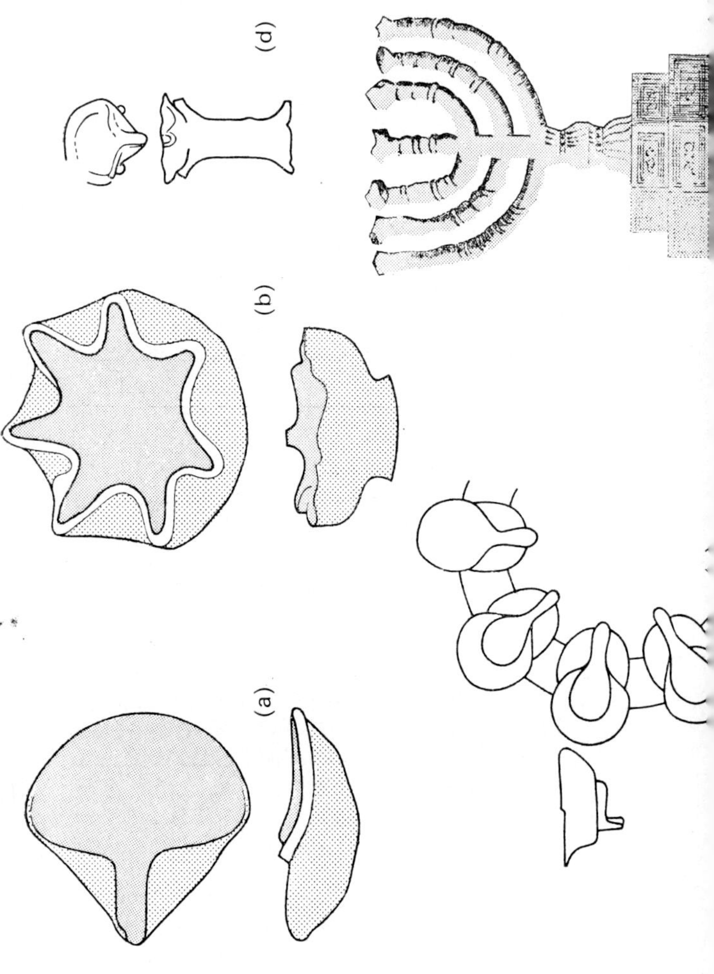
(d)
(b)
(a)

seven indentations or spouts for wicks; or perhaps, more elaborately, a very large bowl or ring on a stand, on which seven lamps stand, each having seven spouts for wicks. It is most natural to suppose that the prophet's vision is linked to a lamp in the sanctuary; but it does not follow that we can make an accurate drawing of it, since, as we may see in Ezek. 1, vision is likely to transcend reality. The theme of the lamp is interpreted in v. 10*b*; the lamp with its sevenfold form corresponds to *the eyes of the* L*ORD*, all-seeing (*seven* here suggests completeness), and watching all that goes on in the world. In the context, this would seem to indicate divine care rather than mere awareness of what happens. A second theme accompanies this, namely that of the two olive trees. Since the temple area may well have been quite large, though not necessarily as large as the later Herodian temple area (and compare the modern *Haram esh-sherif*, see plan, p. 256), trees may actually have grown there as they do in the modern courtyards of the holy area; or the theme may have been suggested by the temple decoration (cf. the description of Solomon's temple in 1 Kgs. 6–7). The two olive trees stand beside the lamp, and they are interpreted in v. 14 as being *two anointed* leaders, namely Joshua and Zerubbabel, the anointed high priest and the divinely chosen leader of the Davidic line. This interpretation is, however, overlaid with yet another element, for in v. 12 there is also a reference to *branches* and to *pipes* through which the oil flows (the text of this verse is not at all clear). Here the symbolism has shifted, the thought being that of the mediation of God's blessing to his people through the agency of the

---

LAMPS AND LAMPSTANDS. The simple type of lamp (*a*), with a place for one wick, is known from many periods in a variety of forms. From an early date, multiple-wick lamps (*b*) are also known. The compound lamp (*c*) shows one way in which we may picture the lamp mentioned in Zech. 4. Lamps, especially for cult use, whether in a shrine or a house, are sometimes provided with stands (*d*). The seven-branched candlestick (*e*), here copied from the Arch of Titus in Rome, which commemorates the capture of Jerusalem and its temple in A.D. 70, is attested by Exod. 25^{31-40}; 37^{17-24}, though the precise details do not entirely correspond. It is very difficult to see how such a lamp is intended in Zech. 4.

leaders of the community. The interpretation must not be pressed literally. It would appear that the prophet—or is it perhaps his followers—has seen more than one meaning in this symbol of the lamp, and has worked it out in more detail than the original vision would have suggested.

Such a portrayal of divine care and blessing is a fitting setting for the stress upon the divine power by which Zerubbabel is to rebuild the temple (vv. 6*b*–10*a*). It is by the power of God, not by human power, that all will be done (v. 6). Is there here a warning against political engagement? The difficulties of the time will be overcome and the completion of the temple celebrated with rejoicing (v. 7). Those who doubt are assured that the temple will be completed, and then the prophet's authority will be clearly seen (v. 9). Doubts of the working of God in an age of disappointment will be resolved (v. 10. The precise meaning of the word translated *plummet* is by no means clear). Everything points to the achievement of the rebuilt temple; it was a generation in which faith was evoked, a new age of hope.

6[9–15] *The token of a new age*

This short passage describes a symbolic action which is to be performed by the prophet. As so often, the precise detail of its meaning remains unknown to us, since we cannot know who the various persons were who are mentioned in vv. 10 and 14. (This latter verse is very difficult. For *Heldai*, the text here has 'Helem'—a name not otherwise mentioned in the passage. Joshua is not actually named, though his name should be supplied. The text is in some disorder, and another possible way of reordering it would be to render 'the crown shall be . . . as a sign of grace and as a memorial'.)

The central feature of the symbolic action is the making of a crown—strictly the text has a plural—and the setting of this crown on the head of the high priest. As in chapter 3, the high priest then appears to be a sign of the coming of the *Branch* (v. 12), and the function of this divinely appointed leader is shown to be the rebuilding of the temple. The plural 'crowns' may be a simple textual error, or it might indicate a complex object for which the plural term would be appropriate. But most often it has been thought that originally the text meant that both leaders were to be crowned. The present form of the text might be due to accidental dislocation, or the name of Zerubbabel might have been deliberately removed. Deliberate alteration could be due to a desire to avoid the political implications of a crowning of the Davidic leader; but in this case, one might have expected a much more thoroughgoing editing of the texts of both Haggai and Zechariah. Accidental omission is quite possible. But it is also possible that the crowning of Joshua appropriately symbolizes the coming glory of a new age under the leadership of the *Branch*, and the correspondence with chapter 3 would then be very close. Verse 13 expresses the position of the two leaders, the governor and the high priest, who work together in amity for the well-being of the community. Such a concept of dual leadership, adumbrated in Ezekiel's description of the prince who has his sphere of influence alongside the priesthood, may be seen also in other Old Testament passages, as for example in the promise of a true king and priest in 1 Sam. 2^{35} and in the way in which the relationship of Moses and Aaron is portrayed in some narratives. It was an ideal which remained, though in actual fact Judah appears to have had no consistent pattern of government. At a later stage, under Greek rule, we find the high priest fulfilling both religious and civil functions. The Qumran community in New Testament times expressed its hopes in terms of a dual messiahship which may be related to these ideas.

Verse 14 suggests that the symbolism of the crown is further related to the fulfilment of the community's hopes; it is to be a reminder (perhaps also 'a sign of divine grace'; cf. above, p. 230) before God in the shrine.

Verse 15 introduces an important emphasis on the part to be played in the restoration by those who return from exile. It recalls $2^{6\,\text{ff.}}$ with the emphasis on escape from Babylon and new life in Jerusalem. It suggests that the reference to the exiles in

v. 10 is also intended to stress their part in the rebuilding and the establishing of the new age.

8^18–23 *The new age*

The whole of chapters 7–8 is concerned with the nature and establishment of the new age. In warning and exhortation, the community is called to obedience (so especially 7^8–14, 8^14–17); to those whose faith is dim, the promises are set out and assurance is given of divine favour (so 8^1–13). Now the climax is reached. First in vv. 18–19, the promise is declared that fasting is to be replaced by festivals of joy. These verses really provide the answer to the query posed in 7^1–3. This is a difficult passage. The text as it stands may be rendered: 'Bethel sent Sharezer and Regem-melech and their men . . .'. RSV offers an attempt at explaining this by inserting the words 'the people of' before Bethel; this assumes that the place-name 'Bethel' can be used to indicate its inhabitants, which is certainly not impossible. But it is more likely that the original sense of the passage was: 'Bethel-sharezer and Regem-melech [this may in fact conceal the title of an official—"the royal officer"] and their associates sent . . .'. This would suggest that the inquiry came from certain officials, at least one of whom had a Babylonian name (as did Zerubbabel), concerned about the meaning of fasting now that restoration has taken place. Subsequently the text appears to have been understood to refer to Bethel, the ancient religious centre, and hence to the carrying out of alien practices there, and vv. 4–7 develop the theme of wrong practice. 8^18–19 points to the nature of the new age as one of true worship, and also one of *truth and peace*—right dealings between men and the full life which comes with divine blessing.

8^20–23 looks to a wider horizon. Like Isa. 2^1 ff. (cf. also Mic. 4^1 ff.) it stresses the centrality of Jerusalem to the life of the world. The experience of the Jewish community, who become a sign of blessing (cf. v. 13 and Gen. 12^3) because of the favour shown to them by God, leads the representatives of other nations to acknowledge that God is with them, and to ask that they too may share in that favour. The hopes expressed in Ezekiel and the Second Isaiah are very much alive; the restoration of Judah is not for herself alone, but that all nations may be brought to knowledge of the God whose power and love are revealed in her.

F. ISAIAH 56–66

It is now common practice to divide the second part of the book of Isaiah into two main sections: 40–55 and 56–66. Concerning the first of these, there is almost complete agreement that it belongs to the last years of Babylonian power, though there have been some suggestions that parts of it are later. The origin of 56–66 is, however, much more under discussion. On the one hand, a difference of tone and in some measure of style and vocabulary suggests that it should be separated from what precedes, and its lack of coherence could indicate more than one author. On the other hand, the many points of relationship in the thought could perhaps be explained as due to the same author working in a different situation. If the prophet of 40–55 returned to Palestine in the years after the fall of Babylon and was directly involved in the many frustrations and difficulties of the period of restoration and of the rebuilding of the temple, might not this be just the kind of thing that he would say? The questions remain unresolved, and decision is difficult because of the different ways in which the evidence can be interpreted. But what seems quite clear is that just as we may best explain the connections in thought and language between the teaching of Isaiah of Jerusalem in the eighth century and the Second Isaiah in the sixth as deriving from a prophetic tradition into which the latter entered and which he further continued and developed, so too we must recognize that, whether or not the same author was involved in 56–66, whether indeed it is the work of one author or several, there is a similar continuance of that same prophetic tradition. There is a unity of tradition in the book of Isaiah, in spite of the fact that more than 200 years probably separate its earliest from its latest sections (i.e. *c.* 740 B.C.–*c.* 500 B.C.); some parts may even have to be assigned to a much later date (e.g. 24–27, see Vol. 5, pp. 213–18).

We may most conveniently here examine certain passages in Isa. 56–66, considering the kind of situation to which they appear to refer. In doing this, we need to be very careful that we do not argue in a circle, for it is very easy to find in a passage certain ideas which suggest that it belongs to the early Persian period, reflecting the situation while the temple was being restored or shortly after, and then to derive from it what is believed to be further precise information about that period. At no point can we be so sure of the dating as that. By and large, however, we may note enough similarities of situation to that which is reflected in the prophecies of Haggai and Zechariah, and perhaps also to those which can be traced in Malachi, to allow us to see here the kind of problems which confronted the generation of the restoration. The hopes and frustrations of that period had a considerable effect on the development of life and thought in the years that followed; so the content of Isa. 56–66 may be seen as expressing the kind of concerns in which the community in Palestine was involved both shortly after the exile and during the often difficult years that followed.

The situation is one of both frustration and hope. It is a moment when judgement is to be passed on certain aspects of the people's life—not least on lack of faith, on wrong religious practice, on alien worship. These chapters are a reminder that the evils castigated by earlier prophets—so especially Jeremiah and Ezekiel—still needed to be checked. Even the Second Isaiah's ridiculing of manufactured idols (Isa. 44^{9-20}, see pp. 118 ff.) did not mean that all such wrong practices came to an end. We get a rather depressing picture of the undercurrents of religious life in the years after the exile.

At a number of points it appears clear that the temple is in use, but it is at the same time evident that the sense of desolation which was brought about by its destruction had not entirely passed. In a long psalm-like passage in 63^{7}–64^{12}

distress at the destroyed temple is strongly expressed (see especially 64[10 f.]); but although it is quite possible that this passage reflects an earlier situation, perhaps even shortly after the destruction of 587, it is always difficult, as we have seen, to give a precise date and historical occasion to poetic utterances of this kind. Even after the rebuilding, the observances of a fast-day, with lament at men's failure and at the many distresses of human experience, could well include words like these; the recall of the disaster of 587 could become a pattern for the expression of penitence and of urgent appeal to God for renewed mercy and grace.

There is in these chapters a strong sense of the reality of a new age, about to dawn or even already present. Against the background of a lack of faith which appears to doubt God's action, there is proclaimed the coming of God himself in glory, a transformation of the land and a new Jerusalem. But this is tempered with the warning that men's failures can frustrate the purpose of God for his people, and delay the saving action which he intends. An alternating pattern is found of hope and warning, promise and judgement.

56[1–8] *The community of true worshippers*

The difference in tone from the Second Isaiah is very evident in this first passage, and this change is one of the factors which suggests that the division should be made at this point in the book. Yet the sense of the immediacy of the coming salvation is here, and the reminder that right action belongs to the moment of that salvation is timely. In such a critical moment, obedience is vital, and it involves the keeping of the sabbath—perhaps this is a brief way of saying that men should properly observe all the demands of true worship—and abstention from evil—which is a way of summarizing the demand for right action. In the new age, as from ancient time, obedience consists in a right approach to God and a right way of dealing with one's fellow men (vv. 1–2).

To this point, two special statements are added, concerning those who might feel themselves to be outcasts from the true community. *The foreigner who has joined himself to the* LORD (v. 3) is one who has accepted membership of the community in obedient allegiance. The term used for the second class, *the eunuch*, generally denotes a court official, but appears to have acquired a special meaning because of the position of officials in charge of the women's quarters in royal palaces (cf. Esther 2^{3}). The Old Testament stress on the blessing of children who preserve a man's name makes the position of the eunuch a sad one; but the promise to the obedient is of a blessing and a memorial which far exceed the blessing of children. Deut. 23^{1} further indicates that, according to some regulations, the eunuch could have no part in the life of the worshipping community. So this passage emphasizes that obedience and faithfulness are of greater weight than ritual regulation.

Similarly, the position of the foreigner is assured, and it is made clear that the temple is the focal point for all peoples (vv. 6–8). So there is expressed here a breadth of view which forms an apt continuation of the stress in the Second Isaiah on the purpose of God's call of Israel for the whole life of the world. (We may also compare Zech. 8^{20-23} and Mal. 1^{11}.)

58^{1-9a} *True fasting*

Much of chapter 57 is concerned with disobedience and idolatrous practice; it suggests that the situation within the life of the community was far from well. The note of judgement continues in the opening of 58, where there is a sharp contrast drawn between the vigour with which worship is practised and the failure which provokes the proclamation of an oracle of condemnation. The theme is not unlike what is found in the book of Malachi, for the people are depicted as complaining that all their faithful worship is of no avail. God, it appears, pays no heed to their fasts and their submission of themselves to him. But the truth is (v. 4) that the fasting which is offered is no fasting at all; it may be outward observance, but it is marked by hostility within the community. The contrast is drawn between the outward observances of fasting—set out in some detail in v. 5—and its true nature—set out in vv. 6–7. One of the psalmists expresses the same conviction:

> The sacrifice acceptable to God is a broken spirit;
> a broken and contrite heart, O God, thou wilt not despise.
> (Ps. 51[17])

words which find an echo in Isa. 57[15]. Fasting is obedience; it is to be expressed in that concern for the oppressed, the unprotected, the poor, which is so characteristic of Old Testament ethical demand. The full relationship with God and the revealing of his glory will follow upon this; he will respond to men's worship because the hindrances of disobedience are removed (vv. 8–9*a*).

60[1–7] *The coming new age*

The group of chapters 60–62 stands in many respects very close to the writings of the Second Isaiah, and includes a series of themes all related to the coming of a new age, of which the centre is the re-establishment of Jerusalem as the centre of the world's life. The opening verse addresses Jerusalem (the subject of the invocation is not in fact named, but the feminine singular verb and the general context make it sufficiently clear). The wording recalls themes to be found in chapter 40; the good news for Jerusalem, its central point the coming glory of God which brings light to the city, contrasts with a gloom on the nations. We may see here an allusion to the theme in the Exodus narratives, where all Egypt is in darkness while there is light in the dwellings of Israel (Exod. 10[21 ff.]). To Jerusalem, restored and glorified by the presence of God, will come the nations and their rulers (cf. Isa. 2[2–4]).

In vv. 4–7 there is a further development of the idea of the new Jerusalem, as the gathering-point for all who belong to her. The scattered members of the Jewish community are to be restored, as sons and daughters to a rejoicing mother. This is to be accompanied by the gathering of wealth, as the tribute offered in worship to God by the nations (so clearly in vv. 6*b*, 7*b*). It is a new and glorious day for city and temple; the thought is close to that of Hag. 2^{6-9}.

In the verses which follow on this opening, we may trace the development of the different ideas. Thus vv. 8–9 elaborate the thought of the return of the scattered members of the community; vv. 10–16 take further the idea of the restoration of Jerusalem and the offering of tribute by the nations, a reversal of fortune for the city which has been through bitter suffering; vv. 17–18 elaborate the theme of wealth and of peace and prosperity, the new city by its very walls and gates acknowledging the nature of God; vv. 19–22 concentrate on the presence of God, and the consequent purification and blessing of his people. Such an interwoven pattern of ideas closely resembles the style of presentation in the Second Isaiah, and the same approach may be undertaken here. When the themes of one passage have been noted, the reiteration and development of these same themes may be traced in other passages where the emphasis may be slightly different and the texture more complex.

61 *The year of the* Lord*'s favour*

It has been noted (p. 124) that the opening verses (1–4) of this chapter have been seen to be especially close to the so-called 'servant' passages in the Second Isaiah. What has been said about their interpretation should be borne in mind as this passage is read. The opening lays emphasis on divine call, the possession of the divine spirit (RSV prints *Spirit*, but this is to anticipate a more fully developed idea which belongs really to a rather later period; the thought here is of that 'breath of God' which fills a man and inspires him, whether to speak or to act, in the divine power). Who is speaking here? The use of the term *anointed* suggests a royal or priestly figure, and a comparison might be made with the royal oracle in Isa. $11^{1\text{ff.}}$ As in the comparable passages in the Second Isaiah, we should certainly also allow for the probable influence of the prophet's own vivid sense of his calling. But the context strongly suggests that it is Jerusalem which is confessing its function; it is Jerusalem the bringer of good news to captives and oppressed, proclaiming a special year of divine favour, when God looks in mercy on his people. As so often in such poetic passages, there is a movement of thought from this so that in the following verses we see the restoration of the ruined places, and from the city we move over to consider the good fortune of the whole people.

The opening proclamation is followed by a characteristic development of themes. Verses 5–7 stress the reversal of fortune, with the whole people appointed as priests, as those who stand in the sanctuary to lead the worship of the nations, accepting as their due the tribute which is offered. A similar picture is drawn in Zech. 14[16ff.]. Verses 8–9 picture the removal of all evil from the people's life, and their consequent reputation as blessed by God. The section reaches its climax in an act of praise, close in its language to many of the psalms, and picturing the new age in terms of righteousness, acknowledged by all nations.

The coming age is here proclaimed as being at hand. It is a moment when God shows favour to his people, in contrast to the long years of exile; it is a day of restoration, of reversal of fortune. The central place is to be occupied by God's people, but their position of privilege is that of priests who facilitate contact with God, and their blessing is recognized by the nations. Thus older elements of more narrow nationalistic thought are preserved, but they are given a deeper meaning; privilege involves obedience and the acknowledgement of God. The 'day of the Lord' still has its element of judgement; but the presence of God brings blessing and life. It is not difficult to see how appropriately the themes of this passage could be made the basis for the interpretation of the moment of Jesus' proclamation as it is described in Luke 4[16ff.]

62 *The new Jerusalem*

In this chapter, the theme of the new city, rebuilt and renamed, is further developed. In vv. 1–5 the reversal of fortune for the city is approached from various aspects. The prophet—or is it perhaps God himself who speaks?—announces his concern for Jerusalem, his determination to speak unceasingly until the restoration takes place. We may compare the distress at the long-continuing desolation and the confidence in restoration expressed in Zech. 1^{7-17}. The vindication of the city will be acknowledged by the nations; it will be a change of situation expressed in the abandoning of the old names—the city named *Forsaken*, and the land termed *Desolate* will now be known by new names, *My delight is in her* and *Married* (v. 4. The RSV margin supplies the actual Hebrew words, *Azubah*, *Shemamah*, *Hephzibah*, *Beulah*; the last two continue to be used in areas where biblical names are in favour, and they also find a place in such biblically based writings as Bunyan's *Pilgrim's Progress*. The translation is necessary to bring out the meaning, which expresses the new purpose of God in grace towards his people.) The marriage analogy which is detectable in all four names and which was used most effectively by Hosea and Jeremiah (though also by Ezekiel, and in the interpretation of the Song of Songs and elsewhere) is brought out in the explicit comments of the last lines of this section.

The city theme is continued in vv. 6–9 in which a primary motif is that of divine protection (cf. Zech. 2^{1-5}). The watchmen are both guardians of the city so that there will be no danger from enemies, and also 'remembrancers' before God, continually drawing his attention to the needs of his city so that he will not rest until it becomes *a praise in the earth* (v. 7)—the word may suggest a song of praise, a psalm, or perhaps more appropriately an object on account of which praise is offered. Though the nations are not here mentioned, we may detect the same concern that the restoration shall be seen throughout the world as an indication of divine favour and as a stimulus to praise God and acknowledge him.

Verses 10–12 echo a theme found in Isa. 35 and 40—the building of a processional way by which men return to Zion; and with this is combined the renaming theme already used in the opening verses of the chapter. The people is renamed (v. 10) as

The holy people and as *The redeemed of the* LORD (a different word, translated 'ransomed', is used in 35^{10}; this latter is linked with ransom from slavery where the former is linked with the action of the kinsman who redeems a man's property or family—cf. Ruth 4); the city is renamed as *Sought out* (*Derushah*—not given in RSV margin) and *Not forsaken* (*Lo-azubah*). For such a reversal of names we may compare also the naming and re-naming in Hos. $1^{6, 9}$, 2^{23}. As we have seen, 'name' often means virtually 'person', and the naming of a person or an object conveys intention and hope; so the ancient Israelites gave names to their children which were meaningful, expressive of situation, or of intention or of hope.

65^{17-25} *New heavens and a new earth*

The last chapters of this book continue with similar themes. The urgent hope that God will come and deliver ($64^{1\,ff.}$) follows on a passage expressing distress at desolation and destruction. The willingness of God to be with his people is described as encountering rebellion and apostasy ($65^{1\,ff.}$). Idolatrous practices, barely identifiable now—perhaps because later scribes carefully removed much of the precision of reference lest the pious reader and worshipper should be led astray—mar the day of hope of which so many passages provide an echo (so in $65^{8\,ff.}$ and much of 66). But through all the uncertainty, there is a clear and confident note. What God did at creation he will do again. The new creation will transcend the old, and there will be a perpetual day of rejoicing and peace.

This hope for the future centres on Jerusalem; here is the focal point of the life of the people and it is here that the divine promise is revealed. So in these verses of chapter 65, and particularly in vv. 19 ff., there is one picture after another of the nature of the new age. The different themes are built together, more closely knit but similar to those of Zech. 8. All distress is gone, life is blessed abundantly, men will enjoy the fruit of their labours, they will live in close relationship with God. The final verse echoes Isa. 11^{6-9}, though in a much briefer form. The holy mountain of God's dwelling is the centre of a new garden of Eden from which all that is hurtful has been removed.

66^{1-2} *The true temple of God*

The rebuilding of the temple after the exile raised in the minds of some men questions about the nature of God's dwelling-place. The ancient poem quoted in 1 Kgs. $8^{12 \text{ f.}}$ (RSV gives the full form of this; part of it is missing in the Hebrew text) hints at the problem of the relationship between the God who by his very nature dwells in 'thick darkness'—for is he not the creator, the one who 'set the sun in the heavens'? —and also in the 'house' built for him by man. The longer, and later, prayer of Solomon which follows poses the question explicitly in v. 27: 'Will God indeed dwell on the earth? Behold, heaven and the highest heaven cannot contain thee; how much less this house which I have built!' Isa. 66^{1-2} puts the question again. It is a reminder that the temple had stood for centuries and, in spite of the attempts at making clear the nature of the relationship between God and his temple, many had come to believe that somehow the temple's existence guaranteed the presence of God (cf. Jer. 7^{4}). To those who rebuilt, there was an equal danger. That they must rebuild is rightly expressed by Haggai and Zechariah; but that they should view the temple as compelling God to be with them was to fail to understand his nature. God may choose to reveal his presence there, as he may choose to accept a sacrificial offering. But the relationship is not thereby limited. Worship and obedience go hand in hand, and in the last resort, if a choice must be made, the Old Testament comes firmly down on the side of saying that the externals of religion are nothing by comparison with the humility and contrition and awe which come properly upon a man at the very presence of God (cf. also Ps. 51^{17} quoted on p. 237). This passage is not, as some have thought, a protest at the very idea of rebuilding; it is a warning that the most prosperous externals for worship are meaningless if those who come before God do not do so with a proper regard for who he is.

G. MALACHI

We have already noted (p. 218) that the collection of prophecies called 'The Book of Malachi' in the English Bible has a heading 'Oracle' like that at Zech. 9^1 and 12^1; and that this suggests three short collections at the end of the 'Book of the Twelve'. This collection has been given a separate title, and has been ascribed to a prophet supposedly called Malachi. But in reality, this is not the name of the prophet, but simply a word extracted from the text at 3^1 where it is correctly translated 'my messenger'. That the name of the prophet was not known can be seen from the fact that the Greek translators rendered the word in the opening verse as 'his messenger'; and the Targum, the translation, often with much paraphrase, designed for the use of Aramaic-speaking Jews, actually identifies the author with 'Ezra the scribe'.

We have simply to recognize here an anonymous collection, and it provides little really precise evidence for its date. The temple is clearly in use—there are many references to ritual practice—so the collection is later than Haggai and Zech. 1–8. The strictures on mixed marriage (2^{11}) and on slackness in religious observance (1^6–2^9 and 3^{6-12}) suggest a period before the reforms of Nehemiah and Ezra, though we can hardly suppose that those reforms removed everything that was wrong. Analogies to the various collections of law suggest a closer affinity with Deuteronomy than with the Priestly Work; but we do not really know how far these may have existed side by side. The generally accepted date of between 500 and 450 B.C. is probable enough. A more precise definition could perhaps be given if we knew more about the history of Edom (cf. notes on 1^{2-5}).

Two main points emerge from this little collection. On the one hand, there is the strongly negative impression created by the repeated criticisms of lack of faith, of slovenly religious practice, of the disobedience of the priesthood, of insincerity in worship, of contacts with alien religion. It is certainly a moment when religion is at a low ebb. But we need to see this in perspective and to recognize that a prophet may be sharply critical without implying that all is evil. For, on the other hand, there is a strong sense of coming judgement and promise; it will be a judgement which destroys all that is evil and which refines the life of the community. It finds a response in the hearts of those who fear God, and for them, as they respond in obedience, there is life and hope and healing.

1^2–5 *The mystery of God's love*

This passage raises acutely the problem of how God's special relationship to Israel is to be understood. The whole idea of a special relationship is difficult; for how can God show partiality? The Old Testament frequently expresses the idea of God's choice of Israel in terms which both imply particular favour for Israel and rejection for other peoples. But it was also possible to present the idea of special choice in terms of special responsibility (cf. Amos 3^2 and the emphasis on Israel's place in the whole purpose of God in Ezekiel, the Second Isaiah, Haggai, and Zechariah). Certainly this prophet is not limited in his outlook if we may judge by 1^11, though he is also strongly conscious of the special position of Israel and of the need to preserve her distinctive character (cf. 2^11).

The relationship between Jacob and Esau forms an important ancient tradition (cf. Gen. 25^21–34, 27); the mystery of God's choice of Jacob as the ancestor of his people is unexplained. Paul could use the motif, quoting Mal. 1^2 f., to stress that no man can claim status with God, for all is of his grace (Rom. 9). So here, to those who doubt the reality of God's care and ask for evidence of his love, the prophet offers the picture of a desolated Edom for which there is no hope of restoration. The indications of his actions will evoke praise of his power.

It looks very much as though the prophet is pointing to a recent disaster to Edom which provides evidence of his contention, but we do not know to what he is referring, nor is it quite certain that a merely historical reference is intended. The book of Obadiah (cf. the notes on pp. 55 ff.) also deals with the problem of Edom, and we have already seen something of the historical conditions in the exilic period and after to which reference may be made here. But Edom in Mal. 1^{2-5} may, as in Obadiah, be understood not merely in historical terms, but also as a symbol of the alien, rejected, evil world outside.

1^{6-11} *Where is God honoured?*

This passage provides one of a number of examples of the polemic in which the prophet is engaged with his people. We may note here as elsewhere the question-and-answer method of presenting the argument. The attack is on the priests, depicted as unaware that their bringing of impure offerings dishonours God; it is a despising of his name, an insult to his person. Men do this; let them try such treatment on the governor and see what will happen!

Verse 10 makes the rebuke even sharper. Such false worship is so evil that it were better for the temple doors to be shut rather than God be treated thus. The point is similar to that made in Isa. 1^{12-17}: better to have no worship at all than to approach God improperly. Verse 11 brings a striking contrast, though opinions differ as to its interpretation. While Israel insults God, he is nevertheless glorified among the nations. It is not clear, however, whether this means that there are faithful members of the Jewish community scattered across the lands and where they worship, God is glorified—with the implication that the other peoples will be able to see this and acknowledge the greatness of God. Or does it mean—an even bolder thought—that while Israel is unfaithful, God nevertheless accepts as genuine the worship which the other peoples offer; all true worship, offered *in every place* (probably meaning 'every shrine'), is really an honouring of him. This is not unlike Jeremiah's contention that the nations which are faithful to their own gods—even though these have no reality—are better than Israel which forsakes the true God (Jer. 2^{11-13}). Whichever sense is right, the judgement is clear.

3^{1-4} *The refiner*

Into the attacks on unfaithfulness there comes suddenly the picture of God's *messenger* (cf. Isa. 40), preparing *the way*, and of God himself coming to his shrine (v. 1). Does the prophet have a specific figure in mind as *the messenger of the covenant in whom you delight*? In 4^5 there is a vivid reference to the coming of Elijah who will lead men back to obedience; is he perhaps here in mind? In 4^4 it is Moses, the law-giver, to whom obedience is enjoined; he too could be appropriately called *messenger of the covenant*. Perhaps we should not try to identify any one individual, but recognize the stress on the coming of God himself in judgement; who is there who can stand in that judgement (cf. Isa. 6 and Ps. 1)? The task of the messenger is that of the refiner; the priesthood will be purified and then worship will be acceptable. Here is a theme closely linked to the thought of the Priestly Work; Israel and her priesthood must be pure and acceptable in the sight of God.

3^{16-18} *God's book of remembrance*

There is a sharp contrast here with the preceding verses which depict the rebellious members of the community. Small wonder that the faithful are anxious when men reverse right and wrong! But God knows men's hearts, and preserves the names of the faithful in his book (cf. Exod. 32^{32}; Isa. 4^3, and other passages). It is these faithful who are the true *special possession* (v. 17) of God (cf. Exod. 19^5; Deut. 7^6), the true chosen people. The present dilemmas will pass and the distinction between righteous and wicked will become clear once more. This coming new age is also the theme of the verses which follow in chapter 4.

H. NEHEMIAH

The book of Nehemiah is part of the large Work of the Chronicler (see pp. 294 ff.), and it contains for the most part narratives concerning Nehemiah the governor, his rebuilding of the walls of Jerusalem and the other measures of reform and rehabilitation which he undertook. The book also contains—in chapters 8, 9 (and perhaps 10)—material concerning Ezra. The problems of chronology and of the relationship between the two leaders are discussed on pp. 191 ff. As a result of the combining of the narratives concerning these two, there is a certain disorder in the Nehemiah material, and the order of the events of his activity cannot be completely clearly discerned. But we must consider this question also in relation to the nature of the Nehemiah narratives, the so-called 'Nehemiah Memoirs' or 'Memorial'.

The Nehemiah material is presented as a first-person narrative, and at first sight we might suppose that this is evidence that the Memoirs were composed by the governor himself. But the analogy of other first-person narratives, both within the Old Testament and outside, suggests that this is by no means necessarily the case. The example of Ezra lies nearest to hand, where we have both first-person and third-person sections of material. From a later date, the book of Daniel offers a first-person presentation at some points. In the prophetic books, we find first-person and third-person passages side by side (cf., e.g., Hos. 1 and 3; Isa. 6, 7, and 8), which suggests that either style may be used without it being necessary to believe that the one is more directly or the other less directly connected with the prophet himself. From outside the Old Testament, we may compare the inscription set up by Mesha, king of Moab (cf. *DOTT*, pp. 195 ff.), and the many royal inscriptions from Egypt and Mesopotamia and other near eastern areas which use first-person style; the scribe is here putting into the mouth of the ruler statements about his achievements. In brief inscriptions found in many different places, ordinary people too have recorded their names and have sought blessing for themselves in such words as:

> May *N.N.* be remembered for ever for good and prosperity.

Such analogies from outside Israel help us to understand various features in the Nehemiah narratives. The setting up of an inscription by an ancient ruler was no doubt partly dictated by the desire for the glorification of the one concerned; but its much more serious purpose was to lay before the deity, to whom the victories or other achievements were attributed, a memorial of what the ruler had done, a continual reminder to the deity so that the ruler's name would be remembered. It is this kind of purpose which we may naturally attribute to the author of the Nehemiah Memorial. He is laying before God the deeds of this great hero, inviting God to keep in perpetual remembrance the achievements of his life and also to remember to ill effect those who set themselves against him and endeavoured to frustrate his undertaking. The words just quoted, inscribed by an ordinary person, are reminiscent of phrases several times used in the Nehemiah material:

> Remember for my good, O my God, all that I have done for this people. [So 5^{19}, and cf. also $13^{14, 22, 31}$, and the negative forms in 6^{14} and 13^{29}.]

It has sometimes been thought that this appeal to God was made because Nehemiah, as an official at the Persian court who could be admitted to the presence of the queen (2^{6}), must have been a eunuch; but nothing else in the text suggests this, and since Nehemiah's opponents are shown as making all manner of attacks on him, we might have expected there to be some reference to this which could well have discredited him in the eyes of some members of his own community (cf. Isa. $56^{4\,f.}$). The more natural assumption is that the compiler of the Memorial, following the familiar pattern of royal and votive inscriptions, set out to glorify one who was to him a hero of the faith, a rebuilder of the life of the community, and to offer this to God as an act of piety and to invoke God's remembrance of him. It is possible, though this is not clear from the content, that there was some element of apologetic in the compiler's purpose. Not all his contemporaries viewed Nehemiah with favour, and it could well be that already existing divisions within the community were in some measure sharpened as a result of what he did; certainly Ezra, coming a generation later, found many of the same problems still existing, particularly in regard to marriage contracts with foreigners with the risks of religious apostasy which these were seen to bring. There may have been some who were ready to dishonour the memory of Nehemiah. For this aspect, an analogy may be seen in the speeches of Job (cf., e.g., 29–31 and also 19^{23-25}) and in some psalms (e.g. Ps. 26) in which one who believes himself wrongly accused sets out his innocence and defends his way of life, calling down judgement upon his detractors and declaring his loyalty and faithfulness to God.

The present order of the narratives is clearly not chronological. A division is made between the first and second periods of Nehemiah's governorship, the latter being covered in chapter 13. But the incidents recounted in chapter 5 are not necessarily in their correct chronological position, and vv. 14 ff. contain a comment on the whole first period of governorship. The dedication of the walls ($12^{27\text{ ff.}}$), instead of following on the rebuilding, is separated from it by other matter concerning the repopulation of Jerusalem (7^{4}, 11^{1-2}). Part of the disorder is caused by the insertion of the list in 7^{6-72}, a list which appears in Ezra 2, and by the Ezra material of chapters 8–9. Chapter 10, which also interrupts the sequence, presents many problems. It appears to offer a continuation of chapter 9 and to set out the covenant undertaken by the people in the light of Ezra's reading and prayer; some such covenant would be in place here. But its list of participants has the name of Nehemiah at the head, and the matters covered by the covenant run closely parallel with those associated with him, particularly in the second period of his activity. Thus it is possible that the Chronicler, or a later compiler if the Nehemiah Memorial was added later than the Chronicler, has moved the account of a covenant which perhaps belongs at the end of the Nehemiah narrative so as to place it where it seemed to belong from its content—perhaps in doing so he displaced a similar story told about Ezra. We have seen (pp. 179 f.) the probability that traditions concerning these two leaders were handed down separately, and that to some extent they are presented as performing very much the same tasks; this would have made the conflation all the easier. The order of the Nehemiah narrative may also have been influenced by the tendency which can be observed in the Chronicler's work as a whole, namely the desire to order material according to content and significance rather than merely according to chronology.

The comments on the passages which follow draw attention to the various aspects of Nehemiah's action as governor; in the description of this period some general points have been made about the setting and about the nature of his achievement (cf. pp. 178ff.). At a crucial moment in the history of the community, when political and economic fortunes appear to have been at a somewhat low ebb, it rested with Nehemiah and those who worked with him to help the people readjust to the experience of being a subject people; he gave a greater coherence to the life of the capital Jerusalem, and he emphasized the relationship between the obedience of a faithful people and the blessings which God gives. It was through such men that the Jewish community was able so to learn obedience and to preserve its distinctive way of life that it could survive the pressures of succeeding years.

1 *The continuing distress of Jerusalem*

The book opens as we might expect a prophetic book to open (cf. p. 178). It describes the visit of a brother of Nehemiah from Judah to the capital city where Nehemiah is a palace official. (At the end of chapter 1 he is described as *cupbearer*; the RSV rightly links this phrase with the narrative of chapter 2.) The description of Jerusalem they bring provokes great distress in Nehemiah: *The wall . . . is broken down*, the *gates are destroyed by fire* (v. 3); and these words provide one of the main themes of the narratives that follow. It is important in these opening verses to see the description of the community in Judah; it is those who *survived*—literally 'those who escaped'—and the following phrase means 'who had been left as a remnant from the exile' (v. 2). Here, as in Haggai and Zechariah, we have the understanding of the post-exilic community as consisting of those who have come through the disaster of the exile.

The response of Nehemiah is in mourning and fasting; vv. 5–11 set out a prayer appropriate to the occasion. Prayers and sermons are frequently found in the writings of the Chronicler (cf. pp. 303 f.); we find one such prayer in Ezra 9. In the book of Esther (see Vol. 5, pp. 189 ff.) prayers of this kind were added in the form which the book has in the Greek translation (cf. the Apocrypha: 'Additions to Esther'). This is a literary device of some importance, for by adding appropriate prayers the author is able to draw out the meaning of the events. We may properly suppose that he made use of the common prayer forms known to him, and partly by quotation and partly by deliberate construction, enhanced the effect of his narrative and drew out its significance. In this prayer we may observe motifs which appear in many of the psalms—the emphasis on the faithfulness of God and the appeal to him to hear his penitent people; acknowledgement of sin, with an appropriate allusion to the warning and promise to Moses (for this cf. Deut. 30^{1-4}). They are God's people, redeemed by him—an allusion to the Exodus but perhaps also to the return from exile. Appeal is made that God will hear, and in particular the general themes are linked to the situation of Nehemiah by a prayer for God's grace when he approaches the king.

2^{1-8} *The commissioning of Nehemiah*

In the opening verses of this passage, we may note a resemblance to the story of Esther. To protect her people from disaster, she risked her life by entering her royal husband's presence (Esther 4–5); Nehemiah, to obtain his desire from the king, does not conceal his distress at the state of Jerusalem, though to intrude his private affairs might evidently be dangerous (cf. v. 2). But Nehemiah's faith is portrayed as stronger than his fear (v. 3). Again when he is asked what his request is, he offers prayer (v. 4). The request that he should be commissioned to go to Judah to rebuild the city is accepted, a time limit for the commission is fixed, and the further request for support and protection is also granted. As the final comment stresses, *the good hand of my God was upon me* (v. 8).

How far may we see in this actual history and how far an imaginative picture? There is nothing improbable in the rise to high office of an alien such as Nehemiah, nor in the giving of generous favours to such a man. As we have seen, the policy of the Persian ruler may have had other motives too, for this was a moment of considerable difficulty in the western part of the empire (cf. p. 175). But we may also recognize that, as in the case of the Zerubbabel story, as it is told in 1 Esd. 4[13–63], and as in the stories in the book of Daniel, there is a poetic licence in the telling.

It has often been suggested that a recent disaster had occasioned the report to Nehemiah and the appeal for action. Such an incident appears in Ezra 4[6–23] which, as we have seen (p. 175), is quite out of place historically in its present position. It is associated with the period of Artaxerxes (most probably Artaxerxes I). In the confused and uncertain situation of *c.* 450 B.C., when the satrap of the province Beyond the River was rebelling, an attempt at rebuilding the walls of Jerusalem might well be construed by opponents as a rebellious act. But it is also possible that we should see here a wider concern of the compiler of the Memorial, who, like the Chronicler, is really much more interested in the restoration of the community and hence of Jerusalem in broader terms. He sees the work of Nehemiah as marking an end to the disaster which came with the fall of Jerusalem in 587 B.C. As we have seen (p. 179), a tradition found in 2 Macc. 1–2 associates Nehemiah with the earlier period of restoration and gives just that kind of emphasis in its interpretation of his activity.

More important than the question of what is historical is the recognition of the point being made: to those who have faith, God gives his blessing. Even the rulers of the great heathen empires acknowledge him, and, whether consciously or unconsciously, they serve his purpose. The same stress is to be found in the Ezra narrative and in the stories of Daniel.

2[9–20] *Rebuilding—support and opposition*

In the opening of this passage, two contrasting themes are brought out. Royal support for Nehemiah's mission—described in v. 8 as the direct result of God's favour—continues in the province Beyond the River; but at once the main opponents of Nehemiah are also introduced, and through the whole of the following narratives, we are shown ways in which the attempt was made by these and others to frustrate his work. Sanballat the Horonite is not given the title of governor of Samaria (though this is hinted at in 4[2]); but we know from the Elephantine papyri (cf. p. 286) that this was his position. From the Samaria papyri (cf. pp. 291 f.) we now know that there were probably three governors of this name, but it is most reasonable to see the opponent of Nehemiah as the first of that name, governor in the mid-fifth century B.C. He had two sons, Delaiah and Shelemaiah, active at the end of the century, presumably because by then Sanballat himself was old. It is important to note that the names of these sons, both ending in '*iah*', the form of the divine name which appears in many Old Testament names (e.g. Jeremiah, cf. pp. 110 f., 281), show that Sanballat was himself an adherent of the faith in Yahweh to which Nehemiah and his associates so ardently belonged. No hint of religious antagonism appears in the narratives, though in chapter 13 such an interpretation could be given. Indeed, 2[10] gives a clear clue to the nature of the opposition: *it displeased them greatly that someone had come to seek the welfare of the children of Israel*, i.e. of the true community in Judah and Jerusalem. Political and economic factors would seem to be the real basis of the antagonism. A full revival of Jerusalem and an independent governor there would reduce the status of the governor in Samaria and of the governors of other surrounding areas. So here we find another opponent named: *Tobiah the servant, the Ammonite*, and subsequently we hear of *Geshem the Arab* (v. 19) and in 4[7] they and their associates are joined by the Ashdodites. It is clear that the revival of Jerusalem was resented on all sides. We know so little about the general circumstances and the personalities involved that we have to be very cautious in assessing the precise situation. We might well suppose that Tobiah was governor of the Ammonite area, east of Jordan; his name too indicates an adherent of Yahweh. That he is called *the servant* or 'the slave' may have been seen by the narrator as a derogatory title; but the word is used of the king (e.g. 'your servant David') and could therefore be used in an honorific sense. (Cf. also the servant in the Second Isaiah.) *Geshem the Arab* might be a leader of another such area; a century later we find the Nabataeans firmly established to the south-east of Judah, particularly around Petra, south-east of the Dead Sea; they or some related group may already have been in control in Edom to the south (cf. pp. 55 f.).

Here again we may ask how far a merely historical account is being given; or how far the idea of a faithful people and leader facing the threat of the surrounding alien nations (cf. p. 92) has shaped the presentation of the history so as to bring out its theological significance. The preservation of the faith of Judah, so urgent and so difficult a matter both at this moment and in the succeeding centuries, may be appropriately pictured as the building up of the city of Jerusalem in the face of opposition, and the exclusion of alien influences from a people being recalled to their faith. History and its theological interpretation are closely interwoven.

Verses 11–16 sketch the survey of the walls undertaken by Nehemiah. Both here and in chapter 3 many topographical details are given, but unfortunately without our being able to identify the exact places on the line of the walls. Although some of the names appear in the later history of the city, and probably the locations remained much the same, the precise area of the city at this time is so different from what it later was (cf. plan on p. 256) that very great caution is needed in attempting identifications. The difficulties of the survey are indicated in v. 14, and the archaeological work of recent years has shown that the lower eastern slopes of the older city were so ruined that they could not be restored. In 3^{20-25}, the description of the parts restored in the rebuilding refers to houses rather than to gates and towers, and it has been thought possible that this indicates that here a new line of wall had to be established, making use of houses near the summit of the slope, because the lower area was too badly damaged (cf. p. 258). It may be that further archaeological work will clarify this point.

Verses 17–20 show how Nehemiah, having so far kept secret his true intentions—subsequent narratives suggest that this may have been because of opposition within Jerusalem to what he proposed to do—now calls upon the people, *priests, nobles, officials, and the rest* (v. 16), to take courage. His testimony is of divine blessing and guidance, and the people make a response in faith. The motif of opposition appears again, as the proposal is mocked and an accusation of rebellion is hinted at; Nehemiah as a royal favourite, acting under the king's protection, was in a strong position, but suggestions that he was aiming at independence could very easily lead to the withdrawal of favour. Nehemiah is depicted, however, as one to whom his confidence in God's protection is such that he can go ahead, and he excludes any claims that his opponents make on the control of Jerusalem.

The scene is set, and the following chapter sets out in detail the organizing of the rebuilding of the walls and gates; it is not without its indications of half-heartedness (cf. 3^5). It is important to note that among those who took part are some from places outside Jerusalem (cf., e.g., 3^7). It is all Judah, the whole true people, which is summoned to this act of faith.

4 *Opposition and faith*

The pattern of opposition and faith continues through this chapter. Verses 1–6 depict a first stage of this, in the ridiculing of the work by Sanballat and Tobiah; the mocking of enemies is a common theme of Old Testament poetry, found in pronouncements upon foreign nations, and no doubt ultimately derived from what we, in modern terms, might call 'psychological warfare'. We need to recall that words of curse and

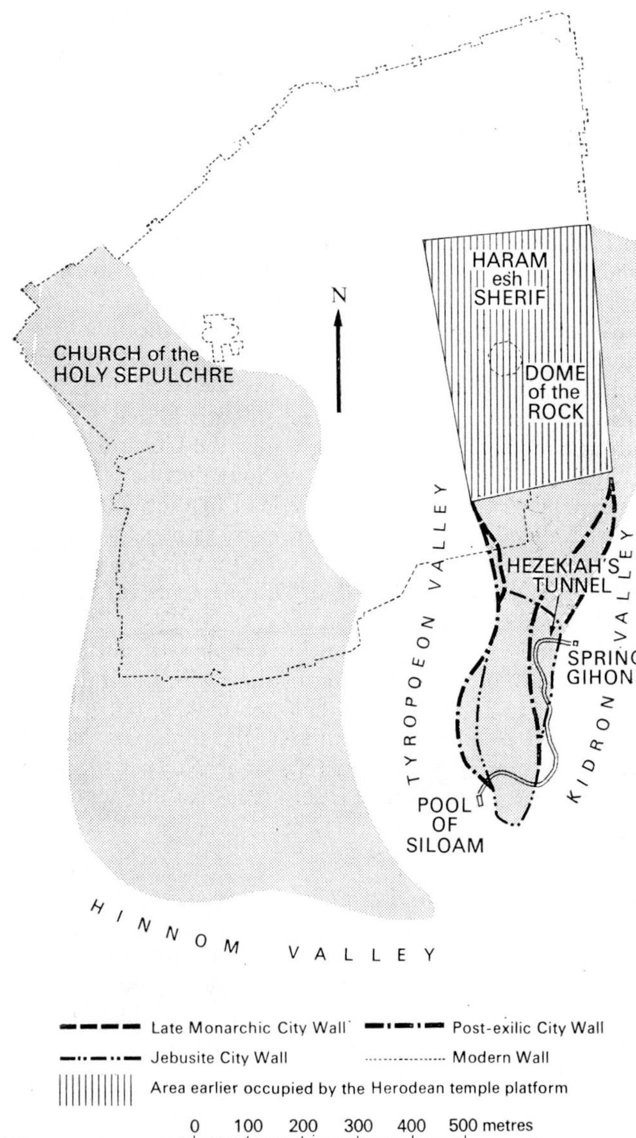
HARAM esh SHERIF
N
CHURCH of the HOLY SEPULCHRE
DOME of the ROCK
TYROPOEON VALLEY
HEZEKIAH'S TUNNEL
KIDRON VALLEY
SPRING GIHON
POOL OF SILOAM
HINNOM VALLEY
Late Monarchic City Wall
Post-exilic City Wall
Jebusite City Wall
Modern Wall
Area earlier occupied by the Herodean temple platform
0 100 200 300 400 500 metres

words of ill omen were felt in the ancient world to be effective, bringing about the purpose for which they were spoken; words of blessing are equally effective for good. The response to this mockery is expressed by vv. 4–5 which use words very much like some of the more violent passages in the psalms to avert the danger (cf. Ps. 109^{6-19}). Such passages present great difficulty to the modern reader, and when the psalms are used in worship they are often omitted. Certainly they cannot be used without explanation, and they need to be set in a context in which their theological meaning is brought out. When men set themselves directly against the will of God, judgement is operative. Faith and courage here meet the threats from outside (v. 6).

Verses 7–23 depict another situation of opposition and faith, but this passage draws out more fully the inner uncertainties of the builders. It is possible that various smaller units have been used to build up a fuller picture of both the opposition and the faith that met it. Thus vv. 7–9 provide a brief statement, perhaps offering a parallel to the mockery theme of vv. 1–6. Verse 10 introduces the despondency of the builders, because of the great accumulation of debris, and this is combined with the threats of the opponents that they will attack. So a division of labour is made within the community, some standing on guard, others proceeding with the rebuilding. The plans of the enemies are frustrated by God's will (v. 15). Verses 16–20 further amplify this by giving another picture of the way in which the

---

PLAN OF POST-EXILIC JERUSALEM. The ancient city of Jerusalem (Jebus) conquered by David was built on a rocky spur running north–south between the deep Kidron Valley and the valley later known as the Tyropoeon: this latter has gradually come to be filled, particularly within the modern walled city and so is not so clearly visible. The plan shows the line of the Jebusite city wall, though some parts of this are not clearly known. The Israelite city followed the same pattern, but extended further north: the wall of the city in the late monarchic period is shown but this too is only conjectural for some parts. The royal palace and temple were evidently part of an extension of the city northwards. After the exile, rebuilding took place in the same area but the city wall on the east was above its older line (cf. pp. 254 f.). How much further the city then extended is still far from clear.

NEHEMIAH'S WALL. The extent of the destruction in 587 B.C. is reflected in the fact that when Nehemiah inspected the walls in 445 he could not ride round (see Neh. 2[14]). It appears that the lower slopes of the south-eastern hill had had to be abandoned, and Nehemiah's wall is to be found on the top of the slope. In the picture it appears in the centre-right. This wall, often repaired and strengthened, remained in use until the destruction by Titus in A.D. 70. It can only be partly traced; it seems very probable that for some parts of its length use was made of already existing houses. For the biblical account, see Neh. 3; identification of the place names remains very uncertain.

builders were on the alert, and a warning system devised so that they could rally to the point attacked. Verses 21–23 summarize the zeal of the workers, and their watching day and night to ensure that the building would not be delayed. The whole passage draws out the relationship between faith and obedience to the call to restore the holy city.

5 *Protecting the life of the community*

The story of the rebuilding of the walls and of the overcoming of opposition is interrupted at this point by another theme concerned with the life of the people. There is no clear chronological relationship shown between this material and the remainder of the narratives; indeed, vv. 14–18 indicate a wider concern with the whole nature of Nehemiah's policy as governor. The chapter serves to remind us that Nehemiah was not just rebuilding the walls of Jerusalem; he was rebuilding the community centred upon that city and the walls are only a symbol of the protection of the community from alien outside influence.

Restoration, as may be seen in so much of the literature of the Persian period, involves more than rebuilding; it demands the rehabilitation of the whole community. So here, not inappropriately, a section concerning the social conditions has been inserted into the story of the walls. The economic problems of poorer people are set out; they have been forced to mortgage their property, some have borrowed to pay the tax to the Persian authorities (v. 4), some have had to sell children into slavery. Nehemiah took firm action against the exploitation of the poorer members of the community by the *nobles* and *officials* (v. 7). Like the prophets before him, he pronounces judgement upon such wrong practice; and, also like the prophets, he performs an action, shaking out his lap (v. 13)—scattering what the fold of his garment contains—as an indication of the judgement decreed upon those who fail to fulfil what is now laid upon them as a covenant, an agreement.

The Old Testament often reveals a concern for the protection of the weak and provides in various of its collections of laws means by which the life of a family (including the family property) may be maintained. The laws on periodic release from debts (Deut. 15^{1-11}; Lev. 25^{8-17}) show this, and so do various laws governing the control of slavery within the community (e.g. Exod. 21^{1-11}; Deut. 15^{12-18}). So here we find Nehemiah taking various measures designed to protect the weaker and poorer members of the community, and in the latter part of this chapter there is an account of various other things that he did—not claiming the governor's allowances, avoiding the kind of grandeur which a governor and his entourage might claim, providing for a large number of officials and guests at his own table (5^{14-18}). Thus he is proclaimed as an ideal ruler and protector of his people.

6^{1}–7^{5}, 11^{1-2}, 12^{27-43} *The walls and the city*

It is convenient to take these three sections together, although they deal with more than one theme. They are now divided from each other by a long list (7^{6-73a}), part of the Ezra story (7^{73b}–9), the list and covenant passage already mentioned (10, cf. p. 249), and a whole collection of other lists (11^{3}–12^{26}). The completion and dedication of the walls form one theme; the other main theme is that of the measures taken to increase the population of the city. Both of these may be seen to contrast with the theme of opposition which appears prominently in chapter 6.

6^{1-14} deal with this opposition, and recount two different points at which an attempt was made to hinder Nehemiah. In 6^{1-9} we are told of various stratagems adopted by his opponents to get him into their hands; when he refuses their invitation to come and meet them, they accuse him more openly of rebellion, even affirming that he has appointed prophets to proclaim him king (v. 7). This recalls how in 1 and 2 Kings, particularly in the northern kingdom, prophetic action is shown to bring new rulers to the throne. In 6^{10-13} a more subtle attack is described in which Nehemiah is shown as resisting the temptation to take refuge in the temple from a threat of which he is warned by a hireling of his enemies. The man concerned, Shemaiah, is described in effect as a false prophet, willing to speak if he is paid. (In v. 10 he is described as *shut up*, the same expression as is used of Jeremiah (Jer. 36^{5}); it is not clear what it means. It suggests some kind of restraint, but whether this is an external one imposed by the authorities or a constraint which is felt to be imposed by God is not certain. Perhaps it simply means that for a time he was—perhaps by reason of illness—confined to his house.) The passage closes (v. 14) with an appeal for judgement upon the opponents of Nehemiah.

6^{15}–7^{3} recount the completion of the walls and the measures taken for the safety of the city by the guarding and shutting of the gates. Two further elements appear in this. One is the awe which comes upon the surrounding peoples at the evidence of God's protection (v. 16); we may recall the way in which the entry of Israel into Canaan is described as accompanied by fear which falls upon its inhabitants (e.g. Deut. 2^{25}). The other is the mention of the internal problems which Nehemiah had to face; there were many within Judah who were in league with Tobiah, himself allied by marriage with important families there. Evidently some of the influential people tried to undermine Nehemiah's confidence by stressing Tobiah's virtues. Subsequently (13^{4-9}) we learn of the way in which Tobiah was given favours during Nehemiah's absence.

7^{4} introduces the new theme of the need for a larger population and for better housing in the city. 7^{5} may really be concerned with a different matter, a measure designed to ensure proper control of the membership of the community; as it now stands it serves to introduce the list which follows, found also in Ezra 2, and both this list and those in chapters 11–12 have been used to provide surveys of the community. There is much concern here with the question of who belongs to the true people, and though this may well seem a somewhat narrow interest, it is nevertheless important for the preservation of the people's values and traditions.

11^{1-2} now stand in isolation, but stress the importance of the city of Jerusalem. As the city of the temple, protected now by rebuilt walls and gates, it must be adequately populated. Just as a tenth of produce and flocks (cf. the laws in Num. 18^{21-32} and Deut. 14^{22-29}, reflecting different types of practice) was to be dedicated to God and holy, so a tenth of the population of Judah is to be in *the holy city* (v. 1). On the regulation of tithes, cf. also Neh. $13^{10\text{ff.}}$.

12^{27-43} describe the actual dedication, with notes of those who took part in the great act of worship, involving processions around the walls and gates in two directions, meeting at last in the temple. It is a description of worship with the emphasis on rejoicing, and such descriptions may be found not infrequently in the writings of the Chronicler; in this respect the Nehemiah Memorial closely resembles the work in which it now stands. The final phrase: *And the joy of Jerusalem was heard afar off* (v. 43), gives to these events their wider meaning; it should not be taken simply to mean that the noise was great, but that what God has done for his people at Jerusalem through Nehemiah was acknowledged far and wide (cf. 6^{16}).

13^{4-31} *Nehemiah's second term as governor*

In a brief narrative, various points concerning Nehemiah's further activity are brought together. They are important for our fuller understanding of his work. First (vv. 4–9), we see the expulsion of a notable opponent of Nehemiah. During his absence, Tobiah had been given a room in the temple by the priest Eliashib to whom he was in some way related, possibly by marriage. Not only was this an insult to Nehemiah, but, more important, it represented a total misuse of the room concerned. The restoration of the room to its proper use for the storage of offerings for the Levites was therefore a significant act of piety. Second (vv. 10–13), there is linked with this a reform of tithing and various appointments to supervise financial concerns. Third (vv. 15–22*a*), we are told of reforms designed to ensure proper observance of the sabbath. Although sabbath observance was of early origin (cf. pp. 29 f., 155 f.), it is in the period after the exile that we find it taking on that special quality which it has preserved to this day in Judaism. Fourth (vv. 23–27), the matter of purity of the people is raised in regard to foreign marriages which bring about loss of the Hebrew language (*the language of Judah*, v. 24). Nehemiah takes strong action, even physical action, against the offenders, for the danger is one to the people's faith. The analogy of Solomon (cf. 1 Kings 11) is used to show the consequences of such behaviour. The theme is also seen in Mal. 2^{11}. Fifth

(v. 28), another opponent is ejected, and again we can see what difficulties faced Nehemiah with the close connections by marriage of the high priest with his enemies; *Jehoiada*, a *son of Eliashib*, was *son-in-law of Sanballat*. It is clear that there were close bonds between Jerusalem and Samaria; but it is also evident that the policy of such a leader as Nehemiah was creating a situation in which there could come about that division which was eventually to be a very sharp one in the religious community, that between Jews and Samaritans (cf. pp. 185 ff.).

These last sections of the Nehemiah story are punctuated by the appeal to God to recall his good works and bring down doom on his opponents. They are drawn together in a final summarizing statement in vv. 30–31, which stresses the purification of the community and the right reorganization of religion. Nehemiah was not only the builder of the walls; he was one of the builders of a true and faithful and obedient people of God.

I. EZRA

The narratives concerning Ezra and his work are to be found in two sections: Ezra 7–10 and Neh. 7[73]–9[37]. We have already noted that the material of Neh. 10, which gives details of a covenant, more probably belongs with the Nehemiah narratives than with those of Ezra, though the climax of Ezra's work may well also have been some kind of undertaking by the community. It appears most likely that in the combining of the Ezra and Nehemiah narratives, the overlap has been reduced and the Nehemiah covenant used to conclude the Ezra material (on these points, cf. p. 249).

The present arrangement of the Ezra narratives derives from two points. First, the separation between the two sections is due to the interweaving of the Nehemiah narratives with those of Ezra; in 1 Esdras, this division does not occur since the Nehemiah narratives are not present, and the words of Ezra 10[44] are immediately followed by a verse which overlaps

Neh. 7^{73} (see 1 Esd. 9^{36-37}). Second, the order of the narratives appears to be due to the desire of the Chronicler to lead up to a climax, the reading of the law and its acceptance by the people. For this reason the account of Ezra's action against foreign marriages (Ezra 9–10), which, from the dates which it contains ($10^{9,\ 16\ f.}$—on this point cf. also p. 193), ought to follow the reading of the law (Neh. 8 and note 9^{2}), has been placed first. The effect is to show the community undertaking an act of purification first, so that then the acceptance of the law is by those who have already excluded from their company the alien influences and religious apostasy which foreign marriages would bring. (For Nehemiah's dealing with this problem, see Neh. 13.) It is in the light of the newly resolved acceptance of the law (cf. Neh. 9^{1-2}) that such firm action could be taken.

Although this rearrangement of the material is necessary to explain its content, it does not by any means solve all the difficulties which are raised by these particular chapters of the books of Ezra and Nehemiah. We observe that Ezra 7^{27-28}, 8, and 9 relate events in the first person singular, with Ezra as the speaker, whereas Ezra 7^{1-26} and 10 and also Neh. 8–9 are related in the third person. We should not overemphasize this difference of narrative technique which can be found elsewhere (cf. the comments on the Nehemiah Memorial on p. 247). Nevertheless, the fact that we may also note some degree of overlap between Ezra 9 and 10 and perhaps also between Ezra 7 and 8, could imply that the Chronicler has made use of different sources of information and has woven them together into the present narrative. In addition, it appears that he made use of an Aramaic source for his account of the commission given to Ezra by Artaxerxes, for 7^{12-26} are in Aramaic whereas the introductory and concluding verses of this chapter are in Hebrew.

The story of Ezra, belonging to the reign of Artaxerxes II (for the discussion of this, cf. pp. 191 ff.), marks the latest element in the work of the Chronicler. (Some later additions have been made, particularly in the lists of names, and this shows a continuing interest in the membership and nature of the religious community in the Persian and Greek periods.) The period of the Chronicler's activity is probably to be placed not long after Ezra; indeed, it has been suggested that Ezra himself was the Chronicler, and traced the history of his people as he saw it up to that moment at which, in the work which he was commissioned to do, a new era could be said to open in the life of the community. Certainly, the presentation of Ezra is very sympathetic, and the emphases in the stories told of him are very much those of the Chronicler's work as a whole. We might even be tempted to suppose that the reference, in the first person narrative of Ezra 8, to Ezra's reluctance to ask for a royal bodyguard—'I was ashamed to ask . . . since we had told the king, "The hand of our God is for good upon all that seek him, and the power of his wrath is against all that forsake him" '(v. 22)—might suggest the honesty of a man who, in telling his own story, does not shrink from acknowledging the hesitations of his faith. We might compare what has been said by New Testament scholars about the connections between the Gospel of Mark and Peter; the revealing of the weaknesses of the leading disciple would come well in a Gospel which in some way derived from his telling of the story. But just as there are doubts about the validity of such arguments for the Gospel, so we may recognize that there is really very little basis on which to regard Ezra as the author of the narrative. And indeed the present arrangement and interpretation of Ezra suggests rather an author who saw in him a great reformer and leader, one under whose influence he himself worked, and one of whom he offered a presentation which did not hesitate to give priority to theological rather than to chronological order.

What was the achievement of Ezra? This must be seen both in the light of the commission which sets out the purpose of his journey to Jerusalem (7^{12-26}) and in the consequences which were to follow for Judaism in the emphasis which he laid. The commission stresses that Ezra was to look into the position of the law in Judah and Jerusalem, and to bring about a wholehearted acceptance of it by all who were to be regarded as the members of the Jewish community. All that follows in the activities in which he is shown to have been engaged is the consequence of this basic concern. The true people of God is to be the obedient people of the law. To a subject people, living under the power of a great empire, with many political uncertainties and no doubt often with wistful glances back at the traditions of a great past history, the recovery and the maintenance of a real national life were of vital importance. In this, Ezra stands in the same line as the prophets and theologians of the exilic age, and as those who in the years of Persian rule—from Haggai and Zechariah to Nehemiah—had sought to explain the meaning of events and to purify and build up the people. It is truly a climax which is reached in Ezra; the promises declared to the people of the past are claimed to be real to those who with him accept the law (cf. especially the prayer in Neh. 9).

In the later development of Judaism, Ezra was revered as the great scribe, the one who again established the law, the successor of Moses. A relatively early indication of this reverence (probably about A.D. 100) is to be found in 2 Esdras, particularly chapter 14, which draws the analogy between Moses and Ezra, and attributes to Ezra the rewriting of the scriptures, supposedly destroyed at the fall of Jerusalem in 587 B.C. To a religious community which, with all the rich development of its life and thought, looked to the sacred writings of the Old Testament as the source from which they derived, the place accorded to one who was associated with the reinstitution and full acceptance of the law was naturally a very important one. Whatever the precise nature of Ezra's achievement, it must be seen not only in historical terms but also in the light of the tradition which grew up around his name.

Ezra 7 *Ezra's commission from the king*

Verses 1–6. We note that the narrative begins without any explanation of the long period of history which has elapsed since the events described in chapter 6. The importance of Ezra is indicated by the genealogy, an incomplete list of the ancestral line, tracing it back to *Aaron the chief priest* (v. 5). This priestly ancestry emphasizes the authority which Ezra has for his people in the delivering and expounding of the law; for while Moses was the giver of the law in the tradition, it was the priests who clarified its meaning by the giving of precise directives (cf. the use of *tōrāh* in Hag. 2[11]). These introductory verses give a brief summary of Ezra's background and work, indicating, without any explanation, that *the king granted him all that he asked*—the pattern is similar to that in the case of Nehemiah, and similar too is the comment, *for the hand of the* L*ORD his God was upon him* (v. 6, cf. Neh. 1–2).

Ezra was priest and scribe (cf. also v. 11). In v. 6 he is described as *a scribe skilled in the law of Moses*. The phrase 'skilled scribe' occurs also in Ps. 45[1]; in the description of an ideal ruler in Isa. 16[5] the same word is rendered 'swift' (to do righteousness). It is natural to think here of the later development of the scribes as interpreters of the law, especially in view of the activity attributed to Ezra in Neh. 8. At the same time, we must note that the term 'scribe' is used in older texts in reference to a royal official, a court secretary (cf., e.g., 2 Sam. 8[15]), and also of other such officials. It would seem that the word developed several meanings, and the suggestion has been made that Ezra was in fact a royal official, though the traditions which evolved about him stressed rather his activity as an interpreter of the law. This suggestion is particularly interesting because of the questions raised by the wording of the commission in vv. 12–26. The passage is very remarkable in its acknowledgement of the God of Jerusalem, and in this it resembles in some measure the decree of Cyrus as that is described in Ezra 1 and 6. We have seen that the latter may be compared with other 'propaganda' documents of the time, particularly the Cyrus Cylinder (cf. pp. 202 f.) If we ask who wrote such documents, then the answer would most probably be that it was an official at the royal court who was either familiar with the language appropriate to the community to which it was addressed or was actually a member of that community, employed at the court for dealing with its affairs. Was Ezra such an official? Was he therefore able to approach the king—or the royal vizier or other executive officer—with a petition for the well-being of his people? Did he then write his own commission, authorized by the king to undertake a journey which also fitted in with Persian policy directed towards improving the situation in Palestine, so vital for the control of a rebellious Egypt (cf. pp. 181 f.)? Was Ezra a sort of 'secretary of state for Jewish affairs'? Or if that is too grand a conception, was he a minor officer whose responsibility was to advise, give information, and when necessary to draft documents for the royal seal? We cannot know the answers to these questions, but the matter illuminates again the probability that the sending of Ezra was in one sense a normal part of Persian policy, undertaken through the normal government channels, while in another sense, relevant to the Jewish community, it would appropriately be interpreted as a divine act, designed to bring about the full establishment and acceptance of the law. Thus Ezra the scribe, the court officer, would become Ezra the scribe, the interpreter of the law.

Verses 7–10 summarize the mission of Ezra, covering matter which is repeated in chapter 8 and looking ahead also to Neh. 8. It emphasizes (v. 10) the intention of Ezra in regard to the law and thus takes a stage further the indications in vv. 1–6.

Verse 11 introduces formally the *copy of the letter*. Although this verse is in Hebrew, both the words used here are Aramaic in form, though both are actually Persian words which have come into the language. The word rendered 'copy' is used (in its closely similar Hebrew form) in Esther (e.g. 3^{14}), similarly for a copy of an official decree.

Verses 12–26 contain the commission itself, beginning with a formal address, and turning with the words *And now* to the substance of the decree. This is a common formula, particularly in letters (cf. the Elephantine letters; note on pp. 283, No. 30, line 4). The commission is extraordinarily liberal, but we have seen elsewhere that the Persian rulers were not averse to giving a broad support in religious matters to subject peoples, particularly where there might be political advantage as well. Ezra is sent on a mission of investigation (v. 14) into the conditions in Judah and Jerusalem, with an ample provision of gifts, both from the king and from Jews in Babylonia. (In vv. 15–16 the opening words of v. 16 may be read as a somewhat exaggerated statement, and this suggests that the author of the story has used, somewhat freely, either a document or a tradition about the decree.) Ezra is to do all that is necessary for the Jerusalem temple, with support from the royal treasury. Verses 21–24 develop the royal support further by instructions to the authorities of the province Beyond the River (cf. Neh. 2[7]), and the point is made in v. 23 that this action is designed to bring upon the Persian empire the favour of the *God of heaven*, a title appropriate to the supreme deity (cf. its use in the Elephantine papyri, p. 283) and one which shows a respect for him comparable with that shown for Marduk, God of Babylon, in the Cyrus Cylinder. For the idea of seeking such favour, cf. Ezra 6[10]. Verse 24 provides for exemption from taxation for the various religious officials. Such a magnanimous act towards the Jews may be paralleled in the account given by Josephus, the Jewish historian, of the policy of Antiochus III the Great in the early second century B.C. (cf. Vol. 5, p. 23), and in the actions of some Roman rulers, notably Julius Caesar. Consideration for the religious susceptibilities of their subjects was sometimes shown by the rulers of the ancient world, though at other times, as in the case of Antiochus IV Epiphanes and others of the Roman rulers, there was a flagrant disregard of such matters.

Verses 25–26 form the most important part of the whole statement. Again, the text as it stands appears to be somewhat exaggerated, since it is hardly to be supposed that the intention is that the Jewish law is to be imposed on *all the people in the province Beyond the River* (v. 25); the next phrases suggest that the intention was that it should apply to all Jewish people, who should be adequately instructed so that they should be obedient to it. Nevertheless, this defining of the Jewish community as those who accept and obey the law, opened the way for non-Jews to come into the community provided they were willing to accept the obligations of the law. While a Jew may be defined as such because of his birth, it is more important that he should be defined in terms of his obedience to the law, and this has been the great strength of the Jewish community through the centuries.

Verses 27–28*a* move over from the commission to the pronouncing of a word of praise at the marvellous act of God, in bringing about such a willingness on the part of the Persian king to show his concern for the temple in Jerusalem. This provides, in the form of a prayer, a comment on the meaning of Ezra's mission. Such a commission was an indication of divine action, and from this Ezra confesses that *I took courage*, and began the work for which he was commissioned (28*b*).

Nehemiah 8¹–9⁵ *The reading and expounding of the law*

(The passage actually begins in the last verse of the previous chapter; it is not quite clear to what context the first part of 7⁷³ belongs but it now provides a link with the preceding Nehemiah material. The different form of this in 1 Esd. 9³⁷ shows how difficult it is to resolve some of the literary problems.)

In this section, a series of celebrations is described, of which the centre is the reading and acceptance of the law.

Verses 1–12 give an account of what happened on the first day of the seventh month—that is in the autumn of the year. An assembly is held in the great open space inside the Water Gate, and a special *wooden pulpit* was constructed in the square. The word actually means a 'tower', and hence in this context perhaps a 'platform', evidently large enough to hold the company mentioned in v. 4 as standing to Ezra's right and left. The assembly consists of *men and women and all who could hear with understanding* (v. 2), i.e. the adult members of the community together with younger people who have now come to an age at which they can hear and accept the law. The occasion is one for ceremonial, the pronouncing of a blessing of God for his goodness, to which the people respond by saying *Amen* (v. 6). This Hebrew word has come over into the language of Christian worship through the Greek translation of the Old Testament and its use in the New Testament; it stresses the truth and sureness of what is said, and signifies an endorsement of it as true by those who make the response. The people stand for the reading, and a company of Levites is at hand to help *the people to understand* (v. 7). Verse 8 should most probably be understood as is indicated by the RSV margin; the reading was accompanied by interpretation, exposition of the law, which would involve not simply explanation of the words but an indication of the consequences of obedience. Another possible explanation is that the reading was in Hebrew and that an interpretation was then given in Aramaic, the language which gradually began to replace Hebrew as the vernacular; this was the language used by the Aramaean peoples to the north-east of Palestine, and it was used as an international language for the whole area by the Assyrians (cf. Isa. 36[11] = 2 Kgs. 18[26]) and Persians (cf. p. 203, and note that Ezra's commission appears in Aramaic). But although at a later date such translation was undertaken and eventually the translations came to be written down and standardized as the Targums (which simply means 'translations'), it does not seem probable that such a procedure was necessary in the time of Ezra. (We may observe Nehemiah's protest at the tendency for children not to speak Hebrew, but this is a protest against alien influences.)

The description of the reading and interpretation of the law here probably rests upon what was already normal practice, though it is clear that a new stress is being laid on its importance. The nearest parallel to the account is found in Deut. 31[9–13] where a seven-year reading is prescribed, in the year of release from debts, at the feast of booths (cf. Neh. 8[13ff.] for this), and we may observe that this reading also includes both the adult members of the community and children who are now to become fully part of the community, being old enough to do so. The Jewish practice of bringing a boy fully into membership at the age of twelve represents a standardizing of this procedure; the Neh. 8 and Deut. 31 narratives do not make any distinction between boys and girls. Verses 9–12 depict the response of the people; the hearing of the injunctions of the law provokes distress at the consciousness of disobedience (cf. the account of the reading of the law to King Josiah in 2 Kgs. 22^{11-13}), but reassurance is given in terms of the law's promises. On Nehemiah in v. 9, cf. p. 192.

Verses 13–18 show a further stage of the reading on the following day, which leads on to a renewed celebration of the feast of booths, the great autumn festival, one of the three major religious occasions of the year (the other two being Passover/Unleavened Bread and Weeks; for one statement of the ordering of the festivals cf. Deut. 16^{1-17}).

The feast lasted seven days, and according to the law in Lev. 23^{33-36} and Num. $29^{12\text{ ff.}}$, where much more detail is given, it was to begin on the fifteenth day of the seventh month; the older legislation in Exod. 23^{16} and Deut. 16 gives no precise date. Nor is a precise date given here in Neh. 8, so that it is possible that the final fixing of a date had not yet been fully accepted. It is expressly mentioned that this celebration marked a revival of the feast, with a renewed making of booths out of branches gathered for the purpose (v. 15), and that it had not been so celebrated since the time of Joshua. Since we find a similar statement in regard to the celebration of the Passover at Josiah's reform (so 2 Kgs. 23^{22}), we may perhaps best take this as a poetic way of saying that what was believed to be ancient custom was now revived, and the failures of intervening years were set aside. Liturgical reform has often been based upon an attempt to recover the purity of ancient practice, though it has always, and quite properly, involved a measure of restatement and reinterpretation.

9¹⁻⁵ describes a day of fasting on the twenty-fourth of the month. In Lev. 16 (and cf. also Lev. 23²⁶ᶠᶠ·; Num. 29⁷ᶠᶠ·; Exod. 30¹⁰) details are given of a special day, eventually to be known as the Day of Atonement, on the tenth day of the month. There is no mention in Neh. 8–9 of this day, and it is probable that we should see the celebration here described as equivalent to it. If so, then we must recognize that in the development of Jewish worship, various practices existed, described in different ways in the various laws and narratives, and that eventually a careful codification and standardization took place so that there should be no uncertainty about the matter. If the Christian churches ever agree on a uniform celebration of Easter, perhaps on a fixed date, it will be possible to trace both the earlier stages of disagreement and the later stages of agreement. A close examination of the festival laws in the Old Testament and of narratives concerning festivals provides us with some part of the history of the worship but does not give us all that we need to know to write a full account. It is possible that what is described in Neh. 9 is a quite different celebration, but if so we have still to account for the entire absence of any mention of the Day of Atonement in the narrative. The celebration here is marked by confession, separation from alien influences (cf. Ezra 9–10), and a renewed acceptance of the law. It issues in a great invitation to praise.

There remains the question as to what law was read by Ezra on the occasion here described. And perhaps we may note first the unsatisfactory nature of attempts at answering this by reference to the supposed length of time the law took to read. Quite apart from the fact that the description indicates a reading which was spread over more than one day and that it involved both reading and study of the law, to put the problem in this way supposes that the account given in Neh. 7 is merely factual, whereas it is clear that it must be regarded as an interpretation of the significance of this major event. The problem then becomes partly one of seeking evidence for the identification of a particular collection of laws, and partly one of examining the history of Old Testament law with a view to determining what might have been available at this moment of time. On the question of evidence of identification, there is really very little on which any firm conclusions can be based. If, as has been suggested (p. 249), Neh. 10 belongs, from its similarities to the Nehemiah material, with his activity rather than with that of Ezra, then the various matters covered there cannot be adduced as evidence. Where in the past this section was used, there seemed to be considerable reason for supposing the law-book to be Deuteronomy; we may note simply that both in the book of Malachi and in the activity of Nehemiah, there is much evidence for the strong influence of Deuteronomy and the ideas associated with it. We may also note that such influence is still strong in the work of the Chronicler. As has been seen (p. 272), the provisions for the celebrations do not exactly tally with any particular law-book, and this suggests that this was a period in which there was still considerable fluidity. So far as the availability of law-books is concerned, we may observe that in the book of Malachi there appears to be some influence from the laws of the Priestly Work, and that this too is strong in the Work of the Chronicler, where the Deuteronomic and Priestly strands come together. Since we have already seen links between Ezekiel and the Holiness Code and hence also the Priestly Work, this would seem to suggest that there was a strong legal tradition in Babylonia; from this, Ezra might be expected to bring a law-book which represented something akin to what we now have in that Work. We should beware of trying to make too firm an identification, for it is evident that some modifications of the laws continued; and even when the written law became fixed, oral tradition went on providing the necessary adjustments to suit contemporary conditions. The important point is to see in the reading and acceptance of the law in Neh. 8–9 an expression of the process by which in the course of time law came to be so deeply influential in the community's life; it is the moment singled out by the Chronicler in his interpretation of the history as the one which was determinative.

Nehemiah 9^{6-37} *The prayer of Ezra*

The Hebrew text begins this long prayer with no mention of the speaker's name. In view of the prominence of Ezra in the narrative and the presence of other prayers of Ezra at significant points (cf. Ezra 7^{27-28a}, 9^{6-15}), it is appropriate that the Greek translation supplies his name. But we should not overstress this, and in any case what is significant is not the name of the person to whom the prayer is attributed, but its content. We have noted the tendency of ancient authors to add such passages (cf. on Neh. 1); such a prayer, which is really very close in content to a psalm, provides a comment on and an explanation of the narratives with which it is set.

It is not necessary to comment on the detail of the prayer, for its allusions are to well-known incidents in the whole history of Israel. We may compare Pss. 78, 105, 106, 135, and 136 which in various ways provide similar surveys. Here is a statement of faith in terms of a recounting of the actions of God in relation to his people in the past. A later example of the same kind is to be found in the book of Judith, 5^{6-21}, where it is put in the mouth of an enemy who uses it to warn Holofernes of the risk he takes in attacking Judah.

After an ascription of praise, the prayer traces God's choice of Abram, his renaming as Abraham, and the promise of the land; it recounts the oppression in Egypt, deliverance and the giving of the law; it comments on the repeated disobedience of the people and the goodness and mercy of God. In vv. 26–31 the disobedience of the people in Canaan is more generally described, the disaster of the exile being indicated without any precise reference. The final verses of the prayer are in the form of a confession of the rightness of divine judgement and an appeal for mercy for the people who are slaves of the imperial power which rules the land.

Whoever composed this prayer made use of forms well known to him. To some extent, the emphasis on distress in the final verses does not accord well with the stress in both the Ezra and the Nehemiah narratives on the goodness of

God revealed through the actions of well-disposed Persian rulers. Perhaps we should therefore see here a prayer designed to comment on the problems of the subject people. The ideals expressed in the work of Ezra must be understood in the light of the realities of a delicate and oppressive political situation; yet the confidence remains the same, for it is God who is creator and who covenanted with his people (cf. v. 6) to whom they may turn. In addition to this, we may see in this passage a clear witness to the kind of confession of faith which was made in post-exilic times. There is an appreciation that God is not by any means a God of past experience alone; he is one to whom they can appeal in every situation. Such a faith was to stand devout Jews in good stead when they faced the pressures of later persecutors and oppressors.

Ezra 9[1]–10[17] *Separation for the people of God*

Ezra's journey to Jerusalem, described in the main part of chapter 8, culminates in the handing over of sacred vessels and the offering of sacrifices. As the text now stands, this appears to be followed immediately by the events described in chapters 9 and 10, but we have seen that it is more probable that they are really the sequel to the reading and acceptance of the law (cf. p. 193). It is as a sequel to this, rather than earlier, that the problem of foreign wives and the introduction of alien belief is raised urgently. (The brief reference to 'separation from foreigners' in Neh. 9[2] could be due to an eventual harmonizing of the different sections.) The opening verses of chapter 9 are closely connected with the wording of Deut. 7[1 ff.] and it is clear that the author of the passage here is making use of older statements about the desirability of avoiding alien worship in order to point to the necessity of the reform associated with Ezra. The Deuteronomy passage, indeed, makes quite explicit the link between such marriages and religious apostasy (cf. vv. 11 ff.). The people of God, according to Deuteronomy, must keep itself pure, and this is expressed in terms of the destruction of its enemies and of their religious objects and sites. The holy people must keep itself holy.

The main part of chapter 9 describes the actions expressive of grief performed by Ezra, and sets out a prayer appropriate to this difficult situation. We may note how this prayer, expressing the consciousness of past guilt (vv. 6–7), goes on to speak of the favour granted by God, *to leave us a remnant*—the returned community often thinks thus of itself—and, though they are a subject people, to show his continuing grace through the agency of the kings of Persia (vv. 8–9). In such a situation, a confession of disobedience is linked with the quotation of words again closely linked to Deut. 7—referred to as what had been commanded *by thy servants the prophets* (v. 11) which is an interesting reflection of the way in which such a collection of laws and their exposition could be viewed by a writer in this period. We may compare the fact that the books from Joshua to Kings are described in the Hebrew Bible as 'The Former Prophets', not because they tell of the activities of prophets earlier in time than 'The Latter Prophets' (Isaiah to Malachi, omitting Daniel), but because they express prophetic judgement on and interpretation of the community's experience. In such a situation of disobedience, the appalling risk exists that even the remnant would be utterly wiped out.

10^{1-17} in some measure repeat the material of the preceding chapter, and it may be that the author is making use of various accounts of the way in which this problem came to light and was dealt with. Its emphasis is slightly different, for here we find a man named Shecaniah exhorting Ezra to be bold and take the necessary action, as if he were showing some reluctance. He and the people join in a covenant, agreeing to put away all foreign wives and the children born to them.

To put into effect the decision thus made, an assembly of all who have returned from exile is called, and judgement decreed on any who disobey the summons (vv. 6–8). We may note here the conception of the community as being in reality only the returned exiles; this is the emphasis so characteristic of the writings of the Chronicler. The true people of God is that which has gone through the experience of exile, or which has accepted a purification comparable with that. Verses 9–15 describe the assembly on the twentieth day of the ninth month —the middle of December—and picture the company as *trembling* both because of the seriousness of the situation and because of the heavy rain (v. 9). The rain is such that the people, while accepting the justice of the accusation and the need for reform, say that they cannot remain in the open; the matter must be handled in due order by appropriate officials. Rain and cold—even heavy snowfalls—are a not uncommon feature of Jerusalem weather in midwinter; at an altitude of 2,500 feet, the modern inhabitant is glad of a solid house and central heating if he is lucky enough to have it. Verse 15 notes that there were only four men opposed to the action—but whether they were opposed to the expulsion of foreign wives or to the method proposed in v. 14 is not said; it is possible that they were even more rigorist than the rest and did not want to see any delay. So, vv. 16–17, the investigation is carried through, and by the beginning of the next year—two months later—all the cases have been dealt with. The remainder of the chapter lists the individuals involved, priests, Levites, and ordinary people.

To a modern reader the story is a harsh one. We may wish to ask what became of the unfortunate women and their children who were thus sent away, presumably back to the families from which they had come. The harshness of the policy is such that it is understandable that some have seen in the stories of Ruth and Jonah (cf. pp. 334 f., 338) protests against such inhuman conduct. We must, however, endeavour to understand the point which is being made and recognize that there is here the same concern with the preservation of a true and faithful people as we have seen in the work of Nehemiah; and indeed that this concern is to be traced further back in the writings of the Deuteronomists and in the great pre-exilic prophets. How is true faith to be preserved, and how is Israel to be a true focal point for men to learn of the love and grace of God? It cannot be achieved if that faith is watered down, or confused with other ideas. The right relation between tolerance and the absolute demands of faith, between the maintaining of one's own position and the sympathetic understanding of the views of others, remains today an acute problem. If Ezra and others like him were harsh and rigid, we must nevertheless see that one consequence of their attitude was the keeping active of faith and the maintenance of the people's existence through periods of great danger.

J. THE ELEPHANTINE PAPYRI

The map (p. 164) shows the position of Elephantine, but a word of explanation about the other names which are associated with it is needed. Elephantine is the Greek name of the island of Yeb in the Nile, an island situated opposite Syene (modern Assuan) which is on the river bank. This latter name appears in Ezek. 29[10], 30[6] as indicating the southern border of Egypt; it probably should also be read in Isa. 49[12]. The name Elephantine, translated from the Egyptian Yeb, probably refers to the importance of this area for the ivory trade, and the position of the island and of Syene are of great significance both for trade and for frontier control. This point marks the first cataract of the Nile, and although a canal had been built, early in the second millennium B.C., to enable ships to pass the cataract, it provided a point for loading and unloading, as well as for customs control. As a frontier point, it was natural that it should have a military post, and it is in this capacity that we find it in the Aramaic documents belonging to the fifth century B.C. which have most often been termed the 'Elephantine Papyri'.

There are in fact two major collections of papyri. One of these came into private hands at the end of the nineteenth century and eventually into the Brooklyn Museum; these were published only in 1953. The other collection was built up of various finds, particularly those deriving from excavations early in the twentieth century, and were published at an earlier date. A note of the most useful books is given on pp. 353 f.

The papyri themselves give us information about the community from which they come. This is described as a 'garrison', the term corresponds to that used for 'army' in the Old Testament. Thus in one letter:

> To my brethren, Yedoniah and his colleagues the Jewish garrison, your brother Hannaniah . . . (Cowley No. 21, lines 1–2. The text, though not quite complete, can be filled out with certainty.)

This Jewish group settled in Elephantine was a frontier guard, employed as a body of foreign mercenary troops on the southern border of Egypt. By the year 419 B.C., when the letter just quoted was written (it is dated in the fifth year of Darius II [423–404 B.C.]), the garrison had been there for more than a century, for in a very important letter to which reference will be made again, we are told that:

> Already in the days of the kings of Egypt our fathers built this temple in Yeb in the fortress and when Cambyses came to Egypt he found this temple already built. . . . (Cowley No. 30, lines 13–14.)

We are not informed how much further back the garrison traced its presence in Egypt; the reason for the mention of Cambyses is to show that he respected it and did not let it be destroyed, so that the possibility that it was much older is not precluded. It is possible that the Jews employed here were recruited from Judah in the period after 587 B.C., or that they came from refugee settlements like that described in Jer. 44; it is also possible that their forefathers had settled there even earlier.

Many of the documents are legal in character, and since certain individuals appear in more than one document, some aspects of their life can be traced and interesting light is shed upon marriage and property law. One whole group of papyri (Kraeling, Nos. 2–12) is concerned with the family affairs of a man named Ananiah bar Azariah, who is called 'servitor (?) of the god Yahu' (on this name, cf. below); it appears that his father Azariah previously held this office. We are told of various property dealings and of his marriage to a slave named Tamut who belonged to a prominent member of the community named Meshullam bar Zakkur; this marriage contract appears to show that the owner of the slave still retained certain rights over her and her children, and a concession appears to be made in the case of her son (perhaps a son by Ananiah). A later document records an act of manumission by Meshullam bar Zakkur which liberates Tamut and her daughter but binds them to service still to himself and his son. These and other documents enable us to get quite a vivid picture of the life and customs of the community.

Of very special interest is the light shed by these documents on the religious life of the community and also on the historical situation in the fifth century B.C. It is of note that here in Elephantine there is a temple to Yahu; this is a form of the name of God known to us from the Old Testament as Yahweh (on this, cf. pp. 110 ff.). Yahu is a form which corresponds very closely to the way in which this divine name appears in proper names in the Old Testament—e.g. Jonathan (properly *Yeho-nathan*), Jeremiah (properly *Yirm-yahu* or *Yirm-yah*). We have already noted that names ending in *-iah* indicate that the one who gave the name acknowledged Yahweh as God (cf. p. 253 on Sanballat's naming of his sons). It is thus evident that this Jewish military garrison preserved its ancestral faith; it also possessed a temple and this indicates that the view that there should be only one temple—as propounded by Deuteronomy (esp. chapter 12) and put into effect by Josiah (cf. 2 Kgs. 22–23)—was not universally accepted or perhaps more probably was not regarded as applicable outside Judah.

But there are strong indications that the worship of Yahu was not strictly observed. We have seen how Jeremiah (44^{17}; cf. p. 38) condemns those who worship the Queen of Heaven alongside the God of Israel. In Elephantine there is considerable evidence of reverence being shown for other deities. Thus a man swears an oath 'by the temple and by Anath-yahu', and in a list of temple contributions it is said that a certain part is for Yahu, another part for Ishumbethel, and yet another for Anathbethel. Personal names appear in which other divine names stand where we might have expected the name Yahu: thus Heremnathan and Bethelnathan (similar in form to *Yehonathan*, Jonathan). What does this signify? In part we can explain the peculiarities by suggesting that particular titles are in reality being applied to Yahu. We know that in the

ELEPHANTINE PAPYRUS—LETTER TO BAGOAS. The first seventeen lines of the letter are shown: of these 1–14 are translated on pp. 283–4 and 15–17 on p. 284. Lines 18–30 (cf. pp. 285 f.) are written on the other side of the papyrus. The rough style of the writing and the corrections—note the word written in above line 5 and the alteration in line 11—suggest that it was either the rough draft or a copy of the actual letter sent to the governor of Judah.

Old Testament, the title Baal—which means 'lord' or 'husband'—is used for Yahweh though often associated with a Canaanite deity. Thus Saul named one of his sons Ishbaal (though later copyists in some cases altered this to Ishbosheth—the latter part being the word for 'shame'). There is evidence of a deity named Bethel; it is possible therefore that in such a name as Bethelnathan, this other name is being used in reference to Yahweh. Ishum is a name which probably appears in Amos 8^{14}; RSV has Ashimah and this form appears in the

Hebrew text and is perhaps due to a pun on the name of the deity and the word for 'guilt'—'*āshām*. But there is no escaping the meaning of Anath, whether alone or in combination with other names or titles; this is the name of a goddess well known in the Palestinian area (particularly from the Canaanite texts from Ras Shamra) and regarded here as the female consort of Yahweh. Yahu is in fact often in these documents described as 'the God of heaven' (cf. Ezra 7[12]), so that it would be quite natural if Anath was thought to be the 'queen of heaven'. The Old Testament is quite firm about the impropriety of there being any female consort for Yahweh (cf. Judg. 6[25 ff.] and the many condemnations in Deuteronomy and in the prophetic books of the intrusion of Canaanite religious ideas into Israelite religion). But popular beliefs die hard, and there was clearly a strong undercurrent of belief in such a female consort. Probably those who worshipped her did not see any disloyalty in what they were doing. The Elephantine community evidently preserved elements of this popular religious belief.

Yet it is clear that they regarded themselves as loyal adherents of Yahweh, and in course of time, when they found themselves in difficulties, they appealed to Jerusalem for help. How this came about is related in the appeal which was made to the governor of Judah:

> To our lord Bagoas, governor of Judah, your servants Yedoniah and his colleagues, the priests who are in Yeb the fortress. The well-being of your lordship may the God of heaven seek after exceedingly at all times, and give you favour before Darius the king and the princes of the palace more than now a thousand times, and may he grant you long life and may you be happy and prosperous at all times.
>
> Now your servant Yedoniah and his colleagues depose as follows: In the month of Tammuz in the fourteenth year of Darius the king, when Arsames departed and went to the king, the priests of the god Khnub who is in the fortress of Yeb were in league with Widrang who was governor here, saying: 'The temple of Yahu the God which is in the fortress of Yeb let them remove from there.' Then Widrang (the scoundrel) sent a letter to his son Nephayan who was commander of the garrison in the fortress of Syene saying: 'The temple which is in

Yeb the fortress let them destroy.' Then Nephayan led out the Egyptians with the other forces. They came to the fortress of Yeb with their weapons, they entered that temple, they destroyed it to the ground, and broke the stone pillars which were there. Moreover five gateways of stone, built with hewn blocks of stone, which were in that temple they destroyed, and their doors they set up (?) and the hinges of those doors were bronze, and the roof of cedar wood, all of it with the rest, of the furniture and other things which were there, all of it they burnt with fire, and the basins of gold and silver and everything that was in that temple, all of it, they took and made their own.

Already in the days of the kings of Egypt our fathers had built that temple in the fortress of Yeb, and when Cambyses came into Egypt he found that temple built, and the temples of the gods of Egypt all of them they overthrew, but no one did any harm to that temple . . .

(Cowley No. 30, lines 1–14.)

It thus appears that certain Egyptian opponents of the Jewish community—motivated perhaps by religious antagonism, perhaps by nationalist fervour—took advantage of the absence of Arsames who was the Persian governor in Egypt and a relative of the royal house. This took place in the fourteenth year of Darius II, i.e. 410 B.C. The letter is a copy (or a rough draft) of the petition actually sent to Bagoas, and it goes on to tell of the sequel:

When this was done, we, with our wives and our children, put on sackcloth and fasted and prayed to Yahu the Lord of heaven who let us see our desire upon that dog Widrang. They tore off the anklet from his legs, and all the riches he had gained were destroyed, and all the men who had sought to do evil to that temple, all of them, were killed, and we saw our desire upon them. (No. 30, lines 15–17.)

No explanation is given of how this retribution came upon Widrang; it could be that a complaint had been made to the Persian authorities in Egypt and that action followed on this. A document that belongs probably shortly after 410 also refers to Widrang's crimes:

. . . When detachments of the Egyptians rebelled, we did not leave our posts, and nothing disloyal was found in us. In the fourteenth year of king Darius, when our lord Arsames went away to the king, this is the crime which the priests of the god Khnub committed here in the fortress of Yeb in concert with Widrang who was governor here, after giving him money and valuables; there is a part of the king's stores which is in the fortress of Yeb, and this they wrecked and they built a wall in the midst of the fortress of Yeb. . . . (Cowley No. 27, lines 1–5.)

This could be an earlier appeal sent to Bagoas (see below), but two points suggest that it may well have been directed to Arsames himself shortly after his return. It refers to 'our lord Arsames', which would be appropriate if he were being addressed (see 'our lord Bagoas' in line 1 of the document previously quoted and subsequent references in that document to 'your lordship'); it also lays its main stress on the rebellious actions of Egyptians, and to the damage to royal installations in the fortress. Subsequently it makes a reference to Egyptians hindering the carrying on of worship in the temple of Yahu and to damage inflicted on the temple. But it would seem that its primary concern is to assert the loyalty of the Jewish garrison, and to encourage action against Widrang and his associates. The report of the retribution which fell upon the latter would seem most probably to refer to government action against disaffected troops. But the problem of the temple remained:

Also before this, at the time when this evil was done to us we sent a letter to your lordship (Bagoas) and to Johanan the high priest and his colleagues the priests who are in Jerusalem, and to Ostanes the brother of Anani, and the nobles of the Jews. They have not sent any letter to us. Also since the month of Tammuz in the fourteenth year of Darius the king till this day we wear sackcloth and fast. Our wives are made as widows, we do not anoint ourselves with oil, and we drink no wine. Also from that time till the present day in the seventeenth year of Darius the king, neither meal-offering, incense, nor sacrifice do they offer in that temple. (No. 30, lines 17–22.)

Thus it would appear that the action against Widrang did not bring about a restoration of the temple, and that the appeal made earlier to Jerusalem had not produced any results. So now the appeal is renewed:

> Now your servants Yedoniah and his colleagues and the Jews, all inhabitants of Yeb, say: 'If it seem good to your lordship, take thought for that temple to rebuild it, since they do not permit us to rebuild it. Look upon (i.e. look favourably upon) your well-wishers and friends who are here in Egypt. Let a letter be sent from you to them concerning the temple of the God Yahu to rebuild it in the fortress of Yeb as it was built before, and they shall offer the meal-offering and incense and sacrifice on the altar of the God Yahu on your behalf, and we will pray for you continually, we, our wives, and our children and all the Jews who are here, if it is so arranged that that temple is rebuilt, and it shall be a merit to you before Yahu the God of heaven more than a man who offers to him sacrifice and burnt offerings worth as much as the sum of a thousand talents of silver. As to gold, we have sent and given instructions. Also the whole matter we have set forth in a letter in our name to Delaiah and Shelemaiah the sons of Sanballat governor of Samaria. Also of all this which was done to us Arsames knew nothing. On the twentieth day of Marcheswan in the seventeenth year of Darius the king. (No. 30, lines 22–30.)

It is not clear what influence Bagoas was thought to wield; perhaps it was simply the case that a request from one Persian governor to another would, other things being equal, encourage action to be taken where a direct approach by subordinates was less likely to succeed. It seems likely from the reference to gold that the letter was to be reinforced with an appropriate gift to the governor. The statement that 'Arsames knew nothing' of the matter simply means that he was absent and in no way involved. We may note the emphasis that an act of piety (helping restore the temple) is regarded as of greater value in God's sight than a multitude of sacrifices (cf. Mic. 6[8]).

Of great interest is the light which the letter sheds on the contemporary situation in Palestine. Sanballat is evidently still governor in Samaria, but it would appear that it is his sons, and more particularly Delaiah, who now exercises the main influence. Bagoas is not mentioned in the biblical narrative, though he is mentioned by Josephus. Johanan is mentioned as high priest, and this would appear to be the priest of Ezra's time (cf. Ezra 10[6]); he was son (or grandson) of Eliashib, the contemporary of Nehemiah (Neh. 3[1]). Thus it appears most probable that Ezra came later, in the early years of Artaxerxes II (cf. the discussion on pp. 191 ff.). Josephus tells a somewhat discreditable story about Johanan, alleging that he murdered his brother Jesus in the temple and that Bagoas took action against the Jews on this occasion. But in view of the very considerable problems which Josephus' account of this whole period raises, it is very uncertain how far we should regard this as historical; it may be a rather garbled account and not belong to these personages at all. In any case he places the whole incident at a much later date.

What followed on this is not precisely known, but a rather carelessly written note appears in another document, probably to be dated shortly afterwards, which records the answer, presumably brought verbally by a messenger and recorded on the spot.

> Memorandum from Bagoas and Delaiah. They said to me: 'Let it be an instruction to you in Egypt to say to Arsames about the altar-house of the God of heaven, which was built in the fortress of Yeb formerly, before Cambyses, which Widrang that scoundrel destroyed in the fourteenth year of Darius the king, to rebuild it in its place as it was before, and they may offer the meal-offering and incense upon that altar as formerly was done.' (Cowley No. 32.)

Apparently one messenger came from both authorities; and this makes even clearer than the previous document that there was no such division between Jerusalem and Samaria as to prevent close collaboration. Indeed, the fact that the Elephantine Jews appealed to both, suggests that they did not know of any deep antagonism such as subsequently appears. Presumably the intention of the message is to encourage the Jews in Elephantine to send a renewed appeal to Arsames and to assure him that what they wish to do has the approval of his colleagues in Jerusalem and Samaria. We note also that this memorandum refers only to meal-offering and incense, and not to burnt-offerings; since another, perhaps almost contemporary note, and perhaps appealing to Arsames though no name appears, affirms that animal sacrifice is not offered but only incense and meal-offering, this would seem to be deliberate. Does this perhaps imply the view of the Jerusalem authorities that there should not be the full sacrificial system in Elephantine, but only those parts of it which could be carried out with propriety away from Jerusalem? This may or may not be the correct explanation.

In connection with the decrees in Ezra 1 and 6, and also the commission of Ezra in 7^{12-26}, mention has been made of the concern which the Persian authorities evidently showed even for the detail of the religious life of their subjects. Such a concern also appears in the letter dated in the fifth year of Darius II (i.e. 419 B.C.) from which a short quotation has already been made (p. 280). The main part of this letter is on the subject of the ordering of worship in the month Nisan. It was sent by a man named Hananiah—his name indicates that he was of Jewish faith—and evidently he was an official of some importance. In another letter which refers to the difficulties of a man named Maʿuziah who had been imprisoned by Widrang—the letter probably belongs not long before the destruction of the temple in 410 B.C.—the mission of Hananiah is mentioned; it is also revealed here that the troubles with the adherents of the Egyptian god Khnub had persisted during the whole of this period: 'Khnub is against us from the time that Hananiah was in Egypt until now' (Cowley No. 38, line 7). Hananiah's letter to the members of the Jewish garrison at Elephantine records that king Darius himself had sent an order to Arsames, the governor of Egypt, giving precise instructions about worship:

> Now therefore count fourteen days of the month Nisan and keep . . . and from the fifteenth day until the twenty-first day of Nisan . . . Be ritually clean and take heed. Do not work . . . nor drink . . . and anything at all in which there is leaven . . . sunset until the twenty-first day of Nisan . . . do not bring it into your houses, but seal it up during those days. (Cowley No. 21, lines 4–9.)

The gaps show something of the uncertainties about the meaning of this letter, and not all of the text given here is completely sure. Some scholars have supposed that there must have been a reference in a missing part of the text to the celebration of the Passover, and for this reason the letter is sometimes called the 'Passover papyrus'. But this is a dangerous assumption in view of all the uncertainties which exist in regard to the religious festivals in Israel. We have seen (pp. 272 f., Neh. 8–9) how the eventual fixing of dates for festivals followed on a long period in which there was variable practice. The two festivals of Passover and Unleavened Bread—the reference to leaven in this letter points to the latter—appear originally to have been separate, and only later came to be fully integrated. 2 Kgs. 23[21–23] record the institution of the Passover in the time of Josiah in a completely new way; it may be that this Jewish community in Elephantine did not observe this. It is possible that Hananiah's letter was designed to authorize their practice, and that the approval of the Persian ruler had been sought perhaps to obviate difficulties which were being created by the local population. The whole matter is shrouded in uncertainties; but one point stands out, namely that such a concern for the detail of the worship of a subject community was shown by the Persian authorities.

Was the temple restored after its destruction in 410 B.C.? This appears very likely. Egypt began rebellion against Persia when a man named Amyrtaeus seized power in 405 B.C.; he gradually gained further control, but did not govern the whole land, and one of the more recently published papyri suggests that the Jewish garrison at Elephantine maintained its loyalty to the Persians as late as 402 or even 401 B.C. Amyrtaeus did not retain control and was replaced by the founder of a new dynasty in 399, Nepherites I. This new line had close associations with the worship of the god Khnub and this fact, in view of the earlier disaster of 410 B.C., would suggest that the temple was again destroyed. At all events, no papyri discovered belong to a later date.

We may trace some indications of these last days of the

Jewish community at Elephantine in the documents. One of them concerns a sale of a house, and refers to 'Anani bar Azariah the servitor [?] of Yahu, and the woman Tpmt [probably Tamut] his wife, the servitor [?] of Yahu the god who dwells in Yeb the fortress . . .' (Kraeling, No. 12, lines 1–2).

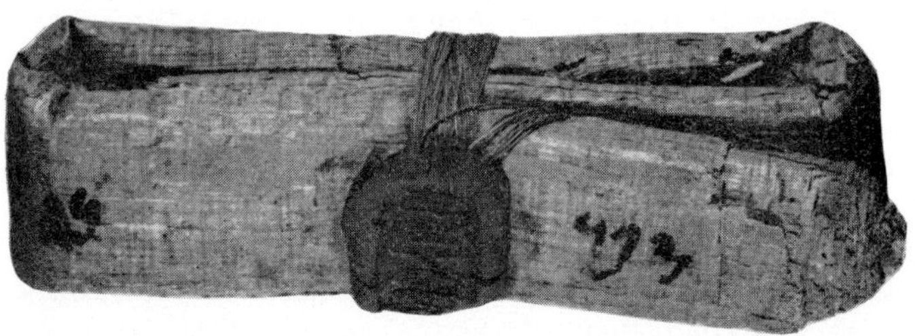

A SEALED CONTRACT FROM ELEPHANTINE. The contract mentioned above (Kraeling, No. 12) is here seen as it was found, rolled, folded, and sealed; when opened out it is about 24 by 12 inches in size and contains over thirty lines of writing. On the outside, there is an endorsement indicating the nature of the document; here the word meaning 'document' (*s*^{e}*phar* [the equivalent Hebrew word is *sēpher*], used broadly for a book, a document, or a letter) appears on the right, and on the left is seen the beginning of the statement 'the house which Anani bar Azariah and Tmpt his wife sold'. The sealed copy ensured that the deed was preserved and was not tampered with; in addition there would be an open copy for consultation (cf. Jer. 32^{9-14} for a description of the normal legal practice).

This expression 'the god who dwells' corresponds closely to Old Testament usage (cf. Deut. 33^{16}; Ps. 135^{21}); this latter passage describes the 'God who dwells in Jerusalem'. This strongly suggests that when the phrase is used at Elephantine it is in reference to the actual existence of the temple which is seen as the dwelling of the deity. This is dated in 402 B.C. (possibly 401). Another letter belongs to 399 B.C. and refers to Nepherites' seizure of power; ominously enough, it mentions Widrang and possibly describes him as 'commander', and if this is correct it is not difficult to foresee that he would take advantage of his restored power to act once more against the Jewish community. Of that community we hear nothing further at all.

K. THE SAMARIA PAPYRI

The paucity of information available to us for the latter part of the Persian period makes the reconstruction of the history of the Jewish community and of Palestine in general extremely difficult (cf. pp. 162 f.). But a welcome small addition to our knowledge has come as a result of the discovery in 1962–3 of a small collection of papyrus documents, some very fragmentary, and of loose seal impressions, some with fragments of papyrus still attached to them. These were found by members of the same bedouin tribe, the Taʿāmireh, who had so much to do with the discovery of the Qumran documents. The excavation of the cave in a valley several miles north of Jericho from which these came, revealed a substantial number of skeletons, deriving from the same period, the fourth century B.C., the documents themselves providing, from such dates as they contain, a range from about 375/365 B.C. down to 335 B.C.

The documents are all legal and administrative, concerned with sales, with slaves and their manumission, contracts and conveyancing of property, divorce, loans, and the like. (One papyrus roll was sealed with seven seals, cf. Rev. 5[1].) They contain many proper names, most of which contain the divine element *-iah*, e.g. Hananiah, and a slave named Nehemiah (cf. p. 281); but others contain elements of alien divine names such as Qōs, a deity known from the Edomite area, Chemosh (Moabite, cf. 1 Kgs. 11[7]), and Nabu, the Nebo of Babylon, who appears in Isa. 46[1]. Clear evidence appears that the documents were, in part at least, written in Samaria; thus one runs:

> . . . Jeshua (?), son of Sanballat, Hanan the prefect . . . In Samaria this document was written.

The mention of Sanballat immediately recalls the stories of Nehemiah, but further documents indicate the probability that there was more than one governor of this name. This had already seemed possible from the evidence of the historian Josephus' rather confused accounts of the period; and it now appears probable that we should find three governors of this name, and that the name was used within the same family, passing each time from grandfather to grandson, a practice known as papponymy and well attested in this period and later (cf. the members of the Oniad and Tobiad families in the second century, Vol. 5, pp. 31 ff.). Thus the line may run as follows: Sanballat (I), the governor of Nehemiah's time, was followed by his son Delaiah, who with his brother Shelemiah was active in about 410 B.C. (cf. the Elephantine Papyri); he was followed by Sanballat (II), whose son Hananiah was governor in *c.* 350 B.C., and he was followed by Sanballat (III) who, according to Josephus (who confused Sanballat III and Sanballat I) was appointed by Darius III (336–331 B.C.).

A linking together of the evidence of these texts with the various accounts to be found in Josephus and the information available from the excavations at Shechem, so closely associated with the Samaritan community for whom Mount Gerizim was sacred, suggests that in the time of Alexander the Great, who brought the Persian empire to an end, Samaritan refugees from Samaria, carrying with them these documents along with such other possessions as they could, went eastwards into the caves north of Jericho and were subsequently massacred there. There may have been some survivors, but at all events, when Samaria was re-established as a Hellenistic city, Shechem took on a new lease of life as the centre in which the Samaritan community was active. This leads us beyond the period with which this volume is concerned, but a fortunate chance has preserved these documents from which some new light is shed on the obscure years of the later Persian period. It may be that more information will yet become available which will assist both in the fuller interpretation of these texts, and also in illuminating the life of the Jewish community and related groups in Palestine during these years.

IV. THE LIFE AND THOUGHT OF POST-EXILIC JUDAISM

IN the course of the preceding pages, references have been made to much of the literature produced during the exilic and Persian periods. This section aims at picking up some of the points already mentioned and putting these into the context of a clearer understanding of the writings in which they are expressed; it also takes up certain themes which have been only briefly mentioned or not touched on at all. We shall look at another great theological-historical work, that of the Chronicler, to which reference has already been frequently made because it is in this work that we have a most important source for the history of the period; we shall consider worship with special reference to the Psalms, the Law and its place in the people's life and thought, and the movement known as Wisdom. Brief comments will also be made on two little books which most probably belong to this period, Jonah and Ruth. But in making this selection, we may be in danger of overlooking other aspects of thought which could shed light on the period. Are there perhaps passages in the prophetic books which belong here? Zech. 9–14 is very difficult indeed to date; it is discussed, quite reasonably, in Vol. 5, pp. 200–12, but with the recognition that it might really belong elsewhere. The book of Joel too might belong here or perhaps somewhat later; it is much concerned with the nature and meaning of the Day of Yahweh, and in this resembles earlier prophecy, particularly that of Amos and Isaiah (cf. p. 30). Joel may contain early oracles reinterpreted and presented in a new context; the reference to the Greeks in 3[6] might indicate this. Other prophecies may also have been reinterpreted in these years, with reference being seen in them to contemporary events. But the uncertainties here are so great that it is hazardous to attempt precise statement. What we need to remember is that the words of the prophets, as well as other earlier Old Testament writings, were not preserved for antiquarian reasons, but because they were believed to speak with immediacy and urgency to contemporary life.

A. THE WORK OF THE CHRONICLER

This last point is of great importance for our appreciation of what the Chronicler was attempting in the historical survey presented in the books now known as 1 and 2 Chronicles, Ezra, and Nehemiah. He was bringing the history more up to date, but he was presenting the earlier period, already covered by the books of Samuel and Kings, in such a way as to show what he believed it to mean for his contemporaries. (He begins with Adam, but covers the period to Saul by means of genealogies.) We may therefore hope to detect in his writings some clues to the way in which theologians of the time were thinking and some of the problems which they and their readers had to face.

There is still much discussion as to how the work as we now have it came into being. Even the view that the books of Ezra and Nehemiah are part of the one larger work is still challenged. But part of this uncertainty derives from asking different questions about what the work is and how it was composed. We should not suppose that an author in the middle of the fourth century simply took up the earlier historical books and rewrote them in a new form, adding material to bring the story up to date. We should rather see the work as the result of a long development, for which we only have information at certain points. The books of Samuel and Kings as we know them represent only one form of the material as it was handed down; the Greek translation and the manuscripts from Qumran make it quite clear that other forms of these books were also in circulation. We may therefore see the first stage in the formation of the Chronicler's work to be a form of the text of these earlier writings in which certain modifications had been made, some additions and omissions perhaps, possibly even in the early years after the exile the addition of some information about restoration and rebuilding. So on the one hand we see the Deuteronomic History, in more or less the form in which we have it; on the other hand, we have other forms of the material, and it has been suggested that one of these may have concentrated on Jerusalem and its fortunes and so have left out passages which did not seem relevant to this main theme. In the years after the exile, as we have observed more than once, Jerusalem became even more a focal point than it had been earlier for the life of Judah; its fate and its future were matters for keen interest.

In the same line of thinking, the author whom we may conveniently call 'the Chronicler' undertook further development of the material, and it is reasonable to suppose that he wrote not so very long after the latest events recorded. Since there is no reference to the overthrow of the Persians, and the work of Ezra has been described (accepting the date of 398 B.C., as we have done), we may place this main point of activity in about 350 B.C. It is not, however, surprising to find indications that some of the Chronicler's successors made further modifications to the work, additions to the genealogies probably and to the material regarding the priesthood under David, some of which show marks of later insertion and perhaps even point to the problems of the priesthood in the second century B.C. A view which is by no means universally held but which is attractive and possible is that the memoirs of Nehemiah were a later insertion (cf. p. 195). This would be quite intelligible, perhaps also in the second century when, as we can see from the references in 2 Maccabees (cf. pp. 179 f.), the figure of Nehemiah was regarded with great respect. Here was a great patriot, a fitting forerunner of the heroes of the Maccabaean time. If this view is right, then whoever inserted the material did so at the points which appeared appropriate, breaking up the Ezra narrative in the process; but he did this in good faith, believing that the same Artaxerxes must be meant in each case and interpreting the activity of the two great leaders as contemporary and complementary.

We have already observed how complicated the traditions regarding the Persian period are, and that further indications of this are to be seen in the other form of the material to be found in the apocryphal book known as 1 Esdras. It is not possible here to go into detailed discussion about this version of part of the work of the Chronicler; it is debated whether we should see it as a fragment which has accidentally survived in its Greek translation, or whether it represents a deliberate selection of parts of the larger work. The latter view has much to commend it because 1 Esdras tells of three great moments in the life of Jerusalem—the reform of Josiah, the rebuilding of the temple after the exile, and the work of Ezra. There is a long addition to the story in chapters 3–5, which serves to glorify Jewish as opposed to other wisdom and in particular to enhance the figure of Zerubbabel. The story of Nehemiah is entirely absent.

If this approach to the work of the Chronicler is the right one, then it is not very appropriate to ask simply 'What sources did the Chronicler use besides the books of Samuel and Kings?' but rather to examine the work as we now have it, recognizing that there may be some passages which have been introduced at a late date while others may represent much earlier matter which had at some stage become part of the historical narrative. This means that we can hardly expect to look at all the differences between Samuel and Kings on the one hand and Chronicles on the other and build up from this a picture of who the Chronicler was and what he thought. We have to make an overall estimate of what the work as we now have it sets out to do.

This is important too from another point of view. This work supplies a great deal of information about the period of the monarchy which is not present in Samuel and Kings. The historical value of this extra material has to be carefully considered, but we must do this with regard to the context in which it is presented. Just as when we study Samuel and Kings we must ask ourselves what particular narratives mean and why they are placed as they are, so too here. And this means that it is not satisfactory to jump from one to another, filling the gaps in Samuel and Kings with what is found in Chronicles; these are two different presentations and they must be taken seriously for what they are, theological interpretations of the history and presentations of its meaning for the readers of the time. The work of the Chronicler has been too little appreciated because it has so often been read in the wrong way; in the Greek translation it is called 'the things left out', and so it has been used to fill gaps. But if we use it in this way, we shall never arrive at a proper understanding of what it is really about. The fact too that some of the Chronicler's statements are quite evidently historically unsatisfactory has made many people think it a rather unimportant work. But if we read it for what it is, then we may gain insights into a way of thinking and interpreting which is very significant indeed.

The theology of the Chronicler has many facets; the fact that he has presented it in the form of a survey of history from creation to his own time means that at no point do we get a precise definition of what he thought. If we pick out here some of the main ideas which appear in the narratives, then these are to serve as guide-lines, to enable the reader of the whole work to enter into it more sympathetically and discover more of the richness of the thought.

A clearly fundamental concern is with the nature of the true Israel, and this comes out at the beginning in the genealogical lists—which make very dull reading. Here use is made of a mass of material, some of which is found elsewhere—in Genesis, for example—to show how the purpose of God begins at the very creation, expressed in the naming of the line of ancestors beginning with Adam (cf. the Priestly Work's view of creation as the beginning of history, pp. 154 f.), and tracing this purpose through the line leading to Israel and within Israel concentrating more and more upon Judah (1 Chron. 4), Benjamin (1 Chron. 8), and the Davidic house (1 Chron. 3). (Cf. Ezekiel's placing of the tribes, pp. 102 ff.). The whole process is brought to a climax in 1 Chron. 9 where the re-establishment of the people after the exile is outlined, largely in lists of names.

After this preface, the historical sequence is followed from the time of the Philistine war and the overthrow of Saul down to the time of Ezra. But it is concerned to emphasize the unity of all Israel in the appointment of David (so 1 Chron. 11^{1-3}, an important statement which offers a reinterpretation of the narrative in Samuel), and stressing the legitimacy and faith of the tribes of Judah and Benjamin as preserving the true line. To them were joined all the faithful, no matter where they might live—at the division of the kingdom the priests and Levites are shown as forsaking their homes in the north to come to Judah where 'they strengthened the kingdom of Judah' (2 Chron. 11^{17}), or in the time of Hezekiah (2 Chron. 30), when admittedly 'Only a few men of Asher, of Manasseh, and of Zebulun humbled themselves and came to Jerusalem'. This true people of God, for its disobedience, went into exile, and it is characteristic of the Chronicler that stress is laid upon the true succession being through those who experienced exile and returned to rebuild. Yet they too could be joined 'by every one who . . . separated himself from the pollutions of the peoples of the land to worship the LORD, the God of Israel' (Ezra 6^{21}; cf. p. 209). In the work of Ezra, the community is purified by the exclusion of foreign wives (Ezra 9–10), because they bring contact with alien peoples 'with their abominations . . . so that the holy race has mixed itself with the peoples of the lands' (Ezra 9^{1-2}). This leads into the reading of the law and its acceptance in a confession of faith and a new covenant (Neh. 8–9). Thus the new community is established. It is an impressive survey of the history of the people of God, in terms of divine grace and human faith.

This people of God is understood in terms of Jerusalem, and with it of the Davidic house and the one legitimate shrine. Worship away from Jerusalem and alien religious practice are utterly condemned. So the history of the northern kingdom appears only when points relevant to this are to be made, and the failure of some southern kings is associated with the northern apostasy (cf., e.g., 2 Chron. 22^{1-9}, 28^{1-4}). The climax of the prologue is reached with the restoration in Jerusalem (1 Chron. 9); it is the city of David and of Solomon, and to these two rulers the largest space is given (1 Chron. 10–2 Chron. 9); it is the centre of the kingdom of Judah and of the restored community (2 Chron. 10–36; Ezra 1–6); here the new community covenants with God (Ezra 7–10; Neh. 8–9).

The reason for the place of Jerusalem is seen first in terms of the Davidic house, Saul being passed over with little mention. David was the conqueror of Jerusalem and there he planned the temple and prepared for its building so that all that remained for Solomon to do was to carry through what was ready to hand. Subsequent history concerns the Davidic line. But this came to an end. Rebuilding of the temple, it is true, was carried out by a member of the family, Zerubbabel. What then becomes of the Davidic monarchy? Here it would seem the Chronicler is offering an interpretation of that monarchy. Its true function is to be seen in relation to the temple and its worship, and as the expression of a united people. Speculation concerning the future of the Davidic house finds an important place in certain parts of the Old Testament and beyond; oracles speaking of a new ruler of the family of David are scattered about the prophetic books (cf. Isa. 9^{2-7}, $11^{1-9\ (10)}$; Jer. 33^{19-26}; Ezek. 37^{24-28}). The loss of the kingship led to a renewed understanding of its more ultimate meaning, and it was to be an important element in the development of messianic thought, as may be seen from the New Testament (cf., e.g., Luke $2^{1\,\mathrm{ff.}}$). Such a current of interpretation is little in evidence during the Persian period, though we cannot be sure of the dates of particular oracles in the prophetic books. It may be that its redevelopment came with the independence of the second century, in part perhaps in contrast to the monarchy of the Hasmoneans and the later rule of members of the Herod family. The Chronicler offers a different and less political interpretation. To those who might ask: Do the promises of an eternal covenant with the house of David mean nothing? (the Chronicler has the passage which corresponds to 2 Sam. 7 in 1 Chron. 17), he is in effect saying: The covenant is expressed in the existence of the now restored temple, the temple which David planned and for which he ordered the worship (for this cf. 1 Chron. 15–16, 21–29), and in the people which takes over the obedience to the law which older tradition had so closely associated with the king (Neh. 8, cf. Deut. 17^{18-20}).

With this non-political interpretation of the monarchy, the Chronicler shows himself to be sensitive to the situation in which the Jewish community found itself. This becomes particularly clear in the last part of the work, where we find a repeated emphasis on the providential care which is evident in the activity of Persian rulers. Cyrus decreed the rebuilding of the temple; when it was questioned, Darius confirmed it even more generously (Ezra 1, 6). Artaxerxes commissioned Ezra and gave him full support and authority (Ezra 7). It was God who brought about this generous action (cf. Ezra 1^{1}, 6^{12}, 7^{6}) and who protected his people (cf. Ezra 5^{5}). It is as a subject people of this divinely guided empire that the Jewish community has to live. In this the Chronicler shows himself as the spiritual descendant of prophets who had seen in trust in God and in submission to his will the meaning of political events, particularly in the teaching of Jeremiah. It is a quietistic line of thought, and one which was no doubt uncongenial to some who still dreamed of independence. The right balance between such faith and a more activist outlook is not easy to hold; the position occupied by the Hasideans in the second century (cf. Vol. 5, pp. 45 ff.) makes clear the tensions involved. The Chronicler affirms the rightful place of such an attitude of trust and obedience.

Sections from the later part of the work of the Chronicler have already been examined in some detail (cf. pp. 201 ff., [246 ff.], 263 ff.). For a full picture of his thought, we need to look at the work as a whole; some suggestions are made here of passages which provide examples of his thinking and of the kind of emphases which he lays. These are intended to facilitate a reading of the whole.

1 Chron. 11[1–3] *The unity of the people at the election of David*

This passage is related to 2 Sam. 5[1–5], but significantly no mention is made of the anointing of David as king at Hebron by the men of Judah alone (cf. 2 Sam. 2[4]). Verse 2 depends on the David/Saul traditions in 1 Samuel which are also not otherwise used by the Chronicler. It is characteristic of his method that he refers to incidents which he does not record, but which it is clear will be familiar to his readers. The prophecy in this verse (cf. 2 Sam. 5[2]) may be compared with Ezek. 34[23–24], 37[24–25] which make the same point in slightly different words, and with Ps. 78[70–72].

1 Chron. 21[28]–22[1] (2 Chron. 3[1]) *The choice of the temple site*

The story told in 1 Chron. 21 differs in some important respects from the earlier version in 2 Sam. 24. But the most significant change comes at the end. In fact, the story has been put in a quite different position in the narrative sequence so as to lead up to this. Whereas the 2 Samuel version simply describes the process by which David was led to purchase the threshing floor of Araunah (Ornan in 1 Chron.) the Jebusite and to build an altar and offer sacrifices there, the Chronicler's version explains that *the tabernacle . . . and the altar of burnt offering were at that time in the high place at Gibeon* (21[29]). But now it is explicitly declared that '*Here shall be the house of the* Lord *God and here the altar of burnt offerings for Israel*' (22[1]). This link is not made in the older form of the narrative, where it is never stated that the temple was built on the threshing floor. The divine provision of the site of the Jerusalem temple is thus underlined. In 2 Chron. 3[1] the developing tradition by which sacred sites are identified with one another leads to the further statement that the temple was built on *Mount Moriah*; this links the temple with the command to sacrifice Isaac in 'the land of Moriah . . . upon one of the mountains of which I shall tell you' (Gen. 22[2]). The Abraham narrative at no point suggests that this mountain is to be connected with Jerusalem, but we can see how the tradition has given a new meaning to it. The Chronicler is here making the claim that the Jerusalem site is not simply the one divinely chosen in the time of David, as an act of grace, but is an ancient holy place linked to the true forefather of Israel. This might well be relevant if there were others at this time claiming that Shechem and Gerizim were more ancient and hence more sacred than Jerusalem (cf. pp. 185 ff.).

1 Chron. 28 *Solomon is designated the temple-builder*

The older tradition knew that David had wished to build the temple but had been forbidden to do so, and preserved a pronouncement that 'your son . . . shall build a house for my name' (2 Sam. 7$^{12-13}$). The Chronicler preserves the same tradition, though he gives a different explanation for the prohibition. '*You may not build a house for my name, for you are a warrior and have shed blood*' (v. 3). The son who is to build is precisely identified as Solomon, *chosen . . . to sit upon the throne of the kingdom of the* L*ORD over Israel . . . who shall build my house and my courts* (vv. 5 f.). In the presence of the whole company of the officials of Israel, on whom the command to be obedient is laid, Solomon is designated, and *David gave Solomon his son the plan . . . of all that he had in mind for the courts of the house of the* L*ORD* (vv. 11 f.), and for all the details of its construction and furnishing. This was in accordance with a *writing from the hand of the* L*ORD* (v. 19; cf. Exod. 25^{9} (P); Ezek. 43^{10}). The narrative continues in chapter 29 by indicating the provision of the necessary materials and the gifts of king and people for the building of the temple.

2 Chron. 13 *Abijah's appeal to the north*

In 1 Kgs. 15$^{1-8}$ Abijam (in 2 Chron. Abijah) is briefly described. The Chronicler has a much fuller account which includes a speech by Abijah before a battle with Jeroboam of Israel. As the two armies face one another, the army of Judah being half the size of that of Israel, Abijah stands on *Mount Zemaraim . . . in the hill country of Ephraim* (v. 4) to make an appeal to the north. His hearers are reminded of the divine choice of David and his dynasty and of Jeroboam's rebellion. '*Now you think to withstand the kingdom of the* LORD *in the hand of the sons of David, because you are a great multitude and have with you the golden calves which Jeroboam made you for gods . . .*' (v. 8). But they have driven out the true priests and accepted false ones. The kingdom of Judah has the true priesthood and the temple in which the regular offerings are made. '*Behold, God is with us at our head, and his priests with their battle trumpets to sound the call to battle against you. O sons of Israel, do not fight against the* LORD, *the God of your fathers; for you cannot succeed*' (v. 12). There is heartfelt appeal here, and warning. The battle is not man's but God's (cf. p. 41 on Ps. 44). The military situation looked hopeless—overwhelming numbers, an ambush which hedged Judah in on both sides. But *they cried to the* LORD, *and the priests blew the trumpets. Then the men of Judah raised the battle shout. And . . . God defeated Jeroboam and all Israel* (vv. 14 f.). The Chronicler has inherited the ancient tradition of the holy war, and he has carried it even further than the narrators in the book of Joshua, indeed right to its logical conclusion. The battle is God's, he gives the victory; men pray to him, the priests blow the trumpets, the enemy takes to flight. This is a recurrent theme, and this presentation of warfare accords well with the Chronicler's interpretation of the situation of his time. The life of God's people rests in the hand of God, and their task is to be faithful and obedient and trusting.

2 Chron. 20^{18-23} *The lesson of faith*

The same point is made in this battle narrative set in the time of Jehoshaphat (*c.* 873–849). But two further points of detail may be brought out in comment on this brief story. First, we find Jehoshaphat the king exhorting the people; his short sermon is based on the text of Isaiah's words to Ahaz (Isa. 7^{9}). The Chronicler introduces a number of such sermon passages, and prayers, put into the mouth of prophets (e.g. Azariah in 2 Chron. $15^{1\text{ff.}}$) or priests (e.g. Jehoiada in 2 Chron.

24[20]) or Levites (e.g. Jahaziel in 2 Chron. 20[14ff.]). They make use of prophetic and other sayings to strengthen their argument, and this strongly suggests that what the Chronicler is doing is quoting the kind of sermons and prayers which he was accustomed to hear; indeed such is his interest in this that we may well wonder whether he was himself a Levite—there is much commendation of the Levites—who exhorted his hearers in this way. Second, we note that the singers who are appointed join in a psalm refrain: '*Give thanks to the* L*ORD*, *for his steadfast love endures for ever*' (v. 21). This appears more than once in the Chronicler's work (cf. 1 Chron. 15[34, 41]; Ezra 3[11]) and is well known as a refrain in the Psalms (e.g. Ps. 136). In a psalm manuscript from Qumran, there is a copy of Ps. 145 with this refrain inserted after each verse. Thus we may see the Chronicler making use of the forms of worship of his own day, and this is important for our understanding of how the psalms were used after the exile (cf. pp. 308 ff.).

2 Chron. 30 *It is God who makes men acceptable in his sight*

The whole story of Hezekiah's reform as it is set out in the Chronicler's narrative in 2 Chron. 29–31 gives insight into his way of thinking. It shows his love of the temple, and his appreciation of the loyalty of the Levites. It shows his missionary spirit, reflecting the view that now the northern kingdom has gone, there was less to stand in the way of a return to the one united Israel centred on Jerusalem; northern apostasy had brought disaster upon itself. It is in a conciliatory spirit that Hezekiah is shown writing *letters also to Ephraim and Manasseh, that they should come to the house of the* L*ORD* *at Jerusalem, to keep the passover to the* L*ORD*, *the God of Israel* (v. 1). Proclamation is made; the people of the north are warmly urged to remember their ancestral faith, as a *remnant* which has *escaped from the hand of the kings of Assyria* (v. 6). God is willing to show mercy. The response is meagre, and the messengers are mocked; but some come to Jerusalem, humbling themselves. But such was the concourse, that adequate preparation for the passover could not be undertaken. *For a multitude of the people, many of them from Ephraim,*

Manasseh, Issachar, and Zebulun, had not cleansed themselves. But Hezekiah had prayed for them, saying, 'The good LORD *pardon every one who sets his heart to seek God, the* LORD *the God of his fathers, even though not according to the sanctuary's rules of cleanness'* (vv. 18 f.). God's blessing was experienced, and the rejoicing was followed by a great campaign against idolatry and a reorganization of worship. The passage is a reminder that those, like the Chronicler and the Priestly Writers, whose concern for purity expressed itself in a firm stress upon ritual correctness and all the elaboration of law which this involves, were not narrow legalists. They were deeply anxious about their people's condition, urgently seeking how the people could be an obedient people of God; but they knew that ultimately the acceptability of the people in God's sight rested with God himself, who would use the forms he had ordained but could not be thought to be limited by them in the action of his grace.

B. WORSHIP AND THE PSALTER

The Old Testament is tantalizingly reticent when it comes to describing worship, and presumably this is for the simple reason that those who engaged in it knew what went on and it was therefore unnecessary to give detailed accounts. We have more precise regulations for the great festivals of the year, and these appear in different forms in the different strands of the material. The regulations of Deut. 16 may well be in some measure early, but in so far as the present form is to be associated with the period of Josiah and the exile, they show us how some at that time saw the meaning of the celebrations. Lev. 23, in the Holiness Code, provides another series of regulations for festivals and sabbaths. Num. 28–29 from the Priestly Work has yet another. In each case, it is likely that much older material is being used and re-presented. Different levels may lie side by side, and it is likely that further changes took place gradually over the succeeding years. Later rabbinic writings suggest this, and indeed the liturgy of a religious community, while it retains certain basic patterns, tends to change slowly, and even where its forms remain much the same, the meaning given to them develops.

Alongside the great public occasions, there were the private and family aspects of worship, and here again our information is very meagre. The regulations for more personal sacrifices in particular moments of emergency are set out. Thus in Num. 6 there are regulations governing special vows, the Nazirite vows which involve abstention from alcoholic drink and special separation from contact with uncleanness. Such personal vows, whether of this type or of others, are known to us later in the story of Paul (Acts 21[17–26]). Lev. 13–14 covers a whole series of problems of uncleanness, described under the general term of leprosy. This is likely to include a very wide range of skin diseases and also covers mildew in materials. Much of what is included in the mass of regulations is what in modern times is covered in quite other ways in the life of society, but for the member of the Jewish community every aspect of life was brought under religious regulation. Life was ordered. Its daily needs were covered. The emergencies of sudden death and disease had their appropriate rituals. The stages of human life were governed by practice. This produces a certain rhythm and order and security. The maintenance of this orderliness was felt to hang together with the very existence of the community's life; so we may appreciate that when this order was threatened, there could be great upheaval. Nehemiah and Ezra were concerned about the preserving of order when they sought to exclude foreign wives who would bring in alien customs. The community was to meet severe shocks in the religious pressures of the second century B.C.; to many devout Jews of the first century A.D. the shock of Christian upheaval was understandably dangerous. That such an ordered society is very conservative is of course true; but it is also evident that, in spite of the dissensions which threats to it created, there was a resilience in the Jewish faith of these years which enabled it to adjust to new demands.

Many things contributed to this resilience, and not least the ways in which the more ancient religious traditions were kept continually before the community in its worship. The reading of the scriptures which became so marked a feature of synagogue worship and hence of Christian worship presumably originated at an earlier time. Neh. 8 shows us the people assembled to hear the reading and interpretation of the law (cf. pp. 270 ff.). But we have no precise evidence from the Persian period of other practices of this kind. We have, however, one pointer which is of considerable importance. This is provided by the psalms. Many of these, probably most in the Psalter, originated in an earlier period, but they have come down to us as they were arranged for use in the post-exilic period. In some cases, modifications may be detected or suspected in them; in other cases, simply the change of situation would result in their words being differently understood. Thus psalms which referred to the king continued to be used, but they could be thought to refer to the coming future king, the messiah, or they could be applied to the needs of the community or of the individual worshipper. Psalms which speak of Jerusalem or Zion are likely to have originated in the earlier cultus of the shrine there, or may have been modified for use there, having originated in other religious centres. After the exile, the place of Jerusalem as a focal point for the whole Jewish people made it natural that such psalms should find an important place in the collection which now forms the Psalter. This is a collection which was formulated as we know it during the post-exilic period; it derives in part from earlier collections some of which are indicated by titles or notes at the end of psalms (cf. Ps. 72[20]). The Greek translation, which came into being during the third or second centuries B.C., at some points divides up the psalms differently and it adds an extra one at the end. Manuscripts of the psalms known from Qumran have a different order in some cases, and there are also examples of other psalms included. The Psalter which we have in the Old Testament is most probably a liturgical collection which eventually came to be accepted as standard. To some degree we may deduce from its contents the religious needs of the community to which it belonged.

The Chronicler gives a number of indications of the ways in which psalms were used, in particular in 1 Chron. 15–16 which describes the bringing of the ark into Jerusalem. The position of the guilds of singers and their function is there drawn out. Elsewhere the responsive use of words of praise is noted, as we have already seen (p. 304). The emphasis on rejoicing in worship which characterizes much of this work, and the inclusion of many prayers, shorter and longer (e.g. Neh. 9), particularly of confession and appeal for divine action and often closely related to psalms of lament, reveal the central place occupied by worship in the Chronicler's thinking. The fact that so many of the psalms contain longer or shorter references to the great experiences of faith and divine action in the past, shows the way in which through this worship the community's link with the ancestral faith was kept alive; while psalmody was used in worship, they could not forget what God had done, and each new stage in their experience was thus linked back to what had gone before.

1 Chron. 15–16 *The liturgy for the entrance of the ark*

The Chronicler presents in these chapters his own picture of what happened when the ark was brought into Jerusalem by David. The danger of wrong handling of this sacred object is indicated in the narrative of 1 Chron. 13 (for the older story, cf. 2 Sam. 6). The principle upon which David is here described as operating is the recognition that '*No one but the Levites may carry the ark of God, for the Lord chose them to carry the ark of the Lord and to minister to him for ever*' (15^{1-2}). So the narrative is filled out with a wealth of detail about levitical families and regulations (15^{3-15}), and in particular of *the singers* appointed to *play loudly on musical instruments* (15^{16-24}). When the ark is brought in (15^{25}–16^{3}), those who are appointed *to invoke, to thank, and to praise the Lord*, among whom the guild of Asaph is marked out as chief (some of the psalms have titles suggesting an association with the Asaph guild, e.g. Ps. 50), sing the appropriate psalm of thanksgiving (16^{4-7}).

16^{8-36} contain the psalm. Verses 8–22 correspond to Ps. 105^{1-15}; this psalm, like 106, contains a long survey of Israel's experience in the past, stressing the eternal nature of the covenant and reminding the people of their belonging with their ancestor Abraham, with Isaac and with Jacob the father of the tribes. The promise of Canaan is recalled, and the way in which the patriarchs, *few in number and of little account* (v. 19), were protected in their wanderings. Ps. 105^{16-45} carries on the survey through the experience of Egypt and the deliverance amid the plagues brought upon the Egyptians, the protection of the people in the wilderness and their entry into the land, culminating in a stress on obedience. The same themes are also developed in Ps. 106 which proceeds from the experience of Egypt and sets out in great detail the wilderness traditions with a stress upon Israel's disobedience and God's mercy, recalling his repeated deliverance of the people when they cried in distress. This psalm (106^{47}) culminates in an appeal to God to gather his people home from exile.

I Chron. 16^{23-33} correspond to Ps. 96^{1-13}. (Verses 28–29 are also closely allied to the opening of Ps. 29; this latter psalm very probably presents an earlier form of the material.) In these verses, the summons is to a great act of praise, in which the whole earth and all nations are summoned to join. Verse 34 has the refrain used more than once in the Chronicler's work (cf. p. 304) and often in the Psalter, and this is followed in v. 35 by words similar to those of Ps. 106^{47}, introduced by the words *say also* which makes it appear that the Chronicler has seen it as desirable, writing for the community in the Persian period, to stress the gathering of his people from exile, so that full worship may be offered. Verse 36 (cf. Ps. 106^{48}) is a final word of benediction. In the Psalter, this verse is not really part of the psalm, but the blessing marking the end of one of the five books into which the Psalter is divided (like the five books of the Law). It would seem not improbable that it was customary for a psalm to close with such a blessing, just as Christian usage adds the *Gloria*, but that this is written out only to mark the ending of the separate books. The Chronicler also adds the note that *all the people said Amen and praised the LORD*; from this we can see that it was normal for the psalm to be said or sung by the appointed officers, and for the congregation's part to be a responsive one. It does not follow that this was the only way the psalms could be used.

We should not suppose that the Chronicler made up this psalm by putting together pieces of three different psalms in the Psalter; we should rather see him using a liturgical structure familiar from the worship of his own time, adding, as we have seen, a note at the end, to give it application to this moment, or perhaps simply following a common practice after the exile of offering a special prayer for the scattered community. Some light is thus shed on the way psalm material was used, and it would seem that the psalms, divided up and arranged as we have them in the Psalter, are not presented in the only possible way. In fact, within the Psalter, we have examples of the same passages occurring more than once; thus Ps. 40^{13-17} appears also as Ps. 70, and Ps. 108 is made up of two passages, Ps. 57^{7-11} and 60^{5-12}. The psalms could be used in various ways, and parts of psalms could appear either separately or in different combinations. No doubt there were conventions to which the officiants worked, but we do not know what the procedures were.

Ps. 126 *The restoring of Zion*

The phrase 'restore the fortunes', which is used twice in different forms in this psalm (vv. 1, 4), appears originally to have been used in a general way to express any change of circumstances for the better. In time of famine, or of drought, one might pray for such a change, a reversal of present distress. But it so happens that the words translated 'fortune' closely resembles a word used for 'captivity', and the expression thus lent itself readily to reinterpretation with reference to the exile. Verses 4–6 of this psalm contain a general prayer, mainly centred on the need for a good harvest and for plentiful water supply. Verses 1–3 may represent an amplification of this to apply its words to the exilic situation and to the hope of an eventual complete restoration of those in distant lands to Zion. RSV margin has an alternative translation of the opening *restored the fortunes of Zion*, viz. *brought back those who returned to Zion* which brings out the point. We may note also that this change for Israel is one which is witnessed by the nations, who acknowledge the mighty acts of God.

This psalm indicates how a close reading of the psalms may suggest the way in which older poems have been modified or, even without modification, have been understood afresh. As we read the psalms, we may put ourselves in imagination in the situation of the Jews of the Persian period. What would the words mean to those who lived as part of a scattered community looking with longing to Jerusalem from afar, or looking from Jerusalem with a yearning that those who were scattered should be brought home?

C. THE PLACE OF THE LAW

The Psalter which we have just been considering for the light it sheds on the worship of the community also reveals another and related aspect of the life of the pious Jew in this period. Again it would be hazardous to attempt any precise dating of the psalms in question, but it is convenient to see in them, as they now stand in the Psalter, a testimony to the reverence for the Law which gradually became so characteristic of Judaism. In particular, Ps. 1, which serves to introduce the Psalter, lays stress on love for the Law and sets out the consequences of obedience and disobedience. It has been suggested that its position is intended to direct the devout man to a reading of the psalms as itself part of his discipline of studying the faith and learning obedience to the Law. There is a similar tendency evident in the Wisdom literature (cf. pp. 316 ff.).

The Law (*Tōrāh*) (on this, cf. also Vol. 3 in this series, pp. 197 ff.) is the term used for the first five books of the Old

Testament, but this derives from older use of the same term to indicate a particular kind of religious directive, associated especially with the priests (cf. Jer. 18^{18}), and then, particularly in Deuteronomy, for a more fully elaborated code of conduct and life. It may thus be understood at three levels: the single instruction delivered specially to meet the needs of a situation, directing a particular course of conduct or a particular interpretation of a question (Hag. 2^{11-14} provides a good example, using the word *tōrāh* for the directive sought, cf. pp. 213 ff.); the collection or code of laws, such as is provided by Deuteronomy or the Holiness Code or the Priestly Code, a gathering together of rules governing many aspects of life; the whole Law, the first five books of the Old Testament, which are not to be understood as law in our normal restricted sense of the word, but as the whole record of God's dealings with Israel, embodying divine action and the nature of man's response. When in Ps. 1 the righteous man is described as one whose 'delight is in the law of the LORD', we must see this first as an expression of the wonder evoked at the marvellous dealings of God with his people, and then as a more detailed consideration of the ways in which every part of life is brought under his control.

The great moment of the Persian period as the Chronicler saw it was when the people accepted the Law afresh as it was read to them by Ezra and expounded for their understanding (Neh. 8; cf. pp. 270 ff.). This is only one interpretation of the period, but it is clearly a very important one, for subsequently the Jews looked to this moment as a climax in their history and claimed as their ideal such full acceptance of the Law and obedience to it. From this, two types of development took place, for though their sources are no doubt much earlier, the full development is only attested in much later literature. On the one hand, there is what we may best term the 'legalistic' development; obedience to the Law is central, it must be made applicable to every detail of life, and this involves elaborate interpretation and the development of what came to be known as the 'oral Law', believed by some to have been delivered to

Moses alongside the written Law. At its best this was a genuine concern to see how conduct should be properly regulated; at its worst it could become petty and in its emphasis on detail could obscure the real meaning of the Law. The New Testament provides ample criticism of such a tendency, but so also do Jewish traditions. It could also very easily, as Paul was to emphasize, slip over into the idea that obedience to the Law gives man a status with God, a claim on God's grace. It is this negative development, though it is not by any means all a bad thing, which has often been stressed in the discussion of the place of the Law in the post-exilic period. On the other hand, concern with the Law was the expression of a deep faith and devotion, a love of the scriptures in which it was recorded, a nourishing of life by the contemplation of the actions and words of God as there presented. It is a joyous way of life (cf. Deut. $30^{19f.}$, cf. p. 147), the way by which through centuries of opposition and persecution the Jewish community has maintained its existence, expressed often in customs which are strange to the non-Jewish world but which are the outward dress of an unshaken faith. It is this spirit which breathes in some of the psalms.

Ps. 1 *Law and life*

The psalm contrasts the righteous and the wicked, picturing them as two communities, or two ways of life. The terms used in v. 1, *counsel*, *way*, and *seat*, are suggestive of a kind of conspiracy among wicked men with which the righteous must not associate himself. Often the psalm has been interpreted as if it envisaged a sharp division of the community into parties, and attempts have been made at identifying these; such an application is very understandable, and it may well have been made by users of the psalm. But basically the point is more generally stated. Holding himself away from association with the wicked, the righteous man concentrates his attention on the law. *Meditates* (v. 2) really suggests the reading over of the Law in a half-voice, a repetition of its content continually. The symbol of life in v. 3 is found also in Jer. $18^{7f.}$ and may be seen in the Egyptian 'Teaching of Amenemope':

> 'The truly silent man (contrasted with the hot-head) . . .
> . . . is like a tree growing in a plot.
> It groweth green and doubleth its yield;
> It is before its lord.
> Its fruit is sweet; its shade is pleasant.
> Its end is reached in the grove. (Quoted from *DOTT*, p. 178.)

It is a natural metaphor for life and well-being. By contrast, the life of the wicked is portrayed as impermanent. They will have no standing in the law-courts—there will be no defence for them; nor will they have any membership *in the congregation of the righteous* (v. 5). To be cut off from the community is as a sentence of death. The sense of the word *knows* in v. 6 might be further brought out by rendering as 'cares for', i.e. watches over.

Ps. 19 *The Law and world order*

It is reasonably supposed by many scholars that this psalm really consists of two originally separate elements, vv. 1–6 an ancient poem particularly concentrated on the glory of the sun in the created order, and vv. 7–14 a glorification of the Law, which has been added to it. Opinions differ as to whether the second part had an independent existence or was composed to elaborate the first part. But in any case the two now belong closely together in that the second provides comment on the significance of the first.

Verses 1–6 picture the whole created order glorifying God and offering praise. The precise relation of v. 3 to vv. 2 and 4 is not clear; it could be a comment added later, but perhaps is better seen as an elaboration of the mystery of this praise of God by his creation. It is a 'song without words'. The created order is centred on the sun (vv. 4*c*–6) which is described here in strongly mythological terms, with allusions to the kind of myth which probably underlies at least some elements in the Samson tradition. Verse 6 suggests a relation between the all-seeing sun and the all-seeing deity.

Verses 7–14 appear at first sight to be on a totally unrelated subject, that of the Law; the passage consists of phrases praising the Law (cf. Ps. 119) and showing the way in which the Law can protect the devout man. The relationship is to be seen in a correspondence between the whole creation in its divinely ordered existence and the life of a man which is equally divinely ordered by the Law which God has given. It is the Law which makes for a true order in human life. The various pictures used in vv. 7–10 elaborate the delight in the Law which is indicated in Ps. 1. Verses 11–14 move on from this to the errors into which men fall even though they seek a good life. It is God alone, who is *rock* and *redeemer*, who can ensure that man is *acceptable in thy sight* (v. 14). The terms *rock* and *redeemer* provide an illuminating link with the religious tradition; the former might suggest the wilderness period, the rock from which water was given for Israel, but more probably alludes to the symbol of the rock in Jerusalem (cf. Isa. 28^{16}; and compare with this 30^{29}, 32^{2}); the latter points to the Exodus traditions of God's redemptive action.

Ps. 119 *Delight in the Law*

This immense psalm is, as we have already noted in commenting on the poems in the book of Lamentations (p. 49), constructed on a highly stylized basis. Each group of eight lines begins with the same letter of the alphabet and all twenty-two letters are covered in turn. This imposes a certain limitation on the content, and there is a further restriction in that almost every line contains a word which is a synonym for law—way, testimony, precept, statute, commandment, and so on. It is a masterpiece of ingenuity, but it is also a remarkably deep expression of religious emotion.

This is not a psalm to read straight through; it is best taken in single sections because of its repetitiveness. Yet even so there is variety in the patterns, with concern for right conduct, for the pressures of life, for the distress in which deliverance is needed. We need also to try to get inside the mind of the worshipper who uses such words as these. At times there appears to be a certain arrogance of statement; but this is balanced by the obviously deep desire of the psalmist for closeness to God, by his consciousness of how easy failure is, by his awareness that life can only be enjoyed in obedience to God's law. The confidence which the devout man has lies not in himself but in what God has revealed.

Verses 17–24 may be read for their sensitivity to the words of God's will and the recognition of the Law as a source of life and guidance. Verses 153–60 illustrate the distress of the psalmist and his acknowledgement of the truth of God's word. The variety and interwovenness of the themes should be observed in each section of the psalm.

D. WISDOM AND LIFE. THE BOOK OF JOB

In each of the psalms we have just considered there is an emphasis on the right ordering of life and a contrast drawn explicitly or implicitly between those who live according to law, principle, wisdom, and those who are wicked, who live in accordance with no principle, the foolish. Such a contrast is very characteristic of the Wisdom literature not only of the Old Testament but of the ancient Near East in general, and the language of these psalms, and of others, shows affinities with the language and style of books like Proverbs and Job and Ecclesiastes which are classified as Wisdom literature. These may be numbered among a larger group of such writings, and with them may be associated sections or short passages in every part of the Old Testament in which similar features appear.

It used to be common among scholars to treat Wisdom as a relatively late development within the Old Testament, and to concentrate attention on its marked differences from the style and content of other types of Old Testament literature. Increasingly, however, partly as a result of the study of the literatures of Egypt and Babylonia, now known to us in so much greater detail, and partly as a result of a closer examination of the appearance of what may be conveniently termed 'Wisdom features' in other parts of the Old Testament, it has come to be realized that Wisdom cannot be treated as a totally separate development. In this process of revaluation it is, however, important not to underestimate the differences of thought and style. In particular it is evident that the works classified as Wisdom do not until a very late date (i.e. in writings which can with assurance be so dated) reveal any clear contact with that line of Old Testament thought which concentrates on God's actions in history, the great redemptive tradition which is so prominent in the prophets and psalms as well as in the narratives from Genesis to 2 Kings. (The Chronicler also stands in this tradition, but there is some evidence, as we have seen, of less concern with history and more with meaning and hence a handling of historical tradition with very marked freedom.) The Wisdom literature is also relatively little concerned with another aspect of religious life, namely worship.

We may account for this difference in the Wisdom literature with the recognition that it is a way of thought and writing which came into Israel from the outside. No doubt early Israel had its proverbs and wise sayings, but the fully stylized form of Wisdom is so closely allied to the world outside Israel that it is clear that an impetus came from there. Tradition associates this primarily with the time of Solomon, and in that period the development of government organization, involving the kind of educational needs which were already being met in scribal schools in Egypt and elsewhere, may well have brought a more intimate knowledge of the material used in that educational system. For such wisdom teaches orderly life and good government. Part of the book of Proverbs is also traditionally associated with the time of Hezekiah (cf.

Prov. 25^{1}); this was another period of significant international political contact. But it would be a mistake to suppose that Wisdom remained an alien element. A prophet might ridicule the pretensions of the wise to knowledge and understanding (cf. Isa. 29^{9-16}), but it could also be said that the counsel given by the wise was a revelation of the divine will to be set alongside the word of the prophet and the directive of the priest (Jer. 18^{18}; Ezek. 7^{26}). The function of the wise was very much a practical one, the ordering of life aright, the injunction to right conduct, to proper observance of custom. Under the influence of such a view of life, the story of Joseph is presented as a pattern (Gen. 37–50), and it has been urged that the story of the succession to David in 2 Sam. 9–20; 1 Kgs. 1–2 also owes its particular presentation to this. The observance of Wisdom elements in poetry and prophecy, in narrative and in the exposition of law (particularly in Deuteronomy), is therefore to be seen as a token of the acceptance of this style and outlook as appropriate to the expression of every kind of religious truth. It was only a logical development that in the later period, when Law came increasingly to be seen as the fundamental principle of life, Wisdom too should be so regarded and the two eventually equated (so in Ecclesiasticus and particularly in the Wisdom of Solomon). The two ways of thinking are not really so unrelated. At the same time, the development of a way of looking at the writings of the past as a guide to life and conduct in the present also owes much to the view that conduct should be regulated, life should be ordered; and what eventually came to be precisely recognized as sacred scripture was a ready source for such ordering.

The dating of the Wisdom literature presents almost insuperable problems. Only in the case of some very late writings can we be sure. Ecclesiasticus, or, to give it its proper title, 'The Wisdom of Jesus Ben Sirach', belongs to about 180 B.C., as we know from the prologue to its translation into Greek made about sixty years later. The Wisdom of Solomon is later still. Probably, though not quite so certainly, Ecclesiastes may be dated to the Greek period. On all these, reference may be made to Vol. 5, pp. 250–80. The book of Proverbs is notoriously difficult to date; its material, consisting largely of single contrasting or comparing sayings, could belong to almost any period, and there is no good reason why much of it may not be quite early in origin. Some parts of the book, notably in chapters 1–9, have generally been thought to be later than the exile; the presentation of the figure of Wisdom, especially in 8–9, is both in style and content very developed, and may be compared with Job. 28. But this does not prove a late date, and the matter remains open. The book of Proverbs has been discussed in Vol. 3, pp. 185–96, and this is preceded (pp. 165–85) by a fairly full account of Wisdom, its international background and its place in Israel. It is there recognized that a majority of scholars would still place some parts of Proverbs in the post-exilic period, and that the final shaping of the book certainly belongs to that time. In view of the fact that the book of Proverbs is not treated in this volume, it must be emphasized that it may still be regarded, at any rate in its final form, as witnessing to the continuing activity of the wise and to the important part played by their way of thought in the evolution of Old Testament ideas.

The remaining Wisdom book of the Old Testament is the book of Job. Here again the date is uncertain. The fact that the author uses a tale about a hero who appears to belong to remote, patriarchal times, led to a belief in some circles that it was written by Moses and the book was sometimes placed immediately after the first five books of the Bible. The name of Job appears in Ezek. 14 along with Noah and Daniel; the former certainly belongs to very ancient tradition, the latter may well be identical with the *Dan'el* known from the Canaanite literature of Ras Shamra (before 1400 B.C.; cf. Vol. 5, pp. 223 f.). This would suggest that the Job tradition itself—embodied in the prose narrative at the beginning and end of the book—is also ancient. But the book itself is likely to be much later. Some scholars would give it a pre-exilic date, but for most the choice is between a sixth-century date, during the period of exile, and a rather later date, perhaps about

400 B.C. The arguments for the exilic date are very much tied up with the problem of the relationship between the poetry of the book of Job and that of the Second Isaiah; but most probably the affinities are to be explained as due to both making use of well-known forms, particularly psalm forms. The arguments for the later date are partly linguistic—a very difficult criterion—and partly theological. It is often felt that it was after the teaching of Deuteronomy and the great prophets that the particularly acute form of the problem of retribution and the suffering of the innocent came to be felt. Dating from ideas is often hazardous, but there is some validity in the view that theological notions hardened after the exile and the book of Job, like the later Ecclesiastes, is in part a protest against a too narrow theology. It is also not impossible that the experience of exile, looked back on from a somewhat later time, might have provided some of the elements which make up the author's thinking. In this, he to some extent resembles the author of the book of Jonah (cf. pp. 337 ff.), presenting the meaning of his people's history in part in terms of the character through whom he gives his message.

The book of Job is a difficult one to understand. The detail of its poetry presents many problems to the interpreter, for many of its words are strange and not used elsewhere in the Old Testament. The peculiarities of the language are such that it has been thought possible that the author lived outside Palestine—in Edom, or North Arabia, or in an Aramaean area. But the amount of Hebrew literature we have in the Old Testament is so limited that we have to be very cautious in such matters as this; so many factors can influence the vocabulary that a writer uses. In regard to style and form, the book of Job has many points of contact with other Old Testament writings.

The book consists of a prologue (1–2) and an epilogue (42^{7-17}) in prose; the remainder is in poetry. Since the name of Job is known as belonging to ancient tradition and there are certain striking differences in style between the prose and poetic sections—and some would say marked differences of conception of the figure of Job—it is generally supposed that the author was making use of a folk-tale, no doubt well known to his contemporaries, as a vehicle for his teaching. To some extent this use of a known story may have imposed limitations on his treatment of his subject; but his choice of this particular tradition as the basis of his exposition suggests that he saw it as an appropriate starting-point for the discussion. It is therefore not improper to see what the prologue and epilogue say, and recognize that the author of the poetry may be utilizing their particular contribution. In the same way that the later creation narrative in some measure reinterprets the older one with which it is placed (cf. pp. 154 ff.), so the poetic material in the book of Job is not simply set within the framework of the prose, it offers a comment upon it and an interpretation of it.

The prologue presents us with an almost fairy-tale situation, the picture of a rich and righteous man, prospering and acknowledging the source of his prosperity in God's blessing. In a heavenly court scene at which the divine beings ('sons of God') come to report, one of them—for so it is natural to read the text—the adversary, the Satan, invited by God to comment on Job, affirms that his piety is the outcome of his prosperity. If he loses his goods, he will lose his faith. (The Satan—note the definite article, for this is not a personal name—is here one of the members of the divine court—cf. 1 Kgs. 22^{19-23} and Zech. 3 (p. 225)—whose function appears to be the general examination and questioning of human conduct. From this he develops into a negative figure, cf. 1 Chron. 21^{1} and later mythological developments.) So Job is subjected, with God's permission, to the loss of all his wealth and of his sons and daughters, he laments and mourns, but accepts what God has done. In a second scene in heaven, the Satan is challenged and maintains that a man will sacrifice property and family but will give up faith when he himself is touched; he is permitted to afflict Job with illness but not to take his life. So Job is 'afflicted . . . with loathsome sores', but resists the temptation to renounce God, rejecting this as folly. He is joined by three friends who come to comfort him, and in their distress they sit in silence 'for they saw that his suffering was very great'.

The epilogue shows God, after he has spoken with Job, pronouncing a harsh verdict upon the friends 'for you have not spoken of me what is right, as my servant Job has' (42^7). They are to offer sacrifice and Job will pray for them; this leads to their reconciliation with God. Then Job is restored to his prosperity, with a new family to replace the one he has lost, and he dies in old age, richly blessed.

The ending too has all the air of a fairy-tale, and to a modern reader seems too simple a solution. But we must remember that once the author of the book used the story, he could hardly leave out the end. It had in any case the merit of declaring a verdict on Job, and thus of endorsing the effect of the poetic centre of the book. But some points in it suggest that in the original tale the middle section, now replaced by the poetry, may have portrayed the three friends in a manner somewhat different from that which now appears in the book. Here we can only speculate.

The main interest clearly lies in the long poetic section, and this consists of several elements. The largest part is made up of a series of speeches in what may be described as three cycles. In the first (3–11) Job speaks three times followed by each of the friends in turn; the same pattern is found in the second (12–20); the third begins in the same way but is either incomplete or in disorder (21–27). In reality there is no division between the groups of speeches; it is merely a convenience to refer to them as cycles. Chapter 28 interrupts the sequence, being a poem on wisdom; it is not in any way directly related to the interchange between the speeches, though it is not altogether irrelevant to the whole theme of the book. It is followed (29–31) by a long final speech by Job, culminating in an appeal to God to answer him. The answer appears only in chapter 38, the intervening 32–37 being taken up by the unexpected intervention of a hitherto unmentioned personage named Elihu. He is not referred to in the conclusion to the book, and it is quite evident that these chapters are not part of the original plan. The speech or speeches of God are found in 38–41, with a response by Job at 40^{3-5} and again at 42^{1-6}.

This is an elaborate structure and some few points of importance may be mentioned briefly here. First, the present form of 21–27 may suggest that the book was unfinished, or that it has come to be disarranged; it has been argued that the author deliberately silenced the friends, but this seems less likely. Is there perhaps here a clue to the formation of the book? Was it shaped over a period of years, perhaps in the first instance in oral discussion, the discussion of a wise teacher with his pupils, in which he elaborated and worked over his interpretation of the Job legend, and himself wrote it up or left it to his followers to do so? Second, 28 is intrusive, but could have been inserted by the original author or by a later follower because its theme, the nature of wisdom, is fundamental to the whole question of whether there can be intelligible discussion about the meaning of life and experience (cf. pp. 324 f.). Third, 32–37 are likewise intrusive. It seems not impossible that the author or much more probably, in view of differences of language and content, some later writer, added these speeches by Elihu, endeavouring thereby to provide a clearer answer to the questions raised by the book. There is some overlap of content with the speeches of God, and this may suggest that this author thought of Elihu (= 'My God he is') as spokesman for God. Was he perhaps motivated by ideas of reverence for God, providing someone who should speak for him rather than portraying him as speaking direct? It is difficult not to feel that, interesting as these chapters are, they weaken the effect of the book. Fourth, the speeches of God are overloaded with long poetic passages only very loosely connected with the main theme, in particular the poems on 'Behemoth' in 40^{15-24} and on 'Leviathan' in 41; these have been much discussed, and it is not possible to decide whether they are poems on the hippopotamus and the crocodile, or whether the two beasts are really mythological. Perhaps there are elements of both in the language used. In the remaining material of these speeches there is much repetition, and we have perhaps a combination of more than one form of the same material; the same may be said of Job's replies. Each of these points needs to be borne in mind as we read the book.

But what is the book about? It used to be said fairly simply that it was about the suffering of the innocent, and this theme is certainly present. But it appears to be really the occasion rather than the theme. This problem is raised in the psalms and in the prophetic writings; it is a common theme of psalms of lamentation, and there is a great deal of overlap between the speeches of Job in the book and such psalms. He, like the writers of the psalms, uses strong language in complaining of the inequities of life.

More fundamental than this question is the issue of knowledge of God and relationship to him. The suffering of the innocent raises this kind of question. If good men suffer and wicked prosper, something is wrong with the world. If God is in control, then he is responsible. But the even deeper question arises as to whether man can know God if there is this disparity in life, and whether man can establish any lasting relationship with God. To a considerable extent, the friends, in differing ways and with differing emphases, present the view that God is knowable even if holy and mysterious; they in effect regard God as definable. Job, on the other hand, questions their confidence and is in distress not simply because he suffers or because other innocents suffer but because the whole relationship with God appears to be in doubt. His final speech makes the whole problem clear. In 29–30 he contrasts his past life—secure in the faith of a relationship with God—with his present distress, in which such a relationship appears to be denied. In 31, with great boldness, he takes upon himself total responsibility for what he is, uttering curses upon himself if he has infringed God's law, but appealing directly to God for an answer. The decisive point then is that God does answer. That his answer is in the form of questions to Job about the limits of man's understanding does not alter that fact. Job recognizes the danger of his attempt at getting a clear definition of God; in a re-established relationship, made possible by the direct approach of God to him, he sees that life can be lived. The answer to his dilemma is in a reaffirmation of faith. The result is that the inadequacy of any human statement about the nature and purpose of God is shown up, not least those over-confident affirmations which appear in the speeches of the friends. But the author does not oversimplify the issues; the friends are given reality, they are shown to be deeply rooted in the religious tradition, conscious of the ways in which God makes himself known to man.

The book of Job is in many ways an elusive work. As a result many varieties of interpretation have been given to it, and differing estimates of the points which it sets out to make. Part of the problem lies in the way in which the thought is presented. We may recognize three important elements in this.

(1) It is clear that in the speeches of Job, the author makes very large use of the psalm-form normally described as the lament; this is particularly evident in chapter 3, the opening of Job's statements. The result is that a very large use is made of stereotyped language, phrases which derive from much older poetry. It is as dangerous to seek for precise references in such language as it is in the psalms or in Isa. 53 (cf. pp. 131 ff.); this is highly poetic, allusive, rich in metaphor. To attempt to find in the speeches of Job an exact description of the disease from which he is suffering—and then perhaps to conclude that this is not the same disease as the prologue indicates—is to misuse the poetry.

(2) The interchange between Job and his friends is hardly dialogue or drama or debate. One analogy suggested for it is that of the Hebrew legal procedure, with Job representing the defendant presenting his case in lament style while the friends make accusations also in a conventional style. Such a view would help to explain why it appears that at times the friends are addressing Job in a way which is totally unrealistic. Of what use is it to say to a man who has lost all his family and possessions:

> You shall know that your tent is safe,
> and you shall inspect your fold and miss nothing.

You shall know also that your descendants shall be many,
and your offspring as the grass of the earth.
You shall come to your grave in ripe old age,
as a shock of grain comes up to the threshing floor in its season (5^{24-26}).

But if this is conventional language, then the difficulty is removed. Whatever precise analogy is suggested, it is clear that each of the speakers in turn is presenting a case; it is argued out on certain well-defined lines, and it is designed to convince by its general coherence and the weight of its effect. Reference back to the previous speaker is for the most part minimal, and often consists merely of a few derogatory phrases at the beginning. Thus Job:

No doubt you are the people,
and wisdom will die with you (12^2).

Such irony is designed to undermine the opponents' security.

(3) The whole presentation is to be classed with the Wisdom literature; its style and language make this clear over and over again. This means that much of the argument is presented in proverbial form. The proverbs of a people are an important source of information about their way of thought, but for an outsider they are particularly difficult to understand. Many of the Old Testament proverbs have come, through the Authorized Version, to be so much a part of our own language that we do not always recognize their source; their familiarity may suggest that we know precisely what they mean. But a close study of the book of Job reveals how proverbial language can be used allusively, suggesting a truth without stating it, approaching it from various angles so that different aspects of it are revealed. The result is cumulative, but always with some uncertainty remaining about what exactly the author means. For this reason, and also because of the problems of interpreting the language itself, it should be emphasized that the general view of the book's purpose and outcome sketched earlier is designed only to help the reader enter a difficult area; it does not sum up all that the book contains, and prolonged

study and repeated reading will not exhaust the treasures of poetry and thought which are to be found here.

Something has already been said of the international character of the Wisdom literature. In the case of the book of Job analogies have been found in other ancient literatures. An Egyptian 'Dispute over Suicide' (for the text see *ANET*, pp. 405–7, cf. also *DOTT*, pp. 164–6) expresses disillusionment and weariness with life; it goes back to at least 2000 B.C. A Sumerian work 'I will praise the Lord of wisdom' (cf. *ANET*, pp. 434–7) and various Babylonian writings (for parts of one of these, cf. *DOTT*, pp. 97–103), also reveal concern about the problems of life and of relationship between man and the gods. It is clear that the device of setting out the problems of theology and of life in dialogue or discussion form was already a familiar one. The author of Job, and his successors who developed what he had written, were taking further a method which they had inherited from the past.

(The notes on the passages which follow have been kept brief since a full discussion of the difficulties of the text and interpretation would be out of proportion here. Reference may be made to the commentaries for detail, but the important point is first to get a general impression of the book and the main lines of its thought.)

3 *Job's lament*

3–10. A close analogy to these verses may be found in Jer. 20[14–18] and it is clear that both make use of already well-known motifs. The day of Job's birth is poetically thought of as having a life of its own; it is to be excluded from the calendar so that it will not be remembered. Verse 8 is difficult; perhaps since the second clause refers to Leviathan, one of the names for the power of chaos, the first line should have 'Sea' for *day*—Sea (*Yām*) being another name which is given to the hostile power, particularly in the Canaanite texts. In a number of

Old Testament passages this meaning appears (cf. 38^{8-11}), often with an added reference to the crossing of the sea at the Exodus (e.g. Nah. 1^{4}).

11–19. There is a natural move over to a longing for death; even at the very moment of birth, he might have died and been at peace. These verses give one picture of what the world of the dead is like; it is a realm of sleep, where the great are reduced to nothing, where all troubles come to an end. For the most part in the Old Testament, the realm of the dead is a shadowy world, with no reality (cf. on $19^{23\,\mathrm{ff.}}$, p. 329).

20–23 continue this theme, but with an emphasis on the distress of those who suffer, for whom death seems the only desirable outcome. Phrase after phrase suggests the state of anguish in which Job finds himself. A comparison may be made both here and elsewhere in the speeches of Job with Ps. 88 where many of the metaphors of the book of Job are found. It provides a clear indication of the relation between the psalm language and that of Job.

11 *The first speech of Zophar*

The first speech of Eliphaz (4–5) has at its centre a recounting of a divine revelation, a mysterious experience of the presence of God, which indicates both the speaker's authority and his sense of the gulf between man and God. He is confident that an appeal to God will meet with response, and that in God there is disaster for the wicked and hope for the righteous. The first speech of Bildad (8) appeals to the order which is attested by the life of the world, and to the authority of traditional wisdom, for these show that the wicked and righteous will gain their proper reward. This first speech of Zophar makes similar claims.

2–3 provide an introductory derogatory statement in comment on what has been said by Job.

4–12 point to the depths of divine wisdom in contrast to man's and to the effect that divine revelation of that wisdom would have upon the pretensions of men.

13–20 appeal for repentance and promise restoration to the penitent. The whole speech is very conventional in tone, and although it is not among the more exhilarating parts of the book, it serves as a good example of the way in which conventional statement is used. At the same time, we may recognize how the author in presenting the ordinary views of the pious and wise does not really caricature them; and in fact what Zophar says here is echoed in the final speeches of God where the immensity of divine wisdom is set forth. There is a subtle difference between the repetition of religious truths and the recognition that they are an inadequate and yet essential way of suggesting the reality which lies behind them.

19[23–27b] *Wherein does hope lie?*

These verses are often seen as providing a climax in the discussion, though the difficulties of understanding the text are so great that a sure interpretation can hardly be offered. Job is shown to be aware of the impossibility of man engaging in debate with God, for God is in absolute control. He is shown as challenging the order of the world which appears to deny the control in which he believes. In the verses leading up to this passage, the estrangement of Job from every other person is stressed (cf. Ps. 88); his friends have failed him. In this extremity an utterance of confidence is made.

23–24 express the hope that what Job has said will be recorded so that posterity will know just what his perplexities were.

25–27*b* affirm the reality of one who will redeem and the confidence that Job will know of his vindication.

Discussion of the meaning of these verses turns around several problems: There is the problem of the actual meaning of the words of v. 26. Does it mean that after death Job will see vindication, and if so what does this involve? Or does it simply mean that there will be a great restoration for Job so that 'from' his body, i.e. within this life, he will know that he is vindicated? Neither is entirely satisfactory. The hope of a real life after death, which appears clearly only in the second century B.C. in Dan. 12, is so firmly denied in 14^{7-14} that it is difficult to find it here. Mere physical restoration seems less than is intended. Perhaps what is envisaged is a moment in the future at which the memory of Job will be cleared, he will be vindicated, and although by then he will be in the realm of the shadowy dead, he will know that this is so. Then there is the question of who is meant by the term *Redeemer*. Here the answer is not so uncertain, for although there are those who have thought that some otherwise unnamed person must be meant, someone who can act on Job's behalf, this is very unlikely. Earlier we find Job saying that were he to come before God as in a law-court, there could be 'no umpire between us, who might lay his hand upon us both' (9^{33}). God in the court is both accuser and judge. So here the idea of some human mediator is improbable, and it is clear that we should see in the *Redeemer* God himself; such language is used of God in the Exodus traditions (e.g. in Exod. 15^{13}). The term in secular use refers to the kinsman who has a responsibility towards a destitute member of a family or towards a widow (cf. Ruth 4^{1-12}, p. 336). The movement of Job's thought is from his distress and feeling of alienation from God to his consciousness that in God alone is hope, and that God will not lightly set aside the bond which he has created.

28 *Where is Wisdom to be found?*

As has already been indicated, this chapter is an independent poem interrupting the sequence of thought; it breaks the connection between the last stage of the discussion and the final appeal by Job in 29–31. But it is very unlikely that its inclusion here is purely accidental; whether the author himself added it or one of his successors, it serves two purposes. On the one hand, quite simply, it provides a sort of breathing-space between the long-drawn-out discussion, with its repetitions, and the final appeal. There is artistic advantage in such a pause, as if whoever put it here is inviting the reader to consider the problem in a larger manner and not to be overwhelmed by the sheer weight of words which has preceded it. On the other hand, at a deeper level, it serves to emphasize a point fundamental to the whole book. Wisdom is an elusive thing, its possession is precious; but where can it be found? Those who claim to have wisdom have in considerable measure in the preceding chapters been shown to lack true wisdom. This belongs to God—here there is a foretaste of the final speeches of God—and man cannot attain this as man. Yet the situation is not a pessimistic one, for there is a way to a wisdom which man can have. The poem ends in a climax of confidence:

Behold, the fear of the Lord, that is wisdom;
and to depart from evil is understanding (v. 28).

The whole poem is a sensitive treatment of the subject; we are led in the opening verses into the mysteries of human experience—that of the mining of metals hidden in the earth, of the ways of birds and animals, of man's control of rock and water (vv. 1–11). The elusiveness of wisdom is pictured in a series of questions; its value not to be assessed by any known standards (vv. 12–19). The secret of wisdom remains; neither the heights to which the birds fly disclose it, nor the depths of Abaddon and Death—names used for Sheol, the realm of the dead. It is God who in his created order sets it out (cf. for a different relation of wisdom to creation, Prov. 8^{22-31} and on this Vol. 3, pp. 188–92), but to man he has declared the way in which wisdom is to be gained (vv. 20–28).

The way is opened up for the reader to move on towards the revelation of God, who alone can disclose the nature of his being and purpose.

38^{1-38} *The mystery of ordered creation*

The first speech of God extends from 38^{2} to 39^{30}; it falls into two parts, the one here considered and the remainder from

38^{39} which consists of a group of short poems in question form dealing with different members of the animal creation—the lion, the mountain goat, the wild ass (onager), the wild ox, the ostrich, the horse, and hawks and eagles. These poems pick out particular wonders or strange elements in the world of animals and birds and may be compared with parts of Prov. 30; it is this kind of wisdom, commenting and illustrating, which is referred to in 1 Kgs. 4^{33} where it is said of Solomon that 'he spoke of trees . . . of beasts, and of birds, and of reptiles, and of fish'.

The first part of the speech similarly consists of smaller elements built together, and likewise in question form, dealing with the whole order of the created world. It is a rich source of information about the pictorial way in which ancient Israel thought of creation, with a wealth of mythological allusion—e.g. in vv. 7, 8, 17. A comparison may be made with Prov. $8^{27\text{ff.}}$, $30^{3\text{f.}}$; Amos 4^{13}, $5^{8\text{f.}}$; and many passages in the Second Isaiah. The writer is drawing on well-known tradition. The whole tenor of the poem is that of the wonder of divine control, the orderliness with which the natural world proceeds. This may be appreciated more clearly if we remember that there was a firm belief in the forces of chaos, expressed often in terms of the great waters or the various monsters of the deep, Leviathan and Rahab and the like, which, if not held under control, might break loose and bring disaster to the world. The order of creation is not just placid; it is an order imposed on opposing force. Palestine is an earthquake area; insecurity is therefore a matter of experience. A great earthquake in the time of Uzziah (cf. Amos 1^{1}) left a deep mark in the people's thought (cf. the late passage Zech. 14^{4-5}). The dry wadis of summer which became raging torrents in the heavy winter rains and could sweep away man and beast were also a reminder that the blessing of rain was an ambiguous blessing, bringing also disaster and death.

The comparison with Prov. 30 may again be made in regard to the whole purpose of the speeches of God in the book; this passage opens with the confession of ignorance and lack of wisdom on the part of the speaker, and leads on into the acknowledgement of the wisdom of the divine creator. So too in the book of Job, the revelation of God himself in his wisdom provokes the response of humility and acceptance.

Is this just an overwhelming of Job with a show of divine power and a mocking of human pretensions? That this is not so seems to be made clear by the last words of Job in 42$^{5-6}$:

I had heard of thee by the hearing of the ear,
but now my eye sees thee;
therefore I despise myself,
and repent in dust and ashes.

The difference between a mere show of power and a revelation of God in person is here brought out; Job responds to the recognition that he has been privileged to meet with God, and in that meeting all pretence and all claim fall away. He simply accepts. And the point is confirmed by the epilogue, for the restoration of prosperity, part of the original tale and therefore indispensable, is not simply a redressing of the balance. It is a token of the reality of that relationship in which a man may stand with God, expressed in the only terms in which this can be stated within the confines of a this-worldly view.

E. THE BOOK OF RUTH

In the English Bible, this little story is placed immediately after the book of Judges with which it is naturally associated because of its opening phrase: 'In the days when the judges ruled' (1^{1}). In the Hebrew Bible, it stands with Lamentations (cf. p. 46) in the group of five 'scrolls'. It is believed by most scholars that the book is a relatively late work; the very general reference back to the Judges period does not suggest a precise historical setting, and its account of and comments on the customs of the time in chapter 4 strongly indicate a much later period when these practices had ceased to be in use. Some features of the language have also been thought to suggest a late date.

As the book now stands, it leads up to the birth of a child who is described as the ancestor of David. Thus the story of Ruth is given a primary importance in tracing the family of the one who was to be Israel's greatest king and a leading figure in her religious thought. But it is very much debated whether the concluding verses which make this connection with David are original to the story or show the interest of a later editor. The point is difficult to resolve. The analogy of other famous men and the stories which come to be connected with them—we might instance the birth story of Moses for which there are counterparts—would make it very probable that a story quite independent of the Davidic family has come to be so attached. The Moabite background has been seen to correspond with David's connections in Moab during the time of his outlawry in the reign of Saul (1 Sam. 22^{3-4}); but this is rather far-fetched, and it is more natural to suppose that David went to the king of Moab not because he could claim a relationship with the Moabites but because the Moabite ruler would not be averse to protecting a rival of the king in Israel. What is much more striking about the story of Ruth is the very fact that a Moabite woman could be regarded in such a favourable light and that she could come to be regarded as an ancestress of the Davidic line. Hostility to Moab is very strong in certain parts of the Old Testament; we may instance the ridiculing of Moabite and Ammonite ancestry in Gen. 19^{30-38} and the exclusion of all Moabites and Ammonites in Deut. 23^{3-6}, where, by comparison, the Edomites (23^{7-8}) are treated much more kindly. But generalization is dangerous, since we know that there are other traditions violently hostile to Edom. Particular periods and particular situations may have produced animosity to Moab.

This consideration also weighs against seeing the book of Ruth as a polemical document directed against the policies of Nehemiah and Ezra. If the book belongs to the fifth century, which is not impossible, then we might legitimately comment that there were some at that time who could look differently at the problem of the community, and see it as right to acknowledge the piety of non-Israelites and the possibility of their accepting full membership. For this is just what the story of Ruth shows her as doing: 'your people shall be my people, and your God my God' (1[16]). In so far as the policy of Ezra meant that membership of the community was defined as being for those who accepted the obligation of the law, one could just as well see the book of Ruth as complementary to that policy as in conflict with it.

If the book is making out a case, this is not at all obvious; there is no evident polemic, no stressing of particular points. But here may lie the skill of a story-teller who first and foremost is a great literary artist—the story is so simple, so beautifully interwoven, moves so gracefully to its climax—and his more immediate purpose in telling the story, if there was one, arises naturally out of what is told.

4[1–12] *The right of the kinsman*

For the two widows, Naomi and Ruth, coming to Bethlehem with no support and no protector, a valuable addition to their meagre living would be gleaning. We must not ask of a story that it should explain why since 'the whole town was stirred because of them', the wealthy kinsman Boaz should not have been moved to offer them some help. For the essence of the story depends on the point that Ruth, who does not know this wealthy kinsman, should be divinely led to the field of Boaz. His help is then given, but its further development is brought about only by the skill of Naomi. The mention in 4[12] of a more remote ancestor of Boaz, Perez son of Judah and Tamar, makes allusion to another story in which a woman preserves the family line by stratagem (cf. Gen. 38). Boaz then accepts his obligation as kinsman and the last chapter reveals how this will operate.

1–2 provide the setting in the gate of the city, where Boaz stops another kinsman of Naomi who has the nearer right to the act of redemption. With them ten *elders of the city* are asked to sit down. Here is a portrayal of what is aptly described as 'justice in the gate' (cf. L. Koehler, *Hebrew Man* (London, 1956), pp. 149 ff.).

3–6 set out the problem and its solution. The duty of the kinsman the *gō'ēl* (v. 3; the same term as in Job 19[26] and there translated 'redeemer') is to ensure the continuity of the family, to keep alive the family name. Naomi's husband and her two sons are dead, but through a kinsman a child may be borne by Ruth who will belong to her dead husband and preserve his name. At the same time, there is family property which can be redeemed (cf. for another example, Jer. 32[6–15]). The position of the land is by no means clear, since Naomi is said to be *selling the parcel of land which belonged to our kinsman Elimelech.* If she actually owned the land, then we may wonder if she was really as destitute as the earlier part of the story implies. Perhaps we should suppose that the land was encumbered by debt. The other kinsman is willing to redeem the land but not to undertake the responsibility of *buying Ruth the Moabitess* (v. 5). Our knowledge of the details of the laws governing such matters is sketchy. The custom of 'levirate marriage' (Latin *levir* = husband's brother) involves the brother of a dead man marrying the widow for the sake of his name (cf. the nonsense story in Matt. 22[23 ff.]). In the Judah–Tamar story, the custom appears to involve the dead man's father as well as his brothers. In Ruth 4 it would appear that a remoter relative could and should act. Redemption of land is a separate issue, but it is not surprising to find the two coinciding in one case. But whether the two had to be kept together as Boaz decrees (v. 5) is not otherwise known to us. One cannot help feeling that this is a device of the story for ensuring that Ruth will marry Boaz, because otherwise the romantic circumstances (as we should describe them) of their meeting in the fields and of her secret excursion to the threshing-floor at night would lead to the wrong result.

7–8 allude to a custom belonging to *former times in Israel* (v. 7). But the only other record we have of such a custom is in Deut.

25^{8-10} and there it is quite different. The widow, if her brother-in-law refuses to carry out his responsibilities in the levirate marriage, is to pull off his sandal and spit in his face and pronounce a curse on him. Of course, the custom may have changed, and we know so little, relatively speaking, of Hebrew law that we must not expect to be able to state it in detail. But it does look rather as though a later story-teller is simply using a reference to an ancient custom as another picturesque detail. The whole function of the taking off of the sandal is totally differently understood.

9–12. Here the function of *the elders and all the people* (v. 9; the latter now brought into the action) is to act as official witnesses of the legal transaction. We may note that they are pictured as active participators in the event and not as passive spectators (cf. on the nations as witnesses in Ezekiel, p. 100). They pronounce not only their witnessing of the transaction but their prayer for divine blessing upon Ruth, upon Boaz and his house, using allusions to the two ancestral wives of Jacob, Rachel and Leah, and to Tamar. This latter reference is indeed a little odd, for it invokes blessing upon the house of Boaz that it may *be like the house of Perez* (v. 12); according to 4^{18}, the house of Perez was really the same as that of Boaz, for the latter was a direct descendant of the former.

F. THE BOOK OF JONAH

Jonah the son of Amittai (1^{1}), with whom this little narrative book is concerned, is known to us otherwise only from a brief statement in 2 Kgs. 14^{25}. He is there described as a prophet who promised the restoration of prosperity and an extension of territory to the northern kingdom in the reign of king Jeroboam II (786–746), in a passage which preserves a positive statement about the north and an assurance of divine salvation for it. It is not impossible that other traditions had been preserved concerning this prophet, and perhaps these included pronouncements about Nineveh the capital of the Assyrian empire; but of such we have no knowledge. The book of Jonah is quite clearly a late story told about this prophet, in which his name—and perhaps the tradition of his nationalist fervour—is used to make certain points about the life of the contemporary Jewish community.

In form the book is quite unlike the other prophetic books. The story is made up of various elements—the theme of the reluctant messenger of God who has to be brought back to perform his task, the theme of the miraculous rescuing and restoration of a man from the sea by the agency of a great fish, exaggerated ideas of the immensity of the city of Nineveh which suggest that to the writer it was known only from remote hearsay. But the detail of the story is of little account by comparison with the message which it quite evidently is intended to convey. God cares for the people even of wicked Nineveh, the symbol of the hostile world of the nations; by comparison with his compassion on 'Nineveh, that great city, in which there are more than a hundred and twenty thousand persons who do not know their right hand from their left, and also much cattle' (4^{11}), how petty is the pride of Jonah, and how selfish his concern for his own comfort. That this book too was written to counter the narrowness of Nehemiah and Ezra has been maintained. This seems much more probable than the comparable suggestion for the book of Ruth, but once again, rather than placing the two views in direct opposition, we should endeavour to see what the book is concerned to do, and to understand its place in the life of a community which could be both narrow and open, and in which the problem of what the community was to be and how it was to be preserved was not one which admitted a simple answer. The book of Jonah sees the real meaning of Israel's history in the light of the wider purpose of God.

Much unnecessary attention has been given to the miraculous element of the great fish. It is possible that this is based on some ancient wonder-tale; perhaps possible that it represents a displaying of the function of the great monster of the deep turned into a beneficent agent of the divine will. In the context of the book, this element is in one sense purely a matter of the mechanics of the story—it serves to get Jonah back from the voyage he has undertaken to the point from which he started. In another sense, we may tentatively see here an allusion to the fortunes of the whole people, with the sojourn in the fish—in the deep—a symbol of the exile. As the people went through the exile, tasting the depths of experience, and was brought (so the Second Isaiah in particular) to a true understanding of its function within the purpose of God, so Jonah symbolizes that people's reluctance to see the outside world accept the mercy of God, and the narrowness of its nationalistic policies. The psalm in chapter 2, which is a real psalm used here as a prayer by Jonah—and it really does not greatly matter whether it was put there by the author of the book or by someone else—suggests this interpretation too, for it is a psalm of lament full of allusions to distress in terms of the forces of Sheol (the realm of the dead) and the deep waters.

1^{4-16} *The reluctant prophet and the devout sailors*

The prophet's attempt to escape from his appointed task by setting sail in the opposite direction is frustrated by a divinely created storm. While the sailors, pious in their own religions, pray to their gods, Jonah sleeps; perhaps we should see this as suggesting heedlessness and insensitivity. When the sailors cast lots to find the one *on whose account this evil* ('calamity') *has come upon us* (v. 7) and discover that it is Jonah, and he reveals who he is and why he is on this journey, they are terrified, more sensitive to the will of his God than he. When Jonah tells them to throw him overboard, they hesitate, not wishing to sacrifice his life, and when they see no other way out, they offer their prayer to his God, and when calm is restored, they sacrifice and make vows. This contrast of the sailors and Jonah paves the way for the response of Nineveh to the prophet's message of doom.

3^{10}–4^{11} *The wideness of God's mercy*

3^{10}–4^{5}. The city of Nineveh, in which Jonah has proclaimed the coming doom because of its wickedness, has repented, seeking divine forgiveness. To this, God responds in mercy. But the prophet is angry. His prayer in anger is a statement of his understanding of the nature of God: *gracious . . . and merciful, slow to anger, and abounding in steadfast love, and repentest of evil* (4^2). The excuse for his flight was his knowledge of this will of God to forgive. There is here a profound recognition of the fact that the idea of a God who is a strict adherent of a rigid system of justice, reward, and punishment, is an easier concept than that of a God of love and mercy. Jonah's desire is for death, because he sees his position made ridiculous by God's mercy. But, as if still hoping for the worst, he makes a shelter from which he can watch the city's fate.

4^{6-11}. The writer adds a new motif to re-emphasize the point. The statement that Jonah has built a shelter is ignored, and shade is now given by a rapidly growing plant. But equally speedily God brings about its withering, and brings the hot east wind, the *hamsin* so well known in Palestine, which stifles the atmosphere, so that Jonah is reduced to despair. His outcry is interpreted as showing concern for an ephemeral plant *for which you did not labour, nor did you make it grow* (v. 10). Yet he cannot understand the concern of God for Nineveh; and the implication is that this city and its people is God's creation, and it is no plant of a day, but a place of many people. The reference to those *who do not know their right hand from their left* may be to children too young to discern, to whom no possible blame could attach; and the same point is made with the reference to *much cattle* (v. 11). So great is the mercy of God (cf. Ps. 103^{8-14} for a similar sentiment).

Additional Note on the extent of Persian influence on Old Testament thought

The closeness of the relationships between the Persian authorities and Jewish leaders—Sheshbazzar, Zerubbabel, Nehemiah, Ezra—during the period of Persian rule has often suggested that it would be reasonable to see in the Old

Testament some evidence of Persian influence upon the thought of this period. But when the matter is more closely examined, it is clear that it is very difficult to establish with any certainty precisely at what points such influence may be observed or to define how far what may be seen is due to outside influence and how far to what may be termed normal processes of development.

A PERSIAN HUNTING SCENE. The scene is portrayed on a seal belonging to the fourth century B.C. It gives a picture of Persian life and a reminder that that life consisted of much more than political activities. Persian art is rich and expressive, a worthy successor to the art and architecture of the earlier cultures of the Near Eastern area.

In general principles, it is reasonable enough to look for evidence of influence, for the study of both the earlier and the later stages of the development of the thought—continuing beyond the Old Testament into the later life of the Jewish community and into the early life of the Christian—reveals a great measure of openness. While the Old Testament developments need to be studied in themselves, it is clear that we cannot fully understand them without taking account of the rich life of the Near East to which they belong. Old Testament language and literature, religion and daily life, belong in that context, and the problem is often to distinguish what is the special character of Old Testament thought and material in the context of all that it shares with the ancient world of the Near East.

At one particular level, influence may be clearly stated: the linguistic. A certain number of Persian words—in some cases there may be doubt because of the possibility that the Persian languages have themselves adopted Semitic words—can be seen in the later Old Testament writings. Examples have already been cited from Ezra 7[11] (cf. p. 268); another example is the word *pardēs* (our word 'Paradise') which means an 'enclosure' or 'park' and which occurs in Neh. 2[8] (a reference to royal estates). It is natural to find that—as in modern borrowings from one language to another—it is particular terms, and especially such as would occur in official correspondence, that most readily come to be used in another language. Persian official documents transmitted to the Jewish community would bring such words to the knowledge of the ruling groups and hence to the people at large.

It is much more difficult to determine influence in the realm of ideas and practices. At the more general and cultural level, the limitations of our knowledge concerning the Persian period are considerable; archaeology has still provided all too little evidence of the life of the period. So far as religious ideas are concerned, there is a twofold problem. On the one hand, the nature and growth of Persian religious ideas are as much a matter of discussion among the scholars in that field as are the similar questions for Old Testament religion; the texts and other evidence are not simple to interpret. The relation between older Persian religion and the religion which came strongly under the influence of the great teacher Zoroaster is a complex one. It is therefore very important that any statements made should be carefully checked against the possible interpretations of the Persian evidence. To say too easily, as has sometimes been done, that Persian dualistic ideas—the idea of a great conflict between a power of good and a power of evil—have influenced the later development of Old Testament thought, is not very satisfactory.

The idea of a great conflict between the power of God, the power of good, and an alien power, sometimes depicted as the power of chaos, can be traced far back in Old Testament thought. At a later stage, in the Greek and Roman periods, the reality and activity of demonic powers come to be much stressed. It is possible that this development owed something to the influence of Persian thought, but precise documentation is difficult to find. The figure of Satan—without the definite article—appears in 1 Chron. 21[1]. (In Zech. 3[1] and Job. 1–2 the use of the definite article suggests that we should translate 'the adversary' (cf. pp. 225, 321).) Is there perhaps here some greater degree of personalizing of the power of evil, the power hostile to God, and is this due to the influence of Persian dualism? It is very difficult to give a firm answer.

The position is similar in regard to ideas about angels. At an early stage, the Old Testament narratives introduce angelic beings (e.g. Gen. 18–19); in later material (e.g. Zech. 1–8) there are further and more developed ideas. Later still, in the book of Daniel and in other writings from the Greek and Roman periods, the angelology is much more fully evolved. How far is this due to the influence of the conceptions of angels found in Persian religion and how far to the gradual development and elaborating of ideas already existing within Old Testament thought?

In this matter of Persian influence, as in other cases where there is discussion of the nature and extent of external influences on Old Testament thought, it is important that two points are kept clear. First, the utmost care must be taken to ensure that the external material concerned is very carefully examined and the problems of its interpretation borne in mind; without this, there may be the risk either of misunderstanding the material itself, or of taking note only of interpretations which suggest correspondence with the Old Testament. Second, it may be doubted whether external influence can operate upon a community except where there are points of real contact in the thought. Any discussion therefore of influence must run alongside a consideration of the nature of Old Testament thought itself, so that we may see the nature of its own development and the possible points at which influence may take place. The two examples just given —that of dualism and that of angelology—indicate how external influence may make itself felt, but internal developments are also of very great importance. In the event, there is likely to be a subtle inter-relationship between the two.

In general, it must be said in regard to the question of Persian influence that there is little clear indication of this during the Persian period itself; subsequently, in the Greek period, probably by way of Jewish groups which lived in the eastern areas of Babylonia and elsewhere, some greater degree of such influence may be observable. A case in point is perhaps the book of Esther, in which a Persian tale may have given rise to some of the elements present in the Jewish story; it is probable also, though not certain, that some of the elements of apocalyptic thought and style are due to Persian influences.

CHRONOLOGICAL TABLES

By R. J. COGGINS

In the tables which follow, these points should be noted:

1. Precise dating in the history of Israel is impossible before the ninth century. In particular the biblical dates of the kings of Israel and Judah, given in 1 and 2 Kings, contain inconsistencies which have been resolved in various ways. The dates given here are therefore bound to be approximations. For discussion of the main problems, reference must be made to the appropriate sections of each volume.

2. Where names of prophets are given, e.g. Amos, Hosea, this should be understood as referring to the lifetime of the prophet and *not* to the composition of the book which bears his name. This can very rarely be dated with any certainty.

3. The column headed 'Archaeological Evidence' simply lists the main points at which archaeological discovery has thrown light upon the history of Israel. For fuller information, with translations where appropriate, reference should be made to such works as D. W. Thomas (ed.), *Documents from Old Testament Times* (Nelson, 1958), and J. B. Pritchard (ed.), *The Ancient Near East* (O.U.P., 1959).

DATE		ISRAEL	NEIGHBOURING POWERS	*Egypt*	ARCHAEOLOGICAL EVIDENCE
1800	PATRIARCHAL PERIOD				
1700		Abraham	Babylonian Power *c.* 1700	Hyksos Period *c.* 1720–1550	Mari Documents 1750–1700 Law Code of Hammurabi *c.* 1700
1600					
1500			Hurrian (Horite) Power	XVIIIth Dynasty 1570–1310	
1400		Jacob Descent into Egypt *c.* 1370	Hittite Empire		Nuzu Documents Tablets from Ras Shamra (Ugarit)
1300			⚔ Qadesh-Orontes *c.* 1286	XIXth Dynasty 1310–1200 Rameses II 1290–1224 Merneptah 1224–1216 XXth Dynasty 1180–1065 Rameses III 1175–1144 Defeat of the Sea Peoples	Tell-el-Amarna Letters
1200		Exodus *c.* 1250. Moses Entry into Canaan *c.* 1200 Joshua			Merneptah Stele
1100		Judges Period	Rise of Philistine Power	XXIst Dynasty 1065–935	Wen-Amon *c.* 1100
1000		Saul *c.* 1020–1000. Samuel David *c.* 1000–961 Solomon *c.* 961–922		XXIInd Dynasty 935–725 Shishak 935–914	Gezer Calendar

DATE	JUDAH		ISRAEL	NEIGHBOURING POWERS			ARCHAEOLOGICAL EVIDENCE
				Egypt	*Assyria*	*Damascus*	
	Rehoboam 922–915 Abijam 915–913 Asa 913–873		Jeroboam I 922–901		Revival of Assyrian Power		
900			Nadab 901–900 Baasha 900–877 Elah 877–876 Zimri 876 Omri 876–869			Ben-hadad I ?900–860	Melqart Stele
	Jehoshaphat 873–849	Elijah	Ahab 869–850		Shalmaneser III 859–824 ⚔ Qarqar 853	Ben-hadad II ?860–843	Black Obelisk of Shalmaneser
	Jehoram 849–842 Ahaziah 842 Athaliah 842–837 Joash 837–800	Elisha	Ahaziah 850–849 Joram 849–842 Jehu 842–815 Jehoahaz 815–801		Adad-Nirari III 811–783	Hazael 843–796	Moabite Stone
800	Amaziah 800–783 Azariah (Uzziah) 783–742		Jehoash 801–786 Jeroboam II 786–746			Ben-hadad III ?796–770	
		Amos Hosea	Zechariah 746–745 Shallum 745				Samaria Ivories and Ostraca
	Jotham 742–735 Ahaz 735–715	Isaiah (active *c.* 742–700) Micah	Menahem 745–738 Pekahiah 738–737 Pekah 737–732 Hoshea 732–724		Tiglath-pileser III 745–727	Rezin *c.* 740–732 Fall of Damascus 732	
	Hezekiah 715–687		Fall of Samaria 721	XXVth Dynasty 716–663	Shalmaneser V 727–722 Sargon II 722–705 Sennacherib 705–681		Siloam Inscription Taylor Prism of Sennacherib
700	Invasion of Judah 701 Manasseh 687–642			Sack of Thebes 663 XXVIth Dynasty 663–525 Psammetichus I 663–609	Esar-haddon 681–669 Ashur-banipal 669–633?		
						Babylon	
	Amon 642–640 Josiah 640–609	Zephaniah Jeremiah (active 626–*c.* 580)				Nabopolassar 626–605	
	⚔ Megiddo 609 Jehoahaz 609 Jehoiakim 609–598	Nahum Habakkuk		Necho II 609–593	Fall of Nineveh 612	⚔ Carchemish 605 Nebuchadrezzar II 605–562	Babylonian Chronicle

DATE	JUDAH	ISRAEL	NEIGHBOURING POWERS: Egypt	Babylon	Persia	ARCHAEOLOGICAL EVIDENCE
600	Jehoiachin 598–597 (deported)					
	Jerusalem captured 597. First Deportation		Psammetichus II 593–588			'Jehoiachin' Tablets from Babylon
	Zedekiah 597–587[1]		Apries (Hophra) 588–569			Lachish Letters
	Fall of Jerusalem 587[1]; Temple Destroyed; Second Deportation					
	Third Deportation 581					
	The Exile	Ezekiel				
			Amasis 569–525	Amel-Marduk 562–560		
		'Deutero-Isaiah'		Nabonidus 556–539	Cyrus 550–530	Cyrus Cylinder
	Return of some Jews? 537			Fall of Babylon 539		'Verse Account of N bonidus'
			Egypt conquered by Persia 525		Cambyses 530–522	
	Temple rebuilt 520–515	Haggai			Darius I 522–486	
		Zechariah				
		'Trito-Isaiah'?				
					Xerxes I 486–465	
		'Malachi'			Artaxerxes I 465–424	
	Governorship of Nehemiah 445–433 432–?					
					Xerxes II 423	
	Sanballat I, Governor of Samaria				Darius II 423–404	
400	Ezra's Mission 398[2]		Egypt independent 401		Artaxerxes II 404–358	Elephantine Papyri
					Darius III 336–331	Samaria Papyri
	Alexander the Great conquers Palestine 333–2		Conquests of Alexander: ⚔ Granicus 334; ⚔ Issus 333; ⚔ Gaugamela 331			

[1] or 586.

[2] This may also be dated at either 458 or 428.

HELLENISTIC PERIOD

DATE	JUDAH		NEIGHBOURING POWERS		ARCHAEOLOGICAL EVIDENCE
			Ptolemies	*Seleucids*	
			Ptolemy I Soter 323–285	Seleucus I 312–281	
300	Ptolemies rule Palestine		Ptolemy II Philadelphus 285–246	Antiochus I 281–261	Zeno Papyri
				Antiochus II 261–247	
			Ptolemy III Euergetes 246–221	Seleucus II 247–226	
				Seleucus III 226–223	
			Ptolemy IV Philopator 221–203	Antiochus III 223–287	
			⚔ Raphia 217		
200	Seleucids rule Palestine		Ptolemy V Epiphanes 203–181		
			⚔ Panium 198		
	Profanation of the Temple 167 (?168)			Seleucus IV 187–175	
	Maccabaean Revolt			Antiochus IV Epiphanes 175–163	
	Book of Daniel 167/4				
	Rededication of the Temple 164 (?165)				
	Hasmonean Rulers		*Rome*	*Seleucids*	
	Judas Maccabaeus 166–160	?Qumran Sect established		Antiochus V Eupator 163–162	
	Jonathan 160–143			Demetrius I Soter 162–150	
				Alexander Balas 150–145	
	Simon 142–134	Jewish Independence granted 142		Demetrius II Nicator 145–139, 129–125	
				Antiochus VI Epiphanes 145–142	
				(Tryphon 142–139)	
	John Hyrcanus I 134–104			Antiochus VII Sidetes 139–128	Qumran Scrolls (?)
	Aristobulus I 104–103				
100	Alexander Jannaeus 103–76				
	Alexandra Salome 76–67				
	Aristobulus II 67–63				
	Pompey captures Jerusalem 63				
	Judah added to the Roman Province of Syria				
	Hyrcanus II 63–40				
			Overthrow of Pompey 48		
		Antigonus 40–37	⚔ Philippi 42		
		Herod the Great 37–4 B.C.	⚔ Actium 31		

SUGGESTIONS FOR ADDITIONAL READING

(This is in no sense a complete bibliography; many of the works here included provide indications of the wider range of literature which is available on the various subjects covered in this volume. Simpler discussions are marked *.)

The Revised Standard Version (RSV)

It is convenient to use an edition which includes the Apocrypha. *The Oxford Annotated Bible*, ed. H. G. May and B. M. Metzger (Oxford University Press, New York, 1962) contains the RSV text and much useful introductory and general material.

Introduction to the literature

*G. W. Anderson, *A Critical Introduction to the Old Testament* (Duckworth, London, 1959).

A. Weiser, *Introduction to the Old Testament* (Darton, Longman and Todd, London, 1961).

G. Fohrer, *Introduction to the Old Testament* (Abingdon Press, Nashville, 1968).

O. Eissfeldt, *The Old Testament: an Introduction* (Blackwell, Oxford; Harper and Row, New York, 1965).

General books covering both history and religion

*P. R. Ackroyd, *The People of the Old Testament* (Chatto and Windus, 1959), Parts III, IV.

*B. W. Anderson, *The Living World of the Old Testament* (Longmans, London, 2nd ed. 1967).

*G. W. Anderson, *The History and Religion of Israel* (New Clarendon Bible, Vol. 1, Oxford, 1966).

*J. M. Myers, *The World of the Restoration* (Prentice-Hall, Englewood Cliffs, N.J., 1968).

R. Davidson, *The Old Testament* (Hodder and Stoughton, London, 1964).

P. R. Ackroyd, *Exile and Restoration* (S.C.M., London, Westminster, Philadelphia, 1968).

H. H. Rowley, ed., *A Companion to the Bible* (2nd ed., T. and T. Clark, Edinburgh, 1963).

History of Israel

*E. L. Ehrlich, *A Concise History of Israel* (Darton, Longman and Todd, London, 1962).

J. Bright, *A History of Israel* (S.C.M., London, 1960; Westminster, Philadelphia, 1959).

M. Noth, *The History of Israel* (rev. ed. A. and C. Black, London, 1960).

The Ancient World and its life and thought; archaeology

*D. Winton Thomas, ed., *Documents from Old Testament Times* (Nelson, London, 1958; paperback reprint, Harper and Row, New York, 1961)—abbreviated as *DOTT*.

J. B. Pritchard, ed., *Ancient Near Eastern Texts* (2nd ed., Oxford University Press, Princeton University Press, 1955)—abbreviated as *ANET*.

J. B. Pritchard, ed., *The Ancient Near East in Pictures* (Oxford University Press, Princeton University Press, 1954).

J. B. Pritchard, ed., *The Ancient Near East, Supplementary Texts and Pictures Relating to the Old Testament* (Oxford University Press, Princeton University Press, 1969).

M. Noth, *The Old Testament World* (A. and C. Black, London, 1966).

R. de Vaux, *Ancient Israel* (Darton, Longman and Todd, London, 1961).

W. F. Albright, *The Archaeology of Palestine* (Penguin, Harmondsworth, rev. ed. 1960).

*G. E. Wright, *An Introduction to Biblical Archaeology* (Duckworth, London, 1962).

ADDITIONAL READING

Dictionaries

Hastings Dictionary of the Bible, 1 vol. rev. ed. H. H. Rowley and F. C. Grant (T. and T. Clark, Edinburgh, 1963).

The Interpreter's Dictionary of the Bible, 4 vols. (Abingdon Press, Nashville, 1962).

Atlases

H. G. MAY, ed., *Oxford Bible Atlas* (Oxford University Press, 1962).

†L. H. GROLLENBERG, *Atlas of the Bible* (Nelson, London, 1956).

†G. E. WRIGHT and F. V. FILSON, *The Westminster Historical Atlas to the Bible* (rev. ed. S.C.M., London; Westminster, Philadelphia, 1957).

Y. AHARONI and M. AVI-YONAH, *The Macmillan Bible Atlas* (Collier–Macmillan, London, New York, 1968).

H. H. ROWLEY, *Teach Yourself Bible Atlas* (English Universities Press, London, 1960).

(† Shorter editions of these two atlases are also available)

Commentaries

(i) Commentaries on most or all of the books discussed in this volume may be found in the following:

New Peake's Commentary on the Bible, ed. M. Black and H. H. Rowley (Nelson, 1962).

The Interpreter's Bible, 6 vols. on the Old Testament (Abingdon Press, Nashville, 1952–6).

**Layman's Bible Commentaries* (S.C.M. London; Knox Press, Richmond, Virginia, 1959–62).

**Torch Bible Commentaries* (S.C.M. London, 1951– ; in progress).

Anchor Bible Commentaries (Doubleday, New York, 1964– ; in progress).

The New Century Bible (Nelson, London, 1967– ; in progress).

The Old Testament Library (S.C.M. London; Westminster, Philadelphia, 1959– ; in progress. This series includes general volumes as well as commentaries).

**The Cambridge Bible Commentary* based on the New English Bible Text is due to begin publication in 1971.

(ii) The following, not included in the series just mentioned, cover particular books discussed in this volume:

C. R. North, *The Second Isaiah* (Oxford University Press, 1964).

N. H. Gottwald, *Studies in the Book of Lamentations* (S.C.M. London, Studies in Biblical Theology, No. 14, 1954).

B. Albrektson, *Studies in the Text and Theology of the Book of Lamentations* (Gleerup, Lund, 1963).

H. H. Guthrie, *Israel's Sacred Songs* (Seabury, New York, 1966)—a general introduction to the psalms.

Special topics

(i) Hebrew Poetry

T. H. Robinson, *The Poetry of the Old Testament* (Duckworth, London, 1947).

O. Eissfeldt, *The Old Testament: an Introduction* (Blackwell, Oxford; Harper and Row, New York, 1965), § 6.

Articles in Bible Dictionaries (see p. 351).

(ii) The 'Servant Songs' in the Second Isaiah.

C. R. North, *The Suffering Servant in Deutero-Isaiah* (Oxford University Press, 1948; 2nd ed. 1956).

H. H. Rowley, *The Servant of the Lord and other Essays* (Lutterworth, London, 1952; 2nd ed. Blackwell, Oxford, 1965).

(iii) The Chronology of Ezra and Nehemiah

H. H. Rowley, 'The Chronological Order of Ezra and Nehemiah' in *The Servant of the Lord* (Lutterworth, London, 1952; 2nd ed. Blackwell, Oxford, 1965).

J. Bright, *A History of Israel* (S.C.M. London, 1960; Westminster, Philadelphia, 1959), critically discussed by J. A. Emerton, 'Did Ezra go to Jerusalem in 428 B.C?' *Journal of Theological Studies* 17 (1966), pp. 1 ff.

(iv) The Elephantine Papyri

Selections may be found in *DOTT* and *ANET*.

The texts are published in:

A. E. Cowley, *Aramaic Papyri of the Fifth Century B.C.* (Oxford University Press, 1923)—referred to as Cowley.

E. G. Kraeling, *The Brooklyn Museum Aramaic Papyri* (Yale University Press, New Haven, 1953, 1969)—referred to as Kraeling.

A. E. Cowley, *Jewish Documents of the time of Ezra* (S.P.C.K. London, 1919)—a shorter edition.

Translations in the text are based on those to be found in the editions mentioned, but modified in some slight degree.

B. Porten, *Archives from Elephantine. The Life of an Ancient Jewish Military Colony* (University of California Press; Cambridge University Press, 1968) offers a comprehensive discussion of the material.

(v) Worship

A. S. Herbert, *Worship in Ancient Israel* (Lutterworth, London, 1959).

H.-J. Kraus, *Worship in Israel* (Blackwell, Oxford, 1966).

H. H. Rowley, *Worship in Ancient Israel* (S.P.C.K. London, 1967).

INDEX OF SCRIPTURE REFERENCES

INDEX OF SUBJECTS

PRINTED IN GREAT BRITAIN
AT THE UNIVERSITY PRESS, OXFORD
BY VIVIAN RIDLER
PRINTER TO THE UNIVERSITY